THE SHORT STORY
A CRITICAL INTRODUCTION
Valerie Shaw

THE SHORT STORY:
A CRITICAL INTRODUCTION

THE SHORT STORY:
A CRITICAL INTRODUCTION

Valerie Shaw

LONGMAN
London and New York

LONGMAN GROUP LIMITED
Longman House, Burnt Mill, Harlow
Essex CM20 2JE, England
Associated companies throughout the world

*Published in the United States of America
by Longman Inc., New York*

First published 1983

BRITISH LIBRARY CATALOGUING IN PUBLICATION DATA

Shaw, Valerie
    The short story.
    1. Short stories, English – History and criticism
    I. Title
    823'.01'09   PR829

    ISBN 0-582-48687-4

LIBRARY OF CONGRESS CATALOGING IN PUBLICATION DATA

Shaw, Valerie, 1941–
    The short story, a critical introduction.

    Bibliography: p.
    Includes index.
    1. Short story. I. Title.
PN3373.S384   1983   808.3'1   83-986
ISBN 0-582-48687-4

Printed in Singapore by
Huntsmen Offset Printing Pte Ltd.

CONTENTS

PREFACE

I would willingly call technique simply craftsmanship, but that it involves
something further. As to each new story, once it has been embarked on,
a number of decisions have to be made – as to size (or length), as to
treatment (or manner of handling) and, most of all, as to what is this
particular story's aim? What is, or should be, this particular story's
scope? What is this particular story really about, and how best can what
it *is* about be shown? To an extent, such decisions are made instinctively,
but intellectual judgment must come in also. The first thing the writer
must learn about technique is that there is no such thing as technique in
the abstract or *in vacuo*. Neither is it to be arrived at for good and all.
Each new story (if it is of any value) will make a whole fresh set of
demands: no preceding story can be of any help.

(Elizabeth Bowen, Preface to *A Day in the Dark*)

There are so many different kinds of short story that the genre as a
whole seems constantly to resist universal definition, a situation
which in this study I have taken to be a strength rather than a weakness. The general reader, along with many short-storywriters, seems
to feel no anxiety about the lack of a single definition, and it is with
this in mind that I have made my central question 'What *does* the
short story do especially well?', and not 'What *should* the short
story do?' I have found that short-story form cannot be adequately
characterized solely in terms of its preoccupation with 'unity of
effect', or by offering a history of its favourite devices and eminent
practitioners. Instead, I have tried to blend these considerations and
to highlight various aspects of short-storywriting, illustrated by
specific instances drawn from diverse periods and countries. So the
context in which particular stories are discussed is neither the con-
tinuum of literary history nor the entirety of any individual writer's
career, and the questions continually being asked are straightforward ones: 'What are the special satisfactions afforded by reading
short stories?'; and 'How are these satisfactions derived from each
story's literary techniques and narrative strategies?' Enquiry into
these matters is seen as directly related to the artistic choices which

face the writer before and during the composition of a story, and which are outlined so cogently by Elizabeth Bowen in the passage I have chosen as the epigraph for this book.

My chapter headings correspond to basic types of narrative and to the technical concerns which influence any short-storywriter's decisions about how to shape a brief narrative, the exceptions being Chapter 2, which concentrates on Stevenson as a transitional figure, and the final chapter, where a number of characteristically modern trends in storytelling are considered. In those chapters dealing with a number of writers, I have selected storytellers whose work exemplifies particularly well the issues being discussed. I do not mean by this that any one writer should be confined to the category within which he or she is given most extended consideration, or that the categories themselves are not interdependent.

In the course of my reading I kept being impressed by what seemed to be the permanent capacity of short fiction to return to its ancient origins in folktale and legend; its ability to make completely new uses of apparently unsophisticated literary conventions; its recurrent concern with an audience, thought of as an intimate group or community, and its frequent tendency towards the instinctual rather than the intellectual. These kinds of understanding are reflected in my approach and choice of stories, and I have also tried to keep in view the divergent impulses (between poetry on the one hand and reportage on the other, for example) that are often to be found in the same story. A related concern has been to indicate the short story's affinities with other art forms, remembering that it was by crossing generic boundaries and applying thoughts about lyric poetry to prose fiction that Edgar Allan Poe first realized how powerful a form the short story could be.

My selection of examples has naturally been influenced by the fact that the short story is an international phenomenon, though extending the scope of my study to include literature other than Anglo-Saxon has greatly increased the problem of what to leave out. I have resisted the temptation to multiply illustrations or to offer lists of analogues, and have settled for fewer writers and more close scrutiny than would have been possible in a survey. This has enabled me to give a certain amount of prominence to less familiar writers like Sarah Orne Jewett as well as to acknowledged masters like Kipling, Chekhov and Maupassant. In most cases I have chosen to discuss one story in detail rather than attempt to cover the numerous instances that presented themselves at every stage of my investigation.

Page references to short stories are to collected editions wherever possible, although in several instances use has been made of readily available paperback versions and anthologies. The same principle applies to texts in translation, and on all occasions titles appear in the form used in the edition cited. Unless otherwise indicated, the date given in brackets after the first mention of a title refers to the story's earliest publication in a volume collected under the author's name, information about original appearances in periodicals being given in the Notes to each chapter when I have thought such information likely to interest the reader. Wherever brief reference to a story is made, my practice has been not to repeat the title in the Notes, but where discussion is more prolonged the title appears in both text and Notes. Few references to current critical material occur in the text, but details of relevant background reading are included in the Bibliography; within the text, most of the authorities cited are themselves practitioners of the short story, and this bias is deliberate on my part. In the Bibliography, and in the Notes, the place of publication of all works is London unless otherwise indicated. When quoting, I have observed each writer's practice as to the spelling or hyphenation of terms such as 'short story', 'storyteller', and so on, and Katherine Mansfield's erratic spelling of Chekhov's name has been preserved. One minor liberty taken was to supply apostrophes where Virginia Woolf omitted them in her letter-writing.

It remains to thank Peter Keating, who read the entire manuscript for me, and whose advice and encouragement have been invaluable to me throughout the planning and writing of this book.

ACKNOWLEDGEMENT

We are grateful to the author's agent on behalf of The National Trust for the poem 'The Bisara of Pooree' by Rudyard Kipling, from *Plain Tales from the Hills*, published by Macmillan, London Ltd.

To Peter

Chapter 1

'ONLY SHORT STORIES': ESTIMATES AND EXPLANATIONS

A short-story writer can try anything. He has tried anything – but presumably not everything. Variety is, has been, and no doubt will remain endless in possibilities, because the power and stirring of the mind never rests. It is what this power will try that will most pertinently define the short story. Not rules, not aesthetics, not problems and their solution. It is not rules as long as there is imagination; not aesthetics as long as there is passion; not success as long as there is intensity behind the effort that calls forth and communicates, that will try and try again.

(Eudora Welty)

'It will always be one of the darkest mysteries to me', wrote Kipling to the novelist Mrs Humphry Ward in 1896, 'that any human being can make a beginning, end *and* middle to a really truly long story.' With his own abilities and limitations very much in mind he went on to elaborate the remark:

I can think them by scores but I have not the hand to work out the full frieze. It's just the difference between the deep-sea steamer with twelve hundred people aboard, beside the poor beggars sweating and scorching in the stoke-hold, and the coastwise boat with a mixed cargo of 'notions'.[1]

Kipling's imagery here conveys a view of the novel as a gallant enterprise dignified by toil and hazard, in comparison with which his own endeavours seem pitifully frail and cautious. Despite his achievement as a short-storywriter, Kipling clearly regretted that 'the full frieze' of long fiction, with all its reminiscences of epic breadth, was beyond his powers. It is a regret which no admirer of Kipling's work would share, but it can be taken as typical of the disparaging attitude frequently shown towards the short story.

Comment on the short story has tended to be either rueful or patronizing, even among writers who have proved themselves experts in the form. V. S. Pritchett's admission that he finds stories and essays the most congenial forms to work in, because he is 'a writer who takes short breaths', actually echoes Zola's stern remark that Maupassant would have to produce a novel, 'une oeuvre de longue haleine', in order to fulfil the promise shown in his first collection of stories.[2] The widespread notion that unless it can be seen as useful apprentice work for budding novelists, short-storywriting must be a compromise of some sort is even more starkly evident in Katherine Mansfield's reaction to a friendly enquiry about her work: 'What do you do in life?' she was asked.

> 'I am a writer'
> 'Do you write dramas?'
> 'No'. It sounded as if she were sorry she did not.
> 'Do you write tragedies, novels, romances?' I persisted, because she looked as if she could write these.
> 'No', she said, and with still deeper distress; 'only short stories; just short stories.'
> Later on she told me she felt so wretched at that moment she would have given anything if she could have answered at least one 'yes' to the 'big' things.[3]

Both participants in this conversation are in no doubt about what the 'big things' are – dramas, tragedies, even romances. Compared with these, short stories seem flimsy, calling for apology rather than pride, and subduing the firm announcement 'I am a writer'.

That publishers also prefer 'big things' is often proposed as one reason for the comparative neglect of the short story. Apparently, if it takes ability to become a published storywriter at all, then strong determination is needed to remain one: the writer has to resist what Katherine Anne Porter describes as 'the trap' waiting for 'every short-story writer of any gifts at all' – the novel which 'every publisher hopes to obtain'.[4] Having discovered that his talent is for brief narratives written at full pitch and intensity, the writer, so Porter insists, has to defy the common expectation that his abilities will be all the more powerfully displayed in the roomy spaciousness of a full-length novel. In fact, far from welcoming the chance to expand and elaborate, the committed short-storywriter is likely to flinch at the prospect, as, for example, did A. E. Coppard. Urged by publishers to write a novel, Coppard 'cringed from the awful job of hacking out mere episodes into epic stature, draping the holes in them with bogus mysticism, factitious psychology, and the backchat of a paperhanger'.[5] Wildly distorted as a general description of novel-writing this most certainly is, but it does demonstrate vividly how Coppard would have conceived his task had he succumbed to persuasion, and sacrificed his need 'to see all round and over and under my tale before putting a line of it on paper'.[6] Wisely, he did not tackle a long composition, realizing that 'within my limitations there was no need for me to do any such thing, no point in stretching and inventing'.[7]

Coppard's belief, based on his own experience, that the short story is a totality which the writer as it were 'possesses' before he writes the first sentence is shared by many practitioners of the form. Katherine Anne Porter too has stated that, 'If I didn't know the ending of a story, I wouldn't begin'.[8] Her story-endings are not only foreseen, they are fixed points to steer by: 'I always write my last lines, my last paragraph, my last page first, and then I go back and work towards it.'[9] Similarly, Katherine Mansfield proposed that, 'once one has thought out a story nothing remains but the *labour*'.[10] Despite widely different cultural backgrounds – Coppard a working-class Englishman; Porter an American Southerner and Mansfield a New Zealander – all of these twentieth-century writers recognize the short story as a distinctive form with its own methods of construction. In this they were anticipated by Chekhov, who in 1889 had asserted that, 'the short story, like the stage, has its own conventions', its own need to 'concentrate for the reader an impression of the entire work' at the end.[11]

The argument that the novel and the short story are separate entities which share the same prose medium but not the same artistic methods is crucial to an understanding of short fiction, but it was slow to gain currency, particularly in Britain. Only towards the end of the nineteenth century, when in fact all branches of literature and the arts were becoming acutely self-conscious, did people begin to acknowledge that short fiction might be shaped according to its own principles. Importantly, the practice of the form in a deliberate way coincided with the early stages of short-story theory; writing short stories and discussing them were aspects of a single exciting situation, as H. G. Wells proclaimed when he described the 1890s as the heyday of the short story. Everyone was discussing short stories in the nineties, Wells recalled, and that gave anybody who was writing them prestige and stimulation: 'People talked about them tremendously, compared them, and ranked them. That was the thing that mattered'.[12] But although the short story in the nineties became, as Wells's rival Henry James put it, 'an object of almost extravagant dissertation', there was little inclination to apply the new term 'short story' to indigenous products that had been around for centuries.[13] This places the genre in a rather curious position. Whereas, for example, the German label 'novelle' came considerably later than the well-established practice of the form, an aesthetic for the British short story seemed to develop simultaneously with the genre itself, label and object emerging alongside one another.[14]

One of the lingering consequences of the late nineteenth-century emphasis on discussion as somehow authenticating the storywriter's activity, has been exaggeration of both the newness and the autonomy of the short story. Perceiving aesthetic differences between novels and short stories can easily turn into separating their destinies, which is not the same thing at all. Although Wells's thrill at the attention given to short fiction for its own sake might suggest otherwise, the development of the short story has always been bound up historically with the state of the novel. What has altered is the nature of the relationship: whereas in the eighteenth century short fiction consistently treated the same subjects as novels, the modern short story tends to reflect the diversity of 'component parts' into which Mary McCarthy saw the novel dissolving in 1960 – 'the essay, the travel book, reporting on the one hand, and the "pure" fiction of the tale, on the other'.[15] Furthermore, discussion of the short story in late Victorian England was only one subsidiary element in a far wider debate in which writers like Wilde, James and Conrad were exploring immense questions about the artist's role in a fragmenting and increasingly secular society. The rise of the short story in England is closely linked with the emergence of the characteristic figure of the modern artist, and with anti-Victorianism in its widest sense; in the atmosphere of the 1880s and 1890s it was simply inconceivable that short fiction should *not* have been talked about. Admittedly, when discussion focused on the part fiction could and should play in a changing world, it was the novel, not the short story, which attracted controversy. So much so, in fact, that the American critic Brander Matthews (himself a writer of short stories) was moved to protest against English complacency and grumble that the London debaters were ignoring the short story, a form pioneered by his compatriots and already supreme in American literature for half a century.

In 1884 Brander Matthews made his claim that the short story deserved as much theoretical attention as Henry James and Walter Besant, among others, were giving to the novel, and for years afterwards he worried away at the topic, publishing several versions of what became in 1901 *The Philosophy of the Short-story*. Dignifying the 'Short-story' with a capital letter and a hyphen, Matthews argued that the dominance of the three-decker novel had 'killed the Short-story in England', while in France and America conditions had favoured the development of short fiction which was different in kind, not merely in length, from the novel.[16] There was a nationalistic side to Matthews's purpose, and this led him into some exaggerated contrasts between the Old World and the New. He asserted that, whereas the native American novel had been positively helped into existence by the short story, 'there is not a single British novelist whose reputation has been materially assisted by the Short-stories he has written'; it was a remark Matthews realized he should modify after reading Kipling and Stevenson.[17] All the same, Matthews was making a convincing point when he noted that English writers of the late nineteenth century lacked a tradition of storytelling as a distinct literary art, and that the main reason for this was the supremacy of the Victorian novel.

The shortage of precedents for treating the short story as a separate genre was, however, more intelligently acknowledged by writers working in England than Matthews suggested. For Henry James, the principal comparison was not with America, but with Europe. While admitting that Hawthorne, Poe and Bret Harte had given the 'short tale' eminence in America, James saw France as 'the land of its great prosperity'.[18] To James, a writer like Maupassant was to be envied the quick-witted public he could rely on to get the point of his brief tales: in contrast, 'the little story is but scantily relished in England, where readers take their fiction rather by the volume than by the page, and the novelist's idea is apt to resemble one of those old-fashioned carriages which require a wide court to turn round'.[19] The three-decker novel, it seems, had pampered the English taste for leisurely, discursive fiction, and with hindsight it is possible to argue that the short story could not begin to catch on in England until one-volume novels started to displace the multi-volumed and serialized fiction which dominated the market until the mid-nineties.

The view that the arrival of the short story into English literature was delayed by the Victorian novel is both compelling and persistent. V. S. Pritchett has recently pointed out that English reading habits in the nineteenth century indulged 'the ruminative and disquisitional', inhibiting the short story until Stevenson, Kipling and D. H. Lawrence appeared on the scene.[20] Before then, Pritchett observes, 'we preferred to graze on the larger acreage of the novel and even tales by Dickens or Thackeray or Mrs Gaskell strike us as being unused chapters of longer works'.[21] Free of this bovine self-satisfaction, the American writer's situation, as Pritchett sees it, was rich with an enlivening sense of transience, a restlessness which made instant responses both a condition of physical survival and a source of artistic energy. The association between the short story and transience is axiomatic in Pritchett's approach, and it is questionable whether stories by Victorian novelists do deserve to be excluded from the canon of short stories proper. But what is immediately significant is that the earliest of the innovators named by Pritchett (Stevenson and Kipling) should both have been keenly alive to foreign examples – more so than many of their contemporaries. One consequence of this for the short story in general is implied when Pritchett goes on to suggest that the 'essentially poetic' quality of the literature produced under tense pioneering conditions in America has nothing to do with literary polish, gaining its power from something 'raw and journalistic'.[22]

The poetic and the journalistic are usually taken to be opposed, not complementary, terms, but as many of the stories to be considered here demonstrate, the short story has a marked ability to bring apparent extremes of style together, mingling self-conscious literary devices and colloquial spontaneity within the 'essentially poetic' compression of a single narrative. It is in this respect that the early American short story can be seen as seminal, reflecting as it did prevalent cultural moods. Pritchett's evocation of the joltingly dangerous frontier situation is part of the picture, but only a part. Two tendencies, according to William Dean Howells, characterized the American nation and the literature it produced: 'one a tendency toward an elegance refined and polished, both in thought and phrase, almost to tenuity; the other a tendency to grotesqueness, wild and extravagant, to the point of anarchy'.[23] The first impulse, Howells explained, led to distinctively American fiction, the second to unmistakably American humour, making tendencies which seemed opposites into parallel developments.

It is possible to go further than Howells and suggest that in the American journals which offered ready markets to native fiction-writers humour and elegance actually came together in an entirely new blend. Exactly how new and difficult to analyze in categorical terms is evident from an interesting divergence of views between Howells and his friend Henry James. Both men wrote at various times about Bret Harte, a figure of enormous importance in the development of American short fiction. In Howells's view, Harte belonged with the vigorous writers who exemplified the anarchic tendency of American life and letters. James, on the other hand, cited Harte as a case of the refined and sharpened perceptiveness which made all American writers – amongst whom James was still including himself – 'in a literary way, on our own scale, very delicate', and which 'stimulates greatly our sense of proportion and form'.[24]

Where Howells, and after him Pritchett, see invigorating wildness that passes straight into the American short story and sets it above British efforts, James sees a 'monotonous civilization' which presents such an 'arid blank' that its writers are forced, 'in the way of contrasts, of salient points, of chiaroscuro, . . . to take what we can get'.[25] So although James and Howells agree that Harte is a significant figure in American literary history, they portray him quite differently: whereas James finds a writer who possesses 'pre-eminently the instinct of style and shape', Howells describes a 'delightful humorist' who is inclined to overdo narrative improbabilities and grotesque effects.[26] If the approaches of James and Howells are combined, the parallel tendencies of the artful and the raw converge, suggesting that Harte's achievement was actually to combine spontaneity and artifice within a single form. Here, perhaps, is a clue to the distinctive possibilities of the short story in general, inviting later critics not to choose between Howells's emphasis on content, and James's on shapely form, but to fuse both considerations.

Today, the desirability of a unified approach which can judge form and content together might seem unarguable, but in fact the notion that the short story deserves such respectful treatment was slow to develop, and is still fairly unstable. Ironically, this is partly because of that journalistic quality which some commentators propose as one of the genre's principal assets. The short story's continued involvement with journalism has damaged its standing while ensuring its popularity, creating a dilemma for writers and critics who are anxious to preserve standards. Despite the fact that so many of the best short-storywriters, including Chekhov, Kipling and Hemingway, began their careers as newspapermen, there is a suspicion that a storyteller's artistry may be far too closely tied up with external considerations like space limitations, restrictive house-styles and editorial stipulations. The size of a *Tatler* sheet, not artistic choice, was what set 2,000 words as a maximum for short fiction in that periodical; it was available space that determined features like the amount of dialogue or the use of a first-person narrator who could compress information and provide retrospective summaries of narrative action.[27] Later, the daily 'turnover' of exactly one column and a quarter in the *Civil and Military Gazette*, where Kipling began publishing stories in 1886, provides a comparable case of implacable word-restriction disciplining short-story form, irrespective of who was employing it. These exigencies, however, are not to be regretted if they are seen as the spurs which chafe the art of the short story into existence. The need to strive for what Kipling called '"economy of implication"' in no more than 2,000 words proved invaluable to him, and, through his example and influence, to anyone writing or studying short stories after he had shown what marvels could be achieved in one column and a quarter.[28]

More damaging than unduly romanticized conceptions of the artist as owing allegiance to no one but himself, and certainly not to an editor, is the fear that the magazines which provide the most accessible market for short fiction are by the same token sure to corrupt it. In the 1930s it was in widely available story magazines that Q. D. Leavis found evidence of the contemporary journalist's deplorable 'anxiety to conciliate and flatter "the man in the street"'.[29] Widely available in comparison with books, these magazines, so Mrs Leavis argued, were bound to lower standards by 'providing fiction that requires the least effort to read and will set the reader up in a comfortable state of mind'.[30] The complaint that a highly commercialized literary market is 'explicitly defiant of other standards and ambitions' is of course not applicable to the short story alone, but the argument that good short stories are especially difficult to publish is frequently heard.[31] Francis King says reviewing pays better; V. S. Pritchett calls the short story an inextinguishable lost cause, pointing out that it is difficult to publish stories longer than 7,000 words, and after 10,000, impossible.[32] But there is no consensus about this matter: Alan Ross maintains that the market is not nearly as bad as it is often made out to be and that, despite continued defensiveness about the short story, 'good stories' sell well, the annual anthology of *London Magazine* stories rivalling most novels in its sales figures.[33]

Other writers point out the prolonged earning power a story may acquire through broadcasts or reprintings in anthologies and teaching manuals, and there is plenty of evidence to support the view that markets for excellence are not unduly restricted. Nevertheless, the plain fact that the short story is composed as a single entity but frequently published as one item among many, its artistic tautness perhaps incongruously spaced out and interspersed with advertising copy, has scarcely been to the advantage of any writer dependent on the periodical market. Instances of short stories published by themselves are rare; Virginia Woolf was fortunate in having her own press and so being able to produce 'Kew Gardens' (1918) as an aesthetic object with its own atmospheric integrity, enhanced by her sister Vanessa's woodcut illustrations.

For anybody making a study of the short story, its fugitive existence in ephemeral publications, or, more recently, in a day's radio programmes, does present a problem, especially if it is felt that the qualities needing fresh emphasis are the immediacy, compression and vitality which the short story shares with journalism of the highest standard. Partly because of the influence of New Criticism, literary discussions of the short story have tended to concentrate on specific kinds of formal intricacy, sometimes treating short fiction as though it were always at its best when aspiring to the complex condition of a metaphysical lyric poem.[34] The trouble with this is that cases where the resemblance is more to the fireside chat or the rapid newspaper article – or where the qualities of lyric and anecdote actually merge – are disregarded. Brander Matthews, for example, was so anxious to prove that the short story is a sharply defined form that he undervalued anecdotal and episodic fiction in preference for stories with a symmetrical design. To do this is to favour certain kinds of unity over others, whereas the glory of the short story's single-minded concision is that it can be put to an infinite number of uses in what it is made to say – about human experience, about ideas and emotions. A highly self-conscious form, the short story can celebrate spontaneity and the instinctual, or dramatize a moment of revelation which brings a character to full consciousness for the first time in his life; it can use its intactness to say that life's possibilities are hedged and narrow, or to express a view of life as violent and torn by harsh conflict; deliberate and calculated in aim, it can have the apparent casualness of a snapshot.

H. E. Bates has remarked with justice that, 'any real examination of the story's development of shape would involve dissection of almost every story written'.[35] Nor would the task end there, since the possible analogues for each story-type are endless, and it would be necessary to account for the hybrid nature of a genre which owes, at various stages of its development, something to virtually every other kind of literature, now resembling the medieval sermon, now the polite essay, now the ballad, or again the sonnet. Each age adds more possibilities, and these remain opportunities for short-story-writers in perpetuity. More feasible than the quixotic project of analysing and classifying hordes of short stories, however, is to examine the development of awareness that 'shape' is what makes a short story distinct from a story that happens to be short.

In tracing the advance of belief that the short story has its own aesthetic, it is once again America that provides a starting-point. As far back as 1842 Edgar Allan Poe had formulated basic principles for the composition of short prose narratives, relating the writer's aims directly to the brevity of the form. By a brilliant stroke, Poe applied to prose writing what he had found to be an invariable rule of poetic production. In poetry, he maintained, 'unity of effect or impression' was only attainable in works which could be read at one sitting: 'All high excitements are necessarily transient. Thus a long poem is a paradox. And, without unity of impression, the deepest effects cannot be brought about.'[36] Since, like a short poem, a prose tale could be read in one continuous effort, Poe argued, similar momentum and impact could be achieved by carefully judging the length and pace of narrative fiction. By exploiting opportunities denied to the novelist, and by strictly controlling the reading experience, the storyteller would be able to convey 'high excitements' and profound effects comparable to those created in lyric poetry. And in order to do this, the writer must be sharply conscious of every stage in his composition, a process which Poe saw as beginning, not with plot-construction, but with the conception of 'a certain unique or single *effect* to be wrought out'.[37]

'Unique', 'single', and 'wrought'; the words remain key terms in discussions of the short story. So too does Poe's insistence that only when the desired effect or impression is clear in the writer's mind should he go on to invent incidents and arrange them in the order best calculated to establish this effect. Whatever the subject, the aim is to pull the reader along towards a single moment when he finds impressed on his mind an effect identical to the one 'preconceived' by the writer. Poe's account of the deliberate artistry by which the writer must seize and maintain control gives the short story the status of an exacting and powerful art form: 'If his very initial sentence tend not to the outbringing of this effect, then he has failed in his first step. In the whole composition there should be no word written, of which the tendency, direct or indirect, is not to the one pre-established design.'[38] What matters here is not just that Poe sees the special importance of the way a story begins, but his realization that while every word must contribute to the 'single effect', this may be achieved by indirection, allowing the writer to withhold the full impact of his design until it is complete. Furthermore, Poe shows acute understanding of the special type of pleasure contained in the experience of that completeness; no matter how hair-raising the plot, there is a particular enjoyment, often rather calm and reflec-tive, in store for the reader who sees the image whole:

> And by such means, with such care and skill, a picture is at length painted which leaves in the mind of him who contemplates it with kindred art, a sense of the fullest satisfaction. The idea of the tale has been presented unblemished, because undisturbed; and this is an end unattainable in the novel.[39]

Here, 'contemplates' suggests a measure of aesthetic detachment, while 'leaves in the mind' indicates that delight survives the actual telling of the tale. By means of careful contrivance, the idea has become an image, and reader and writer are brought into a rare state of intimacy as they share an identical perception.

In Poe's view the short story compared favourably with poetry as well as with the novel, because of the 'vast variety of modes and inflections of thought and expression' available to the writer of prose tales.[40] It is precisely the same appealing range and diversity which excited James in the 1890s when he revelled in the thought of learn-ing 'the trick' of writing short stories: 'by doing short things I can do so many', he declared, 'touch so many subjects, break out in so many places, handle so many of the threads of life'.[41] By the time James made that pronouncement he had been writing magazine stor-ies for two decades, although like so many short-storywriters before and since, he found editors obtuse. Writing to Howells in early 1888, for example, he commented ruefully: 'Though I have for a good while past been writing a number of good short things, I remain irremediably unpublished. Editors keep them back, for months and years, as if they were ashamed of them.'[42] And some years later, when *Harper's Magazine* wanted him to supply an 'international' tale, 'a tale of the Daisy Miller order', James chafed at having to tailor his ideas to editorial requirements.[43] Money, he confessed to himself, was the sole incentive for co-operating with a journal which always demanded 'the smaller, the safer, the inferior thing', and where 'the company one keeps is of a most paralyzing dreariness'.[44]

It was against this background that James saw the advent of *The*

Yellow Book (1894), daringly flouting all that was safe and inferior, as the opening of a millennium to the short story, freeing it all at once to 'assume', and indeed 'shamelessly parade in, its own organic form'.[45] The short story needed rescuing from the general ruling that 8,000 words was the upper-length limit, and what thrilled James about *The Yellow Book*'s liberation from length restrictions was the prospect of retrieving 'shades and differences, varieties and styles, the value above all the idea happily *developed*'.[46] Like Poe, James saw that the length of a story was relative to its central motive, its single idea or 'preconceived effect', and although in practice he found it hard to carry out Poe's directive that copiousness is more to be avoided than undue brevity, his contribution to the development of the short story cannot be over-estimated. His greatest achievements came with his experiments in the form of the novel, but his interest in short fiction was in no way diminished by this emphasis: rather, it was an indispensable part of his exploration into the principles of all narrative art.

Although almost everything James had to say about the short story and its organic unity had been anticipated by Poe, he gave entirely new force (as well as a fresh idiom) to a theory which had been dormant for fifty years, by incorporating it into his characteristically modern view of the artist, isolated in priest-like dedication to art, practising a kind of secular religion, and hardly expecting to be read at all – or at least, by only a few like-minded devotees. James passionately enunciated, both in his critical pronouncements and in his own creative work, the aesthetic paradox at the heart of short-storywriting, luxuriating in the form's power to combine richness with concision, 'to do the complicated thing with a strong brevity and lucidity'.[47] James saw no limits to the effects and tones that could be achieved, or to the subjects that could be treated, in an art form which was free to explore depths and complexities precisely because it was restricted in length. Brevity necessitated a 'science of control', acute and highly conscious judgement about how to adjust shape to ideas.[48] But the sacrifice of multiple alternative situations, tones and characters for the sake of one vivid idea 'happily *developed*' was, so James believed, amply justified by the heightened appeal, shared by reader and author alike, of 'the forms of wrought things'.[49] That is to say, one aspect of the delight offered by short stories would be an awareness of something contrived and highly stylized.

Seen as a form which arouses a feeling of wonder at finding so much expressed within such narrow boundaries, the short story is an intrinsically witty genre which has affinities with a wide range of artistic strategies for compressing meaning, including the metaphysical conceit and the Chestertonian paradox. It is a special case. with its own conventions, of art's capacity to make apparently straightforward or familiar things express complexities through metaphor, symbol and implication, and at the same time to bring seeming opposites into elegant and provoking relationship with one another. With or without any mystical intention, the short story does 'see the universe in a grain of sand' and it rests ultimately on an aesthetic principle which reflects the belief that, as Jorge Luis Borges puts it, 'there isn't anywhere on earth a single page or single word that is [simple], since each thing implies the universe, whose most obvious trait is complexity'.[50]

A twentieth-century writer like Borges stands in a direct line of inheritance from Henry James, to whom the short story had the undoubted appeal of being 'delightful and difficult, and with one of these qualities . . . the direct reason of the other'.[51] Beauty, in James's view, arises from the achievement of what looks impossible, and precisely because the brief story 'is an easy thing, no doubt, to do a little with', it becomes increasingly fascinating 'on the approximation of that liberal *more* of which we speedily learn it to be capable'.[52] Furthermore, to add to James's exhilaration about short fiction's possibilities, he realized that even though each single story could cover only a limited field of experience, a collection of stories could be made to reflect life's diversity. Introducing the American edition of Kipling's *Mine Own People* (1891), James praised the young writer for 'seeing so many chances of touching life in a thousand places, taking it up in innumerable pieces, each a specimen an illustration'.[53] Individually, each story might be self-contained and limited in representational power, but when accumulated these 'illustrations' could make up a comprehensive survey, comparable to the inclusive though wandering vision afforded by a camera obscura. James himself drew the visual analogy when he wrote in 1888 to tell Stevenson that for the next years he planned to concentrate on short fiction: 'I want to leave a multitude of pictures of my time, projecting my small circular frame upon as many different spots as possible'.[54]

One of the aims of the present study is to suggest that such comparisons between the short story and the visual arts are not merely rhetorical. When Henry James records, in his notes for 'The Coxon Fund', that, 'The formula for the presentation of it in 20,000 words is to make it an *Impression* – as one of Sargent's pictures is an impression', he is drawing attention to the most significant respect in which short stories differ from longer narrative forms.[55] The suggestive compression of many stories is achieved by summarizing what would, in the realistic novel, be a record of linked events; in place of a discursive sequence of causes and effects, the story can offer a picture. The picture may resemble a domestic interior of the Dutch realist school, a full-length portrait in which the character of the sitter is paramount, or, as the tendency is in the modern short story, an Impressionist painting, where objects are not determinate and surfaces are not organized according to representational outline.

At every stage of its development the short story reveals affinities with the style of painting dominating the period in question, but what makes the parallel between the modern short story and Impressionist art especially important is the extent to which creator and receiver share acute consciousness of form. The impact of many modern short stories resembles the effect of looking at an Impressionist canvas because it leaves a sense of something complete yet unfinished, a sensation which vibrates in the reader's or spectator's mind and demands that he participate in the aesthetic interchange between the artist and his subject. In painting, lessened concern with representation allows emphasis to be thrown onto the richness and variety of colour, one of the principal means by which an essentially static picture held in a frame may be enlivened; similarly, the short-storywriter can concentrate on textures and moods, aiming, as one reviewer said in 1892, 'like a clever impressionist . . . for colour, air, and light', and capturing a 'supreme moment' of perception.[56]

Concern with 'supreme' and inevitably fleeting moments is a marked feature of post-Jamesian storywriting, where the preference is for the unexplained and non-didactic, to suit what Elizabeth Bowen described in herself as a 'mood of aesthetic restlessness'.[57] Introducing a reissue of *Ann Lee's* (1926), Bowen saw her stories as 'questions asked: many end with a shrug, a query, or, to the reader, a sort of over-to-you'.[58] Taking 'human unknowableness' as her subject, Bowen confirmed the tendency of short-fiction technique to rely increasingly on objective demonstration rather than personal narration.[59] When, for example, a writer like Katherine Mansfield denotes a character's qualities by evoking dress or décor, or when Virginia Woolf presents Kew Gardens as a fluid composition of primary colours and indeterminate shapes, both writers are trying to achieve an impressionistic effect of sense data rendered exactly as they are perceived in real life, while at the same time showing how these data arrange themselves into unique forms. We see Bertha in her green dress in Mansfield's 'Bliss' (1920); we see the red, blue, and yellow lights shifting across one another as the summer breeze stirs the flower petals in Woolf's 'Kew Gardens', but no account of the sequential events leading up to these visual events – selecting and putting on the dress, or walking into the park – are provided; rather, they are deliberately eliminated so that the bright focus on the visual moment is kept clear, undimmed by description or elaboration. What is discernible in both writers is a 'sense of the moment's drama', the sense which has been said to make Katherine Mansfield 'sister' to the painter Berthe Morisot.[60]

Appreciation of much twentieth-century storywriting is enhanced by considering influences and analogues from the visual arts, though it is by no means always artists of the highest standing who turn out to matter most in this. Katherine Mansfield did undoubtedly learn from Van Gogh's pictures, which haunted her long after she saw them in Roger Fry's Post-Impressionism Exhibition in 1910; she learned, 'something about writing which was queer, a kind of freedom – or rather, a shaking free'.[61] Mansfield's response seems to bear out the 'fine thought' which had occurred to Arnold Bennett when *he* saw the Post-Impressionists' work: 'I have permitted myself to suspect', Bennett wrote, 'that supposing some young writer were to come along and do in words what these young men have done in paint, I might conceivably be disgusted with nearly the whole of modern fiction'.[62]

But Mansfield was also influenced by more ephemeral art forms. As Antony Alpers has shown, the *Jugendstil* illustrations of stock figures arrested in characteristic poses caught her imagination when she encountered this brand of graphic art in Germany.[63] The bold outlines and striking use of gesture in the work of the *Jugend* artists are discernible in Mansfield's ability to tell a story through vibrant images. These momentarily freeze a character's movements at the peak of expressiveness, a capacity which is apparent too in the work of one of Mansfield's older contemporaries, A. E. Coppard, whose wide-ranging interest in the graphic arts included becoming 'enamoured' of the Munich coloured weekly *Jugend*.[64]

As the twentieth century advanced, however, the most likely source of influence from art forms outside literature became photography, and in 1918 it was an exhibition of naval photographs that Katherine Mansfield was describing as 'wonderful' to her painter friend Dorothy Brett.[65] It has become virtually a commonplace to point out that photography in the form of cinema is closely allied to the short story; Elizabeth Bowen is only one of several people to point out that the two arts are 'of the same generation'.[66] Introducing an anthology in 1937, Bowen summarized the affinities which had bound film and the short story together for thirty years: 'neither is sponsored by a tradition; both are, accordingly, free; both, still, are self-conscious, show a self-imposed discipline and regard for form; both have, to work on, immense matter – the disorientated romanticism of the age'.[67] The origin of this comparison in a single visual image must, however, be kept in mind. In some respects, the short story belongs more, and more lastingly, with photography – in particular snapshot photography, which dates from the same period as the modern short story – than with film. Because the short story often depicts one phase of a process or action, the complete time-structure and experience of duration offered by film can be telescoped into a single striking image in which drama is inherent. If the photographic image is defined as a self-sufficient illumination which does not require the help of 'plot' or 'story' to give it meaning, then it is possible to say that the creation of images which do not need to be elaborated or explained, but which do expand in the reader's mind, is the storyteller's method of achieving a comparable effect. The special appeal of the snapshot is its seeming casualness, its subject caught perhaps in a moment of total unselfconsciousness, creating the illusion that the photographer, unlike Elizabeth Bowen's film director, is included in the artlessness he captures.

To be a snapshot photographer who is also an artist it is necessary to be a guileful opportunist with a technique to match a keen eye for subjects. These are also the attributes required by any short-storywriter who agrees with Sherwood Anderson's statement that the artist's business is 'just to fix the moment, in a painting, in a tale, in a poem'.[68] Anderson's account of the way tales always presented themselves to his fancy could apply equally well to the photographer: 'There was a suggestion, a hint given. In a crowd of faces in a crowded street one face suddenly jumped out. It had a tale to tell, was crying its tale to the streets but at best one got only a fragment of it.'[69] The purpose of the comparisons suggested here is not to merge the boundaries of painting, photography and short-storywriting, but to indicate that a sense of the similarities and differences between words and visual images is part of the experience, and a good deal of the pleasure, of reading modern short stories. Among certain writers there is a strong inclination to make compression an opportunity to push language to a limit where it begins to shed its literary qualities and seek non-verbal ways of communicating meaning. Anderson is again a case in point, his contact with modern art through figures like the photographer Alfred Stieglitz and 'many of the modern painters' helping him towards a 'new feeling for form and colour' which was partly the realization of an ambition deflected by his earlier writing career.[70] 'I had always wanted to be a painter myself', he recalled, 'was always having sensations and seeing forms that could perhaps have been expressed in paint and in no other way.'[71] To try to express such sensations and forms is the aim of many writers who attempt to overcome the limitations of their prose medium.

Virginia Woolf talks about exactly this in her pamphlet *Walter Sickert: a Conversation* (1934), where she describes a show of Sickert's paintings as being 'full of pictures that might be stories'.[72] Even though the figures depicted are motionless on the canvas, 'each has been seized in a moment of crisis; it is difficult to look at them and not to invent a plot, to hear what they are saying'.[73] What prevails, however, is the prose-writer's awe of what the painter can achieve 'in the silent kingdom of paint', making Woolf declare: 'Not in our time will anyone write a life as Sickert can paint it. Words are an impure medium.'[74] There is, she acknowledges, no narrative equivalent to the sensations aroused by details and the way the painter has arranged them; there is a mystery which the group of conversationalists cannot hope to unravel: 'Why did the red petticoat, the yellow chest of drawers, make us feel something that had nothing to do with the story? We could not say; we could not express in words the effects of those combinations of line and colour.'[75]

Dissatisfaction with the medium in which stories are told, made Virginia Woolf cultivate a lyrical style in an attempt to bring words closer to the effects of line and colour which she admired in painting. The result was to dislodge the narrative element of prose fiction so radically in favour of sensations and atmospheres that in Woolf's case it becomes more appropriate to talk of 'sketches' than of 'stories'. Her procedure is open to the criticism levelled by Somerset Maugham at Katherine Mansfield, whom he accused of using atmosphere to 'decorate a story so thin' that it could not exist without its 'trimmings'.[76] The reasons for Woolf's and Mansfield's rejection of the 'well made', strongly-plotted story preferred by Maugham are discussed more fully later in this study, but already it is possible to identify the assumption that underlies all descriptions of short fiction in terms of other art forms. Whether the comparison is with painting, lyric poetry, or photography, the feeling is that the short story is a form which is eternally preoccupied with devising ways to escape its own condition. This is a contention which can be more limiting than liberating, especially if it is taken as a licence for sheer aestheticism. Its real value is that it highlights the extent to which the short story is an independent yet hybrid genre, which connects with other art forms at various points and keeps eluding definition except as an interplay of tensions and antitheses. Short but resonant; written in prose but gaining the intensity of poetry; made up of black words arranged on a white page, but shimmering with colour and movement; literary, yet frequently imitative of human speech: the only common factor seems to be the equilibrium aimed for, a reflection perhaps of a wider belief that the job of art is to reconcile opposites.

If there are cases in which it is fitting to compare an individual short story with a painting, a single perceptual event, then it follows that a volume of short stories can resemble an art exhibition. This notion does appear frequently in short-story criticism, though not always approvingly: William Sansom, for example, maintains that 'short stories in book form, like pictures in galleries, create bad habits: read or seen one after the other they cancel themselves out'.[77] But there is also support for Henry James's belief that a collection of short pieces, separately framed but created by the same artist, could express fully a writer's view of life. This belief originates with the medieval practice of collecting *exempla* into a single cohesive group, and is still evident in the larger unity within which many contemporary short-storywriters present individual stories.[78] In the late nineteenth century it was again to Europe that James had to look for instances of the consistent 'philosophy' which he considered a pre-requisite of all artistic creation: his faith in the short story's capacity to rival the novel's expressive power rested on examples drawn from outside the scope of Anglo-Saxon literature. One incident was particularly encouraging for James; in May 1889 a talk with the French critic Taine did his spirits 'a world of good'.[79] Listening to Taine, who paid tribute to Turgenev's 'depth, his variety, his form, the small, full perfect things he has left, which will live through their finished objectivity', James felt his own dreams 'consecrated'.[80] The Russian's example revived and confirmed in James the desire that his bequest to literature would consist of, 'a large number of perfect *short* things, *nouvelles* and tales illustrative of ever so many things in life – in the life I see and know and feel – and of all the deep and the delicate – and of London, and of art, and of everything: and that they shall be fine, rare, strong, wise – eventually perhaps even recognised'.[81]

These are grand aims, but what has usually been stressed is the formalism implicit in the word 'perfect', used here by both Taine and James. Equally important is James's conviction that the short story could mirror contemporary life and epitomize modern conditions. He envisages short fiction becoming a vehicle for what he calls, in the preface to 'The Lesson of the Master', 'the civic use of the imagination'; the short story could reflect what was happening in society at large.[82] And this is exactly what James's stories do, especially the artist stories of the nineties which depict writers – types of James's ideal 'man of imagination' – heroically opposing materialistic social trends and corrosive philistinism. In London, in art, indeed everywhere, James saw the moral and social fabric disintegrating, and by realizing that the short story was a form which could express better than any other the fragmentation which was taking place, he helped to inaugurate the genre to the office it has held ever since. 'Our modern attraction to the short story', wrote Chesterton in 1906, 'is not an accident of form; it is a sign of a real sense of fleetingness and fragility; it means that existence is only an impression, and, perhaps, only an illusion . . . We have no instinct of anything ultimate and enduring beyond the episode.'[83] The brevity of the form, that is to say, is directly imitative of the modern experience of being alive.

Over and over again, twentieth-century commentators have confirmed Chesterton's perception. H. S. Canby, for example, noted in 1909 that the short story was a clear manifestation of a 'nervous, curious, introspective age', giving this as one more reason why writers should emulate the best journalistic impulses to bring people interesting news about themselves.[84] And more recently V. S. Pritchett has made a similar connection between modern edginess and short-story form:

'The modern nervous system is keyed up. The very collapse of standards, conventions and values, which has so bewildered the impersonal novelist, has been the making of the story writer who can catch any piece of life as it flies and make his personal performance out of it.'[85] Yet although these comments are typical of many suggestions that the short story epitomizes twentieth-century life, the genre has not been assigned any definite role in accounts of modernism, which invariably focus almost exclusively on poetry and the novel. The short story suffers particular disadvantages; it is not readily associated with a developing tradition represented by literary figures about whose major stature there is wide agreement. There is still a good deal of wariness about reputations founded entirely on short fiction, besides which, influences are hard to trace and schools difficult to locate. What is more, in the case of authors whose storywriting is not a brief interlude in a novelistic career, it is by no means easy to chart individual progress. The plan described by James, that mass of illustrations he envisaged, is cumulative rather than developmental; first this aspect of life would be illumined, then another, requiring a change in the writer or photographer's positioning, but not necessarily in his fundamental attitudes. Consequently, the maturity expected of a novelist, dramatist or poet in his later works is scarcely looked for in the short-storywriter. It is for this reason that Elizabeth Bowen describes short-storywriters as 'a sort of democracy: when a man engages himself in this special field his stories stand to be judged first of all on their merits *as* stories, only later in relation to the rest of his work'.[86] And short-storywriting can be an erratic business, the author being 'at his best sometimes, and sometimes not; and this is equally true at any age or in any year at which he or she happens to be writing'.[87] '"Development"', Bowen maintained, might be a feature of any one writer's successful novels, but 'in successful stories, I hold it to be a myth'.[88] One reason given for this is that the short story 'is a matter of vision rather than feeling', and therefore not capable of maturing gradually with age: 'Of vision, one asks only that it should not lose its intensity – and I would say that if the vision is there at all, that wish is usually granted.'[89]

To emphasize that the short-storywriter's success depends more on vision than on feeling or intellect is also to admit that the form is liable to court repetition. And if the wished-for intensity does actually fade, then the danger is that the writer will try to fake it. It must be admitted that the short story does allow, perhaps even invites, sameness, its compressed form making it especially liable to formulaic treatment. The writer who goes on extending his reach and increasing his artistic difficulties, as Kipling did, is the exception rather than the norm; so too is Chekhov, who never settled into tested and tried methods but was always ready to turn his hand to skits, social problem stories or atmospheric mood pieces. More usual is the situation described succinctly by Pritchett: 'As they grow older, short story writers tend to repeat themselves as Maupassant and Maugham did.'[90] For this reason alone, the author who writes a large number of stories is likely to become associated with specific kinds of subject-matter or recurrent techniques rather than with a view of life; it seems proper to talk about the view of life conveyed by, say, Dickens's novels, but more appropriate to discuss 'Maugham's Malaya' or 'Maugham's irony' than 'Maugham's philosophy'.

There is, however, no good reason why the short story should be more prone to repetitiousness or mechanical inflexibility than any other kind of writing, and indeed a writer like Borges can make a positive virtue out of his constant return to essentially the same topic. When Borges apologizes, 'The same few plots, I am sorry to say, have pursued me down through the years; I am decidedly monotonous', his regret is a polite lie, since what he believes is that the human mind is capable of only a limited number of fables and metaphors which can, however, have timeless and universal meaning.[91] It is a question of confidence in the power of a small number of inventions to mean everything to everyone. There is no doubt about which of the two 'Borgeses' who meet in 'The Other' (1975) is meant to be the wiser; when Borges of 1969 encounters his younger self of 1918, he finds that, 'My alter ego believed in the invention, or discovery, of new metaphors; I, in those metaphors that correspond to intimate and obvious affinities and that our imagination has already accepted.'[92] 'Invention or discovery'; the terms are synonymous within the Platonic doctrine of archetypes to which Borges subscribes, leading him into sympathy with William Morris's theory that, by the late 1860s, when Morris wrote *The Earthly Paradise*, 'the essential stories of man's imagination had long since been told and that by now the storyteller's craft lay in rethinking and retelling them'.[93] Although Borges does not go quite so far, he does find that writing a story 'has more of discovery about it than of deliberate invention'.[94]

The view that a storyteller is less a fabricator of original fictions than a combination of adapter and curator, may seem to diminish the worth of what any single writer can contribute to the genre; but in fact, by stressing the elements of allusiveness and recognition in storywriting, Borges is keeping in play the reassuring sense of familiarity which, on the reader's side, often accompanies the experience of being told a story, whether in print or orally. Where originality comes over is in the skill with which a writer can simultaneously meet the demand for comforting sameness and divert it into new and often disturbing areas. And what is true of any one memorable story holds for the genre itself; it is always individual talent that unsettles the short story out of a tired formula and back into the experimentalism which is its forte. The mistake is to think that experimentalism always declares itself as unprecedented, an assumption which merely encourages gimmickry and against which the work of Borges stands as an example, along with that of Kafka, another 'innovator' whose experimentalism consisted in reviving ancient forms like the folktale, parable, and beast fable, and making them new.

The short story, like any other literary form, varies according to the period in which it is being written, but it has a unique ability to preserve and at any time recall its mixed origins in fable, anecdote, fairy-story and numerous other forms. Because individual short stories keep revealing affinities with their forerunners, it is almost impossible to stabilize a definition of the genre; no summary phrase can encapsulate the diversity of possible story types, lengths, and approaches. Consequently, no one theory of short-story form prevails, most delineations of the art having come from practitioners like Frank O'Connor and H. E. Bates, and being accompanied by clear provisos about their partiality and incompleteness.[95] Confronted with a distinct genre which nonetheless has no single English word to denominate it, anyone setting out to define the short story is bound to waver. In the first place, there are very basic problems of terminology involving adjacent terms like 'sketch', 'tale' and 'novella'. Even if it is established that 'sketch' will be used of descriptive short fiction with the static quality of a still-life painting, it remains to draw a clear line between sketch and 'sketch-like short story'. Similarly, 'tale' might be reserved for the kind of short piece which lies closest to the picaresque novel and makes only very rudimentary or casual links between one event and another, but this would preempt the use of the term for highly crafted stories which deserve to be called tales because the writer conveys a sense of a human teller presenting the material.

Views differ too about the exact distinction between the short story and the novella, definitions here sometimes being interchangeable. When, for example, one theorist describes the 'generically distinct' aesthetic effect produced by the novella as simultaneous 'intensity and expansion', many people will feel that they are actually being offered a classic definition of the short story's aim.[96] Nor does it help matters that the English language has no equivalent to 'nouvelle' or 'novella' other than 'novelette', which has acquired a disparaging connotation. The result is that in literature written in English it is especially difficult to fix an aesthetic borderline between short story and nouvelle: Henry James, for example, used the terms 'tale', 'story' and 'nouvelle' quite unsystematically for any fiction where concision and rigorous selection were operative principles.

What are headaches to a critic, of course, matter little to the writer who is actually creating the fiction. L. A. G. Strong, for one, was happy just to accept the variety offered by an art that is influenced by writers as diverse as Flaubert, Chekhov, Maupassant, Kipling, Lawrence, George Moore and Conrad, concluding that, 'We not only do not know what a short story ought to be, but we do not want to know. The only safe thing is to allow each writer to call his work what he likes and to judge it severely, and without favour, by its own standards.'[97] In the same spirit, William Saroyan declared that he didn't care *what* his stuff was called as long as he could go on creating it.[98] And Elizabeth Bowen admitted that most of her novels 'would have contracted into short stories', *The Death of the Heart* (1938) being in fact 'an inflated short story'.[99] More austerely, Katherine Anne Porter has requested: 'Please call my works by their right names: we have four that cover every division: short stories, long stories, short novels, novels. I now have examples of all four kinds under these headings, and they seem very clear, sufficient, and plain English.'[100] These headings have the merit of simplicity, and the 'plain English' term 'short story' is calculated to keep the reader aware of the genre's roots in the primitive art of storytelling; the term implies the activity of making a narrative as well as brevity of duration. It waives, however, a question proposed as 'unanswerable' by Frank Swinnerton: 'unless we have decided what a short story ought to be, how can we say whether a short story is a good short story or otherwise?'[101] Modern critics who argue that delimitation and identification of the genre must precede value judgements would agree that the 'ought' should be settled, but it is not at all certain that this can be accomplished by categorizing the conventions adopted by writers calling their productions 'short stories'.

It seems reasonable to say that a firm definition of the short story is impossible. No single theory can encompass the multifarious nature of a genre in which the only constant feature seems to be the achievement of a narrative purpose in a comparatively brief space. The word 'comparatively' is used deliberately here, since the brevity of a short story is something we recognize by relative, not absolute, means; our sense that any given successful story might have been longer, but in that case would have lost something essential to our pleasure in reading it, is not a quantifiable factor, and nor does it appear to obey fixed laws. No sooner is a definition of the short story formulated than exceptions begin to multiply, insisting on their value as literature and properly upsetting the tidiness of a homogenizing approach. It is for these reasons that I have tended to substitute for the question 'what ought a short story to be?', the question 'what can a short story do particularly well *because* it is short?' In this way, the seamlessness of Katherine Anne Porter's term 'story' is preserved, and emphasis is given to those qualities which are best displayed in short narrative, and which become increasingly difficult to sustain as length increases. The short story's technique is inclined to be oblique, and perhaps it is only possible to describe the short story by indicating what it is not, and remaining flexible as to what it is. This is why I feel we should go no further than a rudimentary working definition of the short story as a stretch of fictional prose which is shaped and controlled so as to leave no margin of error in the way it creates a pleasing, unified impression on the reader's imagination. The shorter the piece, the truer Katherine Mansfield's remark, 'If a thing has really come off . . . there mustn't be one single word out of place, or one word that could be taken out'; but it should be remembered that there are other kinds of unity which do not depend on condensed style, and that Mansfield's strictures apply more to the ideal story than to most actually written.[102] Good stories usually establish their own terms of comprehension and appreciation. They tend to make Swinnerton's recourse to 'intrinsic quality' as the only 'absolute test' of a story's worth, not nearly as evasive as it might seem.[103]

Latitude in establishing a canon of short stories and eliciting the characteristics of its members is essential if the diversity of the genre is to be prized, as it deserves to be. Precisely because it has not been highly regarded in comparison with poetry, the novel or drama, the short story has lent itself to continous experimentation – and to play-fulness. There are in fact advantages in the lack of prestige suffered by short fiction. Out on the sidelines of critical debate and compar-atively untouched by changes of fashion, the short story has been free to cultivate diversity in an uninhibited way. Writing and reading stories are activities which are bound up with play and delight, no matter how rigorous and exacting the art of compression. In a 1959 BBC interview, Elizabeth Bowen declared that writing was 'an extension of the play thing a child has – that life isn't amusing enough, so you build it up with imagination of your own'.[104] And for Virginia Woolf short stories offered the chance to experiment with techniques and ideas which might turn out to reveal new ways of writing novels: Jean Guiget has pointed out that the periods in which she wrote most of her stories corresponded to times when she was exploring fresh possibilities for fiction.[105] So relaxing could writ-ing experimental sketches be for Woolf that on at least one occasion she felt quite guilty about producing them quickly and without undue strain. After the publication of *The Mark on the Wall* in 1917 she wrote to David Garnett:

> I'm very glad you liked the story. In a way it's easier to do a short thing, all in one flight than a novel. Novels are frightfully clumsy and overpowering of course; still if one could only get hold of them it would be superb. Anyhow, it's very amusing to try with these short things.[106]

Rather similarly, Chekhov said that whenever he struck a snag in a 'long tale' he could always switch his attention to a short story, and if that didn't work either, he could turn to something even less demanding, a vaudeville.[107]

The implication might seem to be that short stories are gloriously easy to write, a false idea which theorists sometimes try to correct by drawing comparisons between the short story and the sonnet. The short story, it is said, is the most difficult prose form to manipulate successfully. But as with all writing, there is no single type of difficulty, and too much emphasis on technical expertise can provoke justifiable retorts like Arnold Bennett's, made on the occasion of the Poe centenary in 1909. 'As for the greater difficulty of the short story, ask any novelist who has succeeded equally well in both', Bennett told 'facile gabblers about "the art of the short story"'. [108] Such talk, he declared, was foolery 'of a piece with the notion that a fine sonnet is more difficult than a fine epic'.[109] Elsewhere, Bennett makes the same point less irascibly:

> A short form is easier to manipulate than a long form, because its construction is less complicated, because the balance of its proportions can be more easily corrected by means of a rapid survey, because it is lawful and even necessary in it to leave undone many things which are very hard to do, and because the emotional strain is less prolonged.[110]

Nothing in what Bennett says alters the possibility of short stories being intensely worthwhile creations, but he is right to oppose claims made too strenuously and exclusively in terms of artistic difficulty.

To overstate the case for the short-storywriter's aesthetic labours is actually to separate the artist from what he is saying, a step which cannot but tell against individuality. The writer's personality may indeed be expressed solely through the artistic shaping of his material, but that is not equivalent to saying that his stories are impersonal aesthetic objects. This distinction was most persuasively made by D. H. Lawrence, whose notable contribution to the short-story genre was to break all of Brander Matthews's rules about 'a single character, a single event, a single emotion, or the series of emotions called forth by a single situation'.[111] In his own stories, Lawrence followed the almost offhand procedure he outlined in a letter to Louie Burrows: 'The great thing to do in a short story is to select the salient details – a few striking details to make a sudden swift impression.'[112] There is no anxiety about form here: form, Lawrence maintained, 'is not a personal thing like style. It is impersonal like logic.'[113] That was why Lawrence regretted seeing Thomas Mann praised as an artist, not a storyteller.[114] The Flaubertian craving for form, in Lawrence's view, sprang from a misguided attitude which undervalued the individual and more especially the primitive. No wonder Lawrence admired Giovanni Verga, whose Sicilian stories he translated: here was a writer who had renounced Flaubert's doctrines in favour of 'the vivid spontaneity of sensitive passionate life, non-moral and non-didactic'.[115] But even in Verga's forceful peasant tales Lawrence found too much artful cutting, too many abrupt transitions:

> As a matter of fact, we need more looseness. We need an apparent formlessness, definite form is mechanical. We need more easy transition from mood to mood and from deed to deed. A good deal of the meaning of life and of art lies in the apparently dull spaces, the pauses, the unimportant passages.[116]

At the opposite extreme we find James, no less an individual, calling on the 'spirit of Maupassant' to help him achieve masterpieces of concision and form.[117] Whereas Lawrence delights in the 'unliterary', or even the anti-literary, James rejoices in the beauty of 'wrought things'.

Many of the finest and most durable short stories are capable of satisfying both kinds of pleasure at once, combining a tight narrative framework with the apparently casual effect of colloquial dialogue; or enhancing a sense of organic unity by highlighting a single detail which seems gratuitous, but which yet has a rightness that makes it indispensable, part of a design and at the same time entirely natural and unforced. One mistake *can* put the whole impact of a short story at risk, but in fact it is often the sense of a risk taken and wonderfully survived that marks a writer's originality. The formal and the casual constantly intermingle in short stories, and through this shapeliness emerges a definite impression of the author's personality. Without a distinctive personal voice, as V. S. Pritchett has argued, the writer will be unable to answer the reader's fundamental longing to see significance in experience: 'The good storyteller knows that, orally or writing, he is putting on a personal, individual act.'[118] Only when the 'act' is divorced from the individuality of the performer does the short story dwindle into a negligible genre.

NOTES AND REFERENCES

1. Quoted Janet Penrose Trevelyan, *The Life of Mrs Humphry Ward* (1923), p. 117.
2. Pritchett, *Midnight Oil* (1971), Penguin pbk edn (Harmondsworth, Middx, 1974), p. 191; Zola, 'Alexis et Maupassant', *Oeuvres Complètes*, éd. etablie sous la direction de Henri Mitterand (Paris, 1966–), XIV, 623. Zola's assessment first appeared in *Le Figaro*, 11 July 1881.
3. Quoted Antony Alpers, *The Life of Katherine Mansfield* (1980), p. 381. The conversation was originally included in 'Olgivanna', 'The

Last Days of Katherine Mansfield', *Bookman* (New York) LXXIV (Mar. 1931) 6–13.

4. *The Days Before*, (1st Eng. edn, 1953), p. 105.
5. *It's Me, O Lord!* (1957), p. 33.
6. *Ibid.*
7. *Ibid.*
8. 'Katherine Anne Porter: An Interview', *Paris Review*, XXIX (1963), 101.
9. *Ibid.* See also Foreword to *The Days Before*, p. vii, where Porter says that her stories 'are written in one draft, and if short enough, at one sitting'.
10. *The Letters and Journals of Katherine Mansfield: A Selection*, ed. C. K. Stead (1977), p. 247 (1 Jan. 1922).
11. *Letters on the Short Story, the Drama and other Literary Topics*, ed. Louis S. Friedland (1965), p. 17 (30 Sept.).
12. Introduction to *The Country of the Blind* (1911), p. vi.
13. 'The Story-teller at Large: Mr Henry Harland', *The Fortnightly Review*, New Series, LXIII (Apr. 1898), 652.
14. The evolution of German short fiction is traced in E. K. Bennett and H. M. Waidson, *A History of the German Novelle*, (Cambridge, 1961).
15. See Benjamin Boyce, 'English Short Fiction in the Eighteenth Century: A Preliminary View', *Studies in Short Fiction*, V (Winter 1968), 110, and Robert D. Mayo, *The English Novel in the Magazines 1740–1815* (Evanston, Illinois, 1962), pp. 4–5 and *passim*. Mary McCarthy's comment was made in lectures paraphrased as 'The Fact in Fiction', in *On the Contrary* (1962), p. 270.
16. *The Philosophy of the Short-story* (New York, 1901), p. 60. Matthews's views were first published anonymously in *The Saturday Review*, July 1884.
17. *Ibid.*, p. 57 and n.
18. *Partial Portraits* (1888), p. 264. James's essay 'Guy de Maupassant' was first published in *The Fortnightly Review*, (1888).
19. *Ibid.*
20. *The Tale Bearers* (1980), p. 164.
21. *Ibid.* (For H. E. Bates's similar argument that the nineteenth-century English short story was 'a kind of orphan slavey' to the novelist and that the genre had 'no history' in England before 1900, see 'A Note on the English short story', *Lovat Dickson's Magazine*, II (Feb. 1934), 145.)
22. *Ibid.*
23. 'The Quest for Nationality', *Harper's Monthly* (Nov. 1891), repr. in *W. D. Howells as Critic*, ed. Edwin H. Cady (1973), p. 210.
24. Review of Howells's *A Foregone Conclusion, The Nation*, 7 Jan. 1875, repr. in *Literary Reviews and Essays by Henry James*, ed. Albert Mordell (New York, 1957), p. 214.
25. *Ibid.*
26. James, *Ibid*; Howells, 'My Favourite Novelist and his Best Book', *Munsey's*, Apr. 1897, repr. in *W. D. Howells as Critic*, p. 277.
27. See Boyce, p. 96 (see note 15 above).
28. *Something of Myself* (1937), p. 72. This, and all subsequent page references to Kipling's prose works, are to Macmillan's Uniform Edition.

29. *Fiction and the Reading Public* (1932), p. 26.
30. *Ibid.*, p. 27.
31. *Ibid.*
32. *London Magazine* (Sept. 1966), p. 12; p. 6.
33. Editor's introduction, *London Magazine*, Mar. 1970.
34. Thomas H. Gullason has indicated the inadequacies of New Criticism's approach to the short story in 'The Short Story: An Underrated Art', *Studies in Short Fiction*, II (Fall, 1964), 24. See also Falcon O. Baker, 'Short Stories for the Millions', *Saturday Review of Literature*, XXXVI (19 Dec. 1953), 7–9, 48–9.
35. *The Modern Short Story: A Critical Survey* (1941), p. 219.
36. Review of Hawthorne's *Twice-Told Tales*, in *The Complete Works of Edgar Allan Poe*, ed. James A. Harrison (17 vols, New York, 1902; repr. 1965), XI, 107. Poe's review first appeared in *Graham's Magazine*, May 1842. To avoid confusion between Harrison's edition of the *Complete Works* and the *Collected Works* which is yet to be completed, the former will subsequently be referred to as the 'Virginia' edition.
37. *Ibid.*, p. 108.
38. *Ibid.*
39. *Ibid.*
40. *Ibid.*, p. 109.
41. *The Notebooks of Henry James*, ed. F. O. Matthiessen and Kenneth B. Murdock (New York, 1947), pp. 105–6 (13 July 1891).
42. *Henry James Letters*, ed. Leon Edel, III (1980), 209.
43. *Notebooks*, p. 167.
44. *Ibid.*
45. Preface to 'The Lesson of the Master', in *The Art of the Novel: Critical Prefaces* (New York, 1962), p. 219.
46. *Ibid.*, p. 220.
47. *Ibid.*, p. 231.
48. *Ibid.*
49. *Ibid.*, p. 220.
50. Preface to *Dr Brodie's Report* (1970), trans. Norman Thomas di Giovanni in collaboration with the author, Penguin pbk edn (Harmondsworth, Middx, 1976), p. 11. All subsequent page references to this collection of stories are to this edition.
51. 'The Story-teller at Large', p. 652.
52. *Ibid.*
53. Repr. in *Kipling: The Critical Heritage*, ed. Roger Lancelyn Green (1971), p. 167.
54. *Letters*, III, 240 (3 July).
55. *Notebooks*, p. 160.
56. Gleeson White, *Letters to Eminent Hands* (1892), p. 59. (White's 'Open Letter' to Kipling is reprinted in *Kipling: The Critical Heritage*, pp. 168–72).
57. Preface to Knopf edn of *Early Stories* (New York, 1951), quoted Victoria Glendinning, *Elizabeth Bowen; Portrait of a Writer* (1977), p. 54.
58. *Ibid.*
59. *Ibid.*

60. Elizabeth Bowen, Introduction to *34 Short Stories by Katherine Mans-field* (1957), p. 26, repr. in *Afterthought: Pieces about Writing* (1962).
61. *Letters and Journals*, p. 245 (5 Dec. 1921).
62. 'Books and Persons', *The New Age*, 8 Dec. 1910, p. 135 (under pseudonym 'Jacob Tonson').
63. See *The Life of Katherine Mansfield*, pp. 100–1.
64. *It's me, O Lord!*, p. 164.
65. *Letters and Journals*, p. 125 (20 July).
66. Preface to *The Faber Book of Modern Stories* (1937), p. 7.
67. *Ibid*. Early in her career Bowen was advised by John Strachey, who ran the literary side of *The Spectator*, to make a habit of going to the cinema, which he thought could teach her a lot (see Glendinning, p. 51). Among others who have likened short-storywriting to the art of film are: A. E. Coppard; V. S. Pritchett; and H. E. Bates.
68. *A Story Teller's Story* (New York, 1924), p. 403.
69. *Ibid.*, p. 402.
70. *Ibid.*, p. 374.
71. *Ibid.*, p. 349.
72. *Walter Sickert*, p. 13.
73. *Ibid*.
74. *Ibid*.
75. *Ibid.*, p. 25.
76. *Points of View* (1958), p 186.
77. *London Magazine* (Sept. 1966), p. 10.
78. See H. S. Canby, *The Short Story in English* (New York, 1909), p. 27.
79. *Notebooks*, p. 101.
80. *Ibid*.
81. *Ibid*.
82. *The Art of the Novel*, p. 223.
83. *Charles Dickens* (1906), p. 85.
84. *The Short Story in English*, p. 338.
85. 'Short Stories', *Harper's Bazaar* (New York), LXXXVII (July 1953), 113.
86. Review of Maxim Gorki, *A Book of Short Stories* (1939), in *Collected Impressions* (1950), p. 153. The review first appeared in *The New Statesman and Nation*.
87. Preface to *A Day in the Dark and Other Stories* (1965), p 7.
88. *Ibid*.
89. *Ibid*.
90. *The Tale Bearers*, p. 38.
91. Preface to *Dr Brodie's Report*, p. 12.
92. *The Book of Sand*, trans. Norman Thomas di Giovanni, Penguin pbk edn (Harmondsworth, Middx, 1979), p. 8.
93. *Ibid*.
94. Afterword to *Dr Brodie's Report*, p. 101.
95. See Frank O'Connor *The Lonely Voice: A Study of the Short Story* (1963), and H. E. Bates, *The Modern Short Story*. Another instance of a study written by a practitioner is T. O. Beachcroft, *The Modest Art: A Survey of the Short Story in Englsih* (1968).
96. Judith Leibowitz, *Narrative Purpose in the Novella* (The Hague, 1974), p. 16.

97. 'Concerning Short Stories', *Bookman* (New York), LXXV (Nov. 1932), 712. Strong expressed this view again in *The Writer's Trade* (1953), pp. 85–6.

98. 'What is a Story?', *Saturday Review of Literature*, XI (5 Jan. 1935), 409.

99. Letter to A. E Coppard, quoted Glendinning, p. 82; BBC interview (1959), quoted Glendinning, p. 125.

100. Introduction to *Collected Stories of Katherine Anne Porter* (New York, 1965), p. vi.

101. Preface to L. A. G. Strong, *Travellers: Thirty-One Selected Short Stories* (1945), p. v.

102. *Letters and Journals*, p. 213 (17 Jan. 1921).

103. *Travellers*, p. v.

104. Quoted Glendinning, p. 31.

105. *Virginia Woolf and Her Works* (1962), trans. Jean Stewart (1965), p. 330.

106. *The Letters of Virginia Woolf*, ed. Nigel Nicolson (6 vols, 1975–80), II, 167 (26 July 1917).

107. *Letters on the Short Story*, p. 236 (14 Sept. 1889).

108. *Books and Persons* (New York, 1917), p. 87. This article was first published in *The New Age*, 28 Jan.

109. *Ibid.*

110. *The Author's Craft* (1914), p. 77.

111. *The Philosophy of the Short-story*, p. 16.

112. *Lawrence in Love: Letters to Louie Burrows*, ed. James T. Boulton (Nottingham, 1968), p. 19 (7 Oct. 1908).

113. *Selected Literary Criticism*, ed. Anthony Beal, Heinemann pbk edn (1967), p. 260.

114. *Ibid.* Lawrence's assessment of Mann first appeared in *Blue Review*, July 1913.

115. *Ibid.*, p. 287 (Introduction to Lawrence's translation of Verga's *Cavalliera Rusticana* (1928)).

116. *Ibid.*, p. 289.

117. *Notebooks*, p. 89 (11 Mar. 1888).

118. 'Short Stories', p. 124.

Chapter 2

'A WIDE MARGIN FOR THE WONDERFUL': ROBERT LOUIS STEVENSON

> He leaves so wide a margin for the wonderful that he escapes the
> danger of being brought up by cases he has not allowed for: when he
> allows for Mr Hyde he allows for everything – it is the improbable
> that has most character, because it involves the finest feelings . . .
> (Henry James on Stevenson)

Among short-storywriters capable of taking fruitful artistic risks,
Stevenson provides an exemplary case. He embodies certain forces
that are crucial to an understanding of the way the genre has developed. The amalgam of influences and conditions prevailing in the last
quarter of the nineteenth century is discernible in Stevenson's work,
and for this reason the present brief chapter will investigate his
methods and achievements. Part of the intention is to demonstrate
in relation to a single, transitional figure some of the issues which
pervade this entire study, though of course Stevenson amply repays
study both in his own right and as a major influence on such an
apparently far more sophisticated writer like Borges.

Stevenson's achievement as a writer of short stories is decidedly
uneven. He was adept at turning out rambling blood-and-thunder
stuff like 'The Pavilion on the Links' (1882), which he described as
a 'grand carpentry story in nine chapters and I should hesitate to say
how many tableaux'.[1] This was a story designed to make money, not
to test out any notion of artistic form. Yet he was equally capable
of producing stories which have deservedly become part of British
literary tradition (and to some extent, of popular mythology); most
notable is *The Strange Case of Dr Jekyll and Mr Hyde* (1886), but
there is also the fine 'Thrawn Janet' (1887), which Stevenson 'could
not help' submitting for publication because, even if its Scottish
dialect might deter readers, 'it was *so good*'.[2] To these should be
added 'Markheim' (1887), where macabre effects are deepened by
allegorical seriousness, and 'Will O' the Mill' (1887), in which Henry
James found 'the most fascinating quality a work of the imagination
can have – a dash of alternative mystery as to its meaning, an air

(the air of life itself) of half inviting, half defying you to interpret'.[3] These teasing masterpieces co-exist with ephemeral productions like the comic set-piece 'Providence and the Guitar' (1882), and 'The Misadventures of John Nicholson', which Stevenson was surely right to call 'a silly Xmas story'.[4]

Stevenson's work is such a mixture of the worthwhile and the mediocre that it is tempting to disregard the loose and over-written stories in favour of the handful of narratives which make it plausible to argue that he is actually one of the creators of the modern short story. A case for Stevenson as a deft artificer can certainly be made if emphasis is given to his diverse uses of narrative voice: his ability to shape his material according to the viewpoint of a lonely or isolated outsider provides a basis for following James's lead and claiming that the question of *form* was always a living one to Stevenson. A living question it undoubtedly was, and Stevenson grasped the principle of unity of effect with a firmness that makes him the direct heir of Edgar Allan Poe. But there is nothing drily theoretical about the way Stevenson explores aesthetic topics: when he proclaims the need to attain organic wholeness in short fiction, it is with all the verve of a practising author who is eager to reach an audience. As the following extract from a letter to Colvin shows, Stevenson is unhesitating about how his art works best:

> Make another end to it? Ah yes, but that's not the way I write; the effects that are to follow; that's what a story consists in. To make another end, that is to make the beginning all wrong. The denouement of a long story is nothing; it is just a 'full close', which you may approach and accompany as you please – it is a coda, not an essential member in the rhythm; but the body and end of a short story is the bone of the bone and the blood of the blood of the beginning.[5]

Similarly, and in language that is more overtly reminiscent of James's, Stevenson declares in the Preface to *Familiar Studies of Men and Books* (1882) that the writer of 'short studies', having 'seized his "point of view" must keep his eye steadily to that', for these short pieces 'are, or should be, things woven like a carpet, from which it is impossible to detach a strand'.[6]

As theory, this comes remarkably close to the prevailing twentieth century view that the short story differs from the novel in terms of structure and conception, not merely in length. But Stevenson's practice does not always bear out his insight into formal matters; even in short pieces, he tends to be better at beginnings than endings, and relatively few of his stories have the kind of thematic and narrative drive that make the conclusion a satisfying inevitable consequence of the opening.[7] The best things in Stevenson's short fiction actually have very little to do with form, except as an artistic ideal, and this is not altogether surprising if consideration is given to the circumstances which were bound to restrict any advance he might make towards the truly 'modern' short story. First, there is the straightforward fact that in the nineteenth century it was not thought at all odd to serialize short stories as well as novels: 'Providence and the Guitar', for example, first appeared under the more specific title 'Leon Berthilini's Guitar' in four weekly instalments in the periodical *London* (2–23 Nov. 1878); and the first readers of 'The Pavilion on the Links' would have had to wait a month to discover what befalls the narrator, abandoned at the end of the first instalment, solitary by the windswept pavilion with only a light from a crannied shutter for comfort. Publishing short fiction piecemeal was customary, Thomas Hardy being another author of the period to supply stories for serialization; both 'The Melancholy Hussar of the German Legion' (1894) and 'The Withered Arm' (1888) first appeared in this way. Even when a writer disliked the practice, as Henry James did, there was little he could do about it beyond complaining when his carefully structured stories were chopped up: 'I am sorry you are to publish ['Lady Barberina'] as *three*', James wrote to the editor of *The Century* in 1884, 'the interest is not calculated for that.'[8] On other occasions, when James actually catered for the editorial habit of breaking stories into sections, he still found that his own wishes could be swept aside, as they were when 'The Aspern Papers' (1888), which he envisaged divided into two parts ('no other', he stipulated), was published in three.[9]

Whatever a writer might believe about 'the body and end of a short story' being 'the bone of the bone and the blood of the blood of the beginning', periodical publication meant that the ending would be severed from the beginning, with the result that a tendency to think in terms of episodes or even chapter-like sections was perpetuated. Even James modified his anger about the division of 'Lady Barberina' because it partly justified him in finding 'the process of writing a very short story' increasingly difficult: 'As one grows older, and sees and learns more, it becomes harder to squeeze this enlarged matter into brevity of form, and I find I *must* take elbow-room.'[10] Serialization provided all of these writers and their contemporaries with 'elbow-room', but by the same token it suppressed attempts to achieve compact form. Nor was this problem confined to Anglo-Saxon writers: Chekhov had reason to grumble about publishing conditions and to adopt a defiant stance. 'In only one case', he wrote, 'is it essential to co-operate with the large magazines: – a long work cannot be broken up into bits and must be published as a whole': no other consideration could have made Chekhov seem to be wooing 'the imposing periodicals', the only ones that could be trusted with 'long works'.[11]

A second, though not necessarily a damaging, circumstance restraining Stevenson's innovatory powers, was that behind him lay a tradition of tale-telling as primarily a recreational activity. 'Fiction', writes Stevenson in his 'Gossip on Romance' (1887), 'is to the grown man what play is to the child; it is there that he changes the atmosphere and tenor of his life.'[12] In his belief that fiction offers an amalgam of pleasure and instruction, Stevenson looks backwards more than forwards; he looks back to the early eighteenth-century taste for moral reflections in the cast of simple narrative and typical characterization. The drift of his chosen title for the collection *New Arabian Nights* (1882) is obvious, and it is worth recollecting that it was in the period of *Tatler* and *Spectator* that the original *Arabian Nights* enjoyed a vogue in England, the Oriental tale playing a prominent part in early periodical fiction.[13] Unlike his eighteenth-century predecessors in so many other ways, Stevenson makes comparable use of strange and exotic settings, mingling the manner of moral essayist and storyteller, even though his morality is far more ambiguous and elusive than anything to be found in the didactic tales of Addison or Dr Johnson.

While certain aspects of Stevenson's short fiction are superficially reminiscent of eighteenth-century journalism, however, the deeper inclinations which stamp his work are totally away from neo-classical restraint; *Spectator* writing he found 'all very fine', but 'vapid'.[14] His felt affinity was more with the extravagance which, closer to his own time, had proved a dominant force in the development of the short story, especially in America. Edgar Allan Poe in the 1840s had ensured that fantasy and exaggeration would displace the politely belletristic, and Hawthorne had decisively widened the scope of short fiction by using the solitary viewpoint to explore the dark mysteries of the human heart. Both writers were congenial to Stevenson, though he recognized the greater stature of Hawthorne, in whose work he found the key qualities of 'unity', an 'unwavering creative purpose' and an ability to create a 'vivid and single impression'.[15] America offered stylistic lessons too: to read Thoreau, for Stevenson, was to encounter 'an exaggerative and a parabolic writer', and to understand fully what Thoreau was only 'on the point of seeing' – that 'the proper method of literature is by selection, which is a kind of negative exaggeration'.[16] In all of these writers, working in a foreign tradition but each initially belonging, like Stevenson, to a regional culture, he probably found support for his belief that fiction should constantly return to its primitive origins in fable and fireside entertainment, favouring exaggeration more than discretion and polish. At the same time, American examples taught him the dangers of exaggerating too blatantly, as Thoreau had done, and strengthened his conviction that the way to thrill readers was to omit and select, exaggerating 'negatively'.

Of importance here is Stevenson's own theory of fable, which he outlined in an early review of Lord Lytton's *Fables in Song* (1874).

This essay displays clearly the kind of tension to be found in Stevenson between his awareness that literary possibilities were changing, and his profound love for the ancient simple forms. Stevenson analyzes the typical fable as a form which uses 'a conception purely fantastic, and usually somewhat trivial' to convey some moral precept; essential elements are playfulness and concision, and 'the lesson must be apprehended by the fancy at half a hint'.[17] The value of the original type of fable, according to Stevenson, lay in 'a sort of humorous inappropriateness', a kind of freedom and exuberance which he realized could not easily survive the increasing sophistication and earnestness of modern readers.[18]

What Stevenson seems nostalgic for is the palpable unreality and moral simplicity of the old forms: the 'primitive sort of fable' expressed 'a humanity, a tenderness of rough truths; so that at the end of some story, in which vice or folly had met with its destined punishment, the fabulist might be able to assure his auditors, as we have often to assure tearful children on like occasions, that they may dry their eyes, for none of it was true'.[19] Working against this simplicity Stevenson sees forces which he summarizes in the phrase 'the progressive centralization of modern thought'; new tendencies, he believes, are going to make the fable less fabulous by restricting the playfulness of the author.[20] There will still be brevity, and a moral idea to grasp intellectually rather than through emotional involvement; characterization will still be 'mechanical': but 'the fabulist now seeks analogies where before he merely sought humorous situations. There will now be a logical nexus between the moral expressed and the machinery employed to express it.'[21]

As Stevenson goes on to describe this altered and more rigorous artistic form, it is difficult to tell exactly whether he is elated or depressed by the challenge presented. He notes that the reader of these new stories is going to be left more to himself to resolve 'the vague, troublesome, and not yet definitely moral sentiment' created, and he emphasizes that morality itself will have to become pervasive, diffused throughout the material:

> It ceases to be possible to append [the moral], in a tag, to the bottom of the piece, as one might write the name of a caricature; and the fable begins to take rank with all other forms of literature, as something too ambitious, in spite of its miniature dimensions, to be resumed in any succinct formula without the loss of all that is deepest and most suggestive about it.[22]

So the gain may be a suggestiveness that Stevenson clearly values and imports into the most morally ambiguous of his own stories, but the loss is of something delightful – what he calls 'the incredible element, the point of audacity with which the fabulist was wont to mock at his readers'.[23] Against this background, it is possible to find in Stevenson's short stories a number of attempts to convey his 'modern' sense that morality is not a matter of neat tags, and to do this without renouncing the 'humorous inappropriateness', fanciful illogicality, and playful – if not entirely mocking – relationship between author and reader, all of which he valued in the old-fashioned fable. One minor, but enormously influential, story, 'A Lodging for the Night' (1882) illustrates clearly the techniques by which Stevenson managed to evade 'the logical nexus between the moral expressed and the machinery employed to express it', offering instead a narrative which combines Poe-like grotesqueries and shrewd selectivity, or 'negative exaggeration'. Unsatisfactory in several respects, 'A Lodging for the Night' does nevertheless display features which indicate one direction short fiction was to take, and it is significant that when twenty-four authors were asked by the *New York Times* in 1914, 'What is the best short story in English?', Stevenson's piece, along with Bret Harte's 'Outcasts of Poker Flat' (1870), should have come out favourite.[24] Clearly, it was felt that Stevenson had surpassed the earlier achievements of Poe and Hawthorne in emancipating the short story from the essay.

In this respect it is important to note that for Stevenson himself the story represented a turning point, and also that 'A Lodging for the Night' evolved out of an essay on François Villon which he had contemplated writing as early as 1875, but which did not materialize until two years later. In May 1877, Stevenson, following Leslie Stephen's advice, abandoned the plan to bring out a book of essays, and by August (the month in which his essay-portrait of Villon appeared in *Cornhill Magazine*) he was looking elsewhere for an improvement in his income: 'I begin', he told Mrs Sitwell, 'to have more hope in the story line.'[25] That Stevenson was moving in a new direction is evident, and this impression is strengthened by Roger Swearingen's recent discovery of a Stevenson story called 'An Old Song' which appeared anonymously in four weekly 'Feuilleton' instalments in the magazine *London* (24 Feb.–17 Mar. 1877).[26] Three years before this, Stevenson had planned a 'Book of Stories', but the idea had been dropped; now, it seemed, writing and publishing stories was to become a paramount concern, involving some adjustment of artistic methods, and in particular a fresh determination to avoid fine writing and stylistic embellishments. After publishing his essay on Villon, he wrote, in the same letter to Mrs Sitwell: 'I am glad you liked *Villon*; some of it was not as good as it ought to be, but on the whole it seems pretty vivid, and the features strongly marked. Vividness and not style is now my line; style is all very well, but vividness is the real line of country.'[27] Then, in a rather characteristically throw-away remark that perhaps reflects his poor opinion of the general reading public, he adds the weary truism: 'if a thing is meant to be read, it seems just as well to try and make it readable'.[28]

But although 1877 may be taken as the date after which fiction began to supersede the essay in Stevenson's work, his realization that the power of short fiction may depend on resisting rather than cultivating fine writing had emerged some years earlier. There is a fascinating letter of January 1874 in which Stevenson tells Colvin about problems he is having with a story that he never finished, 'The Curate of Anstruther's Bottle'. Clearly Stevenson is dissatisfied with inherited literary models; he is fretting about the restrictiveness of a convention that strikes him as possibly 'too much in the style of those decadent curiosities, poems without the letter E, poems going with the alphabet and the like'.[29] Stevenson shows how aware he is of the dangers of sheer ingenuity in short fiction, proposing as a necessary curb on decorative and self-displaying tendencies the virtue of credibility. The need to convince the reader, whatever the convention, makes it proper for the writer to 'rely on the essential interest of a situation and not cocker up and validify feeble intrigue with incidental fine writing and scenery, and pyrotechnic exhibitions of inappropriate cleverness and sensibility'.[30] To reinforce his emphasis on the primacy of subject in storytelling, Stevenson recalls a conversation with his cousin Bob about what an artist could make of the quadrangle in Edinburgh University. The episode is worth lingering over because it so forcibly demonstrates three major principles which are evident in Stevenson's most successful and most innovatory narrative strategies.

First, there is his belief that locale and topography should always serve a direct narrative purpose and be made available to the reader not in exposition but through *action*; this has become an article of faith for most later storywriters. Secondly, Stevenson characteristically associates light-effects with the specific situations of individual characters within a story; this device recurs throughout his fiction, where a single (and often vulnerable) point of light is set against surrounding darkness, creating a poignant and dramatic contrast. The wavering candlelight in 'Markheim'; the candle which Mr Soulis in 'Thrawn Janet' carries out from his manse into the darkness, where it burns in the still air with ominous steadiness; and the narrator's lantern in the climactic scene of *The Beach of Falesá* (1892) are notable instances; in all three works Stevenson's artistic concern to light his scene effectively collaborates with his psychological interest in the solitary, subjective viewpoint on events. Lastly, Stevenson's words to Bob reveal his constant attention to narrative integrity and unity. He recollects saying

that the different doors and staircases ought to be brought before a reader not by mere recapitulation but by the use of them, by the descent of different people one after another by each of them. And that the grand feature of shadow and the light of the one lamp in the corner should also be introduced only as they enabled people in the story to see one another or prevented them. And finally that whatever could not thus be worked into the evolution of the action had no right to be commemorated at all. After all, it is a story you are telling; not a place you are to describe; and everything that does not attach itself to the story is out of place.[31]

Like his American predecessor Poe, Stevenson saw how essential it was to make every detail count in short fiction, where narrative momentum had to be maintained if the author were to benefit fully from having the reader's uninterrupted attention during the single sitting at which a story could be read.

Stevenson was obviously aware of the special possibilities, as well as the limitations, of short fiction, but it would be foolish to claim that in practice his stories always attained unity which could be called 'organic'. 'The Merry Men' for example, which he announced to Henley in 1881 as 'my first real shoot at a story', and which he intended to have the effect of music ('a fantastic sonata about the sea and wrecks'), was conceived episodically, in terms of chapters, rather than thematically.[32] 'Like enough, when it is finished I shall discard all chapterings; for the thing is written straight through', he tells Henley, admitting to a procedure which suggests a certain amount of tension between the momentum of writing the story 'straight through' and the traditional Victorian habit of dividing fiction in sections or chapters.[33]

Modern theorists would argue that a short story ought not to be divisible into chapters at any stage of its composition or appreciation, but even in such an early attempt as 'A Lodging for the Night' Stevenson's desire to do something new in the short story is evident. The story does have qualities that bear out Stevenson's claim that he was learning how to be vivid without becoming over-stylish. It begins with an objective description which establishes time and place in a realistic yet portentous way, creating a bleak atmosphere which is appropriate to the events of the single night to be depicted:

It was late in November, 1456. The snow fell over Paris with rigorous, relentless persistence; sometimes the wind made a sally and scattered it in flying vortices; sometimes there was a lull, and flake after flake descended out of the black night air, silent, circuitous, interminable. To poor people, looking up under moist eyebrows, it seemed a wonder where it all come from.

If there is a risk of decorativeness in the description of the snow flakes falling, then it is swiftly counteracted by the simplicity of the poor people's response – 'it seemed a wonder where it all came from'. The initial setting of the story establishes an obvious enough link between extreme cold and physical suffering, an association which functions throughout the story, and encompasses the wordy debate between Villon and the nobleman Brisetout, who offers him shelter, cold mutton, and bracing moral advice. To some extent, the precision with which Stevenson delineates the setting, and Villon's movements within it, rescues this debate from schematism – but only partially. The confrontation between Villon and Brisetout, who preaches that the needs of the heart (honour, faith and love) surpass all bodily desire, is clearly meant to provide a climax, and it is characteristic of Stevenson to set two extreme views of life in irreconcilable opposition. The cynic Villon argues that the moral life is merely the product of fortunate circumstances, while Brisetout affirms the boundless possibility of repentance and Christian grace. But whereas in mature stories like 'Markheim' and *Dr Jekyll and Mr Hyde*, Stevenson was to find ways of dramatizing conflict and dispersing morality throughout the fiction, here the opposition remains inert and stated. Brisetout himself is too much an allegorical figure, his moral stance fully disclosed by the tapestry on his walls, 'representing the crucifixion of our Lord in one piece, and in another a scene of shepherds and shepherdesses by a running stream' – in sum, Christianity and classical-pastoral united.

What makes 'A Lodging for the Night' memorable is not the ideas raised in it by Stevenson's taste for moral analysis, but rather several elements which show him experimenting with the techniques that intrigued him when he discussed with Bob how the University quadrangle could be treated in different artistic media. These elements include his use of light and perspective, as when he makes something sinister and grotesque out of the minor character Dom Nicolas, the Picardy monk 'with his skirts picked up and his fat legs bared to the comfortable warmth. His dilated shadow cut the room in half; and the firelight only escaped on either side of his broad person, and in a little pool between his outspread feet.' Then comes a fairly stereotyped description of the monk's beery face, before Stevenson returns to the uncanny *effect* of the figure: 'So he straddled, grumbling, and cut the room in half with the shadow of his portly frame.' Inconspicuously, Stevenson has prepared for the violent murder with which this scene culminates.

Later in the story, a similarly bizarre effect is created by Stevenson's manipulation of closely registered sense-experience when Villon, in order to hide from the patrol, jumps from the glimmering light of snowy streets into the darkness of a half-ruinous porch: 'he was groping forward with outspread hands, when he stumbled over some substance which offered an indescribable mixture of resistances, hard and soft, firm and loose'. As the give-away word 'indescribable' confirms, this is the unspecified 'something' which is constantly on hand to alarm the senses in countless gothic tales before Stevenson's time, and as many horror films of our own. Villon's reaction is appropriately stereotyped: 'His heart gave a leap, and he sprang two steps back and stared dreadfully at the obstacle.'

But again Stevenson gives a new twist to the time-worn device which might be called 'the collapse of terror into certainty': Then he gave a little laugh of relief. It was only a woman, and she dead. She was freezing cold, and rigid like a stick. A little ragged finery fluttered in the wind about her hair, and her cheeks had been heavily rouged that same afternoon.' Locally, this is an unremarkable bit of sensationalism, suitable for a Stevensonian 'crawler' and an appropriate way of underlining Villon's hardened callousness, but in fact Stevenson deepens the impact of this tableau by repeating it in severely chastened form later, when Villon describes the dead woman to Brisetout: 'as dead as Caesar, poor wench, and as cold as the church, with bits of ribbon sticking in her hair'. What had previously been decorative pathos provided by the author – 'a little ragged finery fluttered in the wind about her hair' – becomes stark and colloquial – 'bits of ribbon sticking in her hair'.[34]

The robust plainness of this diction, and the fact that it really has no contribution to make to the intellectual concerns of the story, might offer a reminder of another influence on Stevenson – John Bunyan. Stevenson admired Bunyan's style for its 'gusto and precision', and for its capacity to serve, but move beyond, the confines of a central allegorical purpose.[35] In *The Pilgrim's Progress*, Stevenson discerned not only what he called the 'rustic privilege of [Bunyan's] style', but also the eventual benefits of an apparent difficulty, namely the division of interest between story and allegory.[36] In his 1882 review of Bagster's illustrated *Pilgrim's Progress*, Stevenson argues that because 'the mere story and the allegorical design enjoyed perhaps [Bunyan's] equal favour' story never lapses into simple subservience to moral design, but asserts its own charm and interest.[37] In fact, what he finds most exciting about Bunyan is a feature which characterizes Stevenson's own storytelling at its best – something he describes as 'triumphant literality of vision', an uncompromising sense of things in themselves.[38] It is a vision which, Stevenson readily admits, risks lapsing into the ridiculous, and actually courts inconsistencies, but it is all the more welcome for that: what Stevenson seems to be urging is the paradox whereby precisely because we are shown details that do *not* fit the allegorical scheme, we are more inclined to give assent to the work as a whole: 'Christina dying "gave Mr Stand-fast a ring" for no possible reason in the allegory, merely because the touch was human and affecting.'[39]

Stevenson would have found examples of 'literality' strengthening, and yet somehow standing outside, an overall allegorical design in Hawthorne as well as in Bunyan, and increasingly in his own work he used vivid literal detail to enhance moral interest. In fact the pathetic 'bits of ribbon' in 'A Lodging for the Night' are directly reminiscent of Faith's pink ribbons in Hawthorne's 'Young Goodman Brown' (1846), where a simple everyday object is given similarly emblematic force. Sometimes Stevenson's intention seems merely to add a touch that is 'human and affecting', like the dead woman's ribbons, but elsewhere, and more ambitiously, literality is used to create effects that suggest the supernatural. An uncanny atmosphere is made all the more chilling when it is shown emanating from purely physical sources, a principle which can be observed in many short stories which aim to unnerve the reader. Modern instances would be those sinister suburban villas in Elizabeth Bowen's stories, which themselves owe something to the settings used by Algernon Blackwood to convey a kind of suppressed supernaturalism. Stevenson was a pioneer of such techniques, and they can be seen at work in 'The Merry Men', particularly at the moment when the narrator, who is searching for a lost treasure-ship, the *Espirito Santo*, comes upon a worthless but eloquent object:

> I clambered back upon the rocks, and threw the plant of tangle at my feet. Something at the same moment rang sharply, like a falling coin. I stooped, and there, sure enough, crusted with red rust, there lay an iron shoe-buckle. The sight of this poor human relic thrilled me to the heart, but not with hope or fear, only with a desolate melancholy. I held it in my hand, and the thought of its owner appeared before me like the presence of an actual man. His weather-beaten face, his sailor's hands, his sea-voice hoarse with singing at the capstan, the very foot that had once worn that buckle and trod so much along the swerving decks – the whole human fact of him, as a creature like myself, with hair and blood and seeing eyes, haunted me in that sunny, solitary place, not like a spectre, but like some friend whom I had basely injured.[40]

The reality and finality of death is borne in on this narrator (a lowlander who has prided himself on his mechanical abilities), not by a jolting spiritual experience but by the pathos of a little object; more alarming than an other-worldly spectre is the 'whole human fact' of the dead man summoned up by the rusty shoe-buckle. Because he confronts the 'actual man', the narrator is made simultaneously aware of mortality and of his own complicity in shabby human dealings.

Stevenson's acute eye for the telling physical detail is very probably related to his retention of a child-like clarity of vision, something he cultivated through an interest in book illustration. It seems no accident that he should, like A. E. Coppard after him, have admired Japanese prints so much. And his directions to Henley about the pictures for *A Child's Garden of Verse* (1885) suggest how deeply ingrained his own 'triumphant literality of vision' was: 'when the artist finds nothing much to illustrate, a good drawing of any *object* mentioned in the text, were it only a loaf of bread or a candlestick, is a most delightful thing to a young child. I remember this keenly.'[41] This is precisely the 'glamour of reality' which Stevenson found Thoreau attempting to capture by writing ardently about ordinary aspects of the external world.[42] Stevenson's use of detail in his fiction is intended to catch the imagination or to recapture a sense of wonder, and for this reason alone he tends to isolate details, adopting a strategy directly opposed to what he considered to be the nineteenth-century realists' 'insane pursuit of completion'.[43] In his famous 'Note on Realism' he laments that after Scott, the poor story 'once, in the hands of Voltaire, as abstract as a parable', declined into feebleness, 'pampered upon facts' and lugging a heavy baggage of detail.[44] In his criticism and letters, Stevenson is extremely clear-sighted about the artistic principle of selection: Balzac, he explained to Bob, allowed himself to become 'smothered under forcible-feeble detail', unable to suppress the impulse to expand descriptions:

He could not consent to be dull, and thus became so. He would leave nothing undeveloped, and thus drowned out of sight of land amid the multitude of crying and incongruous details. There is but one art – to omit! O if I knew how to omit, I would ask no other knowledge. A man who knew how to omit would make an *Iliad* of a daily paper.[45]

Here, with considerable passion, Stevenson asserts the paradoxical ability of stylized and highly compressed prose to attain epic breadth in its impact. In Stevenson's own stories, character, thought and emotion are often embodied in a single act, attitude or gesture, though it is often with a theatricality that recalls the melodrama as strongly as the epic. Particularly where the narrative situation is extravagantly romantic or even grotesque, Stevenson can make stunning use of the most pedestrian and trivial detail.

In 'A Lodging for the Night', for example, he transforms the innocuous fact that Thevenin, one of Villon's associates, has red hair, into a haunting image of obsessive force. The information itself is first given by the author so blandly that it scarcely registers: 'his bald head shone rosily in a garland of red curls'.[46] But when this cherubic figure is, a little farther on in the story, a leering dead body stuck upright in a chair by his murderer, Stevenson uses the detail of the red hair to convey directly the illogicality and the utterly human appropriacy of Villon's reaction to the grisly spectacle: 'Damn his fat head!' he broke out. 'It sticks in my throat like phlegm. What right has a man to have red hair when he is dead?'[47] It requires boldness in a writer to flirt with the absurd at a crucial dramatic moment as Stevenson does here. Villon's outburst has that same simplicity veering towards the comic which Stevenson noted in his essay on *The Pilgrim's Progress*, but Bunyan's is not the only influence discernible here. Stevenson was no doubt further encouraged in this kind of flamboyance by his reading of Poe, whose *Works* he reviewed in *The Academy* (2 Jan. 1875). Poe's theatricality, his disposition towards portentous atmospheres and melancholy presages, his tendency to inflate his prose with learned allusions and decorative cadences, but above all his insistence on precise facts: all of these features have equivalents in Stevenson's short fiction. In his review Stevenson is duly critical of the 'audacious, impudent thimble-rigging' aspect of those Poe stories which 'cheat' us into terror, and he rejects the later tales as repellently pointless, reserving his greatest admiration for the way Poe can, particularly in his earlier stories, make trivial detail produce overtones which seize the reader's imagination: 'He has the true story-teller's instinct. He knows the little nothings that make stories or mar them. He knows how to enhance the significance of any situation, and give colour and life to seeming irrelevant particulars.'[48] The example Stevenson gives to illustrate this point is superbly apposite:

> Thus, the whole spirit of *The Cask of Amontillado* depends upon
> Fortunato's carnival costume of cap and bells and motley. When Poe
> had once hit upon this device of dressing the victim grotesquely he
> had found the key to the story; and so he sends him with uneven steps
> along the catacombs of the Montresors, and the last sound we hear
> out of the walled-up recess is the jingling of the bells upon his cap.[49]

This, Stevenson argues astutely, is a case of an author getting full value for his own fantasies by making the reader's imagination adopt the detail and accept it as true in an artistic sense.

The question of what made Poe's imagination 'sincere' in one story but 'fustian' in another, and the wider question of what makes a story true or false, continued to preoccupy Stevenson. When his volume of tales *The Merry Men and Other Tales and Fables* appeared in 1887 he wrote to Lady Taylor (to whom the collection was dedicated):

> The trouble with *Olalla* is that it somehow sounds false . . . But the
> odd problem is: what makes a story true? *Markheim* is true; *Olalla*
> false; and I don't know why, nor did I feel it while I worked at them;
> indeed I had more inspiration with *Olalla*, as the style shows . . . I
> admire the style of it myself, more than is perhaps good for me; it is
> so solidly written. And that brings back (almost with the voice of
> despair) my unanswerable: why is it false?[50]

Stevenson is actually suggesting an answer to his own question when he makes style the measure of the 'inspiration' he felt while working on 'Olalla': the results show that here inspiration turned out to mean almost its opposite – self-consciousness in his old belletristic manner. Both the terms of Stevenson's question – What makes a story true? – and his continued bafflement about the answer to it, emphasize the instinctual nature of his imagination and the extent to which too much consciousness about technique and style could damage his writing. Instinct was something to be guarded, justifying as it did Stevenson's belief that the writer's task was to restore people to a romantic sphere: 'the great creative writer', he declares in 'A Gossip on Romance', 'shows us the realization and the apotheosis of the day-dreams of common men. His stories may be nourished with the realities of life, but their true mark is to satisfy the nameless longings of the reader, and to obey the ideal laws of the day-dream.'[51] For this reason alone, theorizing was bound to be inimical to Stevenson's activity as a storywriter, and his contribution to the evolution of the short story lay more in his fiction's reminiscent cast than in any clear advance towards 'modernity'. It was by writing stories which recalled the timelessness of fable and kept alive the association between fable and play, rather than by forging any entirely new convention, that Stevenson brought short fiction to life at the end of the nineteenth century. There is in his work a recognition of the part played by recurrence and familiarity in popular literary entertainment, and of the importance of what Katherine Mansfield was to describe in 1919 as the sensation of seeming to half-know and yet not knowing what is coming as a story proceeds: 'to have heard it all before, and yet our amazement is none the less, and when it is over, it has become ours'.[52]

Because Stevenson was constantly attempting to preserve this sensation, which (as Katherine Mansfield noted) recalls the adult reader to a child-like condition, it is unrewarding to look for any clear development in his short fiction. But this is not to say that artifice is not a key factor in his writing: his best stories depend on an invigorating tension between the instinctual or subliminal properties of his subject-matter (pre-eminently anarchic human passion) and the artistic discipline with which the material is shaped and patterned. The blend is powerfully conveyed in the advice Stevenson gave to Trevor Haddon:

> In your own art, bow your head over technique. Think of technique
> when you rise and when you go to bed. Forget purposes in the
> meanwhile; get to love technical processes; to glory in technical
> successes; get to see the world entirely through technical spectacles, to
> see it entirely in terms of what you can do. Then when you have
> anything to say, the language will be apt and copious . . . Art is not
> like theology; nothing is forced. You have not to represent the world.
> You have to represent only what you can represent with pleasure and
> effect, and the only way to find out what that is is by technical
> exercise.[53]

Stevenson's emphasis on technique is balanced by an equal concern for what the artist 'has to say', and his own famous controlled excursions into moral chaos like 'Markheim' and *Dr Jekyll and Mr*

Hyde are not the product of authorial calculation alone. It may be that Stevenson's appreciation of ancient forms gave him scope to create his gothic gnome Mr Hyde, a gnome 'out of a deep mine, where he guards the fountain of tears', as well as to write tales that aimed not to disturb but simply to entertain, as the original *Arabian Nights* had done.[54] As Stevenson wrote to Meiklejohn:

> When I suffer in mind, stories are my refuge; I take them like opium; and I consider one who writes them as a sort of doctor of the mind. And frankly . . . it is not Shakespeare we take to, when we are in a hot corner; nor, certainly, George Eliot – no, nor even Balzac. It is Charles Reade, or old Dumas, or the Arabian Nights, or the best of Walter Scott; it is stories we want, not the high poetic function which represents the world; we are then like the Asiatic with his improvisatore or the middle-aged with his trouvère. We want incident, interest, action: to the devil with your philosophy. When we are well again, and have an easy mind, we shall peruse your important work; but what we want now is a drug.[55]

Since Stevenson's time it has become all the more unacceptable to turn to Charles Reade, Dumas père, and the Arabian Nights while postponing Shakespeare, George Eliot and Balzac 'until we are well again and have an easy mind', as Stevenson recommended. Modernism has given literary sanction to no one having an easy mind, ever again. And the twentieth-century short story arises precisely out of a sense that life can only be rendered in fragments and compressed subjective episodes which stimulate instead of drugging the mind. Nowadays it is among sub-genres like the detective story or thriller, or in non-literary media like film and television, that the strong-lined narrative preferred by Stevenson is to be found, and this in itself indicates the limitations as well as the attractions of his ideas about fiction. The same point has been made from a different angle by V. S. Pritchett, who remarked in an interview that television 'seems an ideal medium for the short story, yet because television relies so heavily on the plot, a lot of very good short stories aren't considered suitable'.[56] Certainly, in the popular visual media Stevenson's stories have continued to flourish, a phenomenon which may actually diminish, rather than enhance his reputation as an artist. S. S. Prawer has argued that *Dr Jekyll and Mr Hyde* has been filmed so often and interestingly because the cinema is most at home with minor works of art 'taken from the undergrowth of mass publication' and then 'developed into significant works of art' by filmic treatment.[57]

By no means all short stories worth reading emerge from 'the undergrowth of mass publication', which in any case is not an equally murky tangle at all stages of literary history; most of the writers considered in this study aim to please readers who are capable of appreciating Shakespeare as well as Dumas père – and of distinguishing between their relative greatness. But although a view of the short story as pure anodyne is clearly inadequate, it remains true that the short-storywriter who follows, as many of the best do, Stevenson's dictum that the artist's task is 'not simply to convince, but to enchant' may be tacitly renouncing 'the high poetic function which represents the world' in favour of more modest, though immensely worthwhile, aspirations.[58]

NOTES AND REFERENCES

1. *The Letters of Robert Louis Stevenson*, ed. Sidney Colvin (5 vols, 1924), II, 79 (Oct. 1879).
2. *Letters*, II, 151 (June, 1881).
3. 'Robert Louis Stevenson' (1887), *Partial Portraits*, p. 160.
4. Letter to Henry James, *Letters*, III, 115 (Jan. 1887). 'The Misadventures of John Nicholson' first appeared in *Yule Tide . . . Cassell's Christmas Annual*, Dec. 1887 and was not reprinted in any collection during Stevenson's lifetime.
5. *Letters*, IV, 95 (Sept. 1891).
6. *The Works of Robert Louis Stevenson*, Tusitala edn (35 vols, 1924), XXVII, p. xiii; p. xiv. Unless otherwise indicated, all subsequent references to Stevenson's prose writings are to this edition.
7. For Stevenson's ideas about how to begin stories 'in a good way', see *Letters*, III, 9–10.
8. *Letters*, III, 23.
9. *Ibid.*, p. 85.
10. *Ibid.*, p. 23.
11. *Letters on the Short Story*, p. 228 (12 Jan. 1888).
12. *Works*, XXIX, 129. The essay was first published in *Longman's Magazine*, Nov. 1882.
13. See Mayo, p. 40 for an indication of the 'tremendous prestige' lent to oriental narratives by *the Spectator*.
14. *Letters*, II, 93 (26 Dec. 1879).
15. *Works*, XXVII, 8–9.
16. *Works*, XXVII, 93.
17. *Works*, XXVIII, 138. Stevenson's review first appeared in *The Fortnightly Review*, New Series, XV (June 1874), 817–23.
18. *Ibid.*, p. 139.
19. *Ibid.*
20. *Ibid.*
21. *Ibid.*
22. *Ibid.*, p. 140.
23. *Ibid.*, p. 141.
24. See Blanche Colton Williams, *A Handbook on Story Writing* (1921), p. 20.
25. *Letters*, II, 32.

26. See Swearingen, *The Prose Writings of Robert Louis Stevenson: A Guide* (1980), p. 26.

27. *Letters*, II, 32.

28. *Ibid.*

29. *Letters*, I, 133.

30. *Ibid.*, p. 134.

31. *Ibid.*

32. *Letters*, II, 160, 159–60.

33. *Ibid.*, p. 160,

34. 'A Lodging for the Night', *Works* I, 219–40 *passim*. 'A Lodging for the Night' was first published, unsigned, in *Temple Bar*, LI (Oct. 1877) and subsequently included in *New Arabian Nights* (1882).

35. *Works*, XXVIII, 156.

36. *Ibid.*, p. 154.

37. *Ibid.*

38. *Ibid.*

39. *Ibid.*, p. 155.

40. *Works*, VIII, 28. 'The Merry Men' was first published in two parts, *Cornhill Magazine*, XLV (June 1882) and XLVI (July 1882).

41. *Letters*, II, 230 (Mar. 1883).

42. *Works*, XXVII, 94.

43. *Works*, XXVIII, 70.

44. *Ibid.* The essay first appeared in *The Magazine of Art*, VII (Nov. 1883).

45. *Letters*, II, 270–1 (Oct. 1883).

46. *Works*, I, 221.

47. *Ibid.*, p. 224.

48. *Works*, XXVIII, 181; 179.

49. *Ibid.*, pp. 179–80.

50. *Letters*, III, 114.

51. *Works*, XXIX, 123.

52. *Novels and Novelists*, ed. J. Middleton Murry (1930), p. 113. Mansfield was reviewing Constance Garnett's translation of Dostoevsky, *An Honest Thief: and Other Stories*.

53. *Letters*, II, 251–2 (5 July 1883).

54. *Letters*, III, 67 (2 Jan. 1886).

55. *Letters*, II, 104 (1 Feb. 1880).

56. 'A Sense of Strangeness', *Book Choice*, No. 9 (Sept. 1981), 20–1.

57. *Caligari's Children: The Film as Tale of Terror* (1980), p. 86.

58. *Works*, XXIX, 117; *Letters*, II, 104. It was Dumas who exemplified for Stevenson the writer's duty 'not to be true merely, but to be lovable' (*Works*, XXIX, 117).

Chapter 3

'ARTFUL' NARRATION: FROM THE SENSATION STORY TO THE SCENIC METHOD

The path of narrative with care pursue,
Still making probability your clue,
On all the vestiges of truth attend,
And let *them* guide you to a decent end.
Of all ambitions man may entertain,
The worst that can invade a sickly brain,
Is that which angles hourly for surprize,
And baits its hook with prodigies and lies.
Credulous infancy or age as weak
Are fittest auditors for such to seek.

*   *   *   *

A tale should be judicious, clear, succinct,
The language plain, and incidents well-link'd,
Tell not as new what ev'ry body knows,
And new or old, still hasten to a close,
There centring in a focus, round and neat,
Let all your rays of information meet:
What neither yields us profit or delight,
Is like a nurse's lullaby at night,
Guy Earl of Warwick and fair Eleanore,
Or giant-killing Jack would please me more.

(William Cowper, 'Conversation')

If a short story's aim is to achieve a single concentrated impression, then it must move swiftly; it cannot linger to unfold for the reader the little incidentals and wayward episodes, the dull patches and uneventful intervals through which he actually experiences time. All of these things can undoubtedly be suggested in a short piece, but only obliquely, in much the same way as a painting or photograph of a figure caught in an expressive posture can capture an entire life, compressing biography into image. Because a short narrative cannot reproduce, can only imply, extended periods or lapses of time, very often what is shown is one phase of an action, perhaps an ordinary event cut out and framed to epitomize a life of continuing ordinariness; or possibly a crisis which momentarily halts the flow of time, leaving everything permanently altered once it has passed. Where the intention is to depict humdrum dailiness, it is the author who puts a frame around the incident by selecting it and inviting the reader to share in what he has noticed. The story of crisis, on the other hand, deals with an event which declares its own specialness; in essence an interruption, the crisis or dilemma frames itself by virtue of its very nature, and the author's urgency is matched by the fictitious situation of his central character.

Broadly speaking, these are the most divergent possibilities for the short-storywriter, bringing with them differences in narrative point of view, characterization, mood and style. In his review entitled 'The Story-teller at Large' (1898) Henry James identified two distinct effects attainable by the 'rigour of brevity', leaving no doubt as to which type he himself found most rewarding:

> The one with which we are most familiar is that of the detached incident, single and sharp, as clear as a pistol-shot; the other, of rarer performance, is that of the impression, comparatively generalized – simplified, foreshortened, reduced to a particular perspective – of a complexity or a continuity. The former is an adventure comparatively safe, in which you have, for the most part, but to put one foot after the other. It is just the risks of the latter, on the contrary, that make the best of the sport.[1]

But whichever of these alternatives is chosen – detached incident or foreshortened impression – the writer must show more than he tells, hint rather than explain, offer scenes where the novelist might provide description and narrative explanation. Complexity, if it is there at all, does not accumulate gradually throughout an extended time-structure as it usually does in the novel. Even when no more than a single day is encompassed in a novel, Virginia Woolf's *Mrs Dalloway* (1925), for example, reading-time is not purposely confined to the single sitting which Poe saw as a marvellous resource for the short-storywriter, capable of making the reader's hour (or half-hour) of 'perusal' memorable. The short-storywriter must bear in mind Chekhov's observation that, 'long, detailed works have their own peculiar aims, which require a most careful execution regardless of the total impression. But in short stories it is better to say not enough than to say too much, because, – because – I don't know why!'[2] The clue to 'why' surely lies in Chekhov's own phrase 'total impression', a phrase which indicates sustained concentration on the part of reader and writer alike.

The short story's narrative intensity has frequently been contrasted with the novel's more leisurely manner, vividly so by H. G. Wells in his essay 'The Contemporary Novel' (1911):

> A short story should go to its point as a man flies from a pursuing tiger: he pauses not for the daisies in his path, or to note the pretty moss on the tree he climbs for safety. But the novel by comparison is like breakfasting in the open air on a summer morning; nothing is irrelevant if the writer's mood is happy, and the tapping of the thrush upon the garden path, or the petal of apple-blossom that floats down into my coffee, is as relevant as the egg I open or the bread and butter I bite.[3]

Maybe so, though only if the novel is not of the carefully formed and unified kind actually being written at this time by Wells's contemporaries, James and Conrad, whose self-conscious artistry is as prominent in their novels as in their short stories – in Conrad's case, noticeably more so. Furthermore, if Wells means to say anything more than that the short story disdains irrelevancies (and his imagery of the man frantic to escape a pursuing tiger suggests that he does) then this too applies only to certain kinds of story – those which have a point as definite as the branch of the tree the man is heading for, a refuge where safety is perceived as the reverse of sheer terror.

That Wells has in mind a particular brand of rapid narrative movement is clear too from his statement earlier in the same essay that in order to produce its 'one single, vivid effect', the short story must 'seize the attention at the outset, and never relaxing, gather it together more and more until the climax is reached'.[4] Necessarily limited by the reader's capacity to bear such tension, the short story, so Wells asserts, 'must explode and finish before interruption occurs or fatigue sets in'.[5] This is Poe's theory revived, as Wells readily acknowledges. Nevertheless, the vocabulary Wells chooses heightens considerably Poe's account of the reader 'contemplating' a single idea; for the later writer, a kind of imaginative explosion is involved. Words with connotations of suddenness or even violence recur throughout discussions of short-story form: Wells's 'seize' and 'explode' are only slightly varied in V. S. Pritchett's description of the short story as 'a flash that suddenly illumines, then passes', or Sherwood Anderson's notion of the writer being 'swept along' by 'some passion of the flesh or spirit'.[6] Connected with this is the stress many writers put on inspiration as the first stage of composition; Elizabeth Taylor, for example, explained that whereas a novel was something she schemed, ideas for short stories came to her without any search.[7] This view was shared by Elizabeth Bowen, who argued that in order to convey an impression of inevitability, a story's 'conception should have been involuntary, a vital fortuity', no matter how 'voluntary and careful' the effort required to transfer that conception to paper.[8] Initially, it seems, much depends on what James once referred to as 'the luck of the conception that imposes itself *en bloc*'.[9]

The notion that short stories spring from subliminal sources is amenable to more overtly mystical accounts of creativity. Kipling gave a supernatural twist to the inspiration theory when he depicted himself as the obedient servant of a 'Personal Daemon' who appeared early in his career; there Kipling sat, 'bewildered among other notions', until the Daemon came and ordered him 'Take this and no other'.[10] Kipling then 'learned to lean upon' this guide and to 'recognize the sign of his approach'.[11] A similar passivity and suspension of the conscious will is essential to the creativity of Borges, who describes the experience as a kind of epiphany:

> Walking down the street or along the galleries of the National Library, I feel that something is about to take over in me. That something may be a tale or a poem. I do not tamper with it; I let it have its way. From afar, I sense it taking shape. I dimly see its end and beginning but not the dark gap in between. This middle, in my case, is given me gradually. If its discovery happens to be withheld by the gods, my conscious self has to intrude, and these unavoidable makeshifts are, I suspect, my weakest pages.[12]

The belief that the short story involves revelation is bound to affect the kind of narrative dealt with. Considered as an explosion, whether in the reader's mind, the writer's – or indeed both – the short story might be expected to deal best with an intrinsically tense situation, a state of affairs which itself challenges the powers of the conscious will. If this is so, then narrative method is likely to be strung to a correspondingly high pitch. Poe's story 'The Pit and the Pendulum', completed by the summer of 1842, is probably the most celebrated instance of narrative wrenched away from the gradually emerging patternings characteristic of longer fiction. Poe's nameless narrator, totally alone (except for the rats which at one point leap on him in their hundreds) desperately uses his intellect and reason at full stretch to discover what in normal experience could be taken for granted – where he is, and what movements he can make. His historical situation as a victim of the Spanish Inquisition provides a reason for his imprisonment, but beyond that it has little importance. What Poe is really interested in is the nightmarish situation in which a man under sentence of death is deprived of all the usual means by which people locate themselves in time, as well as in space. Poe uses the compression of the short story to investigate experience outside normal time and consequently he summarizes all the information a reader might require about preceding events, packing it all into a single allusive sentence: 'I was sick – sick unto death with that long agony; and when they at length unbound me, and I was permitted to sit, I felt that my senses were leaving me.' Instantly, focus is held on the man's state as his dreadful ordeal begins.

From this point on the narrative moves through successive psychic phases as the narrator's senses bear in on him one ghastly aspect of his helpless predicament after another – sound, touch, the sight of the pendulum ('massy and heavy') descending relentlessly towards him; the blazing eyes of the portraits, and later the smell of heated iron as the walls begin to close in. Whatever the sense-experience, the deduction is the same; the 'dread sentence of death' which he has just heard as the story opens is not a prediction of what is to come, but a description of what 'they', unseen but in total control, are doing to him moment by moment. To be 'unbound' in such a situation is a grimly ironic joke. There can, however, be no suspense about whether the man eventually escapes, since his presence as a narrator using the past tense is an assurance that he does. The only question can be, 'how?', and Poe answers it with an abrupt ending, the out-stretched arm of General Lasalle thrusting into the tale to snatch the narrator from the edge of the abyss: 'The French army had entered Toledo. The Inquisition was in the hands of its enemies'.[13] Rescue comes from outside in every sense of the word, the internal concern of the story being totally centred on the narrator's psychological reactions. In one paragraph alone, these swing like the pendulum itself from fatalistic acceptance of death, through insensibility followed by hope, to utter imbecility. Like the *Blackwood's* tales of effect Poe started out by parodying in the 1830s, 'The Pit and the Pendulum' eliminates variables of time, character and an outside world, choosing instead to deepen progressively an initial impression of terror. By definition, terror is a unified emotion; it must either persist, varying only in intensity, or cease. Nothing in between is possible. That is why stories like this one conform to an extremely simple narrative structure which divides into two discrete and unequal parts: an horrific situation is evoked and exploited for utmost effect, then totally reversed, often in a brief sentence or two.

This simple pattern can be found in countless other stories, and indeed it could be said that a problem which can be stated in terms of stark alternatives provides the core of most short-story narrative. In 'The Pit and the Pendulum', life or death are the alternatives, and this story belongs with a large group of narratives which put a single character in some dreadful predicament and then combine microscopic, almost clinical, attention to his thoughts and sensations with painstakingly technical descriptions of his attempts to evade what seems inevitable death. The basic principle was that enunciated by Poe himself in his high-spirited piece 'How to Write a Blackwood Article', in which Signora Psyche Zenobia is advised how to produce stories 'of the sensation stamp':

> The first thing requisite is to get yourself into such a scrape as no one ever got into before. The oven, for instance, – that was a good hit. But if you have no oven, or big bell, at hand, and if you cannot

conveniently tumble out of a balloon, or be swallowed up in an earthquake, or get stuck fast in a chimney, you will have to be contented with simply imagining some similar misadventure.[14]

Such stories often have great verve, a highly emotional style, and more often than not they are totally absurd. The eerie tales of another nineteenth-century American writer, Charles Fenno Hoffman, display all of these qualities: in 'The Man in the Reservoir', ingenuity is finally rewarded when the narrator climbs up his own fishing rod, the pound pickerel he has caught providing a useful grappling hook; while in 'Ben Blower's Story, or How to Relish a Julep', it is unquenchable hope and a handy mallet that save the stoker from being cooked alive in his own ship's boiler.[15] These tall tales resemble Poe's grotesque experiments in how much the character – and the reader – can stand, and along with fascinated measurement of exact dimensions, distances and physical movements, go equally meticulous records of the victim's meditations on huge metaphysical questions. Life, death, immortality; these questions preoccupy the narrators every bit as much as the practicalities in hand.

It is difficult to see how a story set inside a ship's boiler could fail to be unified. In an exaggerated manner, Hoffman and Poe demonstrate how a single effect can be achieved by inventing situations the very nature of which is to separate characters from the sequential flow of time. Once the situation has been established, probability becomes entirely a psychological matter, although horrific effects are invariably rooted in realistic detail or, in Poe's case, arcane scientific data. This is all in accordance with 'Mr Blackwood's' stipulation that his authors should have 'the actual fact' to bear them out in their sensation stories: 'Nothing so well assists the fancy, as an experimental knowledge of the matter in hand', he remarks.[16] Of course Poe's theory of 'unity of effect' said nothing about the incidents related having to serve anything other than the author's preconceived idea – or 'thesis' as he called it in the 1847 version of his essay on Hawthorne's tale-writing – and his fellow-sensationalists, no matter how idiosyncratic, were not actually contravening the rules he articulated for all storytelling.[17] But powerful (or in Hoffman's case, amusing) as tales of terror can be, they do reveal the limitations of Poe's theory of effect. Involving far more calculation than inspiration, Poe's intention of transmitting an idea 'unblemished, because undisturbed' actually encourages the writer to manipulate his audience so thoroughly that it becomes hard to draw the line between artistry and tyranny.[18] If narrative movement is made to conform to a logic which determines the reader's response at each stage, then there is the danger of success in Poe's terms being gained at the expense of flexibility. The techniques which, in stories like 'The Pit and the Pendulum' or 'The Fall of the House of Usher' (1840), so

51

strenuously control emotional and intellectual reactions turn easily into stereotype, capable of eliciting stock responses and allowing the reader too much detachment; from the moment he recognizes the familiar elements of horror fiction, he can keep his poise, wondering only how, this time, fear is going to be made aesthetically delightful.

As a unique work of a bizarre imagination, a story like 'The Fall of the House of Usher' is certainly a formidable achievement: between the opening – when the narrator, one 'dull, dark, and soundless' autumn day, first sees the melancholy house, surrounded by decayed trees and eerily mirrored in the still waters of the tarn – and the final crash as 'the deep and dark tarn at my feet closed sullenly and silently over the fragments of the "*House of Usher*"', Poe draws a taut atmospheric line. The narrative is actually very loose, but the portentous mood is not diminished by the fact that events cover far more than a single day; nor by the narrator's vagueness about whether the 'terrible night' of Madeline's reappearance occurs on the seventh or the eighth day after he and Roger have placed her body in the vault. The author shows a fine economy of narrative when it matters most, notably at the climax, where exactitude of description fuses with theatricality. Roderick's death is made syntactically as well as factually simultaneous with Madeline's:

> For a moment she remained trembling and reeling to and fro upon the threshold – then, with a low moaning cry, fell heavily inward upon the person of her brother, and in her violent and now final death-agonies, bore him to the floor a corpse, and a victim of the terrors he had anticipated.

The wavering figure on the threshold, then the stark precision of 'fell heavily inward', and the quick transition from 'him' to 'corpse': all of these devices contribute to the sentence's onward drive, accentuating the sense of fatality conveyed by the whole story.[19]

Repeated or imitated, however, the features which make 'The Fall of the House of Usher' memorable become pallid. Readers quickly learn the conventions according to which individual devices produce particular effects. Fascination with effect, so D. H. Lawrence maintained, made Poe more 'a scientist than an artist'.[20] Instead of a rhythm, Lawrence explained, Poe offered a 'concatenation of cause and effect'.[21] The 'chain' might be intricate, as it was in 'The Murders in the Rue Morgue' (1845) or 'The Gold-Bug' (1845); but a chain it was, belonging properly speaking to 'tale', not story.[22] Behind Lawrence's objections to the mechanical quality of Poe's technique is the feeling that art can become the enemy of life. Poe actually expressed this very perception in his emblematic story – almost a parable – 'The Oval Portrait', which first appeared in 1842 and was later to enjoy a vogue among English aesthetes in the 1890s. At the very instant when the painter captures the life of his beloved sitter, he realizes that she is dead.[23] It is a chilling story, but its emotional impact is lessened by the neatness of its construction, which is logical rather than imaginative.

Lawrence was not the first to note the dominance of deduction and 'analytic fantasy' in Poe's work. An entry for 1856 in the diaries kept by Edmond and Jules de Goncourt records the feeling that to read Poe was to enter a world where 'things' played 'a more important part than people; and where interest was 'transferred from the heart to the head, from the passion to the idea, from the drama to the denouement'.[24] The Goncourts' discernment of 'something monomaniacal' in Poe's writing is a useful reminder that the power of his best work derives from a highly individual talent, making it difficult to base generalizations about the craft of short fiction on his example.[25] Nevertheless, the Goncourts' rather apt description of Poe's stories as 'fables on the pattern A+B' does suggest the limitations of stories which adhere too narrowly to a fundamentally simple narrative structure of problem plus solution – or in Wells's terms, man flees tiger, man reaches tree.[26]

Because of its brevity, the short-story form lends itself to an essentially two-part construction, though individual stories will obviously differ in the way they are proportioned. Broadly speaking, the more concerned with climax and denouement a story is, the greater the disproportion between the exciting race from the tiger and the final leap to safety. As in the case of 'The Pit and the Pendulum', the character's relief at finally escaping from danger receives no elaboration. The reader can imagine that for himself, and in any case, the only calmed feelings he is expected to care about are his own. On the other hand, when emphasis is less on action than on motive, replacing crisis with dilemma, an author will probably aim to divide the phases of his narrative more equally. Poe gained a unified effect by extending a single atmosphere or sensation, but other writers working to similarly simple formulae seek unity through symmetry and balance. Differences of subject-matter are involved here. Whereas Poe's method is particularly well-suited to fantastic themes, pushing narrative to an extreme point where both reader and protagonist find dream merging with reality, finer adjustments of proportion are required when the purpose is more realistic.

O. Henry's stories of New York life exemplify this principle well.[27] In one of these, 'The Gift of the Magi', symmetrical construction is what allows the themes of love, poverty and selflessness to be unified within the narrow compass of a story less than three thousand words long. Setting the story on Christmas Eve, O. Henry starts from a ready-made and emotionally charged point of narrative focus against which he can place his poignant opening picture: Della Dillingham Young is sobbing – and as the realist insists, 'sniffling' – in her shabby furnished flat because she has only a pittance to spend on her husband's Christmas present. Early on, O. Henry signals clearly that meaning in this story is going to emerge through contrasts and pairings: having evoked Della's miserable situation he directs attention to two things (one mechanical, the other natural) which the reader knows instantly are destined to be brought into close connection before the story ends: 'Now, there were two possessions of the James Dillingham Youngs' in which they took a mighty pride. One was Jim's gold watch that had been his father's and his grandfather's. The other was Della's hair.' When Della proceeds to sell her hair in order to buy a fob chain 'worthy of The Watch', the expectation of a parallel action on Jim's part is aroused. The narrative is confined to Della until almost exactly half-way through the story, when O. Henry creates a pause, freezing the image of the young woman waiting and fretting about whether Jim will still find her pretty. The second half of the story reveals that Jim has sold his watch and bought combs worthy of Della's 'beautiful vanished hair', an outcome which offers the reader the satisfaction of seeing two pieces of a simple puzzle interlock. The story works by means of a simple ironic reversal in which each character's expectations of giving pleasure are defeated, while the reader derives pleasure from the neatness of the pattern.

O. Henry, however, wants to make larger claims for his story, as the ending makes clear:

> And here I have lamely related to you the uneventful chronicle of two foolish children in a flat who most unwisely sacrificed for each other the greatest treasures of their house. But in a last word to the wise of these days, let it be said that of all who give gifts these were the wisest. Of all who give and receive gifts, such as they were the wisest. Everywhere they are the wisest. They are the magi.[28]

The failure of this attempt to open the story out into wide significance is instructive. It is not due solely to its tone of sentimental irony, nor to the superficiality of the comparison between the Dillingham Youngs and figures from sacred history, though these are symptomatic of the muddle into which O. Henry's need to point a moral leads him. No matter what imagery had been used, this story would have been unable to support a final coda precisely because its narrative structure is so symmetrical that there are no ragged edges from which to unravel a sense of mystery, least of all spiritual mystery. The narrative and the issues it raises are effectively closed as soon as Jim reveals that he no longer has a watch to go with the chain Della has bought; any additional comment inevitably comes over as a moral tag appended in the hope of transforming a realistic story into a fable. Far from dignifying his carefully shaped story with new profundity, O. Henry's ending merely increases the reader's consciousness of artifice.

'The Gift of the Magi', one of O. Henry's shortest stories, illustrates the pitfalls of restricting narrative development too tightly within a two-term system of contrasts, parallels and ironic reversals. Two characters tackle the same problem independently and the single point of the story emerges when the two lines of action converge, and the characters discover that the solutions they arrive at, though morally and emotionally identical, actually cancel each other out. So tidy is the pattern that more is expressed about the author's dexterity than about human generosity, O. Henry's ostensible subject.[29] But although overt moralizing makes the limitations of symmetry in storytelling glaringly apparent, it does not cause them. Even when the reader is left to draw his own moral conclusions from the case depicted, the pleasure offered by O. Henry's clever plots invariably arises from his manipulation of a simple narrative pattern consisting of situation evoked, then reversed. Sometimes it is the trick ending in which he specialized and which, once the vogue was established, made 'the strain of living up to his inventiveness . . . frightful'.[30] Sometimes the pattern involves the idealization of young love's triumphs over shabby circumstances, epitomized by rooming-houses full of transient and impoverished people; at other times it is pastiche treatment of ancient storytelling devices like the talking animal: always, the technique relies on poignant contrasts and simple substitutions.

The principle of substitution pervades O. Henry's fiction. In 'A Cosmopolite in a Café' the talkative E. Rushmore Coglan's boastfulness about his wide travels is overwhelmed by his belligerent defence of his small-town home; at the end of 'The Skylight Room', the name 'Billy Jackson', given to a distant star by a romantic girl, is translated into the full title – 'Dr William Jackson' – of the doctor who snatches her from the edge of starvation. 'Memoirs of a Yellow Dog' is proposed as an alternative to Kipling's animal stories, and the point of one of O. Henry's most famous stories, 'The Last Leaf' (1907), is that art can take the place of nature so convincingly that a young girl regains her will to live, although the old artist who paints the ivy leaf outside her window has sacrificed his life in saving hers.[31] Whatever his subjects, O. Henry keeps his readers aware that he is controlling narrative movement, conveying a strong authorial presence through palpable structural manoeuvres. His style accentuates this effect: high-flown allusions and breezy interruptions simultaneously inflate and domesticate O. Henry's authorial manner, making a virtue out of showing his hand – or pretending to. 'A Service of Love', for example, a sentimental story which follows the same pattern and pivots on exactly the same ironies as 'The Gift of the Magi', opens with a cut-and-dried statement of intent: 'When one loves one's Art no service seems too hard. That is our premise. This story shall draw a conclusion from it, and show at the same time that the premise is incorrect. That will be a new thing in logic, and a feat of story-telling somewhat older than the Great Wall of China.'[32] The candid but teasing opening puts the story firmly in the tradition of the riddle, the quizzical joke based on hidden paradox, and, as O. Henry says, its literary heritage is ancient and venerable.

The main drawback to stories which gain narrative compression by making plot serve a single realization, however ironic in quality, is that like most jokes or anecdotes they can never arouse the same bafflement and surprise twice over. Consequently, if a story with strong plot-interest is going to survive its first telling, then it must offer additional attractions which will justify repeated scrutiny. For this reason, a practitioner like Frank O'Connor would like to see the idea that a short story always has a point, 'smothered at birth'.[33] The notion of 'point', O'Connor argues, 'belongs to the basic anecdote', whereas 'the surface of a great short story is like a sponge; it sucks up hundreds of impressions that have nothing whatever to do with the anecdote'.[34] Yet many of the most durable short stories owe their impact to the anecdotalist's desire to excite and surprise, irrespective of plausibility. The test, as Somerset Maugham observed of Maupassant's art, is whether the author can get away with sacrificing verisimilitude to effect.[35]

To instance Maupassant here is to be forcibly reminded of the extent to which his example lies behind the type of O. Henry story being discussed: it was Maupassant's name that writers of short-story manuals constantly invoked from the 1890s onwards.[36] But as a comparison between O. Henry and his French predecessor demonstrates, the influence was not entirely beneficial, similarities being limited to the sphere of technique and narrative method. Few people would dispute that Maupassant's celebrated story 'The Necklace' (1885) is superior to anything achieved by O. Henry, even though it resembles the American's work in the way it depends on a plot which is conceived in terms of opposites and one major ironic reversal. Once a reader knows that the jewels which Madame Loisel replaces at terrible cost to her life and her marriage were actually false, he can never again read the story in innocence of the central irony that once produced shocked surprise. What were thought to be real diamonds are paste; Madame Loisel has replaced the false with the genuine, priding herself on an effort which is revealed in the last sentence of the story to have been totally misdirected. The necklace is easily lost, but terrible strain is involved in replacing it. An entire life has been determined by a single accident which mocks the woman's sacrifices: 'How strange life is', she ponders, 'how fickle. How little is needed to ruin or to save!'[37] Reduced to its bare outline, 'The Necklace' is fairly crude. What is it about the story that lifts it above its simple narrative scheme?

In form, 'The Necklace' displays all of the qualities which Maupassant in his preface to *Pierre et Jean* (1888) attributed to outdated romance. In a definition which recalls Poe's theories, Maupassant lists the elements of romance. He indicates a series of ingenious combinations leading directly to a denouement; the disposition and graduation of incidents towards a single culminating point (normally a decisive event) and the final satisfaction of all curiosity raised at the beginning, so that no reader could possibly want to know more about the characters' destinies. All of these features appear in 'The Necklace', yet the manner in which Maupassant disposes his material recalls with equal force his definition of realism. Characters moved from one period of their lives to another by means of natural transitions, attention to the influence of environment, the elimination of irrelevant detail, and most of all the communication of an individual vision of the world: the aims of the realist are evident in 'The Necklace' alongside its romantic ingenuity.[38] Maupassant groups incidental facts about his characters, summarizing ten years of hardship in Madame Loisel's daily drudgery, and capturing the relentless rhythm with which she carries sweepings from garret to street, then brings water back up to the garret, pausing for breath at every landing. The result is a compelling fusion of fanciful plotting and realistic portrayal. Furthermore, the view of life expressed by this story runs counter to its highly deliberate structure. Chance is shown to be more powerful than human resolution, a melancholy perception of the random quality of life which suits the brevity of short stories.

There is, then, a tension between the artistic control exerted over all Maupassant's stories and the philosophy they convey. This is one reason why, although they often depend on plot and straightforward narrative ironies, their interest does not necessarily die with the final sentence, as was seen to be the case with O. Henry's stories. In the American's tales a rather arch effect is produced by the disparity between the ornate style of his authorial intrusions and the banal realism of his material. Collectively, O. Henry's stories offer a series of narrative stunts; the author keeps one eye on his audience as he juggles with his characters' lives or conjures a trump card to lay down at the last minute. Everything is explicable. In contrast, Maupassant's view that life is swayed by irrational forces, against which humans struggle feebly, yields more ambiguities. Through Maupassant's transparent style ironies emerge unostentatiously, gaining their own momentum.

Nevertheless, simple contrasts and violent reversals abound in Maupassant's fiction. Sometimes this is a matter of demonstrating peasant guile, as in 'The Devil' (1887), where Mother Rapet, afraid that she has made a bad deal with an equally avaricious peasant, manages to come out on top: hired at a fixed rate instead of her usual day-rates to watch over the peasant's dying mother, she dresses up as the devil and scares the old woman to death in time to make one franc profit. Elsewhere, the irony produced by patterns of reversal is more pathetic: there is poignancy in the switch from the picture of Boule de Suif sharing her basket of food with her fellow travellers to the final cameo which shows her weeping, hungry and rejected, in the darkness. The contrast puts into clear visual terms the deeper satiric point that this social misfit is the only true patriot in the group of travellers. An unusually long story for Maupassant, 'Boule de Suif' employs similar techniques to those found in his briefer *contes*, where the material as well as the treatment is often reminiscent of Poe.[39] Obsession, a topic which recommends itself to short-storywriters by automatically providing narrative intensity, is the theme of many Maupassant stories. The effect varies from the macabre in a story like 'Fear' (1883), to the humorous in 'The Umbrella' (1884); or it can be melancholy, as in 'A Son' (1883), where laburnum fragrance triggers off a comparison between nature's effortless profusion and transient human passions.

But although the majority of Maupassant's stories are built on contrasts – between the obsessive and the normal, the honest and the hypocritical – it would be wrong to suppose that he imposes patterns on his material for the sake of narrative completeness. Rather, he discovers and dramatizes the conflicts which are inherent in his material. This is particularly marked in Maupassant's peasant tales, many of which deal with revenge, a passion which requires no embellishments to yield compact narratives; victim and oppressor exchange roles and a satisfying resolution is achieved. But Maupassant's ability to exploit inherently dramatic situations is by no means confined to stories with a rural setting. Throughout his fiction he chooses subjects which to some extent provide their own unity, a strategy which is related to his characteristic authorial stance. Unlike O. Henry, Maupassant is not the showy master-of-ceremonies treating his reader to a variety of narrative tricks: he is the dramatist who stands somewhat aloof from the antics of his characters.

Because Maupassant consciously followed Flaubert's teaching that the artist's duty was to reveal the unique qualities hidden within everyday reality, he was committed to subduing decorativeness and self-display. In the Pre-Raphaelite painters too he must have found examples of the keen attention to detail recommended by Flaubert. The result was what Conrad described as Maupassant's ability to refrain from 'setting his cleverness against the eloquence of the facts'.[40] Conrad's admiration for Maupassant's austere talent and artistic honesty is important as an individual judgement, but more importantly still it illuminates the direction the short story was to take in the twentieth century. Maupassant's objective method anticipates the ways in which the short story progressively freed itself from more personal forms like the essay, the anecdote, or the subjective prose poem. Frequently invoking Maupassant as a model, short-storywriters from the 1890s onwards began cultivating the qualities summarized by Conrad in 1904 as, 'a point of view consistently preserved and never obtruded for the end of personal gratification'.[41] A crucial aspect of this development was the greater demand made on the audience; more and more, the reader must be able to emulate the artist's 'scrupulous, prolonged and devoted attention to the aspects of the visible world'.[42] Conrad specifically distinguishes between Maupassant's art, which renders facts so perfectly that they call for a rare faculty of observation in the reader, and the kind of fiction in which 'words alone [are] strung upon a convention'.[43] His disdain for 'empty phrases requiring no effort, demanding from us no qualities except a vague susceptibility to emotion' places Conrad in his period, when all art was increasingly seen as legitimately difficult.[44] It also aligns him with everyone who believes that the special difficulties of the short-story form should be shared by author and reader instead of being, as Poe's theory and O. Henry's practice suggest, solely the author's province.

Once it is accepted that the reader is to be made to work hard in ways comparable to the writer's efforts, new attitudes to the construction of short narrative become possible. Instead of the story's meaning being something to marshal into paired contrasts, or else to be withheld until the climax, it can become diffused throughout the story and made to inhere in the fabric of the prose rather than in the order of fictional events. Plot may not be entirely dispensed with, but attention to it ceases to be paramount. Again, Flaubert's influence is crucial, diverting interest from plot to texture: 'When I write a novel', he remarked, 'I aim at rendering a colour, a shade'.[45] The comment applies equally to his short fiction. But if significance is to be diffused without creating an effect of diffuseness, then compression must be achieved by some means other than the swift progress towards a culminating event or insight. One solution to this problem is exemplified by Flaubert's *conte* 'A Simple Heart' (1877), in which an entire life is dramatized in a rhythm which alternates between descriptions of habitual actions and vividly realized scenes. Félicité's routine at various stages of her life gives an impression of continuity, but every so often the flow of continuities is interrupted and redirected by a dramatic event.

By nature repetitive, Félicité's domestic routine lends itself to a narrative method which summarizes long periods of time. Throughout the story Flaubert prefaces descriptions with phrases like, 'Every day . . .', 'All the year round . . .', or 'For several months . . .'. Within this sameness, striking events are announced with the simple formula 'One day . . .', whenever adventure, or more often, shock, temporarily disrupts the even tenor of Félicité's obscure life. Instead of a single crisis, Flaubert offers a number of events which carry the force of a tiny explosion, a discrete moment which halts the story's easy progress but then – unlike a Poe climax, which has no sequel – passes, leaving surfaces unchanged. For Félicité, events take the form of partings and loss: as a young woman, she loses her lover, who simply disappears; later, the partings without farewells are sudden deaths. Her young nephew, Victor; her mistress's child, and finally her beloved parrot Loulou: all of these vanish abruptly from Félicité's loving gaze. Yet in recording Félicité's sorrows, Flaubert brilliantly preserves a detached style which allows emotion to be expressed, not by the author, but through the pictures he makes. Félicité pounding the washing on the river bank, surrounded by empty fields and choking back her grief at the news of Victor's death; the dead child Virginie, 'her head tilted back under a black crucifix that leant over her, her face whiter than the curtains that hung motionless on either side'; Madame Aubain and Félicité accidentally coming across the mourned-for child's 'little chestnut-coloured hat, made of plush with a long nap', and later the colourful religious procession, its sounds and its silences counterpointing Félicité's death throes: these and many other strongly visualized scenes fuse narrative action and human response. Event, setting and character are merged, creating a unity which is both lucid and rich with meaning.

Not fitting in with the Brander Matthews definition of a short story, 'A Simple Heart' attains unity of effect by quite other means than the 'single episode' formula. It manages to encompass a life as unvarying as the great Church festivals which mark the passing of the year in Félicité's community. Historic event is of no significance here; as Flaubert indicates, the points of reference that matter to Félicité are domestic adventures, like the whitewashing of the hall or the collapse of a piece of roof. For the reader, the points of reference which save the story from monotony are the scenes and pictures which express meaning through colour, gesture, and subtly contrasted shades. Typical is the room where Virginie's body lies: 'Three candlesticks on the chest of drawers added touches of red to the scene, and fog was whitening the windows'.[46] Singly and cumulatively, each picture achieves what William James saw his brother Henry consciously aiming to do in his early stories, namely, 'to suggest a mysterious fulness which you do not lead your reader through'.[47]

The 'mysterious fulness' of Flaubert's art is all the more arresting for being derived from lowly subjects and ordinary life. 'A Simple Heart' can be seen as part of a widespread development towards the 'democratic art' described by Mario Praz: 'lacking heroes and heroines, attention becomes concentrated on the details of common life, and these aspects of life are closely studied; the most ordinary things, by dint of being looked at with intensity, acquire an important significance, and intimate beauty of their own, more profound for the very reason that it is muted.'[48] Praz was comparing George Eliot's realism with the 'realism, warm, shot through with muted poetry' of Vermeer, but his remarks about the transformation of minute realistic observation into 'intimism' apply equally well to Flaubert.[49] In wider terms, they can be used to characterize the capacity of the realistic short story to irradiate ordinary things with 'intimate beauty'. The short story which presents a picture (or, like 'A Simple Heart', a series of pictures sharing a similar manner and tone) is able to use its brevity to intensify the reader's gaze and to produce a rare brand of intimacy between reader and story. The beauty of Félicité's 'simple heart', and its significance, arise 'by dint of being looked at with intensity'.

Of course the fundamental constancy of Félicité's character and the stability of her position in the Aubain household facilitate the achievement of unity in recounting her story, pervaded as it is by muted feelings and a mood of suppressed grief. Precisely because her life *is* prosaic, its depiction would be falsified by any suggestion of melodrama, and indeed it is part of Flaubert's realism here to show that the only fitting conclusion to such a story is the natural and universal one – death. But Flaubert's method of picture-making is amenable to more melodramatic subjects, as his disciple Maupassant demonstrates. The climax of 'Two Little Soldiers' (1886) is a suicide, but the violence of this ending is absorbed into a texture which interweaves the customary and the unusual, linking them together through understated detail and repetition. While the soldiers are bound together in friendship and shared homesickness they sit, every Sunday, side by side on the grass, 'their red-trousered legs mingling with the bright colours of the wild flowers', an image so simple and yet so expressive that when this harmony is destroyed by sexual passion, Maupassant need do no more than to show Jean watching Luc and the dairymaid 'disappear side by side, the red trousers of his friend making a scarlet spot against the white road'. The picture is framed for both character and reader, and it communicates so reticently Jean's feelings of loss and exclusion that when he and Luc stop, as they do every Sunday, on a bridge over the Seine, his action seems natural and inevitable:

> Jean leaned over the railing, farther and farther, as though he had seen something in the stream that hypnotised him. Luc said to him: 'What's the matter? Do you want a drink?' He had hardly said the last word when Jean's head carried away the rest of his body, and the little blue and red soldier fell like a shot and disappeared in the water.[50]

Scarcely an action at all, the head carrying away the body because the heart is wounded, the climax makes no disturbance in the objective, highly visual style used throughout.

More adventurous still is Maupassant's stylized technique in a late story, 'The Olive Orchard' (1890). Several stock devices are used, including the arrival of a mysterious stranger, who turns out to be the main character's illegitimate son; and inset narratives are employed to summarize information about the past. But these conventional elements are accommodated within a succession of vivid scenes to which the olive trees are constant silent witnesses. Maupassant skilfully introduces items of décor naturalistically and then later makes them contribute to a dramatic scene: the Chinese gong used to summon the abbé's servant Marguerite, and the green-shaded white china lamp which she brings in just after the stranger has announced histrionically, 'I paid him out for you, Papa'; both of these objects heighten the effect of terror when, after a long ominous silence, the gong rings out stridently and Marguerite rushes in to find, first the stranger lying on the floor, then the overturned lamp, and finally, almost surrealistically, 'the black feet and black-stockinged legs of Abbé Vilbois'. Striking use is made of visual perspective, both in this scene and in Maupassant's later description of the forces of law and order approaching the abbé's pink-washed cottage, their lanterns sending out streaks of yellow light in which the gnarled trunks of the olive trees take on macabre shapes.

But most impressive of all is the scene Maupassant did *not* write. He omits what might have been expected to form a climax, the scene which bridges the struggle between the abbé and his son and Marguerite's discovery of its outcome. What this scene would have needed to show is the abbé's inner struggle with despair, a crisis which earlier in the story is actually anticipated by an allusion to Christ's agony on the Mount of Olives. Instead of including this scene, Maupassant uses a technique of cutting. However much the writer can show, he can also withhold, and here the intention is clearly not to tease but to provide an ironic comment on the narrow view of events the abbé's community will take when his death is discovered. In 'The Olive Orchard' Maupassant means to convey that, against the writer's reserve of knowledge about his characters, rational deduction falters: the morally naive crowd deduces that the abbé has been murdered, but the author hints at a truth more suited to the shady olive grove: 'It never occurred to any one that Abbé Vilbois might possibly have killed himself.'[51] The crowd's opinion of this unconventional clergyman is exposed as shallow, and here Maupassant's teaching resembles that found in many Hawthorne stories, where the community is often seen as deficient in its judgements and insights.

Maupassant's technique of cutting and compressing narrative in order to heighten mystery was to be taken much further by writers who outlived him, most notably by two writers working in England but unusually receptive to European influences, Kipling and James. In their different ways, both of these artists developed the dramatic methods pioneered in the nineteenth-century French *conte*, bringing the short story into relationship more with drama than with the novel, and consequently helping the short story to independence among prose forms. Of the two, it is James who offers us theoretical grounds for aligning short fiction and drama, and whose narrative approach puts him properly among the 'artful storytellers' considered in this chapter. Unlike Kipling, who extended the principle of cutting and concealing to his autobiography (aptly entitled *Something of Myself*), James has left us a vivid picture of his working methods; he sets down his thoughts about the art of fiction, and meditates on the genesis of individual stories, in his *Prefaces* and in the *Notebooks* which survived his destruction of many papers towards the end of his life. These provide incomparably rich material for anyone investigating questions of narrative unity, and their value goes far beyond what they tell us about James's own art, though that is where we must start.

'The completeness of the drama-quality' was invariably what James aimed for in his mature short stories, many of which began modestly as anecdotes.[52] The *Notebooks* offer ample evidence about the processes by which James transformed shreds of dinner-table gossip into finely-wrought and fully-rounded stories. It was an activity which demanded an increasing amount of his attention in the 1890s, the period of his disastrous attempt to become a successful playwright. In May 1895, with no less than three stories promised to the editor of the *Atlantic*, James found that although he had plenty of possible subjects to hand, it was timely to remind himself that, 'more and more, everything of this kind I do must be a complete and perfect little drama. The little idea must resolve itself into a little action, and the little action into the *essential* drama aforesaid. *Voilà*. It is the way – it is perhaps the only way – to make some masterpieces.'[53] The transition proposed here – from idea into action, then from action into drama – is characteristic of James. Always determined to make an idea the motive force of a story, he realized that an idea, or 'concetto' as he often called it, needed to be 'mated with some action' in order to become worthwhile fictionally.[54]

Like the epic poet summoning his muse, James frequently invokes the name of his chosen guide: 'Oh, spirit of Maupassant, come to my aid! This may be a triumph of robust and vivid concision', he writes, as he plans 'The Patagonia' in 1888.[55] Yet in the same year James was arguing that the compactness of Maupassant's stories resulted less from ruthless artistic selection than from limited vision. Splendidly interfused idea and picture might be present in Maupassant's work, but all the same, something was missing:

> The truth is that the admirable system of simplification which makes his tales so rapid and so concise . . . strikes us as not in the least a conscious intellectual effort, a selective, comparative process. He tells us all he knows, all he suspects, and if these things take no account of the moral nature of man, it is because he has no window looking in that direction, and not because artistic scruples have compelled him to close it up. The very compact mansion in which he dwells presents on that side a perfectly dead wall.[56]

By omitting 'the whole reflective part of his men and women – that reflective part which governs conduct and produces character', Maupassant had 'simply skipped' an area which James found inseparable from the artist's highest responsibilities.[57]

Similar considerations were doubtless involved in James's assessment of Prosper Mérimée, whose 'chiselled and polished little fictions' he admired sufficiently to translate 'La Venus d'Ille', 'Tamango' and 'Mateo Falcone'.[58] In the 1870s James cited Mérimée as 'the most striking modern example of zealous artistic conciseness – of the literary artist who works in detail, by the line, by the word'.[59] Clearly, Mérimée's detached style and his interest in human motive appealed to James; and he would have found his own concerns reflected in the French writer's subject-matter, where something savage often intrudes into the civilized, the supernatural into the ordinary. But enthusiasm had to be qualified by the admission that Mérimée was 'elaborately perfect in a somewhat narrow line', striking James as more impressive for his skilful compression of large amounts of dramatic substance into a narrow compass, than for his choice of themes.[60] Implicitly, James shows Mérimée looking forward to the modern short story in his achievement of a 'pregnant brevity' which leaves 'a kind of magical after-resonance' at the end, but he also notes that Mérimée remained tied to old-fashioned subjects, often brutal and hingeing on 'a violent adventure or chain of adventures'.[61] Nor was so much 'bloodshed and general naughtiness' to James's taste.[62]

In his own fiction, James too depicted violence and 'naughtiness', though not of the costume-drama sort. His interest was in the devious brutalities practised beneath the surface of late Victorian society, in violence masked by social convention and, so James believed, threatening the very basis of English civilization. As an artist, he could glory in Mérimée's ingenuity, but his belief that all art must be imbued with a moral sense compelled him to choose subjects which would be both realistic and exemplary. Each story, for James, must offer at one and the same time an aesthetically pleasing 'extension of the picture, the full and vivid summary', and what he habitually called the 'notation' of contemporary phenomena.[63] Many of James's early stories deal with cultural contrasts between Europe and America, but by the time he was preparing the 'New York edition' of his works (1907–09), stories like 'Lady Barberina' (1884) or 'The Siege of London' (1883) seemed no longer salient.

The 1890s, however, had yielded their own momentous theme – and had seen James produce his greatest short stories. James had found a topic equally ripe with complications and conflicts as his 'international theme', though it was one which chastened his earlier tone of social comedy: the position of the artist in society provided James with a subject which was deeply personal and at the same time part of his diagnosis of grave social maladies. In 1894 James envisaged writing a number of tales about 'the drama, the tragedy, the general situation of disappointed ambition' and his first story for *The Yellow Book* was just such a tragedy.[64] 'The Death of the Lion' (1895) conveys the ironic perception that recognition by the social horde spells death to the genuine 'man of letters', whose true value is disclosed only to the story's narrator. A similar contrast between the overt and the hidden is drawn in 'The Private Life' (1893), where the painter Lord Mellifont is a public 'performer' who seems to have no private identity, while Clare Vawdrey, a Browning-like writer, lacks a public self to correspond to his intensely private individuality. These stories and others of the period, including 'The Coxon Fund' (1895) and 'The Next Time' (1896), have the double force of being realistic human dramas and also heartfelt parables of James's artistic beliefs, a layering that greatly enriches his adoption of the scenic methods he admired in European writing.

The dramatic principle, in James's view, had advantages over and above its power to compress and summarize. Drama allowed interest to be spread over a group of people, differing in this from the anecdote, which James defined as 'something that has oddly happened to someone'.[65] The anecdote must always focus on that 'someone'; it 'always has a question to answer – of whom necessarily is it told?'[66] But if a story is conceived in dramatic terms, James maintains, then what 'happens' affects everyone in the story; things are 'squared' and 'kept in happy relation to each other'.[67] Consequently, if constructed according to a 'planned rotation of aspects' and organized by means of '"scenic" determination', the short story can actually rival the novel in complexity.[68]

It has to be admitted that James's urge to grasp the entirety of a situation often overwhelmed his determination to make his stories 'as admirably compact and *selected* as Maupassant'.[69] He found it very difficult to stop even 'very small ideas' from multiplying, no matter how fiercely he tried to restrain them: in the case of his story

'Glasses' (1896), for example, ten thousand words at first seemed a feasible length, but in the event it doubled in size, leading James to write ruefully to his editor: 'I find, in my old age, that I have too much manner and style, too great and invincible an instinct of completeness and of seeing things in all their relations, so that *development*, however squeezed down, becomes inevitable – too much of all this to be able to turn round in the small corners I used to.'[70] And it should be remembered that the situation of one of his longest novels *The Golden Bowl* (1904) first struck him as suitable for 'a little tale'.[71] The struggle to condense his subjects into 'a fixed and beggarly number of words' always struck James as 'a poor and vain undertaking – a waste of time', and for this reason he found the indeterminate form of the short novel specially appealing.[72]

Nevertheless, despite his impatience with extreme brevity, particularly when it was editorially imposed, James did on many occasions prevent complications from proliferating so much that they couldn't be gracefully contained within a tight little framework, 'with every touch an image, a step'.[73] Among his truly short pieces, 'The Real Thing' (1893) stands as an impressive example of his ability to deal with a group of characters without releasing more suggestions than the narrative could hold. In this instance James's *Notebook* entries make it possible to trace the evolution of an elegantly paced short story from the very first stirrings of the writer's imagination. It is a rare opportunity: the origins of short stories and the processes involved in shaping the final, polished product are usually kept hidden from us (and, in some cases, from the writers themselves), although for purposes of instruction a writer like L. A. G. Strong is prepared to combine an analysis of one of his own stories with information about his sources and raw materials.[74] What is offered by James, however, is a chance to see a great writer's mind working on – and through – the fictional possibilities afforded by an initial idea for a story. Because the *Notebooks* give such a full picture of the way 'The Real Thing' was composed, the story will be given special attention here, the intention being to suggest that it can be taken as a paradigm of the 'scenic' method.

The origin of 'The Real Thing' lies in a trivial incident related to James by the painter and *Punch* illustrator George du Maurier. A couple of 'good-looking gentlefolk' had fallen on hard times and offered themselves as artist's models.[75] James no sooner heard the anecdote than he was struck by the 'little tragedy' of two people discovering, after twenty years of country-house idleness, that their only way of making a living might be to sell their good looks, earning wages for simply being 'the fine, clean, well-groomed animals that they were'.[76] James saw that the situation was pathetic and odd, but he did not see it in a comic light as W. S. Gilbert had done when he created his splendid purveyors of good grooming, the Duke and

Duchess of Plazatoro in *The Gondoliers*. While the point of Gilbert's satire is that there is a market for the faded aristocrats' social acumen, what struck James was that in the specialized realm of painting the would-be models were bound to fail; in du Maurier's anecdote James saw something typical of his period, 'the everlasting English amateurness – the way superficial, untrained, unprofessional effort goes to the wall when confronted with trained, competitive, intelligent, *qualified* art'.[77] The knowledge that any painter would hire professional models in preference to 'the real thing' if he needed to paint 'good-looking gentlefolk' gave James the germ of his story.

It is notable that the first step in James's transformation of an anecdote into an illustrative '*morceau de vie*' should have been to see a potential conflict, but having 'tried a beginning' he became conscious that before devising a narrative which would depict amateurism 'confronted with' professionalism he must 'straighten out the little idea'.[78] An important distinction lies behind James's insistence that the piece 'must be an idea – it can't be a "story" in the vulgar sense of the word. It must be a picture; it must illustrate something.'[79] By 'vulgar' story, James evidently means action that is 'stupid, mechanical, arbitrary' rather than 'something that is of the real essence of the subject'.[80] Inventing a plot is a secondary and comparatively easy matter, James finds; what needs most time and thought is clarifying the purpose of the story. Only when he is sure of the idea does he proceed to devise the symmetries and contrasts which will best represent the 'concetto' of 'The Real Thing'. On this, as on other occasions, he sees no point in noting down a proposed plot except 'so as to give the vaguest skeleton and *enclose* the statement in a definite loop'; the 'statement' is what he must be sure of.[81]

The process of fleshing out the skeleton involves rejections as well as inventions. James briefly considers making jealousy the source of conflict in the story; with his models a married couple, what could be more natural than to make the husband the jealous type who does not appreciate the painter's attentions to his wife? But it is quickly clear to James that this rather conventional approach is a false trail – and as such it survives in the completed story, where the narrator briefly suspects Major Monarch of jealousy and then sees there is nothing in this idea. In fact, James realizes, his conception of 'The Real Thing' is far better served by treating his 'lady and gentleman' as a single unit, and then making complication grow out of a confrontation between this 'genteel pair' and another couple, the antithesis of the gentlefolk; these will be the 'real models', 'little vulgar people who *know*'.[82] Although the point is not made explicitly in the *Notebooks*, what is achieved by this decision is that the painter figure is freed from the clear-cut opposition, amateurish versus '*qualified*' art, and so enabled to act as an observing but not disinterested narrator; he can witness the collision between the amateurs and the professionals and, in the telling of the story, encapsulate what he has learned from it.

Already in James's mind the story is taking on the properties of what he termed ' "foreshortening" – the particular economic device for which one must have a name and which has in its single blessedness and its determined pitch, I think, a higher price than twenty other clustered loosenesses'.[83] Having grasped the simple structural device of opposing one pair of models, male and female, to another, and so restraining the 'space-hunger and space-cunning' of his material, he can now open his imagination to more specific features of the contrast: the professionals can be scruffy, so as to highlight the amateurs' cherished but artistically worthless cleanliness; speech inflexions and mannerisms can be used to emphasize the social gulf between the female model – no lady, but gifted with the ability to pose marvellously – and the 'real thing', the genuine lady who is incapable of being anything but her inflexible self; and since the central contrast is strong enough to hold a variety of details together, the impeccable Major's counterpart can be an ungentlemanly Italian, 'ill dressed, smelling of garlic'.[84]

Having planned this much, James fears for a moment that the single conflict he has generated may not be enough to make 'a story by itself', but his reassurance is that, 'it's an IDEA', and a strong idea, which can be turned into 'a little gem of bright, quick vivid form' if only he can 'make it tremendously succinct – with a very short pulse or rhythm – and the closest selection of detail – in other words *summarize* intensely and keep down the lateral development'.[85] These directives might be taken as a blueprint for all short-storywriting. But what James has so far disregarded is the question, what is he going to do to make the idea as striking and significant to the reader as it is to him? Surely some tension over and above the inherently static contrast between two types of artist's model is needed to give a special edge to his 'statement' that worthwhile art never merely imitates 'the real thing'. As a denouement, the failure of the Major and his wife as models, and their departure 'into the vague again' seems low in narrative punch, and whatever James may say about not writing 'a "story" in the vulgar sense of the word', he is still aware that his story so far lacks a crisis.[86] He knows the truth of what Hardy was to observe in 1893: 'A story must be exceptional enough to justify its telling. We tale-tellers are all Ancient Mariners, and none of us is warranted in stopping Wedding Guests (in other words, the hurrying public) unless he has something more unusual to relate than the ordinary experience of every average man and woman.'[87]

Interestingly enough, consideration of this question comes only when James's self-communings about 'The Real Thing' are fairly well advanced, thus indicating yet again his determination to make narrative serve idea rather than the other way around. When he does turn his attention to the need for a crisis, he hits on a straightforward plan; he will make the painter's whole future depend on the book illustrations he is working on when the Major and his wife arrive. Feeling seven thousand words to be a 'tiny number' which will prove a 'tight squeeze', James realizes that can 'get every grain of "action" that the space admits of' if he makes 'something, for the artist, hang in the balance – depend on the way he does this particular work'.[88] So, tension in the story will arise not merely from the Monarchs' desperation about making ends meet, but also from the narrator's own fear of losing a 'great opportunity'.[89] James has found the perfect narrative pretext for accelerating judgement of the genteel couple's suitability as models, and his *Notebook* entry reflects the way the story immediately tightens when he turns his attention to the painter's situation: 'He is willing to give them a trial. Make it out that *he* himself is on trial.'[90]

James's consciousness of his aims and methods in writing 'The Real Thing' is so full and acute that what might be expected is a schematic demonstration, technically perfect, but lacking in warmth. Nothing could be more remote from what we actually get. The human pathos and oddity which James first saw in the situation as described by du Maurier permeate the story. Probably because James invariably drew his ideas for stories from 'the surge and pressure of *life*', there is not the impression, as there so often is in, say, O. Henry's work, that the author is following the dictates of a good idea about human behaviour.[91] The central contrast between amateurs and professionals that James worked out so carefully in the *Notebooks* directs the movement of 'The Real Thing' from the outset, but subtly, beneath the surface of apparently straightforward social realism. The opening sentence seems casual enough to have come from Mérimée himself: 'When the porter's wife (she used to answer the house-bell), announced "A gentleman – with a lady, sir", I had, as I often had in those days, for the wish was father to the thought, an immediate vision of sitters.' The event is totally innocuous, but at the same time as the narrator relates it to his own situation as a needy painter, James is giving prominence to the characters who are to be central to his story; the arrival of 'a gentleman – with a lady' instantly creates a social ambience, emphasizing the typical qualities of the couple. They have given no name, but the porter's wife has no doubts as to their polite standing, even though her announcement leaves the nature of their relationship uncertain; in fact, James delays naming his characters until his story is well under way, referring to them for about the first thousand words as 'the gentleman' and 'the lady'. This allows for the deepening of the narrator's bafflement about their purpose: he guesses that they have come to have their portraits painted, and conjectures that for reasons of decorum they are shy to speak out: 'Perhaps they were not husband and wife – this naturally would make the matter more delicate. Perhaps they wished to be done together – in which case they ought to have bought a third person to break the news.' In fact, as is soon disclosed, Major and Mrs Monarch have come, not to give work to the painter but to plead for work as models, and James devotes the first section of his story to the gradual emergence of the surprising intention behind the arrival of 'a gentleman – with a lady'. The mode of the story is established as ironic from the outset, and the extent to which the opening is decisive can be further appreciated by comparing the first, magazine version of the initial sentence with its later form in the revised New York edition of James's works:

> When the porter's wife (she used to answer the house-bell), announced 'A gentleman – with a lady, sir', I had, as I often had in those days, for the wish was father to the thought, an immediate vision of sitters.

> When the porter's wife, who used to answer the house-bell, announced 'A gentleman and a lady, sir', I had, as I often had in those days – the wish being father to the thought – an immediate vision of sitters.[92]

The second of these has a more compressed effect, largely because of the removal of the first parenthesis, although this also diminishes the colloquial quality of the opening and reduces the importance of the porter's wife. And the change from 'A gentleman – with a lady' to the blander 'A gentleman and a lady', tiny as it is, removes a flourish from the announcement, which in the original version, the natural emphasis falling on 'with', raises curiosity about the nature of relationship. What is achieved by substituting 'and' for 'with' is that the Monarchs are seen as a pair, an effect which fits the narrator's later observation that 'this union had no weak spot. It was a real marriage, an encouragement for the hesitating, a nut for pessimists to crack'. And perhaps James felt that his first formulation threw undue emphasis on Major Monarch. But what James lost by his revision was in fact a more intriguing way of pairing his characters; the first version's 'with' allowed particularly well for the inseparability of the 'gentleman' and the 'lady', and it also deepened the central irony of the story by hinting that what every gentleman of Major Monarch's type requires is a lady on his arm: there is, in the early version, an impression of the two visitors making up a pair, almost like matching china ornaments or 'sets' of presentation photographs of the kind which we are told the Monarchs have given away in 'quantities'. By presenting the Monarchs as a mutually dependent couple at the beginning of his story, James prepares for the narrator's later observation that although they are of little use to an artist, 'There was something in them for a waistcoat-maker, an hotel-keeper, or a soap vendor. I could imagine "We always use it" pinned on their bosoms with the greatest effect.'

James's later minor revision does not alter the meaning of 'The Real Thing' but it does slightly loosen the pattern of ironies within the story. It also lowers the atmosphere of expectation with which the first version instantly surrounded the announcement by the porter's wife, transferring attention perhaps too rapidly to the second sentence, which picks up only one of the story's key-words 'gentleman' 'lady' and 'sitters': 'Sitters my visitors in this case proved to be; but not in the sense I should have preferred.' This sentence James left untouched, and wisely so, since it confirms the promise of an ironic outcome and, taken together with the first sentence, sets up a witty antithesis between 'arrivals' and 'sittings'. The narrative of 'The Real Thing' turns out to be constructed on an alternating rhythm of arrivals and poses, movement and stillness: in the first section, at the point when the Monarchs' distress has reached such a histrionic pitch that the narrator has agreed to employ them, Miss Churm, the professional model, makes an entrance. She has not come 'with' anyone, and her independence is apparent when we are told that to reach the artist's studio she has to 'take the omnibus to Maida Vale and then walk half a mile'. The wet umbrella she is carrying is meant for use, and it contrasts with the purely decorative umbrella which, in the illustration in *Black and White* of Mrs Monarch 'going through her paces' for the painter, is held horizontally, forming a stylized right angle with the Major's equally redundant umbrella, which he holds firmly to the floor. Miss Churm's arrival, and her disarrayed appearance ('a trifle blowsy and slightly splashed') humorously deflates the Major's lament on behalf of all unemployable gentlemen ('poor beggars, who've drunk their wine, who've kept their hunters!'); and it introduces another contrast vital to the story. In herself, Miss Churm is a glorious self-contradiction; she is not all of a piece like the Monarchs, but a 'freckled cockney' who is utterly convincing when she poses in black velvet, a Japanese fan in her red hands, every inch a Russian princess, 'distinguished and charming, foreign and dangerous'. This is the pose in which the second magazine illustration shows her; standing in front of a sturdy and resolutely unglamorous iron stove, Miss Churm, so the caption tells us, 'took her station near the fire. She fell into position and settled herself into a tall attitude.' The visual contrast between this figure and that of Mrs Monarch accentuates the antitheses on which James constructs his narrative, and a reader of the original magazine version of the story would have had the experience of seeing the amateurs depicted on one page and then, on the next opening, the natural professional, who has the 'faculty' of being 'so little in herself' yet 'so much in others', and who can 'represent everything from a fine lady to a shepherdess'.

After this keenly visualized scene, in which dialogue, gesture and descriptive exposition are combined, James's narrative method can allowably become more iterative in order to suggest the passing of an indefinite period of time. He amplifies the painter's distinction between the Monarchs' stiffness and Miss Churm's 'talent for imitation' by summarizing an unspecified number of sittings in his studio. The story is well past its mid-point, and the Monarchs' presence established as habitual, when the narrator mentions casually that 'one day' he asked Miss Churm to make tea for everyone. This scene is merely sketched in, and a single paragraph emphasizes the impossible situation in which the Monarchs – now 'sitters' in the sense of immovable squatters – are trapping the narrator. Then another unprecedented event is recorded, again with the tag 'one day' (reminiscent of Flaubert in 'A Simple Heart') to signal its importance: 'One day Mrs Monarch came without her husband.' In the scene that follows, Oronte, the Italian whose every movement makes a picture, arrives – the narrator recognizes the knock of an out-of-work model instantly – and is taken on in the double capacity of servant and model. At this point in his narrative, but not before, James has assembled all of the components necessary to his central contrast: rivalry between the two women and between the immaculately tailored Major and the itinerant Italian in his 'tight yellow trousers with reddish stripes' is inherent in the symmetry of the two couples. There is an additional ironic twist to this: whereas the Monarchs are indivisibly a married pair, Oronte and Miss Churm are gloriously independent, their only attachment to one another being through their profession. (Here James departs interestingly from the experience recounted by du Maurier, whose 'trained' models were husband and wife.)[93] Now that all of James's characters are in place, it needs only the narrator's realization that his sympathy for the Monarchs is actually ruining his work to precipitate the reversal on which 'The Real Thing' hinges. The real gentlefolk must serve tea to the real models, an action which upsets the social hierarchy and also dramatizes James's belief that imitative art, being of lower rank, should wait upon its superior – imaginative representation. Again, the first readers of the story would have found the impact of this startling moment augmented by Rudolf Blind's illustration. Oronte is depicted taking a cup of tea from the tray held by Mrs Monarch, and the caption underlines the extent to which both characters have been displaced from their accustomed social 'station': 'Mrs Monarch brought the model a cup of tea and he took it from her as if he had been a gentleman at a party, squeezing a crush-hat with his elbow'.

Adroitly, James reflects a sense of closure at this moment of reversal by recording the narrator's conviction that after such humiliation the Monarchs will never return. But the reversal is not the end of his story, as it would have been for a lesser writer. The Monarchs do reappear, and James gives further unity to a story which has already been unified by a Flaubertian alternation of action and picture, a rhythm which corresponds to the way the plot fluctuates between arrivals and sittings, characters knocking on the narrator's door and characters adopting poses. The story's completeness is ensured when James offers yet another moment, recapitulating the opening scene but emphasizing certain significant differences. The crisis in the narrator's career is passing, because he has now committed himself to Oronte and Miss Churm as hero and heroine in the book illustrations which will guarantee his future. He is no longer alone when the Monarchs arrive this time: cockney and Italian are perfectly posed to illustrate a passage 'in which Rutland Ramsay, drawing up a chair to Artemisia's piano-stool says extraordinary things to her while she fingers out a difficult piece of music'. The tableau comes straight out of the country-house life once enjoyed by the Monarchs, but now Mrs Monarch's expertise as a social belle is directed to rearranging Miss Churm's hairstyle, while the Major sets to work on the painter's unwashed breakfast dishes. Once again, the Monarchs surprise the narrator by asking for employment, through gesture rather than speech, with the result that on this occasion the painter is more moved than amused. The Monarchs themselves are now painfully aware of the contrast which has been set out for the reader; in their mute actions the narrator reads their acknowledgement of the 'perverse and cruel law in virtue of which the real thing could be so much less precious than the unreal'. All their former pride has gone, overwhelmed by the instinct for survival: 'They would reverse the parts – the others would sit for the ladies and gentlemen and *they* would do the work. They would still be in the studio – it was an intense dumb appeal to me not to turn them out. "Take us on", they wanted to say – "we'll do *anything*."' The imagined words, 'we'll do *anything*', echo the Major's cry, 'I'd be *anything*', in the opening scene, the change from 'be' to 'do' matching exactly the realization that the Monarchs' 'being' will not 'do', in its sense of 'suit', as far as the painter is concerned. In still another sense, they were willing to be 'done', that is painted, for nothing.[94] The word-play here and throughout the story emphasizes the degree of control exerted by James in this story. After a week, as the narrator tells us without needing to depict the pitiful spectacle of the gentleman and lady 'doing' for him as domestic servants, he pays them to go away. The story ends by placing the entire experience qualitatively, providing a coda which justifies the first-person narrator's effort to recapture this past episode. His closing statement, to the effect that the memory left him by the Monarchs is ample recompense for any lasting damage to his art, implies that the encounter has been a personally valuable, humanizing one. Dealing with the Monarchs has deepened his sensitivity and perhaps even challenged his belief in art as a supreme and autonomous value.

In 'The Real Thing' James has fulfilled his intention of giving his action 'a very short pulse and rhythm' so successfully that anyone reading the story finds it impossible to abstract his 'idea' from its embodiment in a realistic story. Partly, the rhythm belongs to the narrator's thoughts and memories, but the pulse of these is determined by vividly actualized scenes which alternate with passages of description, analysis, and evocations of time passing. At intervals, movement and process quicken into a pictured scene which both typifies the characters and reveals the adjustments and alterations in the relationships between these characters. Each scene has elements of repetition as well as of change, allowing the reader to watch the central situation being slowly modified until the only possible change left is reversal. Furthermore, by enclosing the pulsation of linked events within two similar scenes, James forces us to consider the changes that have occurred in the longer interval between beginning and ending. Similarities between the first and the last scenes enhance the mood of fundamental stability and calm that is characteristic of much realistic short fiction, a mood which is favourable to the capture of fleeting impressions and transient emotions. Yet although 'The Real Thing' opens and closes with virtually the same situation, differences of attitude – the Monarchs more self-abasing, the narrator more anguished by their bid for help – deepen the story's tone and provoke questions about the changes that have taken place beneath the apparently unruffled surface.

James's success in this story springs from the resolute way in which he has overcome the difficulties he saw as inalienable from the storyteller's art. In his Preface to *The Awkward Age*, he describes the 'trap' laid for the writer who is by nature 'amused and beguiled' by human relationships, and whose 'fine inquisitive speculative sense for them' makes him feel as though he were floundering 'in a deep warm jungle': 'Though the relations of a human figure or a social occurrence are what make such objects interesting, they also make them, to the same tune, difficult to isolate, to surround with the sharp black line, to frame in the square, the circle, the charming oval, that helps any arrangement of objects to become a picture.'[95] Framed in a circle, 'The Real Thing' arranges its 'objects' in such a way as to offer us a complete, but not static, picture. All of James's individual scenes and cameos within the story are painted with the same materials and in the same style, but by the end a reshaping has taken place, putting relationships – between, for example, the narrator of 'The Real Thing' and his real and unreal models – in a fresh and different light. No violent or even radical change has taken place, the figures have only regrouped a little, but lights and shades have altered.

In this respect 'The Real Thing' is typical of all short stories which attempt to overcome the discursive and linear properties of prose by deepening rather than – as happens with Poe – extending a situation. Each scene is a composition in itself, but full understanding is reserved for the moment when the relationship between all the pictures can be discerned. Repetition and alteration are the principles involved, and they could be equally well described in terms of poetic techniques. Affinities between short-story form and the oral tradition of the ballad have long been recognized, though generally in relation to stories considerably less stylish than Henry James's. Yet the unsophisticated ballad-maker's use of refrain and incremental repetition is directly connected to highly literate art like James's. When James repeats and slightly modifies his dramatic scenes he is actually employing a device of ancient origin. He is observing what V. S. Pritchett has declared to be 'one of the great principles of story-telling', whatever the form or medium, namely 'to appear to do the same thing twice, but on the second occasion to make a significant alteration'.[96] James, whose refined artistry and seemingly rarefied subjects often lead people to underestimate his fascination with risk and irrationality, would probably have appreciated Pritchett's analysis of reader-psychology: 'The art of the storyteller lies, of course, in surprise; but the art of surprise must come from the continuous knowledge that the reader, in his anxiety, is always playing for safety. It is the storyteller's business to make the path of safety into a path of change and danger.'[97] In the widest sense, James was committed to steering the English reading public off the safe mid-Victorian path, and in his fiction this took the form of ceaseless experimentation. His most daring attempts were made in his novels, but in his short stories too he diverted the notion of 'surprise' away from plot, where his predecessors had been content to leave it.

For James, the intention behind the 'surprises' in 'The Real Thing' were both social and moral. The scenic method of narration is particularly well-suited to this purpose. One of the particular advantages of framing the entire narrative sweep within two similar scenes is that unobtrusive morality can be fused with social observation. The tightness of the frame actually helps to conceal the author's contrivance of patterns, because within the space marked out the author can appear to investigate the material for its own sake. Inside the frame, looseness can be simulated. In some writers this freedom is chiefly evident in style. To give only one instance, the contemporary Irish writer Mary Lavin has the power to make naturalistic dialogue seem to ramble along while all the time she is using the structure of her stories to convey meaning. 'Frail Vessel' (1956), for example, contrasts two sisters, Liddy and Bedelia, one of them reckless but capable of 'some secret happiness' unexperienced by the other, who is efficient, self-righteous and joyless. A series of scenes traces a number of confrontations, all of them ostensibly concerned with practical matters. At the end of the story Bedelia is inwardly raging, envious of Liddy's serenity in the face of disasters which should, according to social conventionality, make her angry. The final picture of Bedelia reshapes the opening image of the two women at their mother's graveside; then, Bedelia had been congratulating herself on her unselfish plans to marry for her young sister's sake. The outcome is indeed that Bedelia has a 'home' for Liddy to come to, but not at all in the way Bedelia imagined.[98] The story's perceptions about the moral and emotional ambiguities that complicate issues like generosity, selflessness and forgiveness do not emerge bluntly; they are crystallized and released through the reader's awareness that the initial picture has been recomposed. Dialogue and description have been circumstantial and unadorned throughout the story, in perfect keeping with setting and character, but complex moral questions remain at the end.

Although the full significance of a story like 'Frail Vessel' does not emerge until the narrative is complete, there is no single climactic moment when realization breaks over the reader. Meaning is compressed, but individual scenes and the story as a whole have duration; the observations they contain, their texture, and their incidental qualities do not evaporate, obliterated by the final 'point' of the story. This is because everything in the story is dramatized, answering a requirement best expressed by Elizabeth Bowen in her 'Notes on Writing a Novel': 'Story involves action. Action towards an end not to be foreseen (by the reader) but also towards an end which, having *been* reached, must be seen to have been from the start inevitable.'[99] Inevitable, not predictable or sensational; the conclusion of a satisfying short story does not merely provide an answer to a puzzle, it invites the reader to retrace his steps and appreciate the deftness with which the writer has led him towards an unforeseen ending. This is the quality which makes it proper to speak of certain short stories as 'dramatic', as distinct from 'melodramatic', the description required by the sensation fiction considered at the beginning of this chapter. 'It is all one quest – in the way of subject – the play and the tale', wrote James shortly before 'The Real Thing' appeared in *Black and White*: 'It is not one *choice* – it is two deeply distinct ones; but it's the same general *enquête*, the same attitude and *regard*. The large, sincere, attentive, constant quest would be a net hauling in – with its close meshes – the two kinds.'[100] This principle, so well illustrated by 'The Real Thing', can be seen at work in all short stories where the 'scenic' method is successfully adopted, leaving the reader feeling that the artist has managed to give his 'tale' the properties of a good play.

NOTES AND REFERENCES

1. *Fortnightly Review*, New Series, LXIII, 652.
2. *Letters on the Short Story*, p. 106 (22 Jan. 1888).
3. *Henry James and H. G. Wells: A Record of their Friendship, their Debate on the Art of Fiction, and their Quarrel*, ed. Leon Edel and Gordon N. Ray (1958), p. 140. The first book appearance of Wells's paper (originally a talk on 'The Scope of the Novel') was in *An Englishman Looks at the World* (1914).
4. *Ibid.*, p. 136.
5. *Ibid.*
6. Pritchett, *Midnight Oil*, p. 188; Anderson, *A Story Teller's Story*, p. 315.
7. *London Magazine* (Mar. 1970), p. 9.
8. Preface to *Faber Book of Modern Stories*, p. 14.
9. *The Art of the Novel*, p. 205. See also Katherine Anne Porter, *Paris Review*, XXIX, 110; 'I started "Flowering Judas" at 7 p.m. and at 1.30 I was standing on a snowy windy corner putting it in the mail box.'
10. *Something of Myself*, p. 209.
11. *Ibid.*
12. Afterword to *Dr Brodie's Report*, p. 101.
13. 'The Pit and the Pendulum', *Collected Works of Edgar Allan Poe*, ed. Thomas Ollive Mabbott (Cambridge, Mass, 1969) II, 681–97 *passim*. All of the Poe stories referred to will be found in Vols II and III (1978) of this edition. 'The Pit and the Pendulum' first appeared in the annual, *The Gift: a Christmas and New Year's Present*, MDCCCXLIII (1842). An impression of arbitrariness about the ending of the story is borne out by the fact that in the original version the last two sentences occurred in reverse order; Poe was clearly undecided as to which statement would make the most effective conclusion.
14. *Collected Works*, II, 340. Originally entitled 'The Psyche Zenobia', Poe's essay was first published in the *American Museum* (Nov. 1838), where it was accompanied by 'Zenobia's' preposterous story 'The Scythe of Time'. 'How to Write a Blackwood Article' also appeared (as 'The Signora Zenobia') in Poe's collection *Tales of the Grotesque and Arabesque* (2 vols, 1840) and in the *Broadway Journal*, II (July 1845), where 'Zenobia's' composition was called 'A Predicament'. For information about Poe's use of British periodicals, see Michael Allen, *Poe and the British Magazine Tradition* (1969).

15. 'The Man in the Reservoir' first appeared in *The Literary World* (of which Hoffman was the editor), III (21 Oct. 1848), 751–53, and was included in several nineteenth-century anthologies. 'Ben Blower's Story' was first published in *Graham's Magazine*. XXI (Sept. 1842), 132–34, and was selected by R. W. Griswold (the author of an early, now discredited 'memoir' of Poe) for his *Prose Writers of America* (1854). For further bibliographical information, see *Homer F. Barnes*'s biography, *Charles Fenno Hoffman* (New York, 1930).

16. *Collected Works*, II, 340.

17. *Complete Works*, ('Virginia' edn) XIII, 153. Poe's later version of his review of Hawthorne's *Twice-Told Tales* was first published in *Godey's Lady Book*, Nov. 1847, and follows closely the 1842 review referred to in Ch. 1.

18. *Ibid.*, XI, 108.

19. 'The Fall of the House of Usher', *Collected Works*, II, 397–417 *passim*.

20. *Studies in Classic American Literature* (1924), Phoenix edn (1964), p. 61.

21. *Ibid.*

22. *Ibid.*, p. 76; p. 61.

23. For a recent variation on this theme, see Bernard MacLaverty's story 'Life Drawing', in *A Time to Dance* (1982), pp. 69–82.

24. *Pages from the Goncourt Journal*, ed. and trans. Robert Baldick (1962), p. 20.

25. *Ibid.*

26. *Ibid.*

27. These stories were collected in O. Henry's second book, *The Four Million* (1906). All of the O. Henry stories discussed can be found in *The Complete Works of O. Henry* (2 vols, New York, 1953).

28. 'The Gift of the Magi', *Complete Works*, I, 7–11 *passim*. The continued popularity of this story is demonstrated by the fact that in 1939 Harrap issued a single edition, clearly intended for the Christmas market and with illustrations by Stephen Goodman, A. R. A., which deliberately brought out the fairy-tale aspect of O. Henry's narrative.

29. In her *Handbook on Story Writing* (p. 74), Blanche Colton Williams actually provides a diagram representing the plot of 'The Gift of the Magi'. For a condemnation of the story's final paragraph as superfluous to this 'plot of cross purposes', see N. Bryllion Fagin, *Short Story-writing: An Art or a Trade?* (New York, 1923), p. 37; Fagin's advice was to, 'Tell your story . . . and stop.'

30. H. S. Canby, 'Free Fiction', *Atlantic Monthly*, CXVI (July 1915), 61.

31. 'The Last Leaf' is the only O. Henry story discussed which does not come from *The Four Million*. It was included in *The Trimmed Lamp* (1907) and is in *Complete Works*, II, 1455–9.

32. *Complete Works*, I, 24.

33. *The Lonely Voice*, p. 66.

34. *Ibid.*, p. 66, p. 67.

35. See *Points of View*, p. 153.

36. The title of an early handbook on short-storywriting illustrates this practice: A. Sherwin Cody, *How to Write Fiction, Especially the Art of Short Story Writing: A Practical Course of Instruction after the*

French Method of Maupassant (New York, 1894). Cody's guide was studied by H. G. Wells; see Ingvald Raknem, *H. G. Wells and His Critics* (Oslo, 1962), p. 358. N. Bryllion Fagin, who taught short-storywriting at the University of Maryland, also recommended study of Maupassant as a model exemplifying the principle that '"Story" is synonymous with action' (p. 37).

37. 'The Necklace' ('La Parure'), *The Complete Short Stories: Guy de Maupassant*, Cassell edn (3 vols, 1970), II, 432–44 *passim*. Numerous collections of Maupassant's tales have appeared in both French and English, and are widely available in paperback.

38. See 'The Novel', *Pierre and Jean*, trans. Leonard Tancock, Penguin pbk edn (Harmondsworth, Middx, 1979), pp. 21–35 *passim*.

39. 'Boule de Suif' first appeared as one of six stories by different authors making up *Les Soirées de Médan* (1880). Its length is about 13,000 words, and it is classified *as a nouvelle* in Edward D. Sullivan's *Maupassant: The Short Stories* (1962), p. 36.

40. *Notes on Life and Letters* (1921), p. 36.

41. *Ibid.*, p. 35.

42. *Ibid.*, p. 37.

43. *Ibid.*, p. 36.

44. *Ibid.*

45. *Pages from the Goncourt Journal*, p. 58 (17 Mar. 1861).

46. 'A Simple Heart' ('Un Coeur Simple'), *Three Tales*, trans. Robert Baldick, Penguin pbk edn (Harmondsworth, Middx, 1979), pp. 17–56 *passim*. Although first published as one of three *contes*, Flaubert's story later appeared in a single edition, with illustrations (Paris, 1894).

47. Letter to Henry James (Apr. 1868), F. O. Matthiessen, *The James Family* (New York, 1947), p. 318; repr. in *Henry James: The Critical Heritage*, ed. Roger Gard (1968), p. 26.

48. *The Hero in Eclipse in Victorian Fiction*, trans. Angus Davidson, Oxford pbk edn (1969), p. 375.

49. *Ibid.*, p. 374.

50. 'Two Little Soldiers' ('Petit Soldat'), *Tales from Maupassant*, introd. R. B. Cunninghame Grahame (1926), pp. 347–55 *passim*. This text has been used in preference to that in *Complete Short Stories* because of the especially fine way the translator (unknown) has captured the effect of Maupassant's prose.

51. 'The Olive Orchard' ('Le Champ d'Oliviers'), *Complete Short Stories*, III, 326–55 *passim*. This story first appeared in two instalments in *Figaro*, 14 and 23 Feb. 1890.

52. *Notebooks*, p. 198.

53. *Ibid.*

54. *Ibid.*, p. 155.

55. *Ibid.*, p. 89.

56. *Partial Portraits*, pp. 258–9.

57. (*Ibid.*)., p. 285.

58. *Literary Reviews and Essays*, p. 170. James's review, 'Mérimée's Last Tales', first appeared under the title 'Dernières Nouvelles' in *The Nation*, 12 Feb. 1874. He returned to the subject in an article 'Prosper Mérimée' in *Literature*, III (23 July 1898).

59. *Ibid.*

60. *Ibid.*, p. 172.
61. *Ibid.*, p. 170. In his 1934 'Note on the English short story', H. E. Bates named Mérimée as one of the founders of the modern short story: while the story was still a neglected form in nineteenth-century England, Bates noted, 'Turgenev was writing *A Sportsman's Sketches*, Tolstoy such masterly short stories as *Family Happiness*, Mérimée such forerunners of the modern surprise story as *Mateo Falcone*' (*Lovat Dickson's Magazine*, II, 146).
62. *Literary Reviews and Essays*, p. 170.
63. 'The Story-teller at Large', p. 652.
64. *Notebooks*, p. 143.
65. *The Art of the Novel*, p. 181.
66. *Ibid.*
67. *Ibid.*, p. 182.
68. *Ibid.*
69. *Notebooks*, p. 104.
70. Quoted, *ibid.*, p. 206.
71. *Ibid.*, p. 130.
72. *Ibid.*, p. 135.
73. *Ibid.*, p. 107.
74. See *The Writer's Trade*, pp. 98–9, where Strong describes the personal background to 'Travellers'. Strong also examines one of his own stories in *Instructions to Young Writers* (1958), Ch. 9.
75. *Notebooks*, p. 102, (22 Feb. 1891). A decade later James recalled du Maurier speaking to him 'of a call from a strange and striking couple desirous to propose themselves as artist's models for his weekly "social" illustrations to "Punch"', in *The Art of the Novel*, p. 283.
76. *Ibid.*
77. *Ibid.*, p. 103.
78. *Ibid.*
79. *Ibid.*
80. *Ibid.*
81. *Ibid.*, p. 140 (26 Dec. 1893).
82. *Ibid.*, p. 103. See *The Art of the Novel*, p. 283 for James's first mention of the professional models whom du Maurier would have had to dismiss in order to employ the impoverished gentlefolk.
83. *The Art of the Novel*, p. 278.
84. *Ibid.*; *Notebooks*, p. 104.
85. *Notebooks*, p. 104.
86. *Ibid.*, p. 103.
87. Florence Emily Hardy, *The Life of Thomas Hardy 1840–1928*, Macmillan pbk edn (1965), p. 252. Katherine Anne Porter quotes this extract from Hardy's notebooks approvingly in *The Days Before*, p. 34.
88. *Notebooks*, p. 104.
89. *Ibid.*
90. *Ibid.*, p. 103.
91. *Ibid.*, p. 135 (30 Aug. 1893). For Conrad's opinion that 'The Real Thing' seems 'to flow from the heart because and only because the work, approaching so near perfection, yet does not strike cold', see

G. Jean Aubry, *Joseph Conrad, Life and Letters* (2 vols, 1927), I, 270 (Letter to John Galsworthy, 11 Feb. 1899); repr. in *Henry James: The Critical Heritage*, p. 279.

92. 'The Real Thing', *Black and White*, III (16 Apr. 1892), 502: *The Novels and Tales of Henry James*, 'New York edition' (24 vols, New York, 1907–09), XVIII, 307. 'The Real Thing' also appeared as the title story in volume form in 1893. The earlier version is reprinted in *Nineteenth Century Stories*, ed. Peter Keating, Longman pbk (1981); all subsequent page references to 'The Real Thing' are to this edition.

93. See *The Art of the Novel*, p. 283. In his *Notebook* entry James also remarks that in order to increase the amateurs' 'incomprehensibility' of the professionals' 'usefulness', he must 'bring up the age of the 2 real models' to the '50 and 40' he had decided on as the most 'touching' ages to make the Major and his wife (p. 104).

94. 'The Real Thing', *Nineteenth Century Stories*, pp. 141–65 *passim*. A minor revision to the final paragraph of the New York edition is worth noting: the earlier version began the paragraph dramatically ('When all this hung before me the *afflatus* vanished – my pencil dropped from my hand. My sitting was spoiled and I got rid of my sitters . . .') while the later version aims for a more compressed, colloquial effect ('My pencil dropped from my hand; my sitting was spoiled and I got rid of my sitters . . .').

95. *The Art of the Novel*, p. 101.

96. *Books in General* (1953), pp. 182–3.

97. *Ibid*., p. 183.

98. 'Frail Vessel', *The Stories of Mary Lavin* (2 vols, 1964–74), I, 1–19 *passim*. This story was first collected in *The Patriot Son and other stories* (1956).

99. *Pictures and Conversations* (1974), p. 170.

100. *Notebooks*, p. 113. In the previous entry James had complained of feeling 'wrenched away from the attempt to get on with the drama . . . by the necessity of doing *au plus tôt* some short tales' (5 Feb. 1892). For James's decision, ten years earlier, to do '*short* things, in such measure as I need, which will leave me intervals for dramatic work', see *Notebooks*, p. 44.

Chapter 4
'ARTLESS' NARRATION

> To crack a nut is truly no feat, so no one would ever care to collect
> an audience in order to entertain it with nut-cracking. But if all the
> same one does do that and succeeds in entertaining the public, then it
> cannot be a matter of simple nut-cracking. Or it is a matter of nut-
> cracking, but it turns out that we have overlooked the art of cracking
> nuts because we were too skilled in it and that this newcomer to it
> first shows us its real nature, even finding it useful in making his
> effects to be rather less expert in nut-cracking than most of us.
> (Franz Kafka, 'Josephine the Singer, or the Mouse-folk')

The reader of fully dramatized stories like those of Henry James
occupies the dignified position of an onlooker freed from the contingencies of personality; he is offered the lure of subtle artistry and
his enjoyment comes from finding ideas and emotions treated with
profundity. Many other writers, however, have worked on the different assumption that the hook must be baited with the promise of
less respectable relationships between reader and story; eavesdropping on other people's conversations, peeping over a diarist's or let-
ter-writer's shoulder, or being flattered into supposing that the
reader is the only person who can be trusted with a secret, are
among the experiences offered by stories which deliberately con-
travene Flaubertian rules. Sometimes the writer's strategy is to
flaunt subjectivity: 'I know what is being said about me', declares
the narrator of Truman Capote's story, 'My Side of the Matter'
(1945), 'and you can take my side or theirs, that's your own business.'[1] A diarist's state of mind is put on display in Gogol's 'Diary
of a Madman' (1835), which begins in the arresting manner of a simple anecdote: 'Something very peculiar happened today.'[2] And in
Kipling's story 'A Friend's Friend' (1888), the reader is given instant
access to the narrator's high feelings, the introductory mood being
unequivocally vengeful: 'This tale must be told in the first person
for many reasons. The man whom I want to expose is Tranter of the
Bombay side,'[3] There are countless stories which attain 'unity of

effect' by keeping us constantly aware of a human personality pervading the material. Stories which bring individual personality into play by using techniques like monologue or confession also create a strong illusion of a listener who wants to know, but also to understand.

Stories of this sort are, of course, as capable of diverse tones and effects as any other type, but they can be usefully grouped together as instances which recall strongly the atmosphere in which, according to Somerset Maugham, narrative first began:

> It is natural for men to tell tales, and I suppose the short story was created in the night of time when the hunter, to beguile the leisure of his fellows when they had eaten and drunk their fill, narrated by the cavern fire some fantastic incident he had heard of. To this day in the cities of the East you can see the story-teller sitting in the market-place, surrounded by a circle of eager listeners, and hear him tell the tales that he has inherited from an immemorial past.[4]

In the modern West, our equivalents to the market-place are the pub, the social club, and a variety of similar settings in which jokes and anecdotes thrive. Somerset Maugham's own preference as a writer was for the kind of story 'you can tell over the dinner table or in a ship's smoking-room and hold the attention of your listeners'.[5] Many of his stories are framed so as to evoke some twentieth-century version of the primitive camp fire. Here again, Maupassant was influential; he had frequently used framing devices to give an anecdotal flavour to his tales or, where the topic was especially horrific, to leave open an exit route back into normality. In 'Madame Parisse' (1886) the narrator sits watching a sunset with a friend who proceeds to tell him a grotesque story of modern love; 'Happiness' (1885) begins with a tea-time debate about love, which leads in to narration of a simple but strange adventure; a newspaper report of a tragic love-affair triggers off the Turgenev-like lyricism of 'Love' (1887). Conversely, by cutting the original introductory frame in the second, expanded, version of his weird story 'The Horla' (1887), Maupassant heightened the terror of the piece.[6] As a general rule, the frame of a Maupassant or Maugham story can be detached without affecting the story's meaning, its primary purpose being to establish mood economically and to put the reader in a receptive 'frame of mind' – itself an apposite phrase.

Somerset Maugham's story 'The Facts of Life' (1940) illustrates his characteristic use of a 'frame' which increases the irony of reversed expectations, and signals laughter as an appropriate response, though without altering the significance of the embedded narrative. The setting is a club. Henry Garnet, normally a genial and reliable bridge-player, puzzles his friends with bad play and general grumpiness. When it emerges that he is worried about his son Nicky, who has been competing in a Monte Carlo tennis tournament, his friends give him the perfect cue: 'Let's have a drink and you can tell us all about it. With a KC, a Home Office Official and an eminent surgeon – if we can't tell you how to deal with a situation, nobody can.' Maugham makes no attempt to mystify; he simply announces, 'And this is the story Henry Garnet told them',and then moves straight into third-person narration. Garnet is still a character seen from the outside, dialogue is recorded whether or not Garnet could possibly have heard it, and his wife's thoughts are as open to examination as the experiences of his son in Monte Carlo. In style and texture this is certainly not the story as it was told by Nicky to his father over a glass of port the previous evening, but Maugham's technique of omniscience allows him to bypass individual characters' feelings in the interest of a central narrative irony: by systematically disregarding his father's advice to beware of gambling, lending money, and getting mixed up with women, Nicky has had a splendid time, and even manages to bring home a profit. This irony in no way depends on the relationship between frame and narrative. The only justification for introducing Garnet's distinguished friends, public servants all, seems to be that they prompt the story at the beginning and dissolve it in laughter at the end, giving, as it were, official sanction to the mild moral anarchy invited by Nicky's successes. The story gives the last word to the lawyer, whose advice to Henry encapsulates a comic view of life: 'I wouldn't worry, . . . My belief is that your boy's born lucky, and in the long run that's better than to be born clever or rich.'[7] Frames like the one used in 'The Facts of Life' authenticate the occasion on which a story has been told, the assumption being that this increases the credibility of some 'curious, but not improbable incident' – which was how Maugham described the province of his own kind of story.[8]

So many writers have attempted to recreate the hunters'-fire situation in terms of their own period, that the twentieth-century storyteller William Trevor is really boasting that he is no slave to convention when he says that he has never produced a short story in which 'two strangers on a long non-stop journey find themselves in a railway compartment with the door jammed'.[9] Of course the change from a homogeneous group around the cavern fire, to two strangers forced into one another's company, is itself indicative of vast changes which make the situation of communal storytelling irretrievable, except as a nostalgic literary convention.[10] Nowadays, the child's bedroom or the nursery school are the only places where a circle of listeners, charmed by a blend of the fantastic and the familiar, is likely to be found. Reading, as distinct from listening, is usually a solitary activity, a fact which presents difficulties to the writer who wants his reader to respond as the member of a group would. Poe saw the problem, and believed it to be intractable:

We listen to a story with greater zest when there are others present at its narration beside ourselves. Aware of this, authors without due reflection have repeatedly attempted, by supposing a circle of listeners, to imbue their narratives with the interest of sympathy. At a cursory glance the idea seems plausible enough. But, in the one case, there is an actual, personal, and palpable sympathy, conveyed in look, gestures and brief comments – a sympathy of real individuals, all with the matters discussed to be sure, but then especially, *each with each*. In the other instance, we, alone in our closet, are required to sympathise *with* the sympathy of fictitious listeners, who, so far from being present in body, are often studiously kept out of sight and out of mind for two or three hundred pages at a time. This is sympathy double-diluted – the shadow of a shade. It is unnecessary to say that the design invariably fails of its effect.[11]

But in fact there are narrative procedures which neither isolate the reader, nor 'double-dilute' his sympathy. The frame can be moved into the body of the story, and instead of being required to 'sympathise with the sympathy of fictitious listeners', the reader can be made the single, intimate listener admitted into the experiences of one fictitious narrator.

The principal model here is not Boccaccio's *Decameron*, where each member of a group holds forth to the others in turn, but the literary conversation, particularly as it developed in the fictionalized essays published in English periodicals throughout the eighteenth, and into the nineteenth, century. In provincial magazines like *Blackwood's* (started in 1817) the emphasis was on a kind of gossipy intimacy which embraced essays, reviews and fiction. Boundaries between fiction and non-fiction were shadowy, and one result of this was to delay the emergence in Britain of short fiction as an independent form. Apart from the supernatural tale, or the sensational 'tale of effect' imitated by Poe, there was nothing capable of competing with the serialized novel when it began to take over the fiction sections of the periodicals, gaining new strength with every decade.[12] Only late in the nineteenth century did *Blackwood's* assist the short story directly, notably by encouraging Conrad. But the overall informality of *Blackwood's* did benefit short fiction indirectly by helping to perpetuate the conversational vitality which had flourished in eighteenth-century journals like *The Rambler*, *Spectator* and *Tatler*.

Metropolitan journalists like Charles Lamb recognized that *Blackwood's* owed its popularity to its personal tone, and his own contributions to *London Magazine* (1820–29) united eighteenth-century lucidity with a romantic emphasis on the individual. In the persona of 'Elia', Lamb relives intimate and often introspective moments in order to share them with his reader, achieving what Mario Praz has described as 'exquisiteness of form' combined with an 'anti-rhetorical quality' of understatement.[13] Lamb's unpretentiously personal essays are important in the history of the short story, partly because, as T. O. Beachcroft has argued, Lamb 'at times brings single essays very near to short stories', but also because their 'anti-rhetorical' properties highlight certain advantages in preserving the affinity between story and essay.[14] It was to this kinship that H. E. Bates was pointing when he remarked that 'the artistic teller of tales', apparently nowhere to be found in nineteenth-century England, did possibly exist 'in the guise of the essayist'.[15] A wonderfully flexible form, the essay exploits, rather than wishing away, the discursiveness of prose, achieving compression more by tone than by the concentration of single images. The human personality of the writer is evident, and kept steadily before us.

In fiction, the effect can be to give written words the flavour of speech. This was the quality Henry James was praising when he said that Alphonse Daudet 'tells his stories as a talker; they always have the flexibility of conversation'.[16] Admittedly, James is quick to point out that Daudet's conversation came from a Frenchman and an artist, and was consequently more 'vivid and discriminating' than most people's.[17] When it came to his own writing, James was certainly reluctant to admit that spontaneity and 'anecdotic grace' were enough to justify telling a story.[18] The anecdote is too much the creature of chance for James: 'It is of the essence of anecdote', he wrote in the preface to *The Reverberator*, 'to get told as it can.'[19] But it was precisely the haphazard quality of anecdote mistrusted by James that contributed to the promptness of his American compatriots in developing the short story as a genre. In post-revolutionary America the loosely-structured essay had special appeal because it suggested alternative means of challenging the oppressively successful English novel. When associated with the venerable practice of essay-writing, American literary endeavour could be linked with European precedents which pre-dated the dominating three-decker novel. Montaigne, not any more recent writer, was Howells's point of comparison for a distinctively American writer like Mark Twain, whose informal and apparently desultory manner avoided making things seem 'drilled into line'.[20] This, Howells wrote in 1901, was the basis of Twain's realism:

> Life itself has that sort of appearance as it goes on; it is an essay with moments of drama in it, rather than a drama; it is a lesson, with the precepts appearing haphazard, and not precept upon precept; it is a school, but not always a school-room; it is a temple, but the priests are not always in their sacerdotal robes. . . . An instinct of something chaotic, ironic, empiric in the order of experience seems to have been the inspiration of our humorist's art.[21]

Although Howells is dealing here with Twain's longer works, his perception of that 'instinct of the chaotic, ironic, empiric' holds good for the short stories too, and indeed for fiction well after Twain and outside America. At the turn of the century, however, what Howells thought needed emphasis was Twain's sheer nerve, his freedom 'in a region where most of us are fettered and shackled by immemorial convention'.[22] Howells depicts Twain as the bold individualist who 'saunters out into the trim world of letters and lounges across its neatly kept paths, and walks about on the grass at will, in spite of all the signs that have been put up from the beginning of literature warning people of the dangers and penalties for the slightest trespass'.[23] The signs, of course, had been erected by the British, and Twain's lack of inhibition was welcomed as a gesture of emancipation.

A crucial aspect of Twain's iconoclasm was, as Howells rightly observed, the freshness of his style; he used English 'as if it were a primitive and not a derivative language'.[24] The result was something to be proud of, 'the English in which the most vital works of English literature are cast, rather than the English of Milton, and Thackeray, and Mr Henry James': in other words, English which was fit to express American civilization.[25] When Twain chooses a word, says Howells, 'It is the Abraham Lincolnian word, not the Charles Sumnerian; it is American, Western.'[26]

The anti-literary impulse discernible in Twain is a marked feature of one influential brand of nineteenth-century American writing, and Twain's own belief was that the humour it carried with it could not be exported. In 'How to tell a Story' (first published in 1895) he distinguished between the American 'humorous' story, the English 'comic' story, and the French 'witty' variety.[27] The humorous story is unique because it depends on the manner of its telling, not on its content, giving an impression of spontaneity and artlessness:

> To string incongruities and absurdities together in a wandering and sometimes purposeless way, and seem innocently unaware that they are absurdities, is the basis of the American art . . . Another feature is the slurring of the point. A third is the dropping of a studied remark apparently without knowing it, as if one were thinking aloud. The fourth and last is the pause.[28]

America does offer a heightened version of the development of humorous short fiction, though Twain probably exaggerated the straight-faced quality of every other country's literature in order to make his nationalistic point. Nevertheless, the aggravation felt by American writers eager to establish a national literature doubtless gave impetus to the creation of distinctive comic storytelling. The argument is actually strengthened by one great exception to Twain's remark that the art of telling a humorous story was born in America and kept at home, namely Kipling. Willing to learn from American examples and beginning his own career remote from the English literary establishment, Kipling mastered all of the devices enumerated by Twain – the straight-faced narration of absurd plots, the slurred point, the casually-dropped 'studied remark' and the pause – and provides some of the finest examples of anecdotal art. What this suggests is that, irrespective of nationality, a state of exile from the conventional literary world is favourable to at least one important kind of short-storywriter.

The advantages of keeping the short story on the fringes of recognized literary movements have generally been overlooked, even by writers like Frank O'Connor who acknowledge that outlawry is a fruitful subject for the storyteller. O'Connor's insistence that the theme of human loneliness must be mirrored in the reader's solitary position leads him to undervalue writers who do not speak to us 'as though we were strangers'.[29] The argument that, 'almost from its beginnings the short story, like the novel, abandoned the devices of a public art in which the storyteller assumed the mass assent of an audience to his wildest improvisations', works well for the self-consciously 'literary' writers most admired by O'Connor, but it leads him to underrate Kipling as an artist.[30] Kipling's chief offence, according to O'Connor, is that 'he is not thinking of me in my private capacity as a solitary reader, sitting at home by my own fire with my book; detached, critical, and inclined to resent any assault on my emotions as an invasion of privacy'.[31] O'Connor's approach cannot embrace stories which deliberately set out to break down the reader's 'detached' feeling, or which recall folktales, fables and fairy-tales in their concern with typical rather than individual character. Nor can O'Connor account for the appeal of stories which bear out Borges's conjecture that humour is 'an oral genre, a sudden favour of conversation, not something written'.[32] Narratives which imitate rhythms of speech, often exploiting the dialect of a particular social class, should not be underestimated in favour of the 'absolute purity' and perfect 'artistic organization' which O'Connor sees as the distinguishing mark of the short story as opposed to the tale.[33] The apparent artlessness of stories which owe something to oral narrative may not have the pathos which can make loneliness an all too interesting condition to be in, but they do have other, perhaps more invigorating charms. These stories do not belong to the line inaugurated by Poe and developed throughout the nineteenth century, but they undoubtedly occupy a significant place in the practice of short-storywriting.

The anecdotal short story even has its own theorist. Bret Harte offered in 1899 an account of 'The Rise of the "Short Story"', which proposed an alternative view to Poe's.[34] Harte traced the origins of America's characteristic fiction to bar-rooms, informal gatherings in country stores, public meetings addressed by 'stump orators' and to the newspaper stories which gave currency to the talk that went on in such places.[35] By preserving its 'concise and condense, yet suggestive' quality, Harte argued, stories which dealt with specifically American subjects 'voiced not only the dialect but the habits of thought of a people or locality'.[36] Literary polish was not what mattered most to a nation whose qualities were epitomized by the Wild West, the 'ideal republic' of California, where Harte's own best stories are set.[37]

Coming originally from the East, Harte saw the opening up of the West in the second half of the nineteenth century as the discovery of a mine, rich with 'romantic and dramatic possibilities . . . unrivalled in history' and crying out for literary treatment.[38] But although this new beginning had bred distinctively American humorists like Twain and Ambrose Bierce, Harte had misgivings about the extent to which the stranglehold of British examples had been broken. The American humorists had offered powerful alternatives to the wan imitations of Addison, Steele and Lamb that abounded in the early part of the century, but serious literature still seemed stuck in a European groove. Harte himself made a resolute stand against this situation, first by writing a Californian romance 'The Story of Mliss' in 1866, with the intention of showing that a characteristic Western American literature existed, and then by taking over the editorship of the *Overland Monthly* in 1868. With its unpretentious brown cover, decorated with no more than a small vignette showing a grizzly bear crossing a railway track, this periodical offered a complete contrast to the lavishly-produced magazines associated with the American East and with England. Harte set out to fulfil the promise held out by his paper's full title – *Overland Monthly, devoted to the Development of the Country* – and was quick to see the part fiction could play in this: he began writing about California and its settlers realistically, yet not so topographically that his stories were in danger of being mistaken for travelogues or immigration propaganda. The result was his best-selling piece 'The Luck of Roaring Camp' (1870) and numerous other stories of gold-prospecting life, the professed aim of which was to illustrate 'an era of which Californian history has preserved incidents more often than the character of the actors', an era which Harte described, rather grandiosely, as being 'replete with a certain heroic Greek poetry, of which perhaps none were more unconscious than the heroes themselves'.[39]

What makes Harte's Californian stories remarkable and worth reading today is less their documentary value (though they have plenty of that) than the tact with which at their best they blend diverse viewpoints and styles, faithfully portraying the miners' unfamiliar, 'uncivilized' way of life with all its idiosyncrasies of speech and manners, and at the same time acknowledging, sometimes undercutting, the 'civilized' literate reader's point of view. Sometimes this is done by using a first-person narrator who observes a group of characters outside of civilized society but displaying its own codes, its own civilities. This narrative 'I' both assures the reader of the authenticity of his material, providing dates, circumstantial detail and background information, and establishes a link with his audience by using a style which contrasts with the vernacular diction used by the characters.[40] The contrast is not meant to patronize or disparage the miners' speech, nor to make extravagant claims for its eloquence; the aim seems to be more a balance, a recognition of plenitude and diversity as essentially American subjects, broadly conceived. The spirit in which Harte uses dialect is distinct from the 'orthographic buffoonery' which Howells detected in the work of Artemus Ward; rather, it conforms to a purpose described, again by Howells, as 'the impulse to get the whole of American life into our fiction':

> This impulse, partly conscious and partly unconscious, is what has given us the rank we shall be found hereafter to have taken in the literature of our age, and which, whether it has given us great American novels or not, has expressed the national temperament, character, and manner not surpassed by contemporary fiction in the case of any other people.[41]

Nevertheless, Harte's story 'Tennessee's Partner' is told by a narrator who is obviously capable of writing like any one of those American Addisons, Steeles and Lambs who were blamed for producing '"fine" writing' and so slighting the 'national character'.[42] The narrator's language is formal, with a wry ironic tone which is totally alien from the characters he is describing. The narrator's initial style is probably intended to ease Harte's audience into the story at the same time as providing a contrast to the rough directness of the miners themselves. That Harte felt some compromise was involved here is evident from the introduction he wrote for the English edition of his works, which he supervised in order to show readers the order in which his tales and sketches had appeared in America. Referring to his early poems and stories, he notes that they were 'marked by very little flavour of the soil, but were addressed to an audience half foreign in their sympathies, and still imbued with Eastern or New England habits and reading traditions'; even in California, apparently, what sold best were 'current Eastern literature' and the long-established periodicals, American and English.[43] But however reluctantly made, Harte's concessions to his original 'half foreign audience' have actually benefited these stories in the long run, giving them a literary richness which is absent from his later work.

In 'Tennessee's Partner', one of Harte's best early pieces, the narrator's manner lends an intriguing air of contingency to his account; it is as if there can be no definitive version of events, only interpretations. Early on, for example, the narrator gives a résumé of how

Tennessee's Partner came to be married; 'I am aware', he notes, 'that something more might be made of this episode, but I prefer to tell it as it was current at Sandy Bar – in the gulches and bar-rooms – where all sentiment was modified by a strong sense of humour'. The narrator's judicious candour throughout the story is clearly designed to contrast also with the summary and hypocritical 'justice' which rids the community of Tennessee when his gambling becomes uncomfortably successful: it also serves as a restraint on the sentimentality inherent in Harte's material. After Tennessee's Partner has delivered an emotional funeral oration over his old comrade (who has been hanged in what Harte elsewhere calls 'a spasm of virtuous reaction, quite as lawless and ungovernable as any of the acts that had provoked it') the narrator adopts the viewpoint of the withdrawing crowd.[44] The lonely figure of Tennessee's Partner is framed, and held:

> As they crossed the little ridge that hid Sandy Bar from view, some, looking back, thought they could see Tennessee's Partner, his work done, sitting upon the grave, his shovel between his knees, and his face buried in his red bandanna handkerchief. But it was argued by others that you couldn't tell his face from his handkerchief at this distance, and this point remained undecided.

There is absolutely no doubt that Tennessee's Partner is weeping, but Harte's strategy of making this a matter of conjecture prevents the sentiment from cloying too much. By adopting, or at least affecting to adopt, the standpoint of the Sandy Bar community, Harte poses as the dispassionate historian merely handing on a local legend, disagreements and all.

Despite its strengths, 'Tennessee's Partner' is likely to strike most modern readers as impossibly stagey. There is nothing very restrained about the picture of Tennessee's Partner raising himself up on his deathbed, and setting out to meet his pal one more time: 'Keep on straight up to the pine on the top of the hill. Thar! I told you so! – thar he is, – coming this way too – all by himself, sober, and his face a-shining. Tennessee! Pardner!'[45] The transfiguration of Tennessee seems as affected and distant from bar-room anecdote as any of the fiction Harte condemned for its limited sympathy with the 'rough and half-civilized masses' who were making America's history. Without diminishing Harte's ability to convey the raw vigour of life in the Sierras, it is essential to recognize just how much his celebration of heroism amongst the gamblers, prostitutes and other 'outcasts' he portrayed, actually depends on artificial devices.

For truly uncompromising use of dialect and anecdotal informality, one has to look elsewhere. Significantly, it is in the more patriarchal areas, where social distinctions were entrenched and apparently impregnable, that artlessness can be found developing with greatest verve in the second half of the nineteenth century. By the 1890s the general reader was tiring of dialect in fiction, and from the East in particular came complaints that American literature was irredeemably provincial. But in the American South such criticisms were cheerfully swept aside, notably by another writer whom Kipling admired, Joel Chandler Harris. For his homely 'Uncle Remus' stories, Harris found it natural to use plantation dialect, a procedure which he defended by pointing out that a great writer like Chaucer also made wide use of dialect. Ennobling as the comparison was, however, Harris's approach was unpretentious; 'unadulterated human nature' was what he wanted to depict.[46] Reluctantly announcing his old negro's final appearance in 1892, after eleven years of tale-telling, Harris affirmed the essential simplicity of his aims:

> There is no pretense that the old darkey's poor little stories are in the nature of literature, or that their re-telling touches literary art at any point. All the accessories are lacking. There is nothing here but an old negro man, a little boy, and a dull reporter, the matter of discourse being fantasies as uncouth as the original man ever conceived of.[47]

Sparse the elements may be, but they actually function in ways that might be proposed as paradigmatic of intimate short fiction, whether for adults or, like these stories, for children. Uncle Remus's story-telling techniques conform to certain rules and rituals which are found in many stories in which a narrator firmly controls the amount of information, and its pacing, insisting on his presence as a 'teller' with a highly individual voice.

Usually discovered at work on some simple task – sharpening an axe or perhaps oiling a harness – Uncle Remus tells his stories as accompaniments to the rhythms of his job, rather in the manner of worksongs. He is a stickler for originality, at least as far as the small boy who listens to his stories is concerned. No matter how old and steeped in folklore the story, the child is made to rack his brains and guarantee that he is not eliciting a repeat performance:

> 'When did Brother Wolf want to eat the young rabbit, Uncle Remus?' inquired the little boy, thinking he saw the suggestion of a story here. He was not mistaken. The old man regarded him with feigned astonishment. 'Aint I done tole you 'bout dat, honey? Des run over in yo' min', en see ef I ain't.'[48]

Uncle Remus likes, as any anecdotalist does, to create suspense at critical moments within tales, but evidently he also has ploys for delaying the comfortable moment when the listener can settle into a passive role and be told a story. Sometimes, delaying the beginning is used to teach some simple moral lesson, but more importantly, the pretence that stories must be coaxed out of the teller increases his prestige. As Uncle Remus puts it, when the child asks why he doesn't come up to the big house and tell stories, the spoon 'hatter go ter de bowl', a neat reminder that his fund of lore and wisdom surpasses anything offered by the boy's white family and culture.[49] Why are Brother Fox's legs black? The boy's father 'dunner no mo' 'bout it dan de man in de moon'.[50] Why does Brother Bull growl and grumble?:

> 'Well, he got a mighty good reason fer gwine on dat away; but who'll tell you? You may spit on yo' thumb en turn over de leaves er all de books up dar in Marse John's liberry, yit you won' fin' out in um. You may ax Marse John, you may ax Miss Sally, you may ax a preacher, yit; but none un um'll ever tell you. Den who kin tell you? Me!'[51]

Associated with the specialness of the teller is a counteracting insistence that he is merely a mediator whose powers do not extend beyond the contours of the narrative. When the little boy asks a logical question at the end of 'The Honey Orchard', Uncle Remus exclaims, 'Eh-eh honey! You pushes yo' inquirements too fur. Dat's what's in de tale I kin tell you; dat what ain't you'll hatter figger out fer yo' se'f'[52] And limits are fixed still more clearly in 'Why Brother Wolf didn't eat the Little Rabbits', where any listener with a grain of curiosity would like to know whether Brer Wolf caught Brer Fox:

> 'How I know, honey? Much ez I kin do ter foller de tale when it keeps in de big road, let 'lone ter keep up wid dem creeturs whiles dey gone sailin' thoo de woods. De tale ain't persoo on atter um no fudder dan de place whar dey make der disappear'nce. I tell you now, when I goes in de woods, I got to know whar I'm gwine.'[53]

Uncle Remus makes a distinction between 'reg'lar up en down tales, what runs cross-ways' and simpler narratives which go 'right straight'; but whichever pattern a story follows, the unvarying rule is that 'folks is folks en creeturs is creeturs', different species with entirely different restraints on their behaviour.[54] 'Sense', Uncle Remus gravely informs the boy, must not be confused with goodness: 'De creeturs dunno nothin' 'tall 'bout dat dat's good en dat dat ain't good. Dey dunno right fum wrong. Dey see what dey want, en dey git it ef dey kin, by hook er by crook.'[55] That, of course is precisely the appeal of these tales; with no moral scruples, the animals can trick their neighbours and delight in the cleverness of their ruses. Harris takes us into a cartoon world where nobody gets permanently hurt, a fantasy where the physically vulnerable win the day, craft triumphing over strength as firmly as it did in the medieval beast-epic *Reynard the Fox*.

But perhaps the most interesting aspect of Uncle Remus's skill as a storyteller reveals itself when the child claims never to have heard about the man who caught a possum, and then lost a good

meal because instead of eating it he fell dreaming about how good
it was going to taste. Uncle Remus retorts that the story is so common, of course the boy has been hearing it all his life, going on to
explain,

> 'You des got de idee in yo' min' dat when I set down fer ter tell you
> sump'n hit's bleedz ter be a tale, en when yuther folks tells it 't ain't
> nothin' but talk. I ain't got no secret 'bout dish yer nigger man what had
> de possum, but I tell you right now, 't ain't no tale. Too many folks done
> been fool wid it.'[56]

The distinction between random talk and a structured tale is the key
to Remus's art; that is obvious enough. But his suggestion that to be
good a tale must have about it a flavour of secrecy and individuality
peculiar to the teller is more surprising, especially in view of the
wide provenance of many Remus story-patterns. Remus's scorn for
stories which turn into plantation jokes or popular sayings (elsewhere
he says that a remark about the cow that swallowed a grindstone
'ain't got no tale behime it. Hit's des a sayin''), must have to do with
the nature of storytelling as an especially intimate business, an activity that loses its piquancy if it becomes too public.[57] This deepens the
sense in which anecdotal stories and folktales belong to the teller,
encouraging an atmosphere of confidentiality which flatters the reader
too, since he is supposedly being entrusted with a secret which would
be destroyed if 'too many folks' were allowed to fool with it.

Literature abounds with stories which disclose a secret, offering
the one 'true' version to replace conjectural accounts of events. In
'The Turn of the Screw' (1898), for example, James plays with this
device; he uses a narrative frame to vary the Dickensian Christmas
fireside setting with which the story opens, delaying the story proper
until the house has been cleared of inquisitive women and only a
tiny circle of choice listeners remains. The implication is that only
the few are sensitive enough to be made party to the governess's
strange memoir. Hardy uses a somewhat similar technique in 'The
Melancholy Hussar of the German Legion', another story which
deals with hidden passion. The fact that the memory of Phyllis's
unhappy love affair is passed from one generation of villagers to
another, gives a folklore quality to her story and at the same time
it sets the narrator his task of correcting false interpretations, 'since
such fragments of her story as got abroad at the time, and have been
kept alive ever since, are precisely those which are most unfavour-
able to her character'.[58] Privileged as a boy of fifteen to hear the full
story from Phyllis's own lips, and enjoined to keep silence until she
is 'dead, buried and forgotten', the narrator has waited thirty years
before sharing her secrets with the reader, who is correspondingly
privileged.[59] It is an aspect of Phyllis's fine sense of honour – the
sense which actually produces the tragedy of her story – that she
hides her suffering, and the final reward for her reticence comes long

after her death when the narrator substitutes the whole inner truth for the fragments pieced together into a distorted picture by narrow-minded village gossips.

The theme of intense suffering caused by love also occurs frequently in Kipling's stories, many of which deal with emotional pain being bravely concealed from public scrutiny. Acknowledgement of a character's stoicism, if it comes at all within the story, comes late, and it is often left to a narrator to reveal inner agonies which society at large would condemn. The bereaved protagonist of 'In the Pride of his Youth' (1888) has no right to grieve publicly; only the storyteller can give testimony, confidentially and delicately. In a much later story, 'The Gardener' (1926), recognition seems to come within the story. The ending of this story is open to multiple interpretation, but one possibility is that the final appearance of the Christ-like gardener who knows Helen Turrell's secret, is emblematic of supernatural recognition for her heroism; she has guarded her private truth and foregone earthly consolation, and by refusing to unburden herself to a mortal confidante she earns acknowledgement on a suprahuman plane.

Throughout his career, Kipling was fascinated by suppressed grief and the noble lie, and although a mature story like 'The Gardener' is so complex and oblique that it seems to have come from a different writer than the jaunty author of *Plain Tales from the Hills* (1888), there is actually far greater continuity than is sometimes supposed. And not in theme alone; Kipling's later 'artful' methods can be seen developing out of his early use of an anecdotal narrator-figure who divulges his characters' secrets. Early on, Kipling saw the possibility of using a narrator for more devious purposes than merely to set a story going, and it is in this respect that he may have learned a good deal from Uncle Remus's apparently artless control of 'reg'lar up en down tales, what runs cross-ways'.

Superficially, any similarities between Joel Chandler Harris and Kipling might seem to be restricted to children's fiction; the clearest analogues to the Remus stories are certainly the *Just-So Stories* (1902) with their whimsical humour and mock solemnity. But more than a common love of animal fable is involved, for in Kipling's fiction for adults there are several elements which suggest that here too he belongs more to the line of American 'anti-literary' story-telling than to his native English tradition. Children are not alone in enjoying secrets; in many of his *Plain Tales* Kipling uses his narrator to create a conspiratorial atmosphere reminiscent of Uncle Remus's kitchen, remote from the 'big house' and safe from interruption. At the end of 'Beyond the Pale' we share the narrator's knowledge of the real reason for Trijago's limp, publicly passed off as due to 'a riding-strain'; the effect is not entirely different from being let into the secret of how Brer Fox's legs came to be black.[60]

Although frequently presented as 'only the chorus', Kipling's narrator resembles Uncle Remus in several respects.[61] He signals clearly when the tale proper is going to begin and what its general nature is to be. 'Mrs Hauksbee was sometimes nice to her own sex. Here is a story to prove this; and you can believe just as much as ever you please', begins 'The Rescue of Pluffles'.[62] And 'The Conversion of Aurelian McGoggin' opens with a boastful swagger: 'This is not a tale exactly. It is a Feat.'[63] At other times, compressed summary or sage generalization precedes the tale itself: 'Lispeth', for example, offers a couple of pages of necessary background before 'One day...' indicates the true narrative beginning; and in 'Thrown Away' a rather arch analogy between rearing a puppy and bringing up a son provides a context for the startling announcement, 'There was a Boy once who had been brought up under the "sheltered life" theory; and the theory killed him dead.'[64] More teasingly promising of confidences than any of these examples, 'A Bank Fraud' opens with what looks like an appeal to the reader's baser instinct: 'If Reggie Burke were in India now he would resent this tale being told; but as he is in Hong-Kong and won't see it, the telling is safe. He was the man who worked the big fraud on the Sind and Sialkote Bank.'[65] In fact, the story turns out to offer a redefinition of 'fraud' as benevolent, almost saintly, deception, and it is Reggie's modesty, not his shame, that is being spared. A conceited accountant in Reggie's bank has long been a thorn in his flesh, but when he hears that the man is dying (news that is withheld from the invalid) Reggie devotes himself to sustaining the accountant's ego, feeding his self-esteem with pretences. It is an achievement to allow a fool to die deluded about his own importance.

Lies and subterfuge are every bit as essential to survival in Kipling's India as in Brer Rabbit's cabbage patch, and both the comic and the tragic sides of this situation are explored in *Plain Tales*. In 'Thrown Away', the Boy's suicide is masked by the gigantic lies forged to protect his family from a truth too grim to be handled; a falsely emotional letter ruins the life of a girl back home in "Yoked with an Unbeliever"', while in the comic piece 'His Wedded Wife' a Senior Subaltern gets his come-uppance through a clever use of disguise. The prevailing attitude to lies in *Plain Tales* is summed up in 'The Bronckhorst Divorce-Case', in which Bronckhorst's unpleasantness is indicated by his lack of 'respect for the pretty public and private lies that make life a little less nasty than it is'.[66] The storyteller himself is of course caught up in all this lying, sometimes following the tradition of tall tales by saying that he doesn't expect to be believed. Yet he can also taunt his readers for being sceptical: 'So now you know how the Broken-link Handicap was run and won. Of course you don't believe it. You would credit anything about Russia's designs on India, or the recommendations of the Currency

Commission; but a little bit of sober fact is more than you can stand.'[67] Somewhat similarly, a first-person narrator pops up at the end of 'The Rout of the White Hussars' to claim, 'I happen to know something about it, because I prepared the Drum-Horse for his resurrection.'[68] Kipling's tactics here demonstrate well that he grasped the principles of the humorous story as Twain had outlined them; he adopts a serious mask, sustaining a grave manner and concealing any sense that his story is even vaguely funny, let alone outrageous. Small wonder that Kipling felt he owed Twain something and had 'a debt to square' when he visited the United States.[69]

The impression left by the majority of *Plain Tales* is of adult material being tailored to a child's susceptibilities, which is another way of describing the quality often condemned as Kipling's 'know-ingness'. When, immediately before the superbly grotesque climax of 'The Other Man', Kipling announces 'And here comes the unpleasant part of the story', it may be felt that he is wilfully breaking into the story to patronize the reader with his superior knowledge.[70] From this standpoint any comparisons between Harris and Kipling are bound to seem diminishing, raising the objection that Kipling talks down to us. A more useful approach, however, is to see the narrator's interruptions and nudges as one means of achieving the strict narrative control required of the short story in general, and particularly of stories written for newspapers as Harris's and Kipling's originally were.

Whether he presents himself as a mere choric figure, like the 'Me' of Kipling's 'In the House of Suddhoo', or as the chief protagonist, like Poe's 'William Wilson' (1840), the controlling narrator takes responsibility for the selection of material. His selection has to be justified, and various ploys exist for making omissions excusable. One of these is to show extreme consideration towards the reader. Having promised to reveal the single fated event which made all virtue drop 'bodily as a mantle' from him 'in one instant', the narrator of Poe's 'William Wilson' can get away with pretending to spare us the sight of the aftermath: 'I would not, if I could', he says, 'here or to-day embody a record of my later years of unspeakable misery and unpardonable crime'.[71] At times Kipling can seem equally crude in his protestations about the 'unspeakable'; when the moment arrives for the narrator and the Colonel to deal with the Boy's mutilated body in 'Thrown Away', the door is closed on us: 'I am not going to write about this. It was too horrible.'[72] Of course the omission does not reduce the horror of the story; quite the reverse. The little Kipling does tell us – 'We burned the bedstead and dropped the ashes into the Canal' – is perfectly calculated to increase the grim effect.[73] What makes Kipling's use of this device strong where Poe's is weak and evasive is that by pointedly respecting the reader's understandable squeamishness, Kipling has found a way of reinforcing the theme of his story, which is almost Conradian in its concern with the testing of human nerve. Like Conrad too is the sense left by 'Thrown Away' that conventional morality is hopelessly inadequate when confronted with the unknown. Paradoxically, Kipling's strategy of seeming to pamper the reader becomes a way of initiating us into experiences which it is our good fortune, not a right, to imagine rather than undergo in actuality. There is a veiled reproach in all this, an affront to the reader's complacency, and it is not unrelated to the way Uncle Remus introduces the little boy to a harsh world where violence is the rule: 'It all done been fix, en I ain't see nobody yit what kin onfix it', he says when the child finds Brer Rabbit's treatment of his enemy Brer Fox heartless: 'Creeturs is natchally got ha'sh idees . . . Ef you er too tetchy fer ter set dar whiles I runs on, you kin des go up ter de big house en watch Sis Tempy fret over dat churn.'[74]

Kipling's Anglo-India, Harris's woods and briar-patches, and Bret Harte's California belong on very different maps, yet they are all metaphoric of conditions in which assumptions about human 'civilization' are questioned. Kipling himself saw the similarity between what he and the American writer were offering: 'Why buy Bret Harte', Kipling recalls asking, 'when I was prepared to supply home-grown fiction on the hoof. And I did.'[75] But while it is newness which challenges conventional morality in Harte's California, Kipling's India is daunting because it preserves ancient mysteries: 'All kinds of magic are out of date and done away with, except in India, where nothing changes in spite of the shiny, top-scum stuff that people call "civilization".'[76] New or old, both are areas in which human traits are exaggerated and every tale is likely to seem tall to outsiders. Kipling makes this point in 'Wressley of the Foreign Office': 'One of the many curses of our life in India is the want of atmosphere in the painter's sense. There are no half-tints worth noticing. Men stand out all crude and raw, with nothing to tone them down, and nothing to scale them against.'[77] The painter's curse, in this case, is a blessing for any storyteller who aims to capture bold effects rather than subtle nuances. India is conducive to those crises and obsessions which in themselves give stories fundamental shape and structure, and tension is all the greater because the line between chaos and order is so thin. Kipling prefaces 'In the House of Suddhoo' with lines that could stand as a motto for all of his writing:

A stone's throw out on either hand
From that well-ordered road we tread,
And all the world is wild and strange:
Churel and ghoul and *Djinn* and sprite
Shall bear us company tonight,

For we have reached the Oldest Land
Wherein the Powers of Darkness range.

(*From the Dusk to the Dawn*)[78]

Precisely because his interest is in the experiences which jolt people off the 'well-ordered road', in the extreme states which test character – or, as in Browning's 'Bishop Blougram', an interest 'on the dangerous edge of things' – Kipling's narrative stance of candour and plain-speaking is well-chosen.[79] It allows him to vary his role from that of eye-witness, to humble mouthpiece, merely recording events which baffle normal powers of understanding. Like Uncle Remus, he acknowledges the vanishing point of the tales he tells, reminding us in 'False Dawn', for example, that he cannot provide the woman's version of what happened that hot windy night; the 'exact truth' is locked up in female freemasonry, and so 'the tale must be told from the outside – in the dark – all wrong'.[80] And where supernatural mysteries are involved, as they are in 'By Word of Mouth', the narrator is even more helpless: 'This tale may be explained by those who know how souls are made, and where the bounds of the Possible are put down. I have lived long in enough this India to know that it is best to know nothing, and can only write the story as it happened.'[81] Here, the uncanny nature of the material dictates the narrative method, and the usually bumptious narrator of *Plain Tales* decorously effaces himself.

Kipling's vision of India as a country of shadowy boundaries, the rational and the irrational constantly merging, also makes it imperative for him to control tone very carefully. Otherwise, the reader may be misled into an inappropriate response. One of the features of Anglo-Indian life as Kipling depicts it is the ease with which jokes can tilt into disaster. It is yet another aspect of the sense of contingency which pervades all Kipling's work. Hilarity and despair lie close together, which is why practical jokes are elating when they come off, but worrying when they begin to shade into seriousness. On the surface, 'Watches of the Night' is a farce involving coincidences and confused identities, but the narrator stresses the 'mistrust and the tragedy' underlying the comedy.[82] He even makes the witty but sympathetic proposal that his story may help to reconcile the couple whom the joke has estranged. When a hoax works to perfection, it can seem heartless, as the child in *Uncle Remus* complained Brer Rabbit's was. It is for that very reason that on one occasion Uncle Remus turns with relief from a story about human beings, and begins recounting 'Brother Mud Turtle's Trickery':

'I don't like deze yer tales 'bout folks, no how you kin fix um', said Uncle Remus, after an unusually long pause, during which he rubbed his left hand with the right, in order to run the rheumatism out. 'No, suh, I don't like um, kaze folks can't play no tricks, ner git even wid der neighbours, widout hurtin' somebody's feelin's, er breakin' some law er nudder, er gwine 'ginst what de preacher say.'[83]

Another method used by Kipling to show that only chance separates comedy from tragedy is to make two tales tonal counterparts to one another. 'His Wedded Wife' and 'In the Pride of his Youth' treat the same situation – a secret marriage – but while the first recounts a hoax that 'leaned as near to a nasty tragedy as anything this side of a joke can', the second topples the subject into unmitigated disaster.[84] Dicky Hatt, the central figure of 'In the Pride of his Youth' undergoes the agonies which were played out in masquerade by the earlier story; he anticipates later studies of private suffering, including Mary Postgate and Helen Turrell, characters who also have secret attachments. 'Not being officially entitled to a baby', Dicky can 'show no sign of trouble' when his child dies, a tormenting situation which continued to preoccupy Kipling all his life.[85]

Surviving in India, according to Kipling, depends on preserving a balance between levity and earnestness, the balance actually exemplified by the range of narrative tones in *Plain Tales*. The Boy in 'Thrown Away' makes the pitiful mistake of taking things too seriously, not realizing that in Anglo-India nothing really matters because everything is transient: flirtations, amusements, sickness – they are all in 'the day's work', because everyone is constantly shifting and nobody is irreplaceable, in private or public life.[86] Transience is especially well-suited to short-story treatment, and in Anglo-India Kipling found a culture in which his own storytelling could take its place among a variety of 'amusements' which 'do not matter, because you must repeat them as soon as you have accomplished them once'.[87] Furthermore, disclosing other people's secrets here is not the betrayal it might be elsewhere; as Kipling points out, 'everything in a man's private life is public property in India'.[88] The positive side of so much openness is that it promotes a sense of human solidarity, and in this lies the principal justification of Kipling's pose as the candid and trustworthy narrator. 'Few people',the narrator of 'By Word of Mouth' asserts, 'can afford to play Robinson Crusoe anywhere – least of all in India, where we are few in the land and very much dependent on each other's kind offices.'[89] The mutual reliance expressed here is reminiscent of Bret Harte's story 'The Outcasts of Poker Flat' (1870), in which adversity is the bond uniting the characters. It is interesting too to notice that Kipling, again like Harte, often emphasizes that his characters are types by giving them nicknames which speak directly to the reader's sense of community: both 'The Innocent' in Harte's story and 'The Boy' in Kipling's 'Thrown Away' are more cases in need of the group's protection than they are individuals. 'Thrown Away' is offered explicitly as 'a curious instance of the fashion in which we are all linked together and made responsible for one another', and the trick of keeping 'The Boy' anonymous increases the story's exemplary quality – as well as augmenting pathos.[90]

Kipling has a wide repertoire of devices for conveying a sense of a group, and indeed it is this element in his work which displeases Frank O'Connor, who feels that Kipling speaks too much as one of a gang. Sometimes a group-sense is invoked ironically by reminding us that there are limits to how far our nosiness is going to be indulged. 'The speech that followed is no affair of mine or yours', the narrator remarks tartly when the Colonel's wife is about to unleash her jealous fury in 'Watches of the Night'; and in '"Yoked with an Unbeliever"' speculations about how and where Phil met the Hill-girl he marries are cut short.[91] At other times a sense of solidarity is conveyed simply by assuming that the reader is as familiar as the author with, say, the contours of the Chedputter race-course or the lay-out of the Simla Club dining-room.[92] This type of bland allusiveness is a favourite device of anecdotal storytellers, since it immediately creates an intimate atmosphere. Information which is indispensable to the plot can be given as the story goes on, but meanwhile the reader is treated as someone who already knows his way around the author's fictional world. H. G. Wells is employing exactly this strategy when he begins 'The Moth' (1895) with a blend of surmise and allusiveness: 'Probably you have heard of Hapley – not W. T. Hapley, the son, but the celebrated Hapley, the Hapley of *Periplaneta Hapliia*, Hapley the entomologist.'[93]

In none of the Kipling stories so far mentioned does the narrator depart from the standard English common to his Anglo-Indian characters – and to his readers. His style is laconic and understated, characterized by short paragraphs culminating in very brief sentences: 'She was not pretty to look at'; 'He always prided himself on speaking his mind, did Schreiderling'; and with even more pointed irony, 'He wrote a book on the East afterwards. Lispeth's name did not appear there.'[94] The effect is sufficiently conversational to preserve an anecdotal flavour, but the idiom is deliberately plain. Kipling's style alters on occasions when his narrator-figure becomes a listener within the story, and it is at these times that he keeps his reader most aware of a distinctive narrative voice with its own accents, and often its own dialect.

Bearing in mind Howells's distinction between dialect properly used, and queer orthography, it is possible to see Kipling's use of dialect as an attempt to stir his reader's aural sense – that feeling for 'the weights, colours, perfumes and attributes of words in relation to other words' which Kipling trained in himself from the start of his writing career.[95] Essentially related to a poetic sense, Kipling's consciousness of 'the attributes of words in relation to other words' provides him with an invaluable tool for compressing meaning in his short stories. In *Something of Myself* he claims that, 'There is no line of my verse or prose which has not been mouthed till the tongue has made all smooth, and memory, after many recitals, has mechanically skipped the grosser superfluities'; the final phrase alone suggests that sound and cadencing can be used to attain concision.[96] Kipling's ear for dialect and other forms of speech deviating from the 'normal' is evident throughout *Plain Tales*, not least in his rendering of aphasia in 'The Conversion of Aurelian McGoggin', and his eloquent drunk, McIntosh Jellaludin in 'To be Filed for Reference'; but it was by inventing his three soldier-narrators Mulvaney, Ortheris and Learoyd that he put this resource to most impressive use as regards the structuring of stories.

By using one of his 'three musketeers' as a narrator, Kipling could incorporate the group-situation into the story's form, at the same time as allowing a single teller to speak in a highly individual style without interruption. The device is as ancient as the 'cavern fire' setting described by Maugham, though Kipling would not have had to look far back for recent precedents. Indeed, the first-person narrator who provides the frame for Mulvaney's monologue in 'The Daughter of the Regiment' occupies a position not unlike that of Joel Chandler Harris's child-listener; he sees 'a story in Private Mulvaney's eye' and he sets about getting that story. And there are similarities between Uncle Remus ritualistically settling himself into his armchair and lighting his pipe, and Mulvaney (another teller who is of a lower 'rank' than his listener) adopting a relaxed but stylized posture. The moment preceding his monologue is like the hushed pause just before an operatic aria: 'We came out under the stars. Mulvaney sat down on one of the artillery bridges, and began in the usual way: his pipe between his teeth, his big hands clasped and dropped between his knees, and his cap well on the back of his head.' 'The Daughter of the Regiment' is concerned with bereavement and heroism, and Mulvaney is given a personal reason for his eagerness to impart the truth about 'Old Pummeloe's daughter' to the author: Mulvaney knows what it is to lose a child; 'I lost me own little Shad', he remarks in an aside, 'but no matther.'[97] It is therefore appropriate that Mulvaney and his listener should be alone together. For more boisterous tales the group can be enlarged, as it is in 'The Three Musketeers', where Kipling offers a classic situation for anecdotal storytelling – a railway refreshment room, plenty of beer, and four people waiting for a train. Here the narration is not confined to one speaker, though Kipling's attitude suggests that it is the verve of direct speech that appeals to him, rather than the interplay of individual viewpoints. Either that, or Kipling has taken the pose of artlessness too far, to a point where it degenerates into silly teas-

ing: 'Then Mulvaney and Ortheris spoke together in alternate fragments: Mulvaney leading [You must pick out the two speakers as
best you can].'[98]

Clumsy, and irritating, as this strategy of 'alternating fragments'
is, it does interestingly anticipate a development which Kipling was
to take much further in his art; as his career went on, narration came
more and more to consist of fragments which it was the reader's job
to piece together with little or no help from the author. In Kipling's
work we can actually see 'artless' narration becoming very 'artful'.
The growing complexity of Kipling's narrative methods partly
reflects an increasing sense of moral ambiguities. When Mulvaney
reappears in *Many Inventions* (1893) to tell the compelling story of
destructive passion, '"Hove-O'-Women"' (one of Kipling's most skilfully 'framed' stories), he makes no attempt to sort out 'Fwhat the
right an' wrong' of the affair; *that*, he says, 'I niver knew, an' I will
niver know; but I've tould ut as I came acrost it – here an' there in
little pieces.'[99]

A decade later, another story about obsessive love and haunting
remorse, 'Mrs Bathurst' (1904), carries the method of telling a story
'in little pieces' to an extreme, creating doubt about what, exactly,
occurs in the narrative, let alone 'Fwhat the right an' wrong'. As
Peter Keating has emphasized, this story, 'with its sudden shifts of
narrative and deliberately ambiguous plot' constitutes a 'radical
artistic redirection of the form of the short story'.[100] An effect of
extreme uncertainty and bafflement is produced by what Keating
describes as the story's 'multiple-narration set skilfully within a
frame of reminiscence, gossip, yarns, parallel circumstances, and
modern technology'.[101] From the outset, Kipling undermines any
secure feelings we may bring to the story; the very conditions in
which the narration is supposed to take place emphasize transience:
the 'I' of the story, his friend Inspector Hooper of Cape Government Railways (an official figure if ever there was one), and the two
marines (Pritchard and Pyecroft) who share the burden of the main
narrative, are brought together by coincidence. They are all killing
time in a railway carriage, temporarily marooned in a siding which,
significantly, is drifted by sand and close to the edge of the surf; the
vista is limitless, and no additional pretext is needed for whiling
away the time with reminiscences. But this is no ordinary anecdotal
interlude; along with the men who, within the story, try to piece
together the marines' fragmentary account of their former shipmate
Vickery's love for the irresistible Mrs Bathurst, the reader has to
work extremely hard to discover any pattern at all. The unspoken
counts for as much as the spoken, and meaning passes between teller
and listener allusively, or in little intuitive flashes: '"Why did Vickery
run?" I began, but Pyecroft's smile made me turn my question to
"Who was she?"' Mrs Bathurst is the title character, and yet she is

less a character than a tantalizing image which we struggle to see and hear. Pritchard gives his own account of 'the kind o' woman she was', but we still sympathize with Hooper's admission, 'I don' *see* her yet somehow'; we too want Mrs Bathurst brought into sharper focus and held in a steady light. Instead, Kipling offers the infinitely repeatable image of Mrs Bathurst on the cinematograph screen; for ever approaching the camera, gazing straight out of the picture with her 'blindish look', she is constantly walking out of view into inexplicable mystery, 'like – like a shadow jumpin' over a candle' as Pyecroft expresses it.[102] The insubstantial flickering image of Mrs Bathurst is the most memorable in the story, and fittingly so, since the essence of her nature is that any man who encounters her finds her unforgettable. By making this shadowy image the heart of his story, and furthermore by assimilating it to Pyecroft's colloquial, tough-minded, but finally perplexed narration, Kipling takes anecdotal storytelling to its furthest point. Kipling's inclusion of the cinema newsreel in his story is not just a topical touch but a key to the story's method; and as such it anticipates indirectly the influence on Borges of Josef von Sternberg's early films. When Borges describes the 'sudden shifts in continuity, and the paring down of a man's life to two or three scenes', which characterized Sternberg's work, and which Borges adopted as techniques in the fiction he wrote in the first half of the 1930s, he could be talking about 'Mrs Bathurst', a story produced over twenty-five years earlier.[103]

Philip Mason has named 'the unaccountability of human affairs and the eccentricity of chance' as centrally important themes in 'Mrs Bathurst', and it has already been suggested that short stories which preserve links with spontaneous anecdote and natural speech are especially well adapted to conveying a sense of life's contingency.[104] What makes 'Mrs Bathurst' perhaps the wittiest story in English literature is that the only thing about it to escape pure contingency is the author's resolute excision of any clues unambiguous enough to put an end to controversy about its interpretation. *Plain Tales* taught that hoax and tragedy are closely related; the highly wrought form of 'Mrs Bathurst' makes it impossible to be certain whether Kipling is offering a *jeu d'esprit* or a deeply-felt moral and artistic credo. In this respect the story resembles James's 'The Turn of the Screw'; both Kipling and James appear to be experimenting to see how far well-established conventions (in Kipling's case the colloquial anecdote, in James's the Christmas ghost story) can be stretched without actually breaking. Both authors, dissimilar in so many ways, set themselves the intriguing question, what happens when you give a familiar effect another turn of the screw?

'Mrs Bathurst' exemplifies a narrative principle which has nowhere been more powerfully enunciated than in another work dealing with violent human experience and critical moments of choice, Browning's *The Ring and the Book* (1868–69):

> Art may tell a truth
> Obliquely, do the thing shall breed the thought,
> Nor wrong the thought, missing the mediate word.[105]

Kipling's story can be seen as a fragmented dramatic monologue, dominated by Pyecroft but interrupted and pushed onwards by the listeners who strain to understand what he is saying. Because this story, like Browning's poem (which consists of ten monologues enclosed within the framework of a prologue and epilogue) is constructed so that it 'shall mean, beyond the facts', any search for objective truth is bound to fail; the inner truth of the main characters, Vickery and Mrs Bathurst, can only be guessed at through the mist of Pyecroft's recollections.[106] Pyecroft has found Vickery terrifying, mentally at least, and his state of mind contributes a strong element of subjectivity to the story, bearing out Browning's comment that 'a fact looks to the eye as the eye likes the look'.[107] Yet Kipling disarms the possible conclusion that Pyecroft's testimony is dubious; he makes Pritchard a secondary witness, and also hints that in Hooper's waistcoat pocket is concealed a grotesque piece of material evidence, the false teeth that identify one of the two tramps killed by lightning near a railway line in Rhodesia.

'Mrs Bathurst' is such a totally artful story that despite the presence of a listening group within the narrative, it seems to address itself far more to the solitary reader than to the wider audience which this chapter began by considering. Even though the whole story is not put into Pyecroft's mouth, the narration has a quality of extreme subjectivity which puts us in touch with the reflective side of the speaker's mind rather than with his outward appearance or behaviour. The principle at work here is amenable to a variety of uses by the short-storywriter, who may choose to take subjectivity to the point where it dominates the narrative completely, making the telling *be* the story in a manner comparable to that of a single dramatic monologue. The closest literary ancestor of this type of story is the lyric form perfected by Browning, who managed to fuse character, action and setting within individual poetic monologues, making one speaker's words carry the entire burden of meaning, and leaving the reader or supposed listener to make his own interpretation. It would be hard to name a short-storywriter who could rival Browning for linguistic inventiveness and psychological complexity, but there are undoubtedly cases where similar effects are achieved in prose. Where the short story and the Browning dramatic monologue can be seen to converge most interestingly is in the formal compression which arises out of a shared fascination with extreme

or bizarre states of emotion. In both story and poem the emotionalism of the speaker is often heightened by placing the character in
a situation which puts him under stress, and which justifies the
impression of urgency created by the momentum of his uninterrupted speech. Fra Lippo Lippi, Andrea del Sarto, the Bishop
ordering his tomb at Saint Praxed's Church: all of these characters
are at critical moments in their lives, and so too is the speaker in
Kipling's wonderful piece 'The Gate of the Hundred Sorrows'
(1888).[108]

In this evocation of a Eurasian's life in an opium house hidden
deep in city backstreets, Kipling uses prose to create the mixture of
spontaneity and rigorous artistic control that marks the best of
Browning. As in one of Browning's meditative dramatic monologues, the duration of the story offers us a segment excised from
the flow of time, a moment and a mood held still, yet filled with
fleeting memories, half-formed regrets and random thoughts. The
narration in 'The Gate of the Hundred Sorrows' is shadowed by the
imminence of the speaker's death, though there is no manifest crisis
to initiate the monologue. Residually an outer narrator, Kipling portrays himself as a mere recorder who has listened attentively but
invented nothing: 'My friend Gabral Misquitta, the half-caste, spoke
it all . . . and I took it down from his mouth as he answered my
questions.' The outer narrator's questions and interruptions are
admittedly not as frequent as those implied in 'Fra Lippo Lippi', but
the presence of an auditor in this story does add immediacy to the
speaker's descriptions of his visions, experiences which by their very
nature suspend time. Perhaps Kipling's admiration for Browning is
directly at work in the fine ending he supplies for 'The Gate of the
Hundred Sorrows'; the speaker is imagining the way he would like
his death to happen, but in the midst of these fantasies he abruptly
turns back to utterly practical matters: 'Then I shall lie back, quiet
and comfortable, and watch the black and red dragons have their
last big fight together; and then . . . Well, it doesn't matter. Nothing
matters much to me – only I wish Tsin-ling wouldn't put bran into
the Black Smoke.' There is a deliberate arbitrariness about this,
reflecting stylistically Gabral Misquitta's belief that all existence is
pointless and that 'nothing is strange when you're on the Black
Smoke, except the Black Smoke. And if it was, it wouldn't matter.'

Clearly, we are intended to sympathize with the half-caste's desire
to make a dignified death, 'like the bazar-woman – on a clean, cool
mat with a pipe of good stuff between my lips'. So well does Kipling
capture the blend of hedonism and self-respect in the speaker that
it is inappropriate to condemn the morality of a man who recalls
vaguely that he had 'a wife of sorts' and accepts that he may have
killed her 'by taking to the Black Smoke'.[109] Moral judgement is
suspended in a way that corresponds directly to the dream-like state

of hallucination which characterizes the entire monologue. But in other short stories of this type, the balance between sympathy and judgement is tilted in quite the other direction and a garrulous narrator is made to disclose, inadvertently, truths about himself that modify, or even extinguish, the initial sympathy which he automatically arouses by putting himself so candidly on display. The implied separation between author and speaker makes a particularly sharp type of irony possible, sometimes verging on cynicism as in Ring Lardner's 'Who Dealt?' (1926), a bitter little story which allows no compassion for a woman whose contempt for the privacy of others is never more in evidence than when she coyly reminds her husband not to give away 'our' secrets. To reinforce his point that this woman has no secrets to call 'ours' at all, Lardner constructs the narrative around a card game, drawing a rather obvious parallel between the speaker's inability to play bridge (where success depends on oblique communication and a kind of rule-governed secretiveness) and her total insensitivity to the feelings of those around her.[110] It is all a little bit too neat.

Curiously enough, it is when the imagined speaker is even more obsessively self-concerned than Ring Lardner's in 'Who Dealt?' that the short story's exploitation of the dramatic monologue form turns out to be most stimulating, and to find a way back to Somerset Maugham's 'circle of eager listeners'. It must be admitted that the range of experiences which this 'self-justifying' monologue can express is limited: the very fact that within the story an auditor is virtually superfluous, reflects the speaker's often pathological detachment from social norms, and the shortcomings of this method are all too apparent in macabre grotesqueries like Ambrose Bierce's investigation of perversity 'My Favorite Murder' (1893), or Truman Capote's confessions of a self-righteous killer, 'My Side of the Matter'. But insanity or criminality are not the only aberrant states of mind depicted by writers of monologues, and indeed it is often more shadowy and undefinable obsessions which yield truly chilling and artistically impressive effects. Some of Kafka's narrators, compulsively inventing the very miseries they complain about, provide brilliant instances of the ironies attainable by combining exaggeration and realism within a single speaker's manner: in 'A Little Woman' (written in 1923 along with 'The Burrow'), glimmers of insight emerge through the narrator's boastful inflation of his own importance, but he remains trapped in his delusion that the anonymous woman is tormented by his very existence. Less sombre, though equally accomplished, is the American writer Eudora Welty's portrait of a spiteful and envious spinster, 'Why I live at the P.O.' (1941). The comic pathos of this story derives entirely from the insistence with which a querulous yet self-congratulatory voice penetrates our minds as we piece together the postmistress's woeful tale of the solitary stand she has made against her family, who one by one 'turn against her'. Although there are moments of broad comedy, almost slapstick, the speaker maintains her shocked gravity throughout what are evidently the harmless high-jinks of a warm-hearted family from which she is self-excluded. Everyone is enjoying the fourth of July but her. Tone is everything in this story, and Welty makes powerful use of the vernacular: circumstances are described in straightforward realistic language, and there is scarcely any figurative language apart from colloquial similes like 'as dizzy as a witch', 'as stiff as a poker', 'as sure as shooting'. Irrelevancies abound, as they do in anyone's aggrieved tirade, and the narrator frequently slips into using the present tense, as though the 'perfectly horrible' things which have been inflicted on her are happening all over again as she tells us about them. At the end of the story, after she has furiously picked up all her possessions and removed herself to the post office (which her family intends to boycott from now on), there is only her voice, declaring 'I want the world to know I'm happy'; the story fades into the silence that stretches ahead of this self-persecuting woman who now has only the war news on the radio for company.[111]

It is as a performer, manipulating and twisting words to suit her own view of life, that the narrator of 'Why I live at the P.O.' comes alive for the reader. An extra dimension is added to this experience by listening to a gramophone recording of Eudora Welty reading the story herself; in the spoken version, pace, inflexions, and of course regional accent all convey qualities which in the written text have to be indicated by conventions like italicization, or the breaking up of words into single letters to indicate quirks of intonation.[112] What is brought home to anyone familiar with both the story as first published and as read by the author, is the extent to which modern technology has contributed to the renewal of a possibility that seemed to have disappeared along with the late nineteenth-century English music hall, which, we have been told, 'encouraged the development of dramatized character sketches'.[113] No one can pretend that the depersonalized gramophone is a substitute for 'live' stage performances, or that readings like Welty's restore us to the condition of the listening group. In fact, 'Why I Live at the P.O.' actually contains a moment which seems designed to remind us that for some things both printing and recording are useless; when the narrator pulls a face 'like this' we have only our imaginations to help us, whether reading or listening. Nevertheless, stories which approximate to recitations in the way they are written, or which are actually made available on record, are not just curiosities, but vivid indications of the freedom enjoyed by the short story as a form to make character rather than plot its primary ground of interest. Like the nut-cracking in Kafka's 'Josephine the Singer', from which this chapter's epigraph was taken, talking is in itself 'truly no feat'; but what makes the mouse-folk in that particular story listen with amazement to Josephine's squeaking, and also draws us to applaud Welty's post-mistress for her relentless talking, is the realization that 'here is someone making a ceremonial performance out of doing the usual thing'.[114] And to make the ordinary seem fascinatingly strange is one of the things that the short story does particularly well.

NOTES AND REFERENCES

1. *A Tree of Night and other stories* (1950), p. 174.
2. *Diary of a Madman and other stories*, trans. Ronald Wilks, Penguin pbk edn (Harmondsworth, Middx, 1972), p. 17.
3. *Plain Tales from the Hills*, p. 269.
4. *Points of View*, p. 147.
5. *Ibid.*, p. 152.
6. For discussion of Maupassant's alterations to 'Le Horla' (first published in *Gil Blas*, 26 Oct. 1886) when it appeared as the title story of a volume in 1887, see Sullivan, *Maupassant: The Short Stories*, p. 56.
7. 'The Facts of Life', *The Complete Short Stories of W. Somerset Maugham* (3 vols, 1951), I, 198–215 *passim*. The arrangement of the order in which the stories appear in this definitive edition is Maugham's own. 'The Facts of Life' was first published in *International Magazine*, Apr. 1939, and collected in *The Mixture as Before* (1940). The complete stories have been republished in various forms, and numerous collections exist in paperback.
8. *Points of View*, p. 152.
9. *London Magazine* (Mar. 1970), p. 10.
10. For Frank O'Connor's opinion that 'the novel and the short story are drastic adaptations of a primitive art form to modern conditions – to printing, science, and individual religion', see *The Lonely Voice*, p. 45.
11. 'Marginalia' (No. CCXXII), *The Works of the late Edgar Allan Poe*, with a memoir by R. W. Griswold (4 vols, New York, 1859), III, 595; repr. under the title 'Listeners Lure' In *Poe's Poems and Essays*, Everyman pbk edn (1927, repr. 1969), p. 340.
12 In *The Philosophy of the Short-story*, Brander Matthews distinguished between late nineteenth-century British magazines, where 'the serial Novel is the one thing of consequence, and all else is termed "padding"' (p. 56) and their American counterparts; he also likened conditions in the United States to those in France, drawing attention to the 'many Parisian newspapers of a wide hospitality to literature' (p. 65).
13. *The Hero in Eclipse in Victorian Fiction*, p. 74.
14. *The Modest Art*, p. 86.

15. 'A Note on the English short story', p. 145.
16. *Literary Essays and Reviews*, p. 183. James was reviewing Ernest Daudet's *Mon Frère et Moi: Souvenirs d'Enfance et de Jaunesse* (Paris, 1882) in the *Atlantic Monthly*, June 1882.
17. *Ibid.*
18. *The Art of the Novel*, p. 181.
19. *Ibid.*
20. *W. D. Howells as Critic*, p. 339. First published in the *North American Review*, Feb. 1901, Howells's penetrating critique was occasioned by the appearance of a uniform edition of Twain's writings.
21. *Ibid.*
22. *Ibid.*, p. 340.
23. *Ibid.*
24. *Ibid.*
25. *Ibid.*
26. *Ibid.*
27. *The Complete Essays of Mark Twain*, ed. Charles Neider (New York, 1963), p. 155.
28. *Ibid.*, p. 158. Twain's exemplar here was Artemus Ward.
29. *The Lonely Voice*, p. 107.
30. *Ibid.*, p. 14.
31. *Ibid.*, p. 103.
32. 'A Note on (toward) Bernard Shaw', *Labyrinths: Selected Stories and Other Writings*, ed. Donald A. Yates and James E. Irby, New Directions pbk edn New York, 1964), p. 215. All subsequent page references to the pieces collected under this title are to the New Directions edition.
33. *The Lonely Voice*, p. 37.
34. *The Cornhill Magazine*, New Series, VII (July 1899), 1–8. (Harte's article is reprinted in *Die Amerikanische Short Story: Theorie und Entwicklung* ed. Hans Bungert (Darmstadt, 1972), pp. 32–9).
35. *Ibid.*, p. 3.
36. *Ibid.*
37. *Ibid.*, p. 5.
38. *Ibid.*, p. 6.
39. Preface, *The Luck of Roaring Camp* (1870), p. vi. See also the author's introd., *The Complete Works of Bret Harte* (10 vols, 1880), I, 8–9, where Harte informs his English readers that the gold rush to California produced 'a body of men as strongly distinctive as the companions of Jason'; the emigrants' 'faith, vigour, youth, and capacity for adventure' made them, in Harte's eyes, heroic creators of 'a peculiar and romantic state of civilization'.
40. An 1887 English edition of *The Luck of Roaring Camp and other Sketches* actually offered English readers a 'Gossiping Glossary' of Californian slang, which the editor Tom Hood described as an amalgam of mining jargon, gambling formulae, and words imported by French and Mexican-Spanish settlers, resulting in 'a language very rich and very vivid – in a word, thoroughly poetical' (p. xiii).
41. *W. D. Howells as Critic*, p. 233. Howells's discussion of 'Dialect in Literature' first appeared in *Harper's Weekly*, 8 and 22 June 1895.

42. Harte, 'The Rise of the "Short Story"', *The Cornhill Magazine*, New Series, VII p. 2, p. 3.
43. *Complete Works*, I, 3.
44. 'The Outcasts of Poker Flat' (1870), *Complete Works*, II, 107–20 (p. 107).
45. 'Tennessee's Partner', *Complete Works*, II, 135–46 *passim*.
46. Introduction to *Uncle Remus and his Friends: Old Plantation Stories, Songs, and Ballads, with Sketches of Negro Character* (1893), p. vii. All subsequent page references to 'Uncle Remus' stories are to this English edition.
47. *Ibid.*, p. x. Harris's first collection of legends from Georgia in negro dialect was *Uncle Remus* (1881); *Nights with Uncle Remus* followed in 1883, and displayed more authorial embellishment than the earlier volume, where the original folktales had been virtually untouched by Harris. Although *Uncle Remus and his Friends* was the last Remus volume, Harris later produced *The Chronicles of Aunt Minervy Ann* (1899), where Remus's sister took on the storyteller's role.
48. 'Why Brother Wolf didn't eat the Little Rabbits', *Uncle Remus and his Friends*, p. 47. See also 'Why the Hawk Catches Chickens', where Remus professes exaggerated disbelief at the child's ignorance of such an ancient tale (p. 5).
49. *Ibid.*, p. 45.
50. 'Why Brother Fox's Legs are Black', *ibid.*, p. 77.
51. 'Why Brother Bull Growls and Grumbles', *ibid.*, p. 81.
52. *Ibid.*, p. 23.
53. *Ibid.*, p. 53.
54. 'Brother Rabbit's Money Mint', *ibid.*, pp. 123–4; 'Brother Fox "Smells Smoke"', *ibid.*, p. 68.
55. 'The Man and His Boots', *ibid.*, p. 160.
56. 'According to How the Drop Falls', *ibid.*, p. 149.
57. 'How the King Recruited his Army', *ibid.*, p. 178.
58. 'The Melancholy Hussar of the German Legion', *Wessex Tales and A Group of Noble Dames*, ed. F. B. Pinion, New Wessex ed. (1977), p. 41. Unless otherwise indicated, all subsequent page references to Hardy's short stories are to this edition. 'The Melancholy Hussar' was first published in two instalments in the *Bristol Times and Mirror*, 4 and 11 Jan. 1890, and then collected in *Life's Little Ironies* (1894); for the Wessex Edition of 1912, Hardy transferred the story to *Wessex Tales*, where he felt it belonged naturally.
59. *Ibid.*
60. *Plain Tales*, p. 179.
61. See, for example, 'In the House of Suddhoo', *ibid.*, p. 145.
62. *Ibid.*, p. 54.
63. *Ibid.*, p. 107.
64. *Ibid.*, p. 3; p. 16.
65. *Ibid.*, p. 186.
66. *Ibid.*, p. 247.
67. 'The Broken-link Handicap', *ibid.*, p. 170.
68. *Ibid.*, p. 245.
69. See Kipling, *From Sea to Sea and other Sketches: Letters of Travel* (2 vol, 1900), II, 186.

70. *Plain Tales*, p. 95.
71. *Collected Works*, II, 426.
72. *Plain Tales*, p. 24.
73. *Ibid.*
74. 'Brother Fox still in Trouble', *Uncle Remus and his Friends*, pp. 69–70.
75. *Something of Myself*, p. 71. For Kipling's excitement at travelling through 'Bret Harte's own country' when he visited America, see *From Sea to Sea*, II, 19.
76. 'The Bisara of Pooree', *Plain Tales*, p. 262.
77. *Ibid.*, p. 310.
78. *Ibid.*, p. 144.
79. 'Bishop Blougram's Apology', *Browning: Poetical Works 1833–1864*, ed. Ian Jack (1970), p. 656 (line 395). For discussion of the impact on Kipling of Browning's *Men and Women* (1855), see Philip Mason, *Kipling: The Glass, the Shadow and the Fire* (1975), pp. 256–8.
80. *Plain Tales*, p. 42.
81. *Ibid.*, p. 318.
82. *Ibid.*, p. 92.
83. *Uncle Remus and his Friends*, p. 167.
84. *Plain Tales*, p. 161.
85. *Ibid.*, p. 218.
86. *Ibid.*, p. 17.
87. *Ibid.*
88. 'In Error', *ibid.*, p. 181.
89. *Ibid.*, p. 319.
90. *Ibid.*, p. 19.
91. *Ibid.*, p. 89.
92. See 'The Broken-link Handicap' and 'The Bisara of Pooree'.
93. 'The Moth', *The Complete Short Stories of H. G. Wells* (1927, repr. 1970), p. 302. This story was first collected, along with other 'Single Sitting Stories', under the title 'A Moth – *Genus Novo*' in *The Stolen Bacillus and Other Incidents*.
94. *Plain Tales*, p. 330; p. 95; p. 6.
95. *Something of Myself*, p. 72.
96. *Ibid.*, pp. 72–3.
97. 'The Daughter of the Regiment', *Plain Tales*, pp. 205–12 *passim*.
98. *Ibid.*, p. 73.
99. *Many Inventions*, p. 293.
100. Introduction, *Nineteenth Century Short Stories*, p. 18.
101. *Ibid.*, pp. 199–200.
102. 'Mrs Bathurst', *Traffics and Discoveries*, pp. 339–65 *passim*.
103. Preface to 1st edn of *A Universal History of Infamy* (1935), trans. Norman Thomas di Giovanni, Penguin pbk edn (Harmondsworth, Middx. 1975), p. 15. For discussion of Borges's work as a film critic in the 1930s and of Sternberg's influence, see John Sturrock, *Paper Tigers: The Ideal Fictions of Jorge Luis Borges* (Oxford, 1977), pp. 114–6.
104. *Kipling: The Glass, the Shadow and the Fire*, p. 164.
105. *The Ring and the Book*, ed. Richard D. Altick, Penguin pbk edn (Harmondsworth, Middx, 1971), p. 628 (Book XII, ll. 855–7).

106. *Ibid.*, line 862.
107. *Ibid.*, p. 46 (Book I, 11. 863–4).
108. For Frank O'Connor's use of Browning to illustrate the short-story-writer's need to select 'the point at which he can approach' a human life which cannot be shown in its totality, see *The Lonely Voice*, pp. 21–2.
109. 'The Gate of the Hundred Sorrows', *Plain Tales from the Hills*, pp. 277–85 *passim*.
110. 'Who Dealt?' is included in *The Best Stories of Ring Lardner* (1959), pp. 247–56.
111. 'Why I Live at the P.O.', *A Curtain of Green* (1941), Eng. edn (1943), pp. 73–87 *passim*.
112. *Eudora Welty Reading from her Works*, Caedmon Literary Records (No. TC 1010).
113. P. J. Keating, *The Working Classes in Victorian Fiction* (1971), p. 153.
114. 'Josephine the Singer, or the Mouse-folk', *Wedding Preparations in the Country and Other Stories*, Penguin pbk edn (1978, repr. 1982), p. 176. This story was written in 1924, less than three months before Kafka's death.

Chapter 5

'GLANCED AT THROUGH A WINDOW': CHARACTERIZATION

> The modern short story writer is content if, allowing the reader to glance at his characters as through a window, he shows them making a gesture which is typical; that is to say, a gesture which enables the reader's imagination to fill in all that is left unsaid. Instead of giving us a finished action to admire, or pricking the bubble of some problem, he may give us only the key-piece of a mosaic, around which, if sufficiently perceptive, we can see in shadowy outline the completed pattern.
>
> (L. A. G. Strong)

First-person narration appeals to many short-storywriters because it provides a natural means of focusing elements which might otherwise seem disparate. Verisimilitude and concision can be attained at one stroke, as Somerset Maugham noted when explaining his own liking for the device of 'the first person singular':

> Its object is of course to achieve credibility, for when someone tells you what he states happened to himself you are more likely to believe that he is telling you the facts as they occurred than when he tells you what happened to somebody else. It has besides the merit from the story-teller's point of view that he need only tell you what he knows for a fact and can leave to your imagination what he doesn't or couldn't know.[1]

Maugham then goes on to stress that first-person narrators are indeed a literary convention and not authorial mouthpieces:

> But the *I* who writes is just as much a character in the story as the other persons with whom it is concerned. He may be the hero or he may be an onlooker or a confidant. But he is a character. The writer who uses this device is writing fiction and if he makes the *I* of his story a little quicker on the uptake, a little more level-headed, a little shrewder, a little braver, a little more ingenious, a little wittier, a little wiser than he, the writer, really is, the reader must show indulgence. He must remember that the author is not drawing a faithful portrait of himself, but creating a character for the particular purposes of his story.[2]

114

It is interesting to note that Maugham acknowledges a degree of idealization in the narrator figure, a factor which was evident in several of the stories and yarns considered under the heading of 'artless' narration; in *Plain Tales*, for example, Kipling does often pose as the especially shrewd, wise, and sometimes brave figure. In other cases, where a subjective effect is the aim, it suits the writer for his narrator to be noticeably *less* level-headed and ingenious, in fact altogether less guileful, than he himself is. The creation of a narrating character 'for the purposes of his story' is actually capable of greater diversity than Maugham allows, although his trio of possible roles – hero, onlooker, confidant – does cover many instances.

Maugham's insistence that a narrator is 'just as much a character in the story as the other persons with whom it is concerned' is of particular relevance to the topic of characterization in short fiction, because it draws attention to the fact that here, as in other respects, every constituent of the story must count towards the total effect. Even if he is merely an onlooker, the narrator must participate somehow in the story's action, or in the unfolding of meaning; he cannot be a completely transparent lens, but must have a fictional identity of his own, even if what he is offering us is no more than sketches of the other people in his story. In order to care about those other people at all, we must become involved with the person who is telling us about them. To make characters believable and interesting within the narrow compass of a short story is perhaps the most challenging problem afforded by the genre, and so frequently do storytellers employ first-person narration as a way of mediating character that it is fitting to begin this part of the discussion by considering 'self-portrayals', as distinct from 'portraits'. Many short stories make it very difficult to maintain any clear-cut separation between 'narrators' and 'characters'; there are numerous examples in which narrative method and character are virtually one and the same thing, and where the narrator is the hero of his own story, not as the starting point for a movement outwards into the multifariousness of the world, as is so common in the first-person novel, but rather keeping the focus on himself, even to the exclusion of those concerns which are almost by definition the province of the novel.

It is this capacity to concentrate attention on the understanding of a single character that makes the short story lend itself to particular kinds of playfulness. For illustrations of this, we have to look elsewhere than in Maugham's work, a sizeable proportion of which he described as, 'on the tragic side'.[3] Being an essentially terse form, the short story can exploit the fundamental wittiness of making a character say a great deal about himself in a small number of words. This is markedly the case when the content is farcical or the narrator a comic grotesque who is so lavish with his speech as to seem unstoppable. Part of the wit exemplified by the first-person 'garrulous' narratives referred to at the end of the last chapter, stories like Welty's 'Why I Live at the P.O.', is that in the last resort only the author can save us from the insistent, maybe hectoring presence of a narrator in full flow, buoyed up on a tide of words. The characteristic position of the listener to such monologues is represented by the author-figure in Mark Twain's comic extravaganza 'The Celebrated Jumping Frog of Calaveras County' (1867): the author finds himself trapped, driven into a corner by old Simon Wheeler who proceeds to reel off his loquacious narrative with never a flicker of facial expression and never an alteration in tone of voice. Even when the wild improbabilities seem to be over, and the tale is told of Dan'l the athletic frog and how he was cheated out of victory by being crammed with quail shot, Simon Wheeler is by no means finished. All set to start afresh, he leaves the author no alternative but to beat a hasty retreat:

> 'Well thish-yer Smiley had a yaller one-eyed cow that didn't have no tail, only jest a short stump like a bannanner, and –'
> 'Oh! hang Smiley and his afflicted cow!' I muttered, good-naturedly, and bidding the old gentleman good day, I departed.[4]

The idea of a story being something inflicted on, rather than invited by, listeners and readers is simply one aspect of Twain's complete joke, but seen in wider terms it is an idea which is bound up with every short-storywriter's accentuated consciousness of the need to sustain interest at every point. 'The story teller's first task', L. A. G. Strong told his young pupils, 'is to catch the reader's attention; the second is to keep it.'[5] To be boring in a short story is the one unforgivable fault a writer can commit; a form which shows little if any leniency to the slightest miscalculation of tone or pacing is hardly likely to permit a lapse into tedium. When short-storywriters play with the notion of boredom it is often for purposes of burlesque. Twain offers one instance, Gogol another: in his early story 'Ivan Fydoravich Schponka and his Aunt' (1831), the last of eight tales 'published by Rudy Panko, beekeeper', Gogol created a narrator who is full of breezy confidence that the reader will want to hear more than can be revealed on a single occasion. At the outset of the tale the supposed author has explained that his information is unfortunately incomplete because his housekeeper went and tore up the final pages of his manuscript for her pie paper, and in the closing sentence he makes a promise obviously meant for breaking: 'Meanwhile Auntie has hatched a new plan which you will learn more about in the next chapter.'[6] It is really Twain's joke turned the other way around: instead of the pretence being that the listener wants to escape from the narrator who has collared him, in Gogol's story it is the teller who makes the comic exit, guaranteeing that interest is kept up.

Where boredom becomes a greater risk is in stories which share the marked subjectivity characteristic of first-person narrative, but where comic irony is not as sharply registered as it is in Gogol and Twain. The narrating figure who expects to be taken seriously, placing emphasis on muted inward moods, half-formed thoughts or feelings, offers us a narrative which depends less on plot, exaggerated incident or abnormal psychic conditions, and more on the unfolding of a personal confession. The narrator's own emotional involvement in his story increases the difficulty he may have catching, and then keeping, the reader's attention. In 'The Artist's Story' (first published in 1896), Chekhov evokes the melancholy side of the button-holing situation guyed in Twain's 'Jumping Frog'. As Chekhov's outer narrator restlessly paces the room, bombarded by his friend Belokurov's outpourings about 'the disease of the age – pessimism', he reflects that, 'Hundreds of miles of desolate, monotonous, burnt steppe are less demoralizing than one man sitting and talking if you have no idea when he is going to leave you in peace.'[7] Locally, there is a special irony in this (the narrator is simply longing to make his own confession), but outside Chekhov's purpose in this story, the remark does highlight the problem of making what a person is, as distinct from what happens to him, the main source of interest in short fiction.

Here, perhaps, the short story is more restricted than the novel, where there is more leisure to establish character traits. In A. E. Coppard's view, the difference between the ways each form handles character is bound up with radically opposed principles of construction. Coppard records in his autobiography how the distinction between the novelist's approach and the storywriter's was made plain to him by Turgenev's account to Henry James of his method. Beginning with 'the vision of some person or persons', Turgenev would then search for the situations and complications which his characters 'would be most likely to produce or feel'.[8] This process, according to Coppard, is the complete reverse of the short-story-writer's 'proper method': whereas 'the novel should have a central character around which to drape the episodes that make for its significance', the short story's initial focus is on situation, and its writer is involved in a different search: 'Dealing with a complication or an episode, true or untrue, in which he perceives some significance or interest, the writer has to find the character or characters most likely to bring it to a successful issue.'[9] Coppard's emphasis on 'a successful issue' is a facet of his own need to 'know all, everything', including the outcome of the plot, before beginning to write, and from this it follows that characterization is subject to equally strict control.[10] Once the design of an entire story was grasped, Coppard explains, 'my characters would always be consistent and behave consistently in accord with my plan for them. They were not to impose their personalities on my tale and run away with it, as, for instance, Pickwick did with the marvellous Papers of Mr Dickens.'[11]

Coppard's remarks suggest that character in the short story is secondary in two main respects; in order of invention, and in relation to the author's considered 'plan'. And in fact this is the conclusion to which a reading of many short stories would lead naturally: Hawthorne's protagonist Young Goodman Brown, for instance, is clearly meant to appear more allegorical than realistic; Melville's Bartleby epitomizes a modern condition which it is the author's 'plan' to evince, and there is no danger of any one of Henry James's artist figures taking over and running away with his stories about artistic and literary life. All of these writers, whether romantic or realistic in their methods, are observing a principle which, according to Elizabeth Bowen, was instinctively grasped by Katherine Mansfield, namely that 'the short story, by reason of its aesthetics, is not, and is not intended to be, the medium either for exploration or long-term development of character. Character cannot be more than *shown* – it is there for use, the use is dramatic. Foreshortening is not only unavoidable, it is right.'[12] In other words, the conventions of the stage are more helpful to the short-storywriter than those of the novel, and it is accepted by modern writers that characterization in short fiction involves stylization and a highlighting of the designed quality of each story. Early on in short-story criticism, however, the treatment of character was seen as putting the entire genre at an intrinsic disadvantage to other types of literature. In 1901 William Dean Howells gave as one reason for the comparative neglect of short fiction the impossibility of making 'a lasting acquaintance'with its characters: 'It is a single meeting we have with them, and though we instantly love or hate them dearly, recurrence and repetition seem necessary to that familiar knowledge in which we hold the personages in a novel.'[13] The penalty for perfect form, Howells maintained, was characterization that compared poorly to anything found in the novel, or in drama: 'We can all recall by name many characters out of comedies and farces; but how many characters out of short stories can we recall?'[14] Nor does Howells have in mind only the boldly outlined 'types' in comedy and farce: since 'narrative must give to description what the drama trusts to representation', he believes that short fiction is bound to be weaker in its impact than any play.[15] It is a problem to which Howells saw no easy solution; he hopes vaguely that as it becomes more 'conscious', short fiction may become capable of rendering 'more memorable' characters, but he does not suggest how this is to be done.[16] He can see that a writer of what he terms 'romanticistic short stories', a writer like Bret Harte, supplies us with unforgettable 'types', but is at a loss when it comes to saying how realists – Sarah Orne Jewett or Mary Wilkins

Freeman, for example – are going to make us remember even the names of their characters.[17]

One answer to Howells's misgivings about the short story's power to portray character had, however, already been enunciated in his admired contemporary Henry James's theory of organic form. James argued that character and action in fiction are inseparable; his most celebrated pronouncement about this comes in 'The Art of Fiction':

> What is character but the determination of incident? What is incident but the illustration of character? What is either a picture or a novel that is *not* of character? What else do we seek in it and find in it? It is an incident for a woman to stand up with her hand resting on a table and look out at you in a certain way; or if it be not an incident I think it will be hard to say what it is. At the same time it is an expression of character.[18]

Although specifically concerned with the novel, James's argument has implications for shorter fiction too. His example of the woman caught in a striking and expressive pose is reminiscent of the type of portraiture at which the short story excels, rivalling the way a painted portrait renders a subject through gesture and pose. The woman arrests attention by looking out of the frame, conscious that she is being observed, requiring of the spectator no prior knowledge about what led her to stand up in just this way, or what the sequel to the gesture turned out to be. It is a still moment, a moment outside of the normal flow of narrative time, and while in the novel it can only provide one 'incident' among many, in a short story it may comprise the whole.

The Jamesian fusion of character and action proved stimulating to later writers anxious to escape the narrative obligations imposed by the novel form. Writing to Stephen Spender in 1937 about her most fact-based novel *The Years*, Virginia Woolf complained that she found the need to maintain narrative development exasperating, an enemy to incisiveness: 'once the narrative gets going the impetus is very heavy and difficult to interrupt, that's the horror to me of the novel'.[19] Woolf's distaste for surface events and outward action is notorious: the trouble with novels, she felt, was that they were obliged to 'drag in so many dull facts'.[20] The solution in her own novels was the substitution of extreme subjectivism, making individual feelings and sensations the only true reality: 'I think action generally unreal', she told Spender, 'It's the thing we do in the dark that is more real; the thing we do because people's eyes are on us seems to me histrionic, small boyish.'[21] Similarly, her rival Katherine Mansfield believed that the writer should try to 'go deep – to speak to the secret self we all have – to acknowledge that'.[22]

Methods of avoiding the narrative impetus that Woolf found so oppressively 'heavy and difficult to interrupt' are clearly more readily available to the writer who chooses to work with short lengths than they are to the traditional novelist – and 'traditional' must be stressed, since in this as in so many other regards, Laurence Sterne's *Tristram Shandy* instantly presents itself as a counter-example. The short story seems a form ideally suited to the treatment of 'reality' in the Woolfian sense of inner experience or unhistrionic action: the duration of a short piece can be made to coincide with the span of a character's introspective interlude, consistency being achieved through mood rather than action. But the hazards of going so far into the dark that subjectivity becomes the sole reality must also be remembered; the writing may seem egotistical, wearying the reader by offering only the contents of a single mind. Chekhov's self-absorbed Belokurov is a·salutary figure, and in fact it was the Russian writer who had demonstrated that fiction could explore emotions from the individual's point of view without capitulating to subjectivism. Fifty years before Woolf wrote her letter to Spender, Chekhov was creating characters whose inward reality was directly accessible to readers, but without forfeiting an outer realm of social behaviour, gesture and dress. Chekhov's characters are the best answer to Howells's complaint that short stories do not create a lasting impression of 'persons'. Not only does Chekhov make his characters memorable, he has the superb audacity to call one of his liveliest pieces 'A Dreary Story' (1890), daring the reader to look no further than the surface, the plane where Virginia Woolf thought 'action generally unreal'.

Chekhov's ability to convey simultaneously the inner reality and the typicality of characters like Olga in 'The Butterfly' (1894) and 'Ariadne' (in the story of that name, first published in 1895), has never been surpassed. And what is more, Chekhov's contribution to the art of the short story is utterly independent of any theoretical bias. In general the vitality of the nineteenth-century Russian short story owed nothing to a self-conscious theory comparable to Poe's in America; so casual and natural did the growth of short fiction seem to have been in Russia that Arnold Bennett, who played a decisive role in introducing Russian writing to the British public, found it impossible to trace origins and influences: 'The strange thing is that Russian fiction never did evolve. Barely a hundred years old, it began right off with masterpieces of Pushkin's in the 1820's and masterpieces of Gogol in the 1830's, and went on with masterpieces until 1904, when Chekhov died.'[23] It is significant that Bennett's remarks should have been prompted by the publication in English of *The Enchanted Wanderer* by Nikolai Leskov (1831–95). A government official, Leskov travelled all over Russia and gathered information about a variety of popular customs, types and ideas which he then incorporated into stories full of anecdotes akin to folk-sayings and jokes, and characterized by the appearance of goodnatured cranks. Leskov's heroes are 'wanderers in search of truth', though not in any intellectual sense; rather, they are often gifted craftsmen, like the central figure in 'Lefty' (1881), a story which draws on an ancient legend about the man who could shoe a flea.[24] The vein of folk-humour evident in Leskov's work is typical of the situation in nineteenth-century Russia, where every poet or novelist made it part of his function to write stories, perpetuate folktales, or give new life to legendary characters.

It was, then, a particularly spontaneous kind of art to which the English-speaking public was responding when translations of Russian stories began to appear early in the twentieth century. There is no doubt about the enthusiasm with which people received the thirteen volumes of Chekhov stories translated by Constance Garnett between 1916 and 1922. Perhaps a degree of reaction against *fin de siècle* aestheticism was involved in this; Bennett certainly intended no reproach when he said that Russian writers 'appear to despise form'.[25] On the contrary, it was a point in favour of writers whose achievements still cannot be explained within any theory of fiction as preoccupying itself solely, or even mainly, with questions of 'form'. Among such writers it was definitely Chekhov who provided the most intriguing example, seeming to Bennett a greater writer than Maupassant. Chekhov displays such diversity and unevenness, appears so offhand about formal considerations that, although everyone since Bennett has agreed that his influence on modern short-storywriting is colossal, no one seems able to explain its exact nature in aesthetic terms. Chekhov's stories cannot be made to conform to the standards of unity set by Poe and Brander Matthews, but far from this being a lamentable state of affairs it is actually the key to the invigorating effect of Chekhov's art: holding no single or settled view of life, Chekhov resembles in at least this respect the narrator of 'A Dreary Story', a man in whom 'even the most skilful analyst' could not 'detect any "general conception", or the God of a live human being'.[26]

Chekhov's greatness as a storyteller stems directly from his concern with the individual: that is his sole ideology. In 1899 he wrote in a letter: 'I have no faith in our intelligentsia . . . I believe in individuals. I see salvation in a few people living their own private lives, scattered throughout Russia . . . the individuals of whom I speak play an obscure part in society; they are not domineering, but their work is apparent.'[27] It is a view of man as unheroic but significant, and it is carried over whole into Chekhov's fictional practice. For stories told in the first person he does not rely on the idealized narrator described by Maugham as virtually an artistic necessity. 'I can't bear two-legged gods, especially if they are invented. Give us Life!', Chekhov declares in one of his many letters advising fellow writers, whom he constantly urged to write about 'ordinary love and family life without villains and angels . . . even, smooth, ordinary life as it actually is'.[28] Chekhov's advice was always a reflex on his own experience as a writer: to his brother he gives a warning, 'Write not more than two stories a week, and polish them carefully'; to another person he writes that 'to be condescending toward humble people because of their humbleness does not do honour to the human heart. In literature, the lower ranks are as necessary as in the army'; and to all of his literary correspondents he affirms his unvarying belief that 'the first and principal charm of a story is its simplicity and sincerity'.[29]

Chekhov's general advice, as well as the detailed comments he offered on other people's stories, are thrown into relief by his constant preoccupation with getting his own stories ready, meeting deadlines, and ensuring an income by pleasing the editors of the periodicals, magazines and journals for which he wrote. A letter to Suvorin, who edited and published the St Petersburg newspaper *Novoye Vremya* (*New Times*), deserves to be quoted at length. Written in 1888 when, despite having just won the Pushkin Prize, Chekhov was feeling that everything he had written was 'rubbish in comparison with what I should like to write', the letter illustrates marvellously the mass of tantalizing possibilities and pressing exigencies out of which a Chekhov character eventually crystallizes:

> You write that the hero of my 'Party' is a character worth developing.
> Good Lord! I am not a senseless brute, you know; I understand that.
> I understand that I cut the throats of my characters and spoil them,
> and that I waste good material. . . . I would gladly have spent six
> months over the 'Party'; . . . I could willingly, with pleasure, with
> feeling, in a leisurely way, describe the *whole* of my hero, describe his
> state of mind while his wife is in labour, his trial, the unpleasant
> feeling he has after he is acquitted; I would describe the midwife and
> the doctors having tea in the middle of the night, I would describe the
> rain. . . . But what am I to do? I begin a story on September 10th
> with the thought that I must finish it by October 5th at the latest; if I
> don't I shall fail the editor and be left without money.[30]

No one has described better than Chekhov the influence of extraneous factors on the proportioning of stories: the relaxed early stages of writing, then the fear of going on too long (Chekhov says terror strikes when the middle is reached and he remembers his editor), and lastly the hectic acceleration of the final phase so that the story will fit the allotted space. 'This is why', explains Chekhov, 'the beginning of my stories is always very promising and looks as though I were starting on a novel, the middle is huddled and timid, and the end is, as in a short sketch, like fireworks.'[31] This rueful admission echoes uncannily a characteristic piece of self-criticism from Henry James, who wrote to Howells in 1884 agreeing that the last third of 'Lady Barberina' was 'squeezed together and *écourté*':

> It is always the fault of my things that the head and trunk are too big and the legs too short. I spread myself always, at first, from a nervous fear that I shall not have enough of my peculiar tap to 'go round'. But I always (or generally) have, and therefore, at the end, have to fill one of the cups to overflowing. My tendency to this disproportion remains incorrigible. I begin short tales as if they were to be long novels.[32]

Yet the belief expressed by Chekhov to Suvorin that without the pressure to turn out stories quickly he would have made them better, is open to dispute. Katherine Mansfield, who declared that she would 'give every single word de Maupassant and Tumpany ever wrote for one short story by Anton Tchekhov', found Chekhov's self-defence misguided:

> Tchehov made a mistake in thinking that if he had had more time he would have written more fully, described the rain, and the midwife and the doctor having tea. The truth is one can get only *so much* into a story; there is always a sacrifice. One has to leave out what one knows and longs to use. Why? I haven't an idea, but there it is. It's always a kind of race to get in as much as one can before it *disappears*.[33]

Chekhov's letters certainly contain plenty of evidence to show that he knew very well that there were artistic reasons for making the 'sacrifice' described by Mansfield. His instruction to Alexander Chekhov – 'Abridge, brother, abridge!' – might be taken as his own motto.[34] And his constant emphasis on the need to polish and excise corresponds directly to the 'Higher Editing' by means of which Kipling produced his most compressed tales.[35] A passage from one of Chekhov's letters, set alongside Kipling's account of his method illustrates the point:

> Write a novel for one whole year, and spend another half year in cutting it down; then let it be printed. You complete your work in a mad hurry; a writer should not write, but should 'ornament' the paper, so that his work will be careful and slow.

> Take of well-grounded Indian Ink as much as suffices and a camelhair brush proportionate to the inter-spaces of your lines. In an auspicious hour, read your final draft and consider faithfully every paragraph, sentence and word, blacking out where requisite. Let it lie to drain as long as possible. At the end of that time, re-read and you should find that it will bear a second shortening. Finally, read it aloud alone and at leisure. Maybe a shade more brushwork will then indicate or impose itself. If not, praise Allah and let it go, and 'when thou hast done, repent not'.[36]

Though never as ruthless in his cutting and 'blacking out' as Kipling, who sometimes put tales aside for several years so that they 'shortened themselves almost yearly', Chekhov was equally positive that the 'secret of art' was to 'work over your phrases' and 'reject the superfluous'.[37] With 'a whole army of people' in his head, 'asking to be let out and waiting for the word of command', he was especially aware that it was essential to restrict the number of characters treated in each story, an activity which he likens to selecting the subject for a portrait:

> And so in planning a story one is bound to think first about its framework: from a crowd of leading or subordinate characters one selects one person only – wife or husband; one puts him on the canvas and paints him alone, making him prominent, while the others one scatters over the canvas like small coin, and the result is something like the vault of heaven: one big moon and a number of very small stars around it. But the moon is not a success, because it can only be understood if the stars too are intelligible, and the stars are not worked out. And so what I produce is not literature, but something like Trishka's coat. What am I to do? I don't know, I don't know. I must trust to time which heals all things.[38]

The involved astronomical metaphor expresses perfectly Chekhov's method of focusing on one central character whose significance and 'intelligibility' are enhanced by the presence of a constellation of other, less prominent characters; like the moon shedding the greatest light but depending on other stars for an understanding of its position, a Chekhov protagonist is never supposed to be autonomous. The difficulties involved in giving subsidiary characters enough – but not too much – attention face all short-storywriters who want to make realistic character portrayal the main concern of their art: nowhere is 'unity of effect' likely to be more elusive than in attempts to render the contrarieties and confusions, the indistinct motives and clumsinesses of human behaviour.

Chekhov's response to the problem is not the evasive one of caricature or stereotype. Rather, he makes the bafflement and incomplete understanding expressed through his moon-and-stars image into a narrative virtue. In 'A Dreary Story' (sub-titled 'from an old man's memoirs') the narrator feels so utterly detached from his public identity that he presents his credentials in the third person before concluding lugubriously: 'I'm every bit as dim and ugly as my name is brilliant and imposing.' At the outset, Chekhov creates a dispirited atmosphere which characterizes the hero, whose shifting moods and 'constant evasions, even to himself', were intended to constitute the entire interest of the piece.[39] Chekhov's aim was to unify what might appear to be a 'medley' by providing sustained insight into a man who is so persistent in his intellectual questioning that he lacks any firm inner identity and 'cares far too little about the inner life of those who surround him'.[40] Aware that he was attempting something new, Chekhov provided himself with a way of turning a medley into a short story: by concentrating on the puzzled and gloomy reality lying behind his unheroic hero's illustrious name, he established a basic situation within which he could present a number of episodes, all of them exemplifying an ironic misalignment between the narrator's public eminence and his inner feeling of weakness. Without exception, Nicholas Stepanovich's relationships proceed on false premises: his family life, his university professorship, and, encompassing these, his thoughts about his impending death, are all corroded by a sense of waste:

> Whether the sky's cloudy or aglow with moon and stars, I always gaze at it on my way back. thinking how death will shortly overtake me. One might suppose that my thoughts must be as profound as that sky on these occasions, and as bright and vivid.
>
> Far from it! I think about myself, my wife, Liza, Gnekker, students, people in general. My thoughts are wretched and trivial . . .

Because Chekhov's narrator is a kind of weary exile in his own surroundings, it seems entirely natural to depict the other characters in the story as hollow frontages – which is how Stepanovich himself responds to them. Chekhov varies his focus to suit his purpose: the narrator provides a substantial foreground, and inset are mere sketches of the people who cluster about him, living off his name but never touching his innermost feelings. A faded wife, an empty-headed daughter, a succession of visitors (first the colleague, then the optimist who wants a pass in the examination he has failed five times, and lastly the aspirant who comes 'shopping' for a dissertation subject), one and all they are totally external to the narrator's preoccupations and consequently it is proper to describe them from the outside. Typical of Chekhov's manner here and elsewhere in his fiction is his compact description of Liza's suitor, with its straightforward attention to details of appearance and dress, its brief touch of fantasy and its reminders that even when people are cardboard stooges like Gnekker something about them is sure to remain mysterious:

> He is a fair-haired young man under thirty, of medium height, very stout and broad-shouldered, with ginger dundreary whiskers near his ears and a tinted little moustache which makes his plump, smooth face look like a toy. He wears a short jacket, a gaudy waistcoat, trousers very broad on top, very narrow down below and patterned in large checks, and yellow heelless boots. He has bulging eyes like a crayfish, his tie resembles a crayfish's neck. The young man's whole person gives off a smell of crayfish soup, or so it seems to me. He visits us daily, but no one in the family knows where he comes from, where he went to school, or what his means are. He doesn't play or sing, but he's somehow implicated in singing and music as a salesman for

someone or other's pianos who's always in and out of the
Conservatory, knowing all the celebrities and officiating at concerts.
He criticizes music with a great air of authority, and I've noticed that
people are quick to agree with him.

The emphasis on 'he' is self-evident, but as a whole the passage moves into perplexity about how, exactly, to place him. The definite outlines of caricature are established only to be blurred, retaining a comic effect without sacrificing credibility.[41]

Similar techniques are evident in 'Ionych' (first published in 1898), where the central character's entire life, a dismal journey into grumpy indifference, is unfolded against the stable family life of the Turkins, absurd characters verging on caricature yet offering Ionych his only moments of inexplicable joy. And in 'A Lady with a Dog', which appeared one year later, a lady's-man is jolted out of his cool knowingness into dizzying passion: when Gurov first sees the lady he can classify her instantly by the way she looks, walks, dresses and wears her hair, but by the end of the story he is shaken out of such facile judgements. He has 'well and truly fallen in love: for the first time in his life'. It is a crucial moment in Gurov's life, but Chekhov is daring enough to leave the future uncertain, opening out the story into a multiplicity of conjectures which are distilled in the couple's inability to understand why 'he should have a wife, and she a husband'; the only certainty is that 'they still had a long, long way to travel – and that the most complicated and difficult part was only just beginning'.[42] The impression is of emotion profoundly felt and yet delicately restrained.

Instead of the succession of events offered by a plot-based story, or the intense participation in the workings of an individual mind provided by subjective narration, Chekhov's stories conform to a shape described by Virginia Woolf in 1933 as 'a succession of emotions radiating from some character at the centre'.[43] This applies equally to Chekhov and his compatriot Turgenev, the subject of Woolf's essay, and it captures the way in which everything in a Chekhov or Turgenev story is made to issue from and return to a centre – but a centre which, like the moon in Chekhov's moon-and-stars image, seems dynamic. Superfluous expository material is eliminated, and emotions 'radiate' because the author himself preserves a stance which is consistent in its dispassionate coolness.

Chekhov's methods of characterization cannot be appreciated fully apart from his dislike of self-display in literature. 'Subjectivity is a terrible thing', he wrote to his brother Alexander in 1883; 'it is bad in this alone, that it reveals the author's hands and feet'.[44] A few years later he related the principle of artistic self-renunciation more explicitly to literary technique: 'Best of all is to avoid depicting the hero's state of mind; you ought to try and make it clear from the hero's actions. It is not necessary to portray many characters. The centre of gravity should be in two persons: him and her.'[45] Throughout his letters, Chekhov reiterates his distaste for overt emotionalism: he teaches Lydia Avilov that, 'The more sensitive the matter in hand, the more calmly one should describe it – and the more touching it will be at the last', a principle which he believes especially important when melancholy subjects are being handled: 'when you depict sad or unlucky people, and want to touch your reader's heart, try to be colder – it gives their grief as it were a background, against which it stands out in greater relief. As it is, your heroes weep, and you sigh.'[46] The same rule, whereby 'the more objective, the stronger will be the effect', lies behind Chekhov's criticism of Maxim Gorki (whose work he knew long before the two men actually met in 1899), for lacking self-restraint and behaving in his stories like an enthusiastic theatregoer who makes so much noise that neither he nor anyone else can listen to what's happening onstage.[47]

In his own stories Chekhov applied his wise perception that emotion is most fully aroused by art when the author declines to prompt his readers openly. Authorial coldness often provides a background against which a Chekhov character's sorrow stands out in relief: Katya's grief in 'A Dreary Story' is distanced twice over, first by being compressed into a tight-lipped sentence in a letter – 'Yesterday I buried my baby' – and also by being absorbed into the narrator's calm account of his emotional desiccation.[48] With a lighter touch, the racing thoughts and feelings of the signalman's wife 'Agafya' as she approaches her husband after a night of truancy are evoked but not defined by the narrator's view of her 'zig-zagging across the field, stopping dead, marking time, her legs giving way under her and her arms floundering about helplessly, or walking backwards'.[49] And it is again understatement which gives the force of an epiphany to Ivan's joy when, at the end of 'The Student' (1894), he sees how profoundly moved the uneducated widow Vasilisa is by his spontaneous re-telling of the ancient story about Peter betraying Christ: he imagines time as an unbroken chain, the two ends of which he has glimpsed and managed to touch so that 'when he had touched one end the other vibrated'.[50]

The wonderful economy of Chekhov's characterization is partly the result of a sifting process whereby he used reminiscence to winnow away superfluities, waiting until 'only what is important or typical' remained in his memory 'as in a filter'.[51] Distanced by time, figures could attain outlines sharp enough to be depicted with realism yet free of extraneous detail. The gain for the writer was what Chekhov called 'grace', a concept which he explained to Gorki in 1899: 'When a man spends the least possible number of movements over some definite action, that is grace. One is conscious of super-

fluity in your expenditure.'[52] For Chekhov, grace was a facet of pro-
priety outside, as well as within literature, since to him reticence was
a matter of pride to 'cultured people', who are not given to 'forcing
their uninvited confidences on other people'.[53] Social and artistic
values meet in Chekhov's emphasis on grace, which always involves
muted expression and the avoidance of melodrama. To Olga
Knipper in 1900 he wrote:

> The immense majority of people are nervous, you know . . . but
> where – in streets and in houses – do you see people tearing about,
> leaping up, and clutching at their heads? Suffering ought to be
> expressed as it is in life – that is, not by the arms and legs, but by the
> tone and expression; not by gesticulation, but by grace.[54]

What applied to stage acting was equally valid in writing, the
author's aim always being to remain 'as objective as a chemist' in
depicting human feelings.[55]

The risk of this kind of insistence is that dispassion may be mistaken for indifference, a possibility that Chekhov tries to avert by
distinguishing clearly between art and sermonizing. At times he can
sound almost regretful in presenting the argument that 'conditions
of technique' are what prevent him from letting his own opinions
emerge in the course of a story:

> You see, to depict horse-thieves in seven hundred lines I must all the
> time speak and think in their tone and feel in their spirit, otherwise, if
> I introduce subjectivity, the image becomes blurred and the story will
> not be as compact as all short stories ought to be. When I write, I
> reckon entirely upon the reader to add for himself the subjective
> elements that are lacking in the story.[56]

But he adamantly resisted the suggestion that the views expressed
in 'A Dreary Story' were his own, pointing out that they belonged
to his fictional professor; all Chekhov had done was to 'make use
of my information' to illustrate the snare in which a basically good-
hearted and clever man could become caught.[57] The same concern
for artistic detachment lies behind Chekhov's reply to Suvorin's
complaint that one of his stories did not help to 'solve the problem
of pessimism':

> It seems to me that the writer of fiction should not try to solve such
> questions as those of God, pessimism, etc. His business is but to
> describe those who have been speaking or thinking about God and
> pessimism, how, and under what circumstances. The artist should be,
> not the judge of his characters and their conversations, but only an
> unbiased witness. . . . My business is merely to be talented, i.e. to be
> able to distinguish between important and unimportant statements. to
> be able to illuminate the characters and speak their language.[58]

In this mood, Chekhov presents himself not just as an individual writer trying to make his stories fit magazine slots, but as a representative artist attuned to the needs of the period: 'The time has come', he goes on defiantly, 'for writers, especially those who are artists, to admit that in this world one cannot make anything out, just as Socrates once admitted it, just as Voltaire admitted it.'[59] With the characteristically modern anti-populist stance of writers like James in mind, it is intriguing to find Chekhov in the 1880s setting his own endeavours against 'the mob', who 'think they know and understand everything; the more stupid they are, the wider, I think, do they conceive their horizon to be'.[60] Unlike James, however, Chekhov was still able to envisage 'an artist in whom the crowd has faith' contributing to intellectual progress by admitting that, as he had put it succinctly in 1887, 'Everything in this world is relative and approximate.'[61]

It has already been suggested that the short story is particularly well-adapted to showing life in its 'relative and approximate aspects', but a provoking question remains. If everything is relative, then what compels the writer's choice of this, rather than that, character among the many who could illustrate 'approximate aspects'? The problem is pressing for a writer who believes that art should promote ideals as well as depict the 'ordinary world'. For a writer like Chekhov, the answer seems to lie in a fictional character's power to suggest forces larger than the individual self. His characters have idiosyncrasies, but these are not the product of fantasy or magnified detail, as they tend to be in the work of, say, Gogol. In Gogol's work, as Prosper Mérimée noted, the aim is often to transport the reader into a fantasy realm without letting him realize that he has left the world of reality at all; the transition from 'the grotesque to the marvellous' must be imperceptible, and to this end Gogol used a method which Mérimée evidently found easy to delineate: 'The receipt for a good, fantastic tale is well known: begin with well-defined portraits of eccentric characters, but such as to be within the bounds of possibility, described with minute realism.'[62] The eccentricities of a Chekhov character, on the other hand, are not starting-points for the construction of fantasies; rather, they are clues to the unstated circumstances, trivial perhaps and yet universally potent, which have formed each character and brought him to the state in which we first encounter him in the narrative. Within a Chekhov story the protagonist, or the small group of characters selected, justify their prominence by being typical. It is not enough merely to settle on 'two or three figures'; they must resonate with 'a feeling of the human mass out of which they come'.[63] Otherwise, as Chekhov told Gorki, 'one sees that these figures are living in your imagination, but only these figures'.[64] Seen in the light of his insistence on typicality, Chekhov's recurring concern with themes of personal defeat and painful adjustments to imperfect circumstances is in complete harmony with his method of characterization and his preference for inconclusive endings. Precisely because no man or woman, either real or fictional, can be entirely whole, the individual never dominates, part of the stories' pathos being that the life of the 'human mass' reflected in each character goes on irrespective of personal destinies or the eventual outcome for individual characters.

This was the quality which Elizabeth Bowen rightly discerned in Gorki's own stories, including such undoubted masterpieces as 'Twenty-six Men and a Girl' (first published in 1899). Reviewing a volume of Gorki in 1939, Bowen spoke of his interest in 'philosophic portraiture' and illustrative action: 'Almost all the stories here show the deformation of major natural feelings by impossible circumstances. . . . Gorki identifies happiness, purity, dignity with the *generalized* moment, when man rises clear of his cramping individual consciousness to the full of his human height, forgetting himself.'[65] The justice of these comments shows just how greatly Gorki profited from Chekhov's advice.

Although no British writer was in Gorki's fortunate position of receiving Chekhov's advice direct, there were translations of his stories from which to learn the importance of typicality in fiction. When Constance Garnett's translation of *The Bishop and other Stories* appeared in 1919, Virginia Woolf was simply one of many who responded warmly, though her comments were distinctive in their perceptiveness about Chekhov's aims and methods. Of 'The Steppe' (1888), Woolf wrote: 'as the travellers move slowly over the immense space, now stopping at an inn, now overtaking some shepherd or waggon, it seems to be the journey of the Russian soul, and the empty space, so sad and so passionate, becomes the background of [Chekhov's] thought'.[66] Woolf recognized that the inconclusiveness and intimacy of Chekhov's stories were marks of their 'conformity and form', the fitful light in which his characters are revealed prevailing over the reader's desire for strong plots or explicit judgements: 'Without metaphor, the feelings of his characters are related to something more important and far more remote than personal success or happiness.'[67] Paradoxically, it is because Chekhov's characters remain earthbound, their destinies perplexing, and their thoughts often 'wretched and trivial' like those in 'A Dreary Story', that they expand in the reader's mind and assume universal proportions; by refusing to transpose their emotions onto any plane other than the ordinary world, Chekhov actually places his characters in a cosmic perspective. To Katherine Mansfield, this was an achievement to rival the *Iliad* or *Odyssey*: reading 'The Steppe' she felt that here was a story which had not *become* immortal, for 'it always was. It has no beginning or end. T[chehov] just touched one point with his pen (.————.) and then another point: *enclosed* something which had, as it were, been there for ever.'[68]

The timelessness of Chekhov's stories, and the universality of his characters, arise largely from the way he manages to strike a balance between immensity and triviality, observing standards of realism that were later summarized by another of his admirers, Arnold Bennett, who pronounced: 'You cannot, in the ardour of the search for ideal truth, repudiate the magnificent commonplace world.'[69]

Chekhov's fidelity to the 'magnificent commonplace world' is not confined to his choice of characters. Landscapes, seasonal changes and constantly altering weather play their part too, accompanying the shifting moods of his people, though not, as Woolf had noted, by providing easy metaphors for inner feelings. The effect is of the dexterous creation of what has been called a 'silent character' in the background of each story.[70] Chekhov does not use nature merely as a fund of metaphors and pathetic fallacies, but as part of the action, the part that Katherine Mansfield believed British writers too often left out: 'as in the stories of Tchehov', she advised in 1919, 'we should become aware of the rain pattering on the roof all night long, of the languid, feverish wind, of the moonlit orchard and the first snow, passionately realized, not indeed as analogous to a state of mind, but as linking that mind to the larger whole'.[71]

The question of 'the larger whole' to which characters' minds are linked is an important one that extends far beyond Chekhov as an individual case into considerations of short-story form itself. It is all very well to document (and so celebrate) the commonplace, but where exactly does the boundary between the commonplace and the banal fall? This question is raised by one of Chekhov's early experiments in objective characterization, 'A Lady's Story', which first appeared in 1887. The story resembles an ironic monologue in form, but its tone is not fully under control; when the female narrator recalls experiencing a glorious feeling of life's bounteousness and variety and then says, 'And what happened afterwards? Why – nothing', the story threatens to collapse into bathos, making us wonder whether we should be looking for authorial self-parody rather than trying to understand Natalya Vladimirovna's state of mind.[72] The trouble with making fleeting perceptions and fluctuating moods the main rationale of short stories is that sensations can become dissociated from their larger background. As his art matured, Chekhov found ways of preventing this from happening in his fiction, principally by emphasizing typicality, but inherent in his methods is a tendency which in later (and lesser) writers turns the art of short-story writing into the trick of registering surface impressions without any concern for 'the larger whole'.

Among authors writing in English, Katherine Mansfield was particularly scathing about the 'new way of writing' in post-war Britain.

Instead of trying to relate their perceptions to any kind of background, modern writers seemed to her simply to 'represent things and persons as separate, as distinct, as apart as possible', with the result that the reader felt shut out from the secret shock of recognition the writer was hugging to himself – or more often, *herself*.[73] And how, Mansfield asked, was the poor reader 'to judge the importance of one thing rather than another if each is to be seen in isolation?'[74] It is a good question. With writers like Dorothy Richardson 'darting through life, quivering, hovering, exulting in the familiarity and strangeness of all that comes within her tiny circle', Mansfield had reason to feel that, 'everything being of equal importance to her, it is impossible that everything should ... not be of equal unimportance'.[75] Mansfield poured scorn on writers who. in her view, were passively holding out their minds, as it were, while 'Life hurls objects . . . as fast as she can throw'; her belief was, that until all of the objects perceived 'are judged and given each its appointed place in the whole scheme, they have no meaning in the world of art'.[76] The temptation to present momentary perceptions, sudden insights, and isolated human figures as if they were enough – and more than enough – to supply interest, is especially strong for any one working within the short-story genre, thriving as it does on entities represented as separate and distinct. Mansfield's strictures on her contemporaries are forceful reminders that without that sense of a 'larger whole' or 'whole scheme', passivity will masquerade as sensitivity, avoiding the effort of choosing, weighing and polishing at every stage of writing. The alternative to the hard work and self-forgetfulness taught by Chekhov (and emulated by Mansfield) is a type of fraudulence to which short stories are especially prone. Herself in constant terror of triviality ('It's not good enough', she wrote of *Bliss and other Stories*, 'they are cutting down the cherry trees; the orchard is sold – that is really the atmosphere I want'), Mansfield saw how easy it was to produce undisciplined realism: after all, 'If you do not throw your Papa and your Mamma against the heavens before beginning to write about them, his whiskers and her funny little nose will be quite important enough to write about.'[77]

It would, however, be misleading to suggest that Mansfield always managed to set her own characters against the vast background she admired in Chekhov and believed essential to artistic worth. She was right, for example, in her severe judgement of her story 'Mr and Mrs Dove' (1922): It *is* 'a little bit made up' and lacking in inevitability; the two doves' 'roo-coo-coo-cooing' in their love nest reduce rather than expand the significance of the human couple's callow dialogue.[78] And 'An Ideal Family' (1922) does fail to leave the impression of things held in reserve, the mark of a fine story: it is difficult not to agree when Mansfield comments in her journal: 'This looks and smells like a story, but I wouldn't buy it.'[79] Too often Mansfield depends on satire as a means of attaining objectivity, almost as though she believed that by reducing the stature of her characters through irony she could automatically enlarge their context. Consequently, although a story like 'Mr Reginald Peacock's Day' (1920) is a highly accomplished piece of satirical mimicry which captures precisely the idiom and mannerisms of a vain egotist, it cannot be said to reverberate outwards and give 'a feeling of the human mass' in the Chekhovian sense. Mansfield's gift for imitating quirky turns of thought and speech-patterns contributed so much to her individuality as a writer that there is little reason to regret that she could not be an English Chekhov, but her work undoubtedly suffered from a tendency to seek refuge from sentiment in satire. Those were the alternatives as she saw them: in 1914 she lamented: 'Nothing that isn't satirical is really true for me to write just now. If I try to find things lovely, I turn pretty-pretty. And at the same time I am so frightened of writing mockery for satire that my pen hovers and won't settle.'[80]

Yet Katherine Anne Porter has argued that Mansfield fought in herself what were her real strengths – 'an unsparing and sometimes cruel eye, a natural malicious wit'.[81] There are certainly complex biographical reasons for Mansfield's artistic self-distrust, but even without probing these, it is evident that her talent for stylized impersonation made it hard for her to erase irony even when she wanted to. 'The Daughters of the Late Colonel' (1922) is a case in point. Mansfield was dismayed when readers found this portrait of two ageing sisters 'cruel', 'sneering'. or perhaps worse still, 'drab': to William Gerhardie, one of the few who seemed to have understood her real purpose (and who was to publish a critical study of Chekhov in 1923), Mansfield admitted: 'There was a moment when I first had "the idea" when I saw the two sisters as *amusing*; but the moment I looked deeper (let me be quite frank) I bowed down to the beauty that was hidden in their lives and to discover that was all my desire.'[82] It has already been suggested that the aim of 'discovering'(in the double sense of finding out and also revealing) the hidden beauty of obscure lives is a constant feature of short story writing: Mansfield's statement of her aim in 'Daughters of the Colonel' would be congenial to many of the writers included in this study. Her compassionate aim in writing this story associates her with a tradition of nineteenth-century writing epitomized by Russian writers like Turgenev and Chekhov, but not everyone agreed that it had been a fruitful line. D. H. Lawrence, for example, rejoiced in 1928 that 'the Tchekhovian after-influenza effect of inertia and willessness is wearing off, all over Europe' and thought it a mercy that people were realizing, 'we've had about enough of being null'.[83]

The trouble as Lawrence saw it was an excess of self-consciousness, the response of a democratic age to the dilemma of having no 'heroes' to write about. Lawrence believed that the quandary had not been confronted but dodged by means of 'subjective intensity', substituting 'every-man-his-own-hero' sentiments and 'the phenomenal coruscations of quite commonplace people' for the vivid spontaneity of remarkable people, heroic in their singularity.[84] Extended beyond cultural and historical boundaries, the problem exposed by Lawrence concerns a fundamental anomaly at the centre of literary realism, an anomaly which is magnified for the short-storywriter. 'The trouble with realism', Lawrence states simply, 'is that the writer, when he is a truly exceptional man like Flaubert or like Verga, tries to read his own sense of tragedy into people much smaller than himself.'[85] According to the logic of this, unless realism is practised only by second-rate writers it is bound to falsify the gulf between the author and his characters, dishonestly pretending that artist and characters exist on the same plane. The brevity of the short story makes it all the more possible to cram small vessels with the artist's own perceptions in the way Lawrence deplored – and all the more essential that Chekhov's *dicta* about authorial detachment be followed. Taken to an extreme, Lawrence's argument makes a realistic short story with shape and something to say almost an impossibility, or at least a contradiction in terms.

But there is a positive side to this, for it draws attention to one of the short story's greatest assets, its capacity for stylization. The artificiality of the genre makes authorial distancing a pre-requisite of success, but an enriching one which is capable of taking a staggering variety of forms. In the comic writer like Twain it is the sheer outsize quality of the characters; in early Kipling, the presence of a narrator who both observes and shares experience with his characters: Maugham's manipulation of tone creates an urbane distance between himself and his passion-driven men and women; Chekhov presents his characters as types: examples could be multiplied, but in every noteworthy short-storywriter it will be found that some convention, some device or literary strategy is at work to create a gap between author and characters, and to keep the reader aware of that gap. The distance may be narrow, but it must be there; and since there is no time to eliminate or alter it radically in a short story, it is best made a conscious factor of the reader's experience. In the last chapter we saw Kipling doing exactly this by depriving his characters of names, a practice which goes back to ancient folktales: figures like 'Red Riding Hood' and 'Bluebeard' are more descriptions, abstractions made vivid, than individual people; they are 'nicknames that tell you what a person is rather than who he is', and fittingly so, since 'the folk tale tends to identify by role'.[86] Although they may seem remote from folk literature in most respects, then, Katherine Mansfield's early stories collected under the title *In a German Pension* (1911) adopt a well-established method of typifying characters: 'the Frau', 'the Man', 'the Young Man', are figures which draw attention to the artifice involved in their creation. The stylized nature of the short story also accounts in part for the fact that the earliest distinctive short fiction in post-classical literature was either broadly comic or else horrific, making capital out of fantasy and unreality. So although there might seem to be no connection between the narrator of Poe's 'Black Cat' (1845) and the sweet-natured young man who narrates Chekhov's 'Ariadne', they are in fact both effective products of their creators' understanding that, whether fantastic or realistic, short stories depend on contrivances which mark the author's detachment from his characters.

It was probably her miscalculation of the gap Lawrence discerned between, on the one hand, the sensitive artist capable of discovering hidden beauty, and, on the other, the humble character oblivious of any beauty at all in his life, that made Katherine Mansfield miss her target in 'The Daughters of the Late Colonel'. The 'daughters' are two women whose individuality and happiness have been sacrificed to a dictatorial father of the old colonial school, and there was every reason for readers to misunderstand the relationship between the author and her characters, mistaking what Mansfield intended as a loving portrayal of 'my two flowerless ones' for an ironic story 'poking fun at the poor old things'.[87] As Antony Alpers has pointed out, while Chekhov could rely on familiarity with types, and could rapidly establish characters in terms of social class or profession, Mansfield had to use more devious means to bring her readers into close relations with her characters.[88] This holds true for stories other than those examined by Alpers. Chekhov can begin 'The Artist's Story', for example, with a quick succession of direct statements which orientate his reader within a familiar world:

> Six or seven years ago I was staying in a country district of T—
> Province on the estate of a young landowner called Belokurov. He
> was a very early riser who wore a peasant jerkin, drank beer in the
> evenings and was forever complaining that no one appreciated him.
> He had a cottage in the garden, while I lived in the old manor-house
> in a huge colonnaded ballroom with no furniture except the wide sofa on
> which I slept and the table where I played patience.[89]

Writing in the 1920s, Mansfield can assume nothing about her readers, and so she plunges straight in as if her audience were already acquainted with her characters, leaving essential information to emerge obliquely as the story goes on. This is the opening of 'The Daughters of the Late Colonel': 'The week after was one of the busiest weeks of their lives. Even when they went to bed it was only their bodies that lay down and rested; their minds went on, thinking things out, talking things over, wondering, deciding, trying to remember where . . .' Gradually, the questions raised in the reader's mind (The week after what? Who are 'they' and what do they have to decide?) are answered, and the characters of Constantia and Josephine emerge through dialogue, reported daydreaming, and occasional glimpses from outside (we learn their age, for example, through the maid Kate's view of them as 'old tabbies'). Intimidated by all and sundry – the father who has just died; the nurse with her worryingly robust appetite; Kate, who demands 'Fried or boiled?' and then stamps off to the kitchen to fry the fish regardless – the sisters are Chekhovian in their inability to make the simplest decision. No jam for the blancmange, the clergyman's offer to serve 'a little communion' in the drawing room, how to disguise their father's watch from light-fingered native runners when they post it to their brother in Ceylon: these are some of the dilemmas which alarm the women in a succession of episodes which Mansfield strings together so as to show past and present interweaving. As in Chekhov's 'A Dreary Story', the intention seems to be to 'foreground' the central character (or in this case pair of almost identical characters) and to use subsidiary 'sketched' characters for plot purposes, and also for the sake of contrasts between inner feeling and outward behaviour. In the event, however, Mansfield moves so freely in and out of the minds of all of her characters that they end up existing on the same level, leaving no way of gauging the author's attitude to her subject. It is as though she is helplessly at the mercy of the Keatsian 'negative capability' she once described in a letter to her painter friend Dorothy Brett: 'When I write about ducks I swear that I am a white duck with a round eye floating on a pond' she wrote, going on to explain that she believed firmly in technique 'because I don't see how art is going to make that divine *spring* into the bounding outline of things if it hasn't passed through the process of trying to *become* these things before re-creating them'.[90]

In 'Daughters' Mansfield succeeds wonderfully in 'becoming' the dithery sisters who see their own lives as drab and full of might-have-beens. But quite rightly she wants more. If there is to be a middle way between ridicule and sentimentality, then she needs to provide a perspective wider than the characters' own view of things. And for this, as she told Gerhardie, she relies on the ending: 'All was meant, of course, to lead up to that last paragraph, when my two flowerless ones turned with that timid gesture, to the sun. "Perhaps *now* . . ."'[91] At the end of the story each sister contemplates a stone-and-gilt Buddha. presumably a relic of their Anglo-Indian childhood, and to each comes a vague intimation that their father's death could mean freedom. Both want to declare something about the future, but since neither will be the first to speak, the moment passes:

A pause. Then Constantia said faintly, 'I can't say what I was going to say, Jug, because I've forgotten what it was . . . that I was going to say.'

> Josephine was silent for a moment. She stared at a big cloud where
> the sun had been. Then she replied shortly, 'I've forgotten too.'[92]

Clearly, Mansfield means the Buddha, the sunlight falling in a pale
red patch on the Indian carpet, and finally the obscuring cloud, to
take on symbolic force, an intention which is at odds with her
realism earlier in the story. Once again, comparison with Chekhov
is instructive: whereas in his stories objects and natural occurrences
remain part of the furniture of his character's lives, in Mansfield they
are often called on for grander purposes, sometimes remaining on
the level of expressive aspects of décor, but often being given an
overtly symbolic role to perform. The transition into a symbolic
mode at the end of 'Daughters' is not entirely successful, perhaps
because the sisters' experiences have not been given sufficiently stylized treatment from the outset. In other stories which announce
their figurative uses of language earlier, and where dependence on
metaphor is more pervasive, Mansfield is better able to balance sympathy and judgement and to introduce symbols – Linda's aloe tree
in 'Prelude' (1920), for example, or Bertha's pear tree in 'Bliss' –
naturally, and without seeming to impose a premeditated artistic
design.

The task facing many short-storywriters, then, is to create believable characters and at the same time convey a sense of dimensions
larger than the individual characters themselves. When placed
alongside other stories dealing with similar themes of freedom and
defeated will, 'The Daughters of the Late Colonel' lacks force and
clarity of purpose. Partly, as has been suggested, this is a consequence of the social diffuseness of Mansfield's period making it difficult for her to typify her characters. But it also has to do with her
lack of a cultural standpoint. George Moore in *The Untilled Field*
(1903) and Joyce in *Dubliners* (1914) document a state of 'paralysis'
comparable to that epitomized by the Colonel's daughters; but very
much to these writers' advantage, they have a discernible nationality
which in itself conditions their manipulation of the gap between
author and material. Moore's characters exemplify moods and pre-
dicaments which are not narrowly personal but intended to embody
widespread Irish problems: Bryden in 'Home Sickness', the finest
story in *The Untilled Field*, chooses a noisy bar-room in a Bowery
slum rather than stagnation in Ireland, but he cannot forget the life
he has discarded. Similarly, Gabriel Conroy in Joyce's 'The Dead'
is irked by the narrowness of life in Ireland: like Mansfield's spins-
ters, he longs to escape, but where Mansfield's ironic tone is uncertain in direction, Joyce manages to make Conroy's behaviour at the
Christmas party, and later in the overtly symbolic scene in the hotel
bedroom, representative of more than individual quirks and vani-
ties; he ensures that irony will not be confused with sneering. Taking
up the stance of adversaries to their own native cultures seems to

have benefited Moore and Joyce, giving a bite to their stories that was absent from Mansfield's stories about England. An expatriate rather than an exile, she did not feel the same conflicts as the Irish writers, and it is significant that she produced many of her best short stories when she became increasingly distant, in time if not in attitude, to the New Zealand period of her life.

But it would be misguided to suppose that without the frictions typified by Moore and Joyce the short-storywriter is disabled in his attempts to broaden characterization beyond individual portraiture. The instance of D. H. Lawrence, particularly in stories based on his early experiences of mining life in Eastwood, is sufficient to demonstrate that even when there is no abrasion between the author and the environment he depicts, characters can be made both socially realistic and representative of universal forces. By merging descriptions of people with evocations of their surroundings (themselves a blend of nature and industrialism) Lawrence unifies character and setting, making physical characteristics or individualizing features like name or dress secondary to intensity of effect. In the opening paragraphs of 'Fanny and Annie' (1922), which reverses the theme of escape by showing a young girl's return to her home town, and her eventual subjugation to 'the common people', the man Fanny is destined to marry appears – or rather, manifests himself – as if he were as much a natural phenomenon as a foundry worker:

> Flame-lurid his face as he turned among the throng of flame-lit and dark faces upon the platform. In the light of the furnace she caught sight of his drifting countenance, like a piece of floating fire. And the nostalgia, the doom of home-coming went through her veins like a drug. His eternal face, flame-lit now! The pulse and darkness of red fire from the furnace towers in the sky, lighting the desultory, industrial crowd on the wayside station, lit him and went out.
>
> Of course he did not see her. Flame-lit and unseeing! Always the same, with his meeting eyebrows, his common cap, and his red-and-black scarf knotted round his throat. Not even a collar to meet her! The flames had sunk, there was shadow.[93]

The withholding of Harry's name until later in the story is characteristic of Lawrence's method of storytelling. 'He and she', these are all the characters required to make a story, Chekhov said, and in many of Lawrence's stories the sexual relationship between two characters provides ample narrative tension, the tautness of the short story perhaps affording Lawrence the ideal vehicle for his view of sexuality. Conflict – the aesthetic imperative of short fiction – is implicit in Lawrence's account of sexual relationships, and it can be argued that in his short stories and novellas he managed to convey his beliefs with a forceful impersonality which he forfeited in longer, more discursive, works. Concentration on two characters, as in a very early story like 'The Shadow in the Rose Garden' (1914), allows Lawrence to move easily between two points of view without making the reader feel the need for any fuller sense of actuality. The emotional tension between the characters and their final arrival at a shocked state of impersonality, transcending hatred, are rendered convincingly within the single crisis depicted. 'He' and 'She' confront one another, but nothing is resolved. The analytic intensity and rapidly alternating viewpoints evident in the following passage typify Lawrence's method of conveying the conflict:

> It was difficult for her to endure his presence, for he would interfere with her. She could not recover her life. She rose stiffly and went down. She could neither eat nor talk during the meal. She sat absent, torn, without any being of her own. He tried to go on as if nothing were the matter. But at last he became silent with fury. As soon as it was possible, she went upstairs again, and locked the bedroom door. She must be alone. He went with his pipe into the garden. All his suppressed anger against her who held herself superior to him filled and blackened his heart.[94]

In a novel, where the reader's tolerance of abstractions and unparticularized personal pronouns is more limited, this style would seem too curt, the short sentences wearying, and the author's stance altogether too remote from his tortured people. But curiously enough, it is these features which make the characters credible in the short piece. Although the story is distinctively Lawrentian, its method derives from an earlier period: when the 1890s writer Hubert Crackanthorpe wanted to portray the grimly mechanical quality of a failed marriage in his Zolaesque story 'Embers' (1893), he too chose to reduce his characters to 'he' and 'she', and to create an effect of impersonality by keeping dialogue down to a sparse minimum.

Impersonality here certainly does not reflect any lack of commitment to the issues involved in the subject. 'I can only write what I feel pretty strongly about', wrote Lawrence in 1913, 'and that, at present, is the relations between men and women. After all, it is *the* problem of today, the establishment of a new relation, or the readjustment of the old one, between men and women.'[95] The problem remains unsolved in 'The Shadow in the Rose Garden', but relationships in Lawrence's short stories are not always as bleak as they appear to be in that particular story. Even when couples do attain greater harmony of feeling, however, it is seldom through talk or discussion: Frank O'Connor has pointed out that the crisis in many Lawrence short stories is a decisive moment of physical contact, often establishing a link between violence and love.[96] Among others, two of the stories collected in *England, My England* (1922), 'The Horse-dealer's Daughter' and 'Tickets, Please', show that it is through action, not wordy explanations, that oppositions are over-come. More generally, Lawrence's tendency to see all of life in terms of antitheses made the short story especially congenial to his imagination. Sometimes the conflict is between two ways of life: 'Daughters of the Vicar' (1914), for example, draws a contrast between the stifling respectability of one girl's marriage and her sister's financially imprudent, but emotionally enriching, choice of a miner to be her husband. This entire story turns on an antithesis, an effect that was clearly signalled by the title 'Two Marriages' under which Lawrence first wrote 'Daughters of the Vicar' in 1911. Elsewhere, and particularly in Lawrence's later, more 'abstracted' stories, the clash is between warring elements within the individual self.

But whether a Lawrence story is set in his native Eastwood or in the primitive landscape which provides the mythic background to a piece like 'The Woman Who Rode Away' (1928), it invariably pushes characterization beyond realistic limits. Throughout his storytelling career, Lawrence is far less interested in behaviour, con-scious motives and dialogue than in the perennial conflicts they betray – or perhaps are intended to conceal. The result, according to a later writer, Eudora Welty, is the impression that Lawrence is deliberately, almost wilfully, refusing to get his story told, or to let his characters talk naturally or conversationally – as though he found plot and character minor considerations which he gladly sacrificed to a 'magical world of pure sense, of evocation', a world that tran-scends both plot and character.[97] Because Lawrence's medium is predominantly a sensuous one, Welty contends, his method is to 'break down' character, unlike Chekhov who 'builds up character'.[98] Furthermore, Lawrence's stories ruthlessly disregard any demand for 'perfect and dovetailing structure', preferring to 'make a sham-bles of the everyday world' rather than seek 'the frozen perfection, the marblelike situations' favoured by other writers.[99] Welty com-pares Lawrence's story-world to an untidy room, usefully suggesting that it is his splendidly undutiful attitude which makes him unique among storytellers, Welty herself included: 'We all use the everyday world in our stories, and some of us feel inclined or even bound to give it at least a cursory glance and treatment, but Lawrence does not care. He feels no responsibility there at all.'[100]

There is no doubt that Lawrence did feel his responsibilities to lie elsewhere than in a faithful depiction of everyday people and events, though these actually contribute to his finest stories, espe-cially the ones based on his own Nottinghamshire background. Later stories in which realism is more thoroughly abandoned tend to rely too heavily on the reader's sympathetic intuition: pieces like 'The Woman Who Rode Away' and 'The Man Who Died' (1931) are cut so far adrift from actuality that the principal figures do seem frozen.

Instead of drawing the reader along through fluid states of emotion, characters are emblematic, locked in an esoteric pattern of meaning. The titles of these pieces alone suggest that Lawrence is concerned with universal categories becoming manifest in specific instances. The formula of 'The Man who . . .' recurs in other Lawrence titles ('The Man who Loved Islands', for example), but of course it is not exclusively Lawrentian: other instances abound, including Wells's 'The Man Who Could Work Miracles'; Algernon Blackwood's 'The Man Whom the Trees Loved', and, especially tantalizing in its blend of the general and the highly specific, 'The Man Who Was Milligan'; Kipling's 'The Man Who Would be King', and Mansfield's variation of the formula, 'The Child-Who-Was-Tired'. By drawing attention to the way characters exemplify timeless principles, albeit with striking uniqueness, these titles arouse expectations more of parable than of tale, echoing the cadences of items from ancient folklore such as the old Norwegian story 'The Smith Who Could not get into Hell'. What we find in Lawrence's mature short fiction, then, is a way of treating character that recalls very old narrative practices and, closer to his own time, Kipling's 'cases' and James's 'specimens'. The point is reinforced by setting a title like 'The Man who Loved Islands' beside earlier Lawrence titles which emphasize, variously, family ties ('Daughters of the Vicar', 'The Horse-dealer's Daughter'); objects ('The White Stocking'), or names and occupations ('Fanny and Annie', and 'Tickets, Please').

By making his characters serve the interests of truths that we are meant to see as larger and more permanent than the individual who embodies them, Lawrence seems to be forging a modern alternative to biblical parable; he is using fiction to replace the authority of sacred texts with his own unorthodox spiritual dogma. No matter how opposed to Christian ethics Lawrence was, his impulse is essentially a religious and didactic one. So it is possible to see Lawrence as extricating a well-established type of short fiction, the exemplary narrative or moralized character sketch, from the context of social morality in which it had developed its conventional literary features. For if Lawrence is in one sense returning short fiction to one of its earliest manifestations, the sermon, then it is by paring away the layers of social, as distinct from religious, significance which had accumulated round the 'tale with a purpose' since medieval times. More concerned with the inner essence than the manners and conduct of his 'Man (or Woman) who . . .', Lawrence sets aside the modifications which literary and social history had made to the early narrative technique of depicting a representative 'case' or 'instance'. Yet at the same time, if only in his use of a single emblematic figure to give point to a loosely constructed story, Lawrence helped to perpetuate a continuously changing tradition in which sermonizing techniques were adapted to fictional uses.

The most influential developments in what was essentially a sec-
ularizing process came in a period when precisely those questions
of manners, conduct and taste which Lawrence found superfluous
were prime material for fiction – the eighteenth century. Predominant among eighteenth-century short narrative forms was the charac-
er sketch, which had both the practical advantage of being made
to fit easily into restricted spaces on periodical pages, and the moral
respectability of teaching that beneath surface variations human
nature was everywhere and always the same. The writer of character
sketches claimed a special moral role which was typified by Mr Spectator, with his aim of 'reprehending those Vices which are too trivial
for the Chastisement of the Law, and too fantastical for the Cog-
nizance of the Pulpit', and his related undertaking 'never to draw
a faulty Character which does not fit a Thousand People'.[101]

Before Addison and Steele established the *Spectator* in 1711, they
had of course already enlivened the British periodical press with
their *Tatler* (1709–11), where a variety of character-types was put
on display, often accompanied by a brief illustrative story or anecdote. So, for example, we are shown in one number the prude and
the flirt, and given a little story to demonstrate 'the humour of a
coquette pushed to the Last excess'; the suggestion is that, prim or
fetching, women are all sisters under the skin.[102] Then there is 'Tom
Folio', the epitome of tedious pedantry, whose pretensions to be
'an universal scholar' earn him the succinct description, 'learned
idiot'.[103] The technique used in the portrayal of 'Tom Folio' exemplifies particularly well the way a *Tatler* sketch works: first, the outlines of the character are drawn by means of summary and
generalization; then a turn is made towards the specific, and we are
told about a visit Tom made to the narrator 'yesterday morning
. . . when I discovered in him some little touches of the coxcomb
which I had not before observed'; and finally, just at the stage where
these individual traits are beginning to dominate the piece, the narrator comments that he knows 'several of Tom's class'.[104] What we
have been offered is a portrait which has enough detail to keep us
interested in the subject, but which is also the vehicle for an inclusive satire on 'all men of deep learning without common sense'.[105]

But no matter how lively the style and how vivid the scenes in
which typical characters were presented in eighteenth-century
sketches, the repertoire of eccentricities and recognizable idiosyncrasies was inevitably limited. By the middle of the century most of
the 'types' worth writing about had been used up, though in fact this
did not deter writers from producing character sketches well into the
next century. Ironically, the tradition seems to have lingered most
tenaciously in America, the land which Bret Harte claimed to have
been the birthplace of the short story. There is nothing remotely
innovative about the work of a genteel humorist like the nineteenth-

century writer Joseph G. Baldwin who published a series of sketches called *The Flush Times of Alabama and Mississipi* in 1853. Baldwin held a respected position in the legal profession, and his role as a court judge is doubtless what lies behind his mock-heroic portrait, 'Ovid Bolus, Esq., Attorney-at-Law and Solicitor in Chancery'. Behind it too is the tradition of the English essay, and Baldwin seems to have had no qualms about transferring this urbane form to the pioneer world of log-built houses where his tale is set; nor did he hesitate to make the 'leading vice' of his character Ovid Bolus (who is a genius among liars), the sole pretext for a 'story' which is totally devoid of incident or climax.[106] Baldwin's work demonstrates that the hunt for original 'types' was becoming desperate.

But in England too the legacy of Addison and Steele proved restricting. Robert Mayo has shown that by the late eighteenth century, essay-periodicals had become the refuge of literary reactionaries, good-humoured eccentrics and dabblers in belletristic writing.[107] Until the 'hundred-years spell' cast by Addison and Steele was broken, Mayo argues, periodicals and journals were blandly indifferent to the possibilities of short fiction, a fact which is underlined by their lack of curiosity about the theoretical basis of fiction during a period when the novel was undergoing 'phenomenal development'.[108] And as we have already seen, when the situation did change in nineteenth century, short fiction was so overshadowed by the novel that it did not benefit immediately from new theoretical interests. It is telling that Macaulay, for example, should have found the importance of the *Spectator* essays to be that they 'gave to our ancestors their first taste of an exquisite and untried pleasure' – the novel.[109] 'Every valuable essay in the series may be read with pleasure', Macaulay admitted, 'yet the five or six hundred essays form a whole, and a whole which has the interest of a novel.'[110] From this standpoint, the amalgam of variety with spicy brevity achieved by the *Spectator*, is significant only as an anticipation of the long fiction which was predominant when Macaulay wrote his study of Addison in 1843. Macaulay's eagerness to affirm that 'if Addison had written a novel on an extensive plan, it would have been superior to any that we possess' seems to blind him entirely to the potential of short fiction as an independent form.[111]

Broadly speaking, the belief that fiction should serve a moral purpose was the single most powerful curb on the development of short fiction in Britain. Moralized vignettes of the *Tatler* and *Spectator* brand continued to be the most popular vehicle for examining human conduct, even when novelists had begun to show greater psychological interest in the workings of individual character. It is as though the novel continued to attract innovation and experiment, leaving short fiction with a narrow range of 'special effects', including allegory, the supernatural, terror of all varieties, and – mixed incongruously with all these – moral didacticism. To appreciate how rapidly the novel gained over other fictional forms it is necessary only to place a character from, say, Maria Edgeworth's *Moral Tales* (1801) beside a Jane Austen heroine, or (if Austen's individual greatness falsifies that comparison) with Fanny Burney's Evelina. All three writers work within a moral framework, but in Edgeworth morality coerces the characters into simplified patterns and schematic contrasts, usually involving a struggle between virtue and vice.

It is hard to imagine what progress could have been made in short-story characterization so long as it was acceptable, if not obligatory, to pursue moral objectives through narratives full of awkward transitions, coincidences and other contrivances designed to show virtue earning its reward and vice being triumphantly crushed. A significant advance is discernible only when portraiture and moralizing begin to part company, a separation which occurs first in the visual arts and specifically in the aims announced by the Pre-Raphaelite Brotherhood when it was formed in 1848. A painting like Holman Hunt's 'The Awakening Conscience' (1854) fuses a narrative impulse with a desire to reproduce faithfully the outward appearance of human figures and their surroundings, capturing a moment which has decidedly moral implications, but without making a 'message' explicit. The painter's moral attitude is absorbed into the picture itself, and unity is inherent in the subject, not imposed by the artist. A comparable development in literature takes place in the closing decades of the nineteenth century, with writers like Walter Pater and Henry James. Pater described 'The Child in the House' (which he composed in 1878) as 'a portrait', explaining that he intended readers 'as they might do on seeing a portrait, to begin speculating – what came of him?'[112] Characterization here, or in any one of Pater's *Imaginary Portraits* (1887), is still a matter of typification, but what is typified is moral only in the same sense as Hunt's picture of the girl startled into awareness, or James's 'portrait' of Isabel Archer as the individual who restores significance to the 'type' denoted by the word 'Lady', is moral. In these 'portraits', character is revealed through outward action and detail, and the eighteenth-century assumption that the artist's opinions matter to the reader has disappeared. Whereas Isaac Bickerstaff's personality was an essential component in *Tatler*, setting a normative tone of moral fairness and unifying the paper's miscellaneous contents, the late nineteenth-century artist relied on the finished painting or prose piece to produce its own effect of formal unity, inviting us to speculate rather than attend to a lesson.[113]

The result is concentrated insight which does not depend on an unfolding narrative or plot, or even on the continued presence of the character: in Kipling's 'The Head of the District' (1891), for example, Yardley-Orde dies shortly after the story opens, but we already feel that we know him through and through. 'So sufficiently has Kipling characterized him', wrote Somerset Maugham, looking back to a previous age for a comparison, 'that anyone could write his life-history, after the pattern of one of Aubrey's *Lives*, with a fair chance that it would be accurate.'[114] Even when the subject is of a more psychological nature, as it is in James's 'Brooksmith' (1892), the method of characterization is succinct and objective; the author effaces his own personality and allows the characters to express their inner feelings and moral attitudes through posture and behaviour, obliquely, and in ways that are reminiscent of Chekhov's notion, 'grace'.

When Pater, James and Kipling were writing, it would have been to stage melodrama that people would have looked for Maria Edgeworth's clear-cut moral contrasts. In fiction, things were more complicated: for none of these writers was the relationship between the artist and his contemporary situation straightforward, and in fact the 'type' who dominates James's greatest short stories is the troubled artist-figure who heroically opposes the trends current in his society. Whether the new developments in late nineteenth-century art are attributed to the collapse of social, intellectual and religious stability; to Darwinian science, or to the post-Romantic concept of the artist as 'unacknowledged legislator' instead of urbane preacher, the changes were decisive ones for the British short story. Released from the confines of moral exempla, character in short fiction could now become realistic in more complex ways and, perhaps the true test of liveliness, it could consciously and freely revert to very ancient forms: in the long run a writer like Lawrence could be his own kind of moralist, creating his own distinctive brand of 'moral fable'.

NOTES AND REFERENCES

1. Preface to *Complete Short Stories*, II, vii.
2. *Ibid.*, p. viii.
3. *Ibid.*, III, viii.
4. *The Celebrated Jumping Frog of Calaveras County and other Sketches*, ed. John Paul (1867), pp. 19–20. Twain's enormously popular and widely pirated story was first published as 'Jim Smiley and His Jumping Frog' in the *New York Saturday Press*, 18 Nov. 1865, and has had numerous different forms and titles. Its second collected appearance was in *Sketches Old and New* (1875), where Twain embellished it considerably. The first version has been quoted here because its ending seems superior; the reported speech used in later appearances of the yarn is flat compared with the impatient exit line, 'Oh! hang Smiley . . .'

5. *Instructions to Young Writers*, p. 56.
6. *Diary of a Madman and other Stories*, p. 188. 'Ivan Fyodorovich Schponka' appeared first in *Evenings on a Farm near Dikanka*, but unlike the rest of the stories (which drew on the folklore and legends of Gogol's own district in the Ukraine and were primarily fantastic) it displayed the realism and interest in the anti-hero characteristic of Gogol's later work.
7. *The Oxford Chekhov*, trans. and ed. Ronald Hingley (9 vols, 1964–80), VIII, 105. Vols IV–XI of this edition contain fiction of Chekhov's mature period (1888–1904), translations being based on the text in Chekhov's *Works* (1944–51). Except in the cases of stories not included in *The Oxford Chekhov*, all subsequent page references to Chekhov's fiction are to this edition.
8. *It's Me, O Lord!*, p. 215.
9. *Ibid.*, pp. 215–16.
10. *Ibid.*, p. 215.
11. *Ibid.*
12. *Afterthought*, p. 71.
13. 'Some Anomalies of the Short Story', in Bungert, *Die Amerikanische Short Story*, p. 48. Howells's article was first published in the *North American Review*, CLXXIII, Sept. 1901.
14. *Ibid.*, p. 49.
15. *Ibid.*
16. *Ibid.*
17. *Ibid.*, p. 50.
18. *Partial Portraits*, pp. 392–3. James's essay first appeared in *Longman's Magazine*, Sept. 1884.
19. *Letters*, VI, 123 (30 Apr.).
20. *Ibid.*, p. 96 (26 Dec. 1936).
21. *Ibid.*, p. 122.
22. *Letters and Journals*, p. 232 (Sept. 1921).
23. *The Evening Standard Years: 'Books and Persons' 1926–31*, ed. Andrew Mylett (1974), p. 23 (10 Feb. 1927).
24. Vsevold Troitsky, Foreword to *The Enchanted Wanderer and other Stories*, trans. George H. Hanna, ed. Julius Katzer (Moscow, 1958; repr. 1974), p. 11.
25. *The Evening Standard Years*, p. 31 (10 Mar. 1927).
26. *The Oxford Chekhov*, V, 80.
27. *Letters on the Short Story*, pp. 286–7 (22 Feb.).
28. *Ibid.*, p. 75 (6 Mar. 1891) and p. 230 (11 May 1888).
29. *Ibid.*, p. 70 (6 Apr. 1886); p. 277 (14 Jan. 1887); p. 231 (July 1888).
30. *Ibid.*, p. 12; p. 11.
31. *Ibid.*, p. 11.
32. *Letters*, III, 27 (21 Feb.).
33. *Letters and Journals*, pp. 202–3 (1 Dec. 1920): p. 251 (17 Jan. 1922).
34. *Letters on the Short Story*, p. 72 (30 Aug. 1893).
35. *Something of Myself*, p. 207.
36. Chekhov, *Letters on the Short Story*, p. 98 (15 Feb. 1895); Kipling, *Something of Myself*, pp. 207–8.
37. Kipling, *Something of Myself*, p. 208; Chekhov, *Letters on the Short Story*, p. 99 (3 Nov. 1897).

38. *Letters on the Short Story*, pp. 11–12 (27 Oct. 1888).
39. *Ibid.*, p. 16 (24 Sept. 1889).
40. *Ibid.*, (14 and 30 Sept. 1889).
41. 'A Dreary Story'. *The Oxford Chekhov*, V, 33–83 *passim*.
42. *The Oxford Chekhov*, IX, 140 and 141. This story first appeared in the magazine *Russkaya mysl* (*Russian Thought*) in December 1899 and was later revised for inclusion in Chekhov's first (ten-volume) 'Collected Works' (1899–1902).
43. *Collected Essays* (4 vols, 1966–67), I, 251.
44. *Letters on the Short Story*, p. 69.
45. *Ibid.*, p. 71 (10 May 1886).
46. *Ibid.*, p. 98 (1 Mar. 1893); p. 97 (19 Mar. 1892).
47. *Ibid.*, p. 98 (29 Apr. 1892). For Chekhov's remark about Gorki's 'lack of self-restraint', *ibid.*, p. 84.
48. *The Oxford Chekhov*, V, 51.
49. *Lady with Lapdog and other stories*, trans. David Magarshack, Penguin pbk edn (Harmondsworth, Middx, 1964, repr. 1970), p. 31. 'Agafya' was first published in *Novoye Vremya* in March 1886, one of the earliest occasions on which Chekhov signed a story with his full name rather than using a pseudonym.
50. *The Oxford Chekhov*, VII, 107.
51. *Letters on the Short Story*, p. 32 (15 Dec. 1897).
52. *Ibid*, p. 86 (3 Jan.).
53. *Ibid.*, p. 271 and p. 272 (1886).
54. *Ibid.*, p. 186 (2 Jan.).
55. *Ibid.*, p. 275 (14 Jan. 1887).
56. *Ibid.*, p. 64 (1 Apr. 1890).
57. *Ibid.*, p. 17 (17 Oct. 1889).
58. *Ibid.*, pp. 58–9 (30 May 1888).
59. *Ibid.*, p. 59.
60. *Ibid.*
61. *Ibid.*, p. 59 and p. 275 (14 Jan.).
62. Introduction to *The Mantle and Other Stories*, trans. Claud Field (n.d.), p. 15.
63. *Letters on the Short Story*. p. 90 and p. 91 (3 Feb. 1900).
64. *Ibid.*, p. 91.
65. *Collected Impressions*, pp. 154–5.
66. *Books and Portraits*, ed. Mary Lyon (1977), p. 124. Woolf's review was first published in *TLS*, 14 Aug. 1919.
67. *Ibid.*, p. 125.
68. *Letters and Journals*, p. 137 (21 Aug. 1919).
69. *The Evening Standard Years*, p. 124 (2 Feb. 1928).
70. V. S. Pritchett, *London Magazine* (Sept. 1966), p. 8. For an earlier version of Pritchett's comment on this facet of Russian fiction, see his article in the *New Statesman and Nation*, New Series, XXIII (17 Jan. 1942), 43.
71. *Novels and Novelists*, p. 51.
72. *The Schoolmistress and Other Stories*, trans. Constance Garnett (1920), p. 92.
73. *Novels and Novelists*, p. 41. Mansfield was reviewing May Sinclair's *Mary Olivier: A Life*, in *The Athenaeum*, 20 June 1919.

74. *Ibid.*, p. 138 (*The Athenaeum*, 9 Jan. 1920).
75. *Ibid.*, p. 140.
76. *Ibid.*, p. 4 (*The Athenaeum*, 4 Apr. 1919).
77. *Letters and Journals*, p. 181 (25 Sept. 1920); *Novels and Novelists*, p. 41.
78. *Letters and Journals*, p. 225 (July 1921).
79. *Ibid.*, p. 226 (23 July 1921).
80. *Letters and Journals*, p. 47 (4 Apr.).
81. *The Days Before*, p. 86.
82. *Letters and Journals*, p. 224 (23 June 1921).
83. *Selected Literary Criticism*, p. 288 (Introduction to *Cavalleria Rusticana*).
84. *Ibid.*, p. 275. Lawrence's topic here was again Verga's fiction, but this article on *Mastro-don Gesualdo* was not published until after Lawrence's death.
85. *Ibid.*, p. 273.
86. Angela Carter, Introduction to *The Fairy Tales of Charles Perrault*, trans. Angela Carter (1977), p. 15.
87. *Letters and Journals*, p. 224 (23 June 1921).
88. For Alpers's comparison between the opening paragraphs of Chekhov's 'The Steppe' and those of Mansfield's 'Prelude', see *Katherine Mansfield* (1954), pp. 214–17. See also Alpers's *Life of Katherine Mansfield*, pp. 190–2.
89. *The Oxford Chekhov*, VIII, 97.
90. *Letters and Journals*, p. 84 (11 Oct. 1917). Mansfield's remark echoes something said by Chekhov in a letter of 24 Sept. 1889: 'To write an old man's memoirs one should *be* an old man' (quoted in *The Oxford Chekhov*, p. 229).
91. *Letters and Journals*, p. 224.
92. 'The Daughters of the Late Colonel', *Collected Stories of Katherine Mansfield* (1945), pp. 262–85 *passim*.
93. *Collected Short Stories* (1974), p. 428.
94. *Ibid.*, p. 216. For details about the genesis of this story, which was originally composed as 'The Vicar's Garden' in 1908, and first published six years later, see Keith Cushman, *D. H. Lawrence at Work: The Emergence of the Prussian Officer Stories* (Hassocks, 1978), pp. 28–32 *passim*.
95. *The Letters of D. H. Lawrence*, ed. James T. Boulton (Cambridge, 1979), I, 546.
96. See *The Lonely Voice*, pp. 147–53.
97. 'The Reading and Writing of Short Stories', *Atlantic Monthly*, CLXXXIII, No. 3 (Mar. 1949), 49.
98. *Ibid.*, p. 47.
99. *Ibid.*
100. *Ibid.*, p. 48. Welty's article, which is a continuation of her piece in the previous month's issue of *Atlantic Monthly*, is reprinted in Bungert, pp. 145–66.
101. *The Spectator*, ed. Donald F. Bond (5 vols, Oxford, 1965), I, No. 34 (9 Apr. 1711), 144 and 145.
102. *The Tatler*, ed. George A. Aitken (4 vols, 1899), III, No. 126 (28 Jan. 1710), 69.

103. *Ibid.*, No. 158 (13 Apr. 1710), p. 234 and p. 235.
104. *Ibid.*, p. 235 and p. 236.
105. *Ibid.*, p. 236.
106. Baldwin's 'Ovid Bolus, Esq.' is included in *The Masterpiece Library of Short Stories: The Thousand Best Complete Tales of all Times and all Countries* (10 double-vols, n.d.), XIII and XIV, 688–98.
107. See *The English Novel in the Magazines*, Ch. 2 *passim*.
108. *Ibid.*, p. 84 and p. 77.
109. *Critical and Historical Essays contributed to the Edinburgh Review*, ed. F. C. Montague (3 vols, 1903), III, 365–6.
110. *Ibid.*, p. 365.
111. *Ibid.*, p. 366.
112. *Letters of Walter Pater*, ed. Lawrence Evans (Oxford, 1970), No. 47, p. 29 (17 Apr. 1878).
113. For discussion of Bickerstaff's unifying role, see Richmond P. Bond, *The Tatler: The Making of a Literary Journal* (Cambridge, Mass, 1971), p. 212 and *passim*.
114. Introduction to *A Choice of Kipling's Prose* (1952), p. xxvi.

Chapter 6

PLACES AND COMMUNITIES

Descriptions of Nature must above all be pictorial, so that the reader, reading and closing his eyes, can at once imagine the landscape depicted; but the aggregation of such images as the twilight, the sombre light, the pool, the dampness, the silver poplars, the clouded horizon, the sparrows, the distant meadow, – that is not a picture, for, however much I try, I can in no way imagine this as a harmonious whole. . . . descriptions of Nature are in place and do not detract from the effect only when they are à propos, when they help you communicate to the reader this or that mood, like music accompanying declamation.

(Chekhov)

Although few stories, especially in the modern period, depend entirely – or even largely – on a vividly realized setting for their impact, the short-storywriter can make locale play a significant part in his story by a variety of means; these range from straightforward description of landscapes, architecture and geographical position, to oblique evocations of place through dialogue and action. In some cases, setting may be the first element to present itself to the reader's imagination and the last to leave his memory. Seeing a place in his imagination is actually how composition begins for the contemporary writer Frank Tuohy; first the place, and then the people.[1] In Tuohy's experience, the characters, when they do appear, often turn out to contrast with their setting, a situation which supports the view that conflict is the special province of short fiction. But whatever the relationship between place and people, the scene in which a story is set often contributes in decisive ways to the total effect. Another twentieth-century storyteller, Elizabeth Bowen, attached great importance to this aspect of her work, noting that many of her stories were 'sparked off' by places and 'an intensified, all but spell-bound beholding, on my part, of the scene in question'.[2] Elsewhere, Bowen presents her views about this in wider, less personal terms, which apply to all types of narrative: 'Nothing can happen nowhere. The locale of the happening always colours the happening, and often, to a degree, shapes it.'[3]

In other words (turning Bowen's negatives around), there must be a 'somewhere' for 'something' to happen in a story, an assertion that might appear so uncontentious as to be scarcely worth making at all. But what justifies its emphasis at this stage is the assumption behind it, namely that stories deal with 'happenings'. Obviously, Bowen is talking about the kind of narrative that has a plot in which setting can be made to play a vital role. Latent in her remark is a distinction between fictional places with a dramatic function to fulfil, and settings which operate more like the backcloth of a stage, providing a background for the action, but not serving any greater purpose than that. The difference is between the indispensable and the decorative, and the perception to which Bowen leads us is that the writer has to use discretion if he is to make his 'where' convincing without letting it become distractingly ornate; unless scene-setting in fiction is entirely necessary to the movement of the plot, it remains 'a sheer slower-down', its 'staticness' loading the story with 'a dead weight'.[4] Although she had the demands of the novel form in mind when she made these comments, Bowen's warnings about the dangers of becoming too 'scene-minded' carry additional force for the writer of short stories, who can afford even less than the novelist to freight his narrative with 'dead weight'.[5]

As Elizabeth Bowen saw it, the temptation to compensate for artistic weaknesses by painting rhapsodic word-pictures sprang from the fact that scene, 'much more than character' – more, she insists, than any other fictional constituent – lies within the writer's 'conscious power', always a hazardous situation in her view.[6] It is undoubtedly true that the inferior short-storywriter generally gives himself away by failing to control his power to evoke scenes and images, or by indulging in extraneous descriptions of the kind Chekhov was condemning in the letter quoted at the head of this chapter.[7] Chekhov's strictures, like Bowen's, apply most pertinently to stories which depict natural, as distinct from urban, scenes, the reason being that atmospheric effects and lyrical flights of the imagination seem to be more generously yielded by rural landscapes. But to say such a thing is to indicate precisely those dangers noted by writers who insist that setting must '*materialize* – i.e. must have a palpable physical reality' in obedience to the 'same law' of relevance as character description.[8] In regard to a short-storywriter's choice and handling of setting, relevance is as much a prime consideration as we have seen it to be in matters of plot and characterization. And since individual writers usually display consistency in their views about the various facets of short-storywriting, it is not surprising to find Bowen making the same rules apply to characterization and scenic descriptions, or to discover that Chekhov's pronouncements about settings for stories are in perfect accord with what we have already heard him say about the portrayal of character. The aim is still simplicity made eloquent by means of restraint, and again it is while giving practical advice that Chekhov conveys his aesthetic beliefs with special conviction. To Gorki he wrote this:

> The descriptions of nature are the work of an artist; you are a real landscape painter. Only the frequent personification (anthropomorphism) when the sea breathes, the sky gazes, the steppe barks, nature whispers, speaks, mourns, and so on – such metaphors make your descriptions somewhat monotonous, sometimes sweetish, sometimes not clear; beauty and expressiveness in nature are attained only by simplicity, by such simple phrases as 'The sun set','It was dark', 'It began to rain', and so on – and that simplicity is characteristic of you in the highest degree.[9]

Thirteen years earlier, in 1886, Chekhov had expressed the same desire for stylistic unity and harmony to his brother Alexander, who seems to have needed the lesson more badly than Gorki:

> In my opinion a true description of Nature should be very brief and have a character of relevance. Commonplaces such as, 'the setting sun bathing in the waves of the darkening sea, poured its purple gold, etc,' – 'the swallows flying over the surface of the water twittered merrily', – such commonplaces one ought to abandon. In descriptions of Nature one ought to seize upon the little particulars, grouping them in such a way that, in reading, when you shut your eyes, you get a picture.[10]

The emphasis Chekhov places on 'picture' here, as well as the related concern to avoid equating 'picture-making' with lavish 'word-painting', recurs throughout discussions of short-story technique. In 1910, for example, we find D. H. Lawrence writing to Louie Burrows about a story she had written: 'you want to give more setting: . . . Gather the picture – get the essentials for *description* – present to the eye'.[11] And in 1945 Elizabeth Bowen defined 'setting a scene' as an attempt by the writer to 'direct the reader's visual imagination'.[12]

But although few people would dispute the importance of getting the descriptive essentials right in a story, it is more difficult to establish with any certainty the demarcation line between, to remain for the moment with Bowen's terms, the 'static' scene that interferes with narrative flow, and the scene which 'can be shown, or at least felt, to act upon action or character'.[13] In fact, many short stories of the period in which Bowen did her own apprentice work as a writer call in question the distinction she was to draw in her maturity; for modernist writers, particularly during the 1920s, the 'static' quality of a scene was often made to constitute both the main source of interest and the prime agent shown to be at work on the central character. This is what Katherine Mansfield does in 'The Tiredness of Rosabel' (completed in 1908), where meaning is derived almost entirely from the drab fixity of the girl's surroundings; and Virginia Woolf's little story *The Mark on the Wall* reduces movement still further, restricting both reader and narrator to *one* room, and, while inside that room, concentrating on *one* wall, on which there is *one* mark to monopolize attention. These are stories which offer an altered perspective on Bowen's dictum 'Nothing happens nowhere'; in 'The Tiredness of Rosabel' and *The Mark on the Wall*, 'nothing happens', but there is a 'somewhere', the essence of which is to prevent anything 'happening' in the sense Bowen intended. Setting is neither a background nor a catalyst to action, and each writer's approach – in these stories at least – exemplifies the modernist developments to which Somerset Maugham was responding when he asserted that setting was an old-fashioned element of storytelling, useful enough for putting the reader in a suitable frame of mind or for adding verisimilitude, but dispensable.[14]

But although Maugham is right to say that modern short stories usually omit the scenic descriptions which were characteristic of earlier, more leisurely, fiction, it is not indisputable that such a practice constitutes an improvement over older methods. Stories which cut down setting too radically often lack the tension and conflict which are usually seen as inalienable from good storytelling. What most readers want is not a merging of people and place, but a delineation of the way in which characters stand out in relief from their surroundings. This involves the writer in finding plausible ways of getting his characters moving, a task about which Elizabeth Bowen has some especially interesting things to say in connection with her own work:

> Someone remarked, Bowen characters are almost perpetually in transit. Arguably: if you are to include transitions from room to room or floor to floor of the same house, or one portion of its surroundings. I agree, Bowen characters are in transit *consciously*. Sensationalists, they are able to re-experience what they do, or equally, what is done to them, every day. They tend to behold afresh and react accordingly. An arrival, even into another room, is an event to be registered in some way. When they extend their environment, strike outward, invade the unknown, travel, what goes on in them is magnified and enhanced: impacts are sharper, there is more objectivity.[15]

The idea that the inner lives of fictional characters is 'magnified' when people are shown 'in transit' is of enormous importance to any discussion of 'place' in the short story, as too is Bowen's observation that techniques for sharpening impacts by making characters 'behold afresh' do not necessitate the description of long epic journeys. What matters is the heightening of consciousness, and this can be achieved by moving a character from one room to another; the next room can be every bit as much 'the unknown' as, say Kipling's India or Bret Harte's California.

The principle to be noted is one that has already been seen as constantly operating in short fiction – namely, contrast. This is what made Bowen rejoice as an artist that she had grown up in an age of rapid technological change, the 'intensifications' of which she found to be 'good for art'.[16] Speed, she declares, 'alerts vision, making vision retentive with regard to what only may have been seen for a split second. By contrast, it accentuates the absoluteness of stillness. Permanence, where it occurs, and it does occur, stands out the more strongly in an otherwise ephemeral world.'[17] Once the notion of contrast between the permanent and the ephemeral has been grasped, and with the short story's aim of 'alerting vision' in mind, it becomes entirely understandable that so many writers should choose to locate their characters in settings which draw attention to transitoriness. The bar-rooms and cafés in which Borges frequently places his characters offer clear instances of this, and related examples are the rooming-houses depicted by O. Henry; the shabby-genteel private hotels and boarding-houses where William Trevor sets many of his stories, and the anonymous settings (cafés, waiting rooms, and station restaurants) which are characteristic of Ernest Hemingway's short stories. The reasons for choosing settings like these are self-evident: the scene can be established rapidly, the reader's experience of similar places making it unnecessary to fill in many specific details; the narrative is controlled by the natural 'framing' effect of the setting; and a number of heterogeneous characters can be kept in focus for a short time without straining credulity.

It is among writers whose subjects are primarily urban that the most marked use of transitory environments is to be found, but the technique of bringing together diverse characters within a single setting is not restricted to stories of city life. The most important consideration is the writer's sense of the contrast between the permanent and the ephemeral, the alerted vision which the writer aims to communicate to his reader. A particularly fascinating case of the way this can work is Sherwood Anderson's account of the circumstances in which he wrote his series of stories about small-town life, *Winesburg, Ohio* (1919). In his 1924 'Note on Realism' Anderson recalled the shock with which he heard people say that his book was 'an exact picture of Ohio village life'.[18] Far from it, Anderson explained: 'The book was written in a crowded tenement district of Chicago. The hint for almost every character was taken from my fellow-lodgers in a large rooming house, many of whom had never lived in a village.'[19] The point here is not the justice of Anderson's defensiveness about realism in literature, but that he could transfer his experiences from a city setting to a rural one, giving to Winesburg qualities that are directly comparable to those found in other writers' fictional bar-rooms and temporary lodgings.

Urban or rural, then, many short stories seem to adopt similar techniques for establishing setting economically. And what goes for, say, a Borges interior is also evident when the writer's purpose is to capture the feeling of a vast outdoor environment. In Kipling we have an outstanding exponent of scene-setting methods used to bring a variety of exterior landscapes quickly to life, and to create an instantaneous mood of anticipation in the reader. The opening of '"Love-O'-Women"', for example, demonstrates exactly what Chekhov and Lawrence meant by their emphasis on the selection and grouping of essential details so as to make a picture:

> The horror, the confusion, and the separation of the murderer from his comrades were all over before I came. There remained only on the barrack-square the blood of man calling from the ground. The hot sun had dried it to a dusky goldbeater's skin-film, cracked lozenge-wise by the heat; and as the wind rose, each lozenge, rising a little, curled up at the edges as if it were a dumb tongue. Then a heavier gust blew all down wind grains of dark-coloured dust. It was too hot to stand in the sunshine before breakfast. The men were in the barracks talking the matter over. A knot of soldiers' wives stood by one of the entrances to the married quarters, while inside a woman shrieked and raved with filthy words.[20]

Here, the confines of the barrack-square are instantly narrowed still further with the focus on the closely-observed 'film' of blood, which is so precisely and yet imaginatively described that it makes the abstraction 'blood of man' palpably present, a weird sacrament on an unequivocally secular altar. So powerful is the visual image that the contrast drawn between silence and confused human speech works on us unobtrusively and as an integral aspect of the entire setting.

Not that Kipling is unable to capture the atmosphere of an interior with equal power. The first two paragraphs of 'At the End of the Passage' (1891) deserve to be quoted in their entirety to show how he manages to arouse our expectations of change by evoking an oppressively static mood:

> Four men, each entitled to 'life, liberty, and the pursuit of happiness', sat at a table playing whist. The thermometer marked – for them – one hundred and one degrees of heat. The room was darkened till it was only just possible to distinguish the pips of the cards and the very white faces of the players. A tattered, rotten punkah of whitewashed calico was puddling the hot air and whining dolefully at each stroke. Outside lay gloom of a November day in London. There was neither sky, sun, nor horizon, – nothing but a brown purple haze of heat. It was as though the earth were dying of apoplexy.
> From time to time clouds of tawny dust rose from the ground without any wind or warning, flung themselves tablecloth-wise among

the tops of the parched trees, and came down again. Then a whirling dust-devil would scutter across the plain for a couple of miles, break and fall outward, though there was nothing to check its flight save a long low line of piled railway-sleepers white with the dust, a cluster of huts made of mud, condemned rails, and canvas, and the one squat four-roomed bungalow that belonged to the assistant engineer of the Gaudhari State line then under construction.[21]

An interior, most certainly, but one which takes its colour (or rather its gloomy lack of distinct colour) from the frighteningly spacious Indian landscape within which the assistant engineer's squat bungalow is pathetically dwarfed. More accurate than calling this an interior is to say that Kipling adroitly establishes an indoor setting which is characterized by the outer forces that press in and make the normality of a whist-game curiously unsafe. The total effect is disturbing, and all the more so for the little domestic touches Kipling includes; the clouds flinging themselves 'tablecloth-wise', and the strikingly unusual comparison between a hot dusty day in India and a November day in London, alike in their murkiness, are disorienting, making us feel that we are in transit while the four men sit playing cards, their faces as white as the dust that makes the piles of railway-sleepers ghostly.

Both '"Love-O'-Women"' and 'At the End of the Passage' bear out particularly well Somerset Maugham's remarks about Kipling's ability to transport us out of our normal surroundings, though it was the bustle of Indian life as much as its ominous stillness that Maugham associated with Kipling's stories:

> They give you the tang of the East, the smell of the bazaars, the torpor of the rains, the heat of the sun-scorched earth, the rough life of the barracks in which the occupying troops were quartered, and the other life, so English and yet so alien to the English way, led by the officers, the Indian Civilians and the swarm of minor officials who combined to administer that vast territory.[22]

This ability of Kipling's is perhaps most evident when he actually includes travel in his stories, as he does in 'The Man Who Would be King' (1888), which hinges on a terrifying venture into the unknown, but begins with an apparently routine train-journey undertaken by the outer narrator. We are introduced to the conditions and classifications of the Indian railways, and every word of Kipling's description counts towards a complete impression:

> There are no cushions in the Intermediate class, and the population is either Intermediate, which is Eurasian, or Native, which for a long night journey is nasty, or Loafer, which is amusing though intoxicated. Intermediates do not buy from refreshment-rooms. They carry their food in bundles and pots, and buy sweets from the native sweetmeat-sellers, and drink the roadside water. That is why in the hot weather

Intermediates are taken out of the carriages dead, and in all weathers are most properly looked down upon.[23]

In his later fiction, Kipling was to use a more indirect method of establishing his setting and giving it a role in a story, but what can be seen happening in an early piece like 'The Man Who Would be King' is the concept of 'transit' being extended into the idea of travel: it is not only the fictional characters who are on the move, but the reader as well. And when the short-storywriter deliberately sets out to take us into foreign territory, the genre to which his work is most closely and naturally related is travel-literature, the roots of which lie in periods when the short story was in its infancy.

In its simplest (and also its most discursive) forms, evocation of place shares some of the characteristics of non-fictional travel-writing, particularly in periods when a valid part of the storyteller's purpose was held to be the introduction of readers to geographical areas which they were unlikely to see for themselves. Early in the nineteenth century there was nothing strange about Washington Irving's assumption that the short pieces eventually collected into his internationally popular *Sketch Book of Geoffrey Crayon, Gent.* (1819–20) would appeal only to Americans curious about English life and landscapes. And in his *Cornhill* article on the American short story Bret Harte pointed out the form's special ability to voice 'the habits of thought of a people or locality' and give 'a striking photograph of a community or a section'.[24]

In fact, what we have seen Kipling do for the fictional representation of India's suffocating heat, Harte had already done for the equally inhospitable chill of the Sierras. In 'The Outcasts of Poker Flat', Harte uses natural description to convey a sense of mystery, creating a parallel between the theme of social exile exemplified by his hero Oakhurst, and the 'singularly wild and impressive' landscape into which the group of outcasts travel. Harte uses a blank waste of snow both naturalistically (the sun seeming to warm the scene, but actually revealing 'drift on drift of snow piled high around the hut') and as a symbol of purity. A prostitute and a girl who is a model of chastity nestle in one another's arms:

> The wind lulled as if it feared to waken them. Feathery drifts of snow, shaken from the long pine-boughs, flew like white-winged birds, and settled about them as they slept. The moon through the rifted clouds looked down upon what had been the camp. But all human stain, all trace of earthly travail, was hidden beneath the spotless mantle mercifully flung from above.[25]

Beneath the snow lies the body of Oakhurst, the gambler whose calm equanimity is a facet of high-strung excitement and who is offered as an example of true honour and Christian self-sacrifice. Obviously, Harte is trying to do much more here than to offer a 'photograph' of the Sierras, and what raises his prose above the level of straightforward description is the way it links visual detail to the central themes of his story. To contemporary readers, he seemed to be discovering utterly new subject-matter, leading the 1890s writer Gleeson White, for example, to observe that Bret Harte in the West, and Kipling in the East, were finding themes 'to move a world to laughter or tears where others had but found dull material for dreary books of travel'.[26]

In the twentieth century, however, the demand for Harte's fundamentally romantic treatment of landscapes waned, though stories which depended on the metaphor of travel continued to be written. Arnold Bennett's enigmatic story 'The Death of Simon Fuge' (1907) derives much of its power from the way we are shown the northern industrial town of Bursley through the eyes of a 'serious and fairly insular Englishman'. As the narrator pushes a way through an obdurately physical crowd at the station, he is overwhelmed by the feeling that his links with civilization have been broken: 'So much crude force and naked will-to-live I had not set eyes on before', he declares as he reacts to a scene which in several respects anticipates the opening of Lawrence's 'Fanny and Annie'. Sundry details about the place and the people are added as the story proceeds, and though the figure of the dead artist Simon Fuge remains mysterious, unexplained by the '*milieu* of advertisements of soap, boots, and aperients' in which he grew up, the narrator carries away with him a composite memory which we are enabled to share: often to this day, he tells us, he can be in the midst of 'civilized' society when suddenly 'there rises up before me a complete picture of the district, its atmosphere, its spirit'. The suggestion is left that the narrator's host Mr Brindley is right to say, 'I believe this place will do you good', the additional twist being that Bennett thinks it will do his readers good to see what life in the northern provinces is like.[27]

It is highly significant that 'The Death of Simon Fuge' should take its place in a collection of stories which share a single setting; the very title of the volume *The Grim Smile of the Five Towns* holds out the promise of topographical unity. This places Bennett's work in the line of storytelling in English that was given considerable impetus by Irving's *Sketch Book*, another case of a work with an indication of documentary purpose in its title. The term 'sketch' sets up a direct analogy between pictorial and literary arts, and although this alone might seem to disqualify Irving from inclusion in a study of the 'short story', *The Sketch Book* actually merits consideration as an early instance of a tendency which persisted throughout the nineteenth century and into the twentieth.

The device of grouping tales and stories set in the same location, so as to create a persuasive effect of realism, appears in works as diverse as Sarah Orne Jewett's *The Country of the Pointed Firs*

(1896), which will be discussed later in this chapter; William Faulkner's *Go Down, Moses* (1942); Sherwood Anderson's *Winesburg, Ohio*, and – perhaps most compelling of all story-cycles with a single setting – Joyce's *Dubliners*. In these collections one or more unifying techniques are employed to bind stories together: a single, sometimes markedly regional background; a dominant tone or mood, and often a central character whose reappearance in successive stories produces an impression of continuity. All of these devices extend the scope of each individual piece without pretending to offer the type of progressive development associated with the novel. Such works gain overall unity through linked episodes rather than any sustained narrative or thematic movement, and as William Dean Howells observed in 1887, 'breadth is in the treatment of material, not the amount of it'.[28] Each episode must have its own impact, be capable of standing on its own feet, qualities which Howells found in the New England stories collected in Mary Wilkins Freeman's *A Humble Romance, and Other Stories* (1887): in these, he wrote, 'you have the air of simple village life as liberally imparted as if all the separate little dramas were set in a single frame and related to one another . . . It might all have been interwoven in one texture of narrative; but the work would not necessarily have gained breadth in gaining bulk.'[29] In other words, Freeman might have written a novel, but instead of supplying 'a thread of narrative' to give 'structural unity', she has chosen to put each 'drama' in a separate frame, relying on 'unity of spirit, of point of view, of sympathy' to provide harmony.[30] A strong sense of place undoubtedly contributes to the unified effect of Freeman's collection, helping to create that special brand of intimacy between reader and author which is characteristic of the individual stories and collections selected for consideration in this chapter. In all of them the reader is acclimatized to conditions in a circumscribed locality and so becomes familiar with a particular way of life.

Although an emphasis on locality usually entails a lowering of narrative interest, this does not necessarily result in fiction being overwhelmed by documentary. It is a question of balance rather than alternatives, as Irving's *Sketch Book*, described by its author as a miscellany 'written for different humours' shows.[31] That narrative was secondary among Irving's aims is clear enough: 'I consider a story as merely a frame on which to stretch my materials', he wrote to Henry Brevoort on 11 December 1824, going on to add that he has 'preferred adopting the mode of sketches and short tales rather than long works' because 'in these shorter writings, every page must have its merit'.[32] The content of Irving's heterogeneous work bears this out, with its array of vignettes, character sketches and anecdotes, both humorous and touching; its depiction of rural landscapes, domestic interiors, taverns and numerous examples of civic and church architecture; specimens of the fashionable rich and the sorrowing poor; fragmentary evocations of fleeting experiences (like 'A Sunday in London' which is written in the present tense to achieve a striking effect), and encounters with fantastic beings like the talking book in 'The Mutability of Literature'. All of these appear in Irving's literary tour, and all have direct antecedents in the *Tatler* and the *Spectator*.

Following Addison, Irving uses a fictional persona to link disparate subjects, and his 'Geoffrey Crayon, Gent.' resembles Mr Spectator (himself less sociable than his predecessor Isaac Bickerstaff) in being a solitary. But whereas Addison invented the mask of a man about town whose lack of distinctive colouring allowed him to eavesdrop unobserved, 'rather as a Spectator of Mankind, than as one of the Species', Irving pushes the device further, making Geoffrey Crayon an innocent abroad and a positive amateur when it comes to writing.[33] His qualifications as a writer of sketches are the natural result of the adventurous spirit that since childhood has attracted him into 'foreign parts and unknown regions', first in his native city and later more daringly still in the surrounding countryside: 'I made myself familiar with all its places famous in history or fable. I knew every spot where a murder or robbery had been committed, or a ghost seen.'[34] This man is an explorer with a strong ability to get to know a place and its associations rapidly but intimately, an ability which typifies narrators of stories with a topographical purpose. Crayon is such a speedy traveller and accurate observer that before long he has exhausted the possibilities of America and moved on to Europe, where 'charms of storied and poetical association' remain to satisfy his longing to escape from 'the commonplace realities of the present' and lose himself 'among the shadowy grandeurs of the past'.[35]

Grandeurs he finds in abundance as he roams the English countryside, bringing to 'the shifting scenes of life' the same 'sauntering gaze with which humble lovers of the picturesque stroll from the window of one print shop to another; caught sometimes by the delineations of beauty, sometimes by the distortions of caricature and sometimes by the loveliness of landscape'.[36] The pictorial comparison is entirely appropriate: what Irving offers is a series of prints in prose, a portfolio which resembles that of an 'unlucky landscape painter' described in Crayon's prefatory 'Account of Himself'; when the painter returned from his tour of Europe he had no sketches of St Peter's or the Coliseum to display, only drawings of 'cottages and landscapes, and obscure ruins', the 'nooks and corners and bye places' into which his 'vagrant inclination' had led him.[37] The implication is that the vagrant eye, by avoiding spectacular sights, sees deep into the heart of things.

Crayon's taste for the picturesque leads him most often into English churchyards, where he has a knack of arriving just in time for a funeral. Place and personality merge within the tone of melancholy reflectiveness that provides what little unity *The Sketch Book* has, and to this end Irving's persona of the lonely, homeless stranger observing foreign manners and customs is well chosen. In the sequence describing a traditional Yorkshire Christmas, for example, his position as an outsider excludes him from family tittle-tattle, but it also frees him to concentrate on gathering 'antiquarian lore'.[38] An old English family, he remarks, is 'as well worth studying as a collection of Holbein's portraits or Albert Durer's prints'; and all the more worth recording because, like so many other 'specimens' examined by Geoffrey Crayon, it is threatened with extinction.[39] There is a consistently nostalgic impulse in *The Sketch Book*'s preoccupation with transience; the virtues it praises – joviality tempered with decorum; harmony between different social classes, contentment, piety, and serenity – are constantly shown to be disappearing. As Perry Miller has pointed out, it is ironic that the first American work to gain wide international respect should be anti-progressive, adhering to values totally unlike those embodied in the American pioneer myth.[40]

For his methods, Irving looked back to eighteenth-century ideals of order, symmetry and restraint, using his pose as an amateur writer to enhance his repeated claims that his researches are accurate. His insistence on the truthfulness of his reports recalls Defoe particularly strongly. When Irving's material is purely topographical, Crayon's modest credentials are perfectly adequate, but in cases where realistic landscapes provide the settings for stories of a fantastic turn ('Rip Van Winkle', for example, or 'The Spectre Bridegroom'), or for sharply satirical pieces like 'Little Britain', Irving devises a different strategy. He distances himself still further by inventing a second persona who takes responsibility for the tale, a tactic which is evident throughout the history of the short story. 'Rip Van Winkle' and 'The Legend of Sleepy Hollow' are simply found amongst Dietrich Knickerbocker's papers; Crayon gets the colourful account of 'Little Britain' from an 'odd looking old gentleman' who is later proved to be a reliable witness, and 'The Spectre Bridegroom' is narrated by an old Swiss to a group of travellers around a stove in a Flemish inn, a situation of appropriate internationality.[41] The tale of the ghostly bridegroom shows little originality on Irving's part, and his constant indebtedness to German literature has long been recognised; his probable literary source for this story is Gottfried Bürger's ballad 'Lenore'.[42] But he shows ingenuity in the way he frames a story, combining his evocation of setting with a disclaimer of his own ability to do the material full justice. He meticulously describes 'The Inn Kitchen' where he first heard the tale he is about to recount, and then appears to falter:

> I fear, however, it derived its chief zest from the manner in which it was told, and the peculiar air and appearance of the narrator . . . I wish my readers could imagine the old fellow lolling in a huge armchair, one arm akimbo, the other holding a curiously twisted tobacco pipe, formed of genuine *écume de mer*, decorated with silver chain and silken tassel – his head cocked to one side, and the whimsical cut of the eye occasionally, as he related the following story.[43]

Yet despite the care with which the quaint figure of the Swiss traveller is described, and however many his pauses for arriving guests, fills of tobacco, and the occasional leer at the buxom kitchen maid, he contributes nothing at all to the story he tells. The style is entirely Irving's, down to the choice of a ballad-like epigraph and the footnote glossing the name 'Katzenellenbogen'. Irving seems to be using the setting of a small group whiling away the time to put his readers into a receptive mood for a supernatural tale, something Dickens did in his Christmas Books and which James was to achieve with great subtlety in 'The Turn of the Screw'.

Hardy employed a similar device in his yarn 'A Tradition of Eighteen Hundred and Four', which was first published at Christmas in 1882: the outer narrator has come into an inn to shelter from the rain, and there in the 'yawning chimney-corner of the inn-kitchen' he finds Solomon Selby sitting with others who have gathered there.[44] When Solomon takes his pipe out of his mouth and smiles 'his narrative smile', the scene is set for the oral narration that follows.[45] Perhaps, though, the finest example of a writer who uses an initial setting to prepare the atmosphere for a strange story is Conrad in 'Heart of Darkness' (1902). The principle involved in all of these stories is that a realistic frame increases the mysteriousness of the material framed, an effect that in Irving's case is further heightened by the order in which the tales are arranged: in the collected *Sketch Book* the mysteriousness of 'The Spectre Bridegroom' is increased rather than dispersed by the straightforward tourist description of Westminster Abbey that follows it. At one and the same time, *The Sketch Book* explores realms of fantasy and charts a visible world so compellingly that in 1896 Brander Matthews could declare that, 'no single work has been more potent than the "Sketch-Book" in directing to Stratford on Avon and through Westminster Abbey the unending procession of transatlantic travellers from America'.[46]

Irving is equally concerned to provide an authentic context for 'The Legend of Sleepy Hollow', where the lonely glen is painstakingly located for us, and the narrator's confession that he cannot believe half of the tale himself is deferred until the very end. Similarly, the description of the Kaatskill Mountains, with which 'Rip Van Winkle' opens, has the manner and style of a travel sketch, although as a prelude to the story of Rip's wonderful escape from a nagging wife it is also designed to beckon the reader into an enchanted landscape where dreams come true. The mood of these stories is comic, but at other times Irving's attention to realistic detail has an overtly moral element that makes him belong not only with the eighteenth-century essayists but with the early romantic poets. He was well-read in the works of Scott, Byron, and Robert Burns, and he shared the Wordsworthian aim of startling the reader into moral awareness by disclosing the impressive story that lies behind a banal object. In one of his most emotive, and admittedly one of his most sentimental, stories, 'The Pride of the Village', he uses his pose of humility to challenge the reader and scorn sensationalism: 'Such are the particulars which I gathered of this village story. They are but scanty, and I am conscious have little novelty to recommend them. In the present rage for strange incident and high seasoned narrative, they may appear trite and insignificant, but they interested me strongly at the time.'[47] The same educative motive lay behind Irving's threnodies on America Indian life, 'Traits of Indian Life' and 'Philip of Pokanoket', which were first published in 1814 while Irving was still in America, and only brought into *The Sketch Book* for the composite British edition six years later. Despite their separate origins, these sketches fitted in easily with their companion pieces, taking a part in the entire book's concern to make the reader look beyond mere surfaces. And this was not a concern which disappeared when critical interest in Irving waned after the 1850s: at the end of the century we find Robert Cunninghame Graham writing travel sketches and celebrating the South American gaucho in a manner that recalls what Irving had attempted in his portrayals of American Indians. In 'El Lazo' (1899), for example, Cunninghame Graham laments the inevitable replacement of primitive hunting weapons by the rifle, and he offers his 'short description' more as 'a sort of record of a dream, dreamed upon pampas and on prairies' than as a story proper.[48]

The emphasis of such writing, however exotic the setting, is on something more inward than narrative movement, which for Irving was simply a way of making the 'instruction' he offered more palatable to 'a story-telling and a story-reading age'.[49] Above all other literary merits, Irving valued the 'play of thought, and sentiment, and language; the weaving in of characters . . . the familiar and faithful exhibition of scenes in common life; and the half-concealed vein of humour that is often playing through the whole': these are what he believed made an author 'continually piquant'.[50] Notions of structural compression do not enter into Irving's view of art, and it is inappropriate to look in *The Sketch Book* for any unity beyond that arising from its alternating moods and its preoccupation with mutability. In fact, the only pieces that could stand alone as stories rather than generalized type-cases or episodes are actually those with the strongest elements of unreality. Irving's contemporaries were astute in recognizing the superiority of his fantastic tales, seeing beyond the guileless manner in which 'Geoffrey Crayon' presents them:

> I am always of easy faith . . . and am ever willing to be deceived,
> where the deceit is pleasant, and costs nothing. I am therefore a ready
> believer in relics, legends, and local anecdotes of goblins and great
> men; and would advise all travellers who travel for their gratification
> to be the same. What is it to us whether these stories be true or false,
> so long as we can persuade ourselves into belief of them, and enjoy all
> the charm of the reality?[51]

The suggestion that incredible stories are one of the permissible luxuries of travel is compatible with Irving's association between morality and amusement: his account of an English Christmas, which constituted one of the seven separate numbers in which *The Sketch Book* originally appeared, will be worthwhile, according to Irving, if by entertaining its readers it prompts 'a benevolent view of human nature'.[52] No matter if the customs recorded are as much a part of fantasy as Sleepy Hollow or if, as Hazlitt maintained, 'whatever the ingenious author has been most delighted with in the representations of books he transfers to his portfolio, and swears that he has found it actually existing'.[53]

There is no need to follow Hazlitt all the way into accusing Irving of swallowing 'the tempting bait of European popularity' and meretriciously 'complimenting our national and Tory prejudice', in order to see what prevents *The Sketch Book* from retaining a prominent place in the history of the short story – conservatism of attitude.[54] Irving's artistic methods and the techniques he uses to turn the reader into an armchair traveller persist in later periods, but the tendency of subsequent fiction is away from the tranquil outlook that sees Sleepy Hollow, where manners and customs remain fixed, as an ideal. H. S. Canby argued that the impetus in the rise of the short story came from Poe's weird intensity, not Irving's benign disposition, and from a modern viewpoint this seems highly plausible.[55] Nevertheless, if what is stressed is Irving's desire to make his readers look intensely, albeit at the ordinary and not the bizarre, then the difference between Poe's aims and Irving's are not as extreme as Canby supposed. Both writers attempt to concentrate the reader's gaze, and although concentration in *The Sketch Book* is dispersed because Irving moves between rural and urban settings, he did show how topographical realism could be adapted to fictional purposes, using the story-series to give a feeling of intimacy with lives remote from the reader's own. In a sense, Irving's essayistic stories lead eventually to such sociologically motivated sketches as Arthur Morrison's 'A Street', published originally in 1891 and later collected along with other working-class stories in *Tales of Mean Streets* (1894). Where Irving's outlook in a piece like 'Little Britain' is basically optimistic, and his manner a blend of realism and fancifulness, Morrison offers a bleak picture of 'an oppressive, all-pervading, monotony'; but neither writer pretends to give more than his own view, the result of his personal quest among communities about which he expects his readers to be ignorant, or even prejudiced.[56]

It was this feeling which Howells proposed as amply compensating for epic breadth in fiction. He defended Turgenev against the charge of narrowness by arguing that, 'each man is a microcosm, and the writer who is able to acquaint us intimately with half a dozen people, or the conditions of a neighbourhood or a class, has done something which cannot in any bad sense be called narrow; his breadth is vertical instead of lateral, that is all'.[57] Among English writers whose work might be seen as supporting Howells's case is Mary Russell Mitford, whose 'Sketches of Village Life' began appearing in *The Lady's Magazine* in December 1822 and were first published under the title *Our Village* in 1824. In her first sketch, Mitford invites the reader into what she claims is the 'most delightful' of all situations 'for a constant residence' – 'a little village far in the country; a small neighbourhood not of fine mansions finely peopled, but of cottages and cottage-like houses . . . with inhabitants whose faces are as familiar to us as the flowers in our garden'. What makes this rural simplicity attractive is not the solitude it engenders, but the intimacy it ensures within 'a little world of our own, close-packed and insulated like ants in an ant-hill, or bees in a hive, or sheep in a fold, or nuns in a convent, or sailors in a ship'. To be 'close-packed' is no discomfort here, 'where we know every one, are known to every one, interested in every one, and authorized to hope that every one feels an interest in us'. This is a community where malicious gossip is unknown and privacy needs no guarding. Consequently, morality is effortless and customary, in total harmony with the natural landscape: 'How pleasant it is to slide into these true-hearted feelings from the kindly and unconscious influence of habit, and to learn to know and love the people about us, with all their peculiarities, just as we learn to know and to love the nooks and turns of the shady lanes and sunny commons that we pass every day!'

As in life, so in art: Mitford asserts that the joys of village life correspond directly to the pleasures contained in particular kinds of literature: 'Even in books I like a confined locality, and so do the critics when they talk of the unities. Nothing is so tiresome as to be whirled half over Europe at the chariot-wheels of a hero, to go to sleep at Vienna, and awaken at Madrid; it produces a real fatigue, a weariness of spirit.'[58] The soothing stay-at-home feeling behind this corresponds exactly to the mood in which, more than a century earlier, Addison had asked readers of the *Spectator*, 'Is it not much better to be let into knowledge of ones-self, than to hear what passes in *Muscovy* or *Poland*?'[59] In her turn, Mitford is justifying an impulse that is pervasive among short-storywriters, as well as implicitly opposing the conventions of the romantic novel of her day. A great deal of short fiction starts from the assumption that readers pick up a story because they are already fatigued and 'weary of spirit', and consequently glad of the restful unity of place and limited *dramatis personae* that Mitford admired in Jane Austen's novels, where we can 'sit down in a country village . . . quite sure before we leave it to become intimate with every spot and person it contains'.[60] The attractions of repose and intimacy – these are what Miss Mitford finds in Jane Austen, in Gilbert White's Selborne, or even in distant islands, whether Robinson Crusoe's or Prospero's.

According to this view, intimacy with a small group of people or natural phenomena, whether achieved by realistic or fantastic methods, is preferable to panoramic range and fierce narrative pace. And as Mitford's choice of examples makes clear, stories which concentrate on tiny or remote locales are by no means pastoral escapes. Far from it; they can include the exotic as well as the everyday. What they have in common is the belief that the reader's imaginative energies can be directed towards new perceptiveness by means of intense focus on people and place. As in Irving's work, intimacy becomes an artistic means of expanding the reader's understanding in new and diverse ways. For Mitford and her contemporaries, emphasis lay on moral awareness gently increased, but although the moral aspect of this type of fiction dwindles in later periods, the use of a closely observed setting to create an effect of intimacy persists, retaining many of the features evident in *Our Village*'s affectionate portrayal of country scenes and rural types.

Narrative plays a minor role in Mitford's depiction of life in her idealized Berkshire hamlet, its primary use being to illustrate 'the best part of the English character, its industry, its frugality, its sound sense, and its kindness'.[61] A typical instance is the story of Hannah Bint, one of several resourceful and plucky women in *Our Village*, who saves her family from misfortune and parental fecklessness by the good management of a single Alderney cow. What little action *Our Village* contains usually arises directly from the setting; visits to friends or outings to picturesque spots provide sufficient dramatic interest, as they do in other carefully localized works like Mrs Gaskell's *Cranford*, the first part of which appeared in *Household Words* on 13 December 1851, after Dickens had given it the Mitfordesque title 'Our Society at Cranford'. Rhapsodic nature descriptions predominate, the author's country walks presenting a simple structure within which to demonstrate parallels between natural and human graces – qualities which Mitford assures herself, hurrying past the parish workhouse, are to be found everywhere. Social comment is only part of her purpose in so far as it merges with her setting, and occasional gloomy thoughts or 'unaccountable depression' are dispelled by her belief in moral exertion as 'the true specific for nervousness'.[62] 'We must get on' is her characteristically brisk response to 'morbid fancy', anticipating Mrs Gaskell's rural tale *Cousin Phillis* (1864), where to 'fight your own way back to cheerfulness' is proclaimed the cure for a broken heart.[63]

The simplicity of Mitford's morality is a facet of her sense of community, and it is notable that she insists on people being known and loved with all their foibles. An eccentric like 'poor John Evans', the gardener who went insane when his wife died and now potters around 'full of a child-like simplicity' helps bind the villagers closer together because 'his unprotectedness, his utter defencelessness have an irresistible claim on every better feeling'.[64] Sentimental this may be, but what in Mitford veers into sentimentality, emerges as an important feature of later short stories which use similar methods to explore human behaviour within single and often highly individualized settings. In the compressed form of the short story a firm sense of place provides a stable framework in which to portray the odd and eccentric, or their disturbing counterparts, the grotesque and obsessed. The pattern established by Mitford was liable to become stereotyped, but when modified by the individual talents of writers as diverse as, among others, Sarah Orne Jewett, Kipling, and Sherwood Anderson, it could develop far greater profundity.

The New England world portrayed by Sarah Orne Jewett is every bit as self-enclosed as Miss Mitford's village, and in part she was simply meeting America's keen demand, after the Civil War, for realistic pictures of small corners in its newly re-united vastness; the more local the colour, apparently, the stronger the boost to a feeling of national solidarity.[65] Looking back to the time when her early sketches *Deephaven* (1877) first appeared, Jewett recalled the 1870s as 'just the time when people were beginning to come into the country for the summer in such great numbers', making it appropriate for the storyteller to try to acquaint town and country people so that they would be 'less suspicious of one another'.[66] It was fundamentally the same purpose as Mitford had displayed four decades earlier when in 1830 she edited a three-volume collection of *Stories of American Life* designed to 'show the Americans as they are; or rather to make them show themselves', something which apparently had not been achieved by the 'essentially European' Irving.[67] Mitford's selection from popular annuals and magazines encompassed both the citified and the essentially primitive or rural, and in calling attention to what could be learned about a foreign country by reading of its untutored habits, she was echoing comments made in Number 138 of *The Rambler*. There, on 13 July 1751, Dr Johnson noted that in cities the 'prevalence of fashion' among people anxious to create an impression had the effect of blurring distinctions, and he urged writers to venture into country regions.[68] If they did so, Johnson maintained, 'they might diversify their representations, and multiply their images, for in the country are original characters chiefly to be found'.[69] In America the vogue for topographical fiction with a strongly rural bias lasted well into the 1890s, when Howells was still able to claim that, 'we are an intensely decentralized people in our letters as well as in our politics . . . and there is no section or region without some writer emulous to report its life'.[70] It is to this line of writing that Jewett, who received great encouragement from Howells early in her career, belongs: in her series of sketches *The Country of the Pointed Firs* a small coastal town in Eastern Maine offered her a setting where she could emulate Harriet Beecher Stow, whose tale *The Pearl of Orr's Island* (1862), also set in Maine, she read as a child. She could write about 'people of rustic life just as they were'.[71]

So compelling is Jewett's evocation of life in Dunnet Landing that some critics want to call *The Country of the Pointed Firs* a novel, a stylistic precursor of such works as Dos Passos's *Manhattan Transfer*.[72] But this goes against the experience of reading the work, which retains the episodic quality of its first serial appearance in the *Atlantic Monthly*. Each chapter is a fresh beginning in a familiar place, reminiscent of the new date and altered weather at the start of each section in *Our Village*. Like Mitford, Jewett uses an unnamed female narrator to link her sketches, but with the difference that it is as an outsider, welcomed into, but not essentially part of, the community, that Jewett's narrator returns 'to find the unchanged shores of the pointed firs, the same quaintness of the village with its elaborate conventionalities; all that mixture of remoteness, and childish certainty of being the centre of civilization of which her affectionate dreams had told'.[73] Mention of the 'affectionate dreams' which have haunted the narrator since she first fell in love with the village establish a mood for the entire work, inviting the reader to share experiences which are real but dream-like. Sympathy and wonder are to be the appropriate responses, a measure of Jewett's allegiance to Flaubert, who provided her with the motto, 'Ce n'est pas de faire rire ni de faire pleurer, ni de vous mettre à fureur, mais d'agir à la façon de la nature, c'est à dire de faire rêver.'[74] But at the same time as promising the stability of 'unchanged shores', the narrator introduces a hint of irony which gives a special edge to her descriptions of the village and its inhabitants, with their 'childish certainty of being the centre of civilization'. The narrator's tone, gentle but alert, helps to shape each episode into something close to the modern conception of the short story, enlisting perceptiveness that is not straightforwardly visual or moral. Setting is not elaborated for its own sake, but in order to explain character and raise questions about human choice. The reflective cast of these sketches represents a definite change from Jewett's earlier method in *Deephaven*, where a moribund New England seaport was viewed by a pair of high-spirited young girls on holiday, the inclination being to mock, rather than sympathize with, the antiquated oddities assembled there.

Individual episodes are, in the Mitford manner, often built around visits and excursions, but for all its social activity and self-importance Dunnet Landing clearly represents 'a way of life gradually dying', maimed by national progress and at the best of times lived against a harsh background.[75] Although Jewett's fondness for landscape painting is evident in her loving descriptions of the dark tract of pointed firs and the vibrant autumn colours of swamp-maples, she shows too the poor soil and rocky ground; we see spruces and fir balsams competing with man, and never losing: 'I tell you those little trees means business!' declares the narrator's landlady Mrs Todd, forcing her to acknowledge 'a vigor of growth, a persistence and savagery about the sturdy little trees that put weak human nature at complete defiance'.[76] This conflict between man and nature makes any easy contrast between urban and country life foolish: the narrator is attuned to the 'hidden fire of enthusiasm' which New Englanders reveal only rarely, on 'high days and holidays', and she appreciates how different this is from 'those petty excitements of every day' that consume city-dwellers' energies; but she is also alive to other kinds of waste, closer at hand.[77] Watching Mrs Todd uncharacteristically blossom before an audience, she observes: 'I could see that sometimes when Mrs Todd had seemed limited and heavily domestic, she had simply grown sluggish for lack of proper surroundings. She was not so much reminiscent now as expectant . . .'[78] Love of place does not cloud the realization that in Mrs Todd's case 'a narrow set of circumstances had caged a fine able character and held it captive'.[79] Into her stories, Jewett incorporates a critique of nostalgia and passive acceptance of things as they are – the very attitudes which some people feel the short story in general encourages, and the regional story in particular enshrines.

During a period when, as Miss Jewett's younger contemporary Willa Cather observed, the literary fashion in America was for 'machine-made historical novels', and magazines were full of 'dreary dialect stories', *The Country of the Pointed Firs* demonstrated that the technique of creating intimacy between the reader and a small group of characters in a fixed setting need not be narrowing; large issues about human beings and the effects of their environments are raised.[80] Dunnet Landing is indisputably a small world: men are few, young people fewer still, and everyone is lonely. Many of them long bereaved, the characters are self-possessed; forthright but reticent;

169

hospitable in the best sense, generously surrendering self as well as possessions; formal without being unfeeling. They constitute a community of solitaries, typified by the old fisherman Mr Tilley, whose motto, 'I'd rather tough it out alone' expresses the prevailing view of life.[81] Jewett's presentation of a community where eccentricity is actually the norm does not, however, stay on the level of quaint portraiture. She combines her local observations of the New Englander's 'pettiest indifference to large things', especially during the lull between Independence and the Civil War, with a recognition that human loneliness is a permanent condition.[82] Harmony between historical comment and philosophical reflection is achieved through a style which allows Jewett to expand the significance of her portraiture while still maintaining the homely realism she is so good at. Characteristic of this is the moment when Mrs Todd, having talked with unusual intimacy about past emotions, walks on alone:

> There was something lonely and solitary about her great determined shape. She might have been Antigone alone on the Theban plain. It is not often given in the noisy world to come to the great places of grief and silence. An absolute, archaic grief possessed this countrywoman; she seemed like a renewal of some historic soul with her sorrows and the remoteness of a daily life busied with rustic simplicities and the scents of primeval herbs.[83]

Given the context, the allusion to Greek tragedy is daring, though perhaps it is rather too anxiously followed up by the narrator's generalization about 'the noisy world'. The natural cadencing of the final sentence does, however, create an individual quality of voice which successfully dignifies the humble figure; Mrs Todd ceases to be just an ageing woman renowned for her skilful growing, collecting, and dispensing of herbs – though because of insistence on the prosaic dailiness of these activities she remains that too.

Passages like this are characteristic of Jewett's method, and also, in broader terms, of a great deal of short-storywriting. Human gesture and feeling are placed in a universal perspective, inviting reflection on forces that are ultimately mysterious. The form of the short story favours the principle of revealing the strange in the actual, an illumination which frequently depends on detaching the seer from the seen. In later writers, style and narrative impersonality are the means chiefly used to obtain the aesthetic distance needed to convey the ordinary and the marvellous at the same instant; Sarah Orne Jewett's devices are comparatively simple ones, somewhat didactic in flavour yet capable of fusing setting and character into wholeness, as for example when the author looks down on the village the day she is leaving, and glimpses Mrs Todd for the last time:

> At such a distance one can feel the large, positive qualities that control a character. Close at hand, Mrs Todd seemed able and warm-

hearted and quite absorbed in her bustling industries, but her distant figure looked mateless and appealing, with something about it that was strangely self-possessed and mysterious. Now and then she stooped to pick something, – it might have been her favorite pennyroyal, – and at last I lost sight of her as she slowly crossed an open space on one of the higher points of land, and disappeared again behind a clump of juniper and the pointed firs.[84]

At a distance, both figure and landscape take on significance that is unobtrusively symbolic, while the poignant mood of loss characteristic of the entire work is prolonged. The implication is that although Mrs Todd's life continues in unchanging obscurity, its essential grandeur has been revealed to the narrator at the moment of departing for city life again. The pressure towards symbolism is gentle and unselfconscious, bearing out Jewett's advice to an aspiring writer; simplify, write what you know, and above all 'Don't write a "story" but just *tell the thing*!'[85] She herself had learned from European examples the value of 'just telling the thing'; on her slant-top desk she kept pinned another Flaubert maxim, 'Écrire la vie ordinaire comme on écrit l'histoire.'[86] Her openness to foreign influences was clearly beneficial, and in her turn she was recognized by writers working outside America, notably Henry James, who appreciated her 'sense for the finest kind of truthful rendering, the sober and tender note, the temperately touched, whether in the ironic or the pathetic'.[87] Yet while praising the 'rare personal' quality of Jewett's work, James also registered the 'minor compass' of her fiction, and hinted at the disadvantages of relying so much on touch and tone in any kind of storytelling.[88] The objection that her gift for exact description restricted Jewett's inventiveness was made more bluntly by Edward Garnett: 'She is receptive but not constructive in her talent'.[89] It is a comment that applies to many short-story-writers who depend on mood to supply unity. Although not necessarily a damaging admission, it is true that unity in *The Country of the Pointed Firs* comes from its bittersweet mood: any demand for plot is soon overwhelmed by interest in the feel of life in nineteenth-century Maine, its recluses, and the social rituals which bring solace without denying loneliness. Although what were brief moods of not unpleasant melancholy in Mitford's *Our Village* have darkened into a more consistently sombre impression of human isolation, *The Country of the Pointed Firs* is similar in confining narrative to inset stories, most of which arouse the narrator's moral sympathies by recapitulating experiences from the distant past. Adding one exemplary sketch to another while keeping the setting constant allows Jewett to accentuate mood, a purpose for which loose structure has definite advantages: the reader can share the narrator's observations without having to keep track of a taut story-line. The attractions of this arrangement are evident from Jewett's choice of 'formlessness' when she wrote her most mature work, but the question remains whether comparable unity can be achieved in the single short story, where, in order to play a significant part in the total impact, setting must be rapidly established and its atmosphere sustained without the aid of repetition. A selection of stories written by Jewett in the 1880s and 1890s will demonstrate a variety of uses made of location in pieces which differ from the *Pointed Firs* sketches in several ways, but principally in their self-containment, and in their increasingly oblique use of setting.

'A White Heron' (1886), Jewett's best known and most anthologized single story, uses landscape in a far more symbolic way than anything to be found in *The Country of the Pointed Firs*. Dark woodland (referred to at one point as 'this New England wilderness') is the setting for this story about a sensitive nine-year-old girl who has been brought to live with her grandmother on a lonely farmstead, and whose love of her new surroundings makes her feel 'as if she had never been alive at all before she came to live at the farm'. Sylvia perceives the difference between sickness and health, echoing the venerable distinction between town and country: 'She thought often with wistful compassion of a wretched geranium that belonged to a town neighbour'.Sylvia quickly gets to know the countryside so well that her grandmother can boast, 'There aint a foot o' ground she don't know her way over, and the wild creetur's count her one o' themselves.' So Sylvia seems the ideal person to guide a young ornithologist who comes looking for a white heron. But although the inducements are strong (the jack-knife she is given; a ten dollar reward promised her, and, most tempting of all, the approval she would win from this attractive stranger who stirs 'the woman's heart asleep in the child') Sylvia finds that she cannot betray the lovely bird into the collector's hands. Paradoxically, the crucial action in this story is a silence; when the splendid moment arrives for her to tell where the heron nests, Sylvia says nothing.

Described straightforwardly as a conflict between love of nature and loyalty to an admired fellow-being, the story's theme will seem simple enough. But such an account underestimates the wide suggestiveness achieved by Jewett's elaboration of her initial setting and her arrangement of specific landscape features into patterns, sometimes spatial, at other times composed mainly of colours, but always expressing that Sylvia's real choice lies between different outlooks on the whole of life. Two kinds of approach to the natural world are examined: the instinctual, which is receptive to the shifting boundaries of sense experience, and the scientific, which deals in specimens like the young hunter's trophies, 'put in cases, dozens and dozens of them'. What is 'rare' to the ornithologist is 'strange' to the girl's romantic vision, a contrast that is delicately conveyed through a transition from dialogue to inner thought. The ornithologist describes the heron as 'a queer tall white bird', identifiable by its soft feathers, long thin legs, and characteristic nesting habits, while to Sylvia it is part of a mysterious landscape which mingles danger and loveliness, and which she is seeing in her mind's eye as she listens to the young man, her outward attention apparently concentrated on a hop-toad:

> She knew that strange white bird, and had once stolen softly near where it stood in some bright green swamp grass, away over at the other side of the woods. There was an open place where the sunshine always seemed strangely yellow and hot, where tall, nodding rushes grew, and her grandmother had warned her that she might sink in the soft black mud underneath and never be heard of more. Not far beyond were the salt marshes and beyond those were the sea, the sea which Sylvia wondered and dreamed about, but never had looked upon, though its great voice could often be heard above the noise of the woods on stormy nights.

By carefully selecting details, particularly of strong colour, and then linking the 'strange white bird' with the unknown sea, Jewett establishes, within the idiom of the child's thoughts, associations which are essential to the story's climax. This comes when Sylvia goes out alone before dawn, fully intending to locate the heron's nest for the young hunter. She climbs a huge pine-tree, 'the last of its generation' to survive from the ancient forests and 'a landmark for sea and shore miles and miles away'. The author's comparison between this stately tree and 'a great main mast to the voyaging earth' resumes the earlier merging of land and sea in Sylvia's thoughts, and it is appropriate that from the giddy height of the tree-top she should scan a 'sea of green branches' for the heron's nesting-place. Against the visual uniformity evoked by repeating the word 'green' several times, the sudden appearance of the heron, at first a mere 'white spot like a floating feather', then rising and sweeping gloriously past the landmark pine to settle briefly near the child, occurs as a stupendous event, representative of absolute freedom. The moment is decisive for Sylvia: admitted now to the secret of 'the wild, light, slender bird that floats and wavers and goes back like an arrow presently to his home in the green world beneath' she cannot surrender its beauty to the hunter. But nor is she conscious of what makes her choose to sacrifice her felt desire to win treasures that come only from 'the great world' outside her – and all 'for a bird's sake'.

As in so many other short stories, the experience offered in 'A White Heron' is a moment of revelation, visual in quality but moral in its implications. The beauty of the morning, shared with the solitary heron, compels Sylvia to reject the money that would in fact help alleviate her grandmother's poverty. The full significance of what happens in the story is not accessible to the child protagonist, but is left to the reader's understanding. To convey the story's meaning, Jewett is clearly drawing on traditional colour symbolism, white denoting purity and therefore inviting a parallel between the heron and the young girl, and greenness summarizing the natural world and recalling the pastoral tradition in literature. But because equal attention is given to naturalistic details, including the dry twigs that scratch the child's arms and legs 'like angry talons' as she climbs the tall pine-tree, and the 'shouting cat-birds' which disturb the heron, the story never becomes drily schematic.

Nevertheless, compared with the informality of *The Country of the Pointed Firs*, 'A White Heron' reads self-consciously, leaving an impression of artificiality. The point of view is mainly Sylvia's own, but the language is very much that of an adult author who has analysed what remains inexplicable to the child: to this author belong the alternations between past and present tenses, the praise of Sylvia's heroic tree-climbing efforts, and, rather to the story's detriment, a tendency to underline heavily what has already been dramatized. The ending in particular displays lack of confidence in the reader's ability to interpret the story unassisted; the broad issues of freedom, purity and innocence which have been opened up are suddenly reduced and oversimplified, and Jewett's style collapses into lifeless rhetoric and sentimental apostrophe: 'Were the birds better friends than their hunter might have been? Who can tell? Whatever treasures were lost to her, woodlands and summertime, remember! Bring your gifts and graces and tell your secrets to this lonely country child!'[90] From this it appears that while the brevity of 'A White Heron' made the thematic integrity and richness of the story possible, with setting assimilated into overall meaning, compression also encouraged Jewett to indulge a tendency towards didacticism and decorative writing that is directly at odds with her greatest strengths as a storywriter.

The main flaw of 'A White Heron' is its slightly overwritten quality. This arises from Jewett's 'poetic' personification of nature in order to link Sylvia morally and spiritually to her surroundings: it is not a fault in most Jewett stories. Usually, the relationship between Jewett characters and their environment is earthier, more amenable to comic treatment, and expressive of social as well as moral attitudes. The opening of 'The Only Rose' (1895) is typical, summoning up place and person simultaneously without departing from matter-of-fact statement: 'Just where the village abruptly ended, and the green mowing fields began, stood Mrs Bickford's house, looking down the road with all its windows, and topped by two prim chimneys that stood up like ears.' It is the perfect spot for gossipy intimacy; and that is what moves this and several other Jewett stories forward. The neighbourly visit is possibly her favourite story-situation: the social niceties of visiting provide the entire subject of a story much admired by Kipling, 'The Guests of Mrs Timms' (1895), where two ladies have their hopes of a cordial welcome dashed when they call unannounced; 'Aunt Cynthy Dallett' (1899) contains an inset narrative about a similarly cheerless, but impeccably polite, visit during which a hostess takes genteel revenge on an uninvited guest by leaving her alone in the cold parlour while an elaborate tea is prepared; and hospitality also provides a theme in 'Miss Tempy's Watchers' (1888), in which two women keep vigil in Miss Tempy's kitchen on the eve of her funeral and enjoy her quince preserve exactly as if she had asked them to tea, not to watch over her dead body.

Action is neatly tailored to situation in all of these stories, but the fit is especially graceful in 'The Only Rose', the first section of which is devoted to a conversation between Mrs Bickford and her neighbour Miss Pendexter, both elderly but enjoying very different financial and social positions; and, as the story gradually discloses, with totally divergent personal histories. While the women sit talking in her kitchen, Mrs Bickford is sorting a pile of flowers into three heaps, flowers not of her own growing since any plant of hers manages only the rare bloom under her 'unsympathetic but conscientious care'. Detecting 'unusual signs of emotion' in her normally reticent friend, Miss Pendexter suddenly guesses that the three bouquets are connected with Mrs Bickford's 'bereavement of three husbands', a surmise that piques her 'easily roused curiosity' until the widow discloses plans to visit the burying-ground. From this point on, the conversation focuses on the dilemma facing Mrs Bickford: one solitary rose has managed to survive her attentions, yet there are three graves it might be placed on; three dead husbands – presumably they too have received 'unsympathetic but conscientious care' – and nothing, it seems, to choose between them. 'I respected 'em all', declares Mrs Bickford, 'I don't know but what I think on one of 'em 'most as much as I do of the other.'

The situation is comic, though it strikes the women with the force of 'a great emergency' before which they are powerless. Mrs Bickford's determination to be impartial leads her into recollection of each husband in turn, revealing how very different they really were: the most recent was a successful business man who 'done everything by rule an' measure' and left plenty of wealth behind him; before him, Mr Wallis, a failed inventor who was handsome, excellent company, but 'a dreadful notional man'; and her first love Albert, 'just the kind of healthy young man that goes right off if they get a fever'. The problem of who should have the rose strikes the widow as insoluble: gratitude says it ought to go to Mr Bickford; a degree of remorse for opposing Mr Wallis's dreamy projects makes him the strongest candidate, while by rights of uncomplicated sentiment, the rose belongs to Albert. By the next morning, when the second section of the story opens, the rose has 'ceased to be merely a flower' and become 'a definite symbol of personal choice'; only at the last minute is the situation resolved and a decision side-stepped when Mrs Bickford's nephew, unaware of all this agonizing, takes the stray rose to give to his lover. The outcome satisfies the old woman's nostalgia, identifying her memories of Albert with her hopes for her nephew, and making the story's ending into a celebration of young love's triumph over death. No loose strands are left, and if anything, the story seems finally too tidy, forcing the reader to stand back and admire Jewett's workmanship.

In fact, it is when the reader is an eavesdropper on the apparently aimless conversation in the first section that the story works best. By its very nature, the countrywomen's talk, rendered here in speech forms that combine rural dialect and genteel mannerisms, introduces looseness and profusion into the tight framework of the story. The blend of tautness and spontaneity is always a satisfying one in short fiction, and it occurs frequently in Jewett's fiction. In 'The Courting of Sister Wisby' (1888), for example, gossipy anecdote is embedded in a mass of irrelevant circumstantial detail; names, places, lines of kinship and so on, all contribute to an effect that is authentically full yet at the same time highly allusive. The technique is realistic, but often the aim is ironic, as it is in 'The Only Rose', where Jewett shows a wonderful capacity to reveal undercurrents of rivalry and envy beneath the chatter of mutually sympathetic friends. Setting plays an important place in all this: when, for example, Miss Pendexter passes the parlour with its shut blinds, and the sitting-room (also protected from the light) before entering Mrs Bickford's kitchen, she can't help wishing that 'somebody beside the owner might have the pleasure of living in and using so good and pleasant a house'; the thought captures the spinster's own situation and her attitudes towards housekeeping, at the same time as indicating that 'pleasure' counts for little with Mrs Bickford. And when Mrs Bickford is complaining that flowers indoors give her a headache, and are in any case a bother to arrange, Miss Pendexter's response manages to be not exactly a reproach, but certainly a reminder of her own comparative poverty. There are echoes of Miss Mitford too: '"A garden's a sight o' care, but I don't begrudge none o' the care I give to mine. I have to scant the flowers so's to make room for the pole beans . . . A few flowers gives me just as much pleasure as more would", she added. "You get acquainted with things when you've only got one or two roots."' Details natural to the setting contribute to the impression that the conversation is moving forward by tacit negotiations and harmless suppressions: Miss Pendexter smiles to herself and says nothing when Mrs Bickford pronounces that of course she can't stand the morning sun, but gesture says everything when the spinster moves from her chair at the window, out of the hot sun on her back, 'for Mrs Bickford always kept the curtains rolled high up out of the way, for fear of fading and dust'.

The domestic setting of the story makes it entirely acceptable that only two people are involved, and this in turn allows simple comparisons and contrasts to be highlighted. In Jewett's stories the pairing is usually a capable 'woman of property' with plenty, possibly too much, common sense, and a gallant spinster making the best of limited means. In one instance, 'Miss Tempy's Watchers', it is openly suggested that the dead woman chose prosperous Mrs Crowe and humble Miss Binson as 'watchers' so that the rich might learn to understand the poor. But Jewett does not combine characters with the intention of drawing stark distinctions of class. Rather, she shows how within the close communities depicted in her stories, differences of attitude and social standing are preserved while being somehow absorbed into the fabric of intimacy. Confidential but decorous talk is what works this magic, and in 'The Only Rose' Jewett creates a minor drama of silences and cues, the tension of which coexists with the garrulity of two old women. Detecting 'an overburdening sense of the inexpressible' in her neighbour, Miss Pendexter has to find a way of drawing her out without trespassing on privacy; she must help the other woman past a lull with well-timed questions. On the surface, Mrs Bickford is simply at a loss with her assortment of flowers, but Miss Pendexter sees that really she is signalling for help:

> She glanced out of the window; then gave Miss Pendexter a long expressive look. 'I expect you're going to carry 'em over to the burying ground?' 'Yes 'm', said the hostess, now well started in conversation and in quite her every-day manner.

A little later, another question – 'The rose? Why, are you goin' to pick that too?' – prompts Mrs Bickford to admit what is troubling her, and from this arises a shared moment of understated affection:

> 'Why, 't is difficult for you, 'aint it?' responded Miss Pendexter. 'I don't know's I can offer advice.' 'No, I s'pose not', answered her friend slowly, with a shadow of disappointment coming over her calm face. 'I feel sure you would if you could, Abby.'

Confidences can now proceed, and from this point Mrs Bickford's memories flow with such momentum that at one stage she has to pause, seeming 'to suppress with difficulty a desire to speak even more freely'.

Miss Pendexter has to keep nudging her friend back to the main topic, curtailing self-pitying recollections of the hard times that followed unworldly Mr Wallis's death, and offering another cue: '"Mr Bickford was a very personable man", she hastened to say, the con-

177

fidences were so intimate and interesting.'⁹¹ Her desire coincides with the reader's: everyone wants a good story, the more intimate the better, and Miss Jewett's characters have fine tactics for getting precisely that. Sometimes a lot of patience is required, as for example in 'The Courting of Sister Wisby'; there, lengthy chatter precedes Mrs Goodsoe's confidential narrative, and when she eventually does reach it, the outer narrator is keen to keep her to the subject: '"I have a dim recollection of there being something strange about the marriage", I suggested, after a pause, which began to appear dangerous. I was so much afraid the subject would be changed. "I can tell you all about it", I was quickly answered.'⁹² The delight of being the one who can 'tell all about it' to a receptive audience invariably prevails, and Jewett catches its tones exactly as Mrs Goodsoe responds to the hint.

In the 'The Only Rose' more courage is needed to push narrative further into the most interesting areas; Miss Pendexter is brave when she takes it upon herself to mention Mrs Bickford's first husband. Here, too, however, the widow obliges with a spate of inconsequential details and even some insight into her ungenerous failure to appreciate Albert's glorious singing voice. But self-justification is too ingrained a habit, and, as emotion rises, attention is diverted to practical matters: '"I must hurry now 'an put these in water", she said, in a matter-of-fact tone. Little Miss Pendexter was so quiet and sympathetic that her hostess felt no more embarrassed than if she had been talking only to herself.' The irony is plain. This has in fact been a monologue.

Early in the story, Mrs Bickford's narrowness is suggested by the straight path leading to her kitchen window, where she would invariably be found sitting, 'unless she were solemnly stepping about, prolonging the stern duties of her housekeeping'. And throughout her reminiscences she unwittingly reveals her closed, selfish nature. But egotism only becomes fully apparent when Miss Pendexter, warmed by the confidential atmosphere, offers her own secret in exchange. Jewett's skilful manipulation of tone turns a simple piece of dialogue into a collision of attitudes, the realist's against the romantic's:

'I never was married myself, Mis' Bickford, because it wa'n't so that I could have the one I liked.'
'I suppose he ain't living, then? Why, I wa'n't never aware you had met with a disappointment, Abby', said Mrs Bickford instantly. None of her neighbours had ever suspected little Miss Pendexter of a romance. 'Yes'm, he's livin', replied Miss Pendexter humbly. 'No'm, I never have heard that he died.'
'I want to know!' exclaimed the woman of experience. 'Well, I'll tell you this, Abby: you may have regretted your lot, and felt lonesome and hardshipped, but they all have their faults, and a single woman's got her liberty, if she ain't got other blessin's.'

' 'T wouldn't have been my choice to live alone', said Abby, meeker than before 'I feel very thankful for my blessin's, all the same. You've always been a kind neighbour, Mis' Bickford.'

The widow does not really 'want to know' Abby's sorrows, which are undoubtedly greater than anything undergone by 'the woman of experience', and all the sadder for not conforming with conventional definitions of bereavement. Patronized by neighbours who would never suspect her of a romance, her grief can be brushed aside with a cliché about the satisfactions of staying single, and although invited 'with unusual cordiality' to stay for tea, she knows Mrs Bickford's 'dislike for unexpected company' well enough to understand that she is meant to leave now, her confidences undisclosed, if not actually rebuffed. The story could well have ended with her departure, the sun low and the green fields stretching away 'into the misty distance', and Abby glancing up at the rose, thinking, 'It seemed to belong most to Albert, but she had not liked to say so.'[93] What is left in the reader's mind as this first section closes is an awareness that Miss Pendexter has a story which remains untold, a story of romantic commitment at odds with the conventionality represented by Mrs Bickford, whose money and marriages give her social standing – and consequently the power to humble the spinster into silence. The tantalizing glimpse we have into Miss Pendexter's secret life creates ambiguities by questioning further the grounds of Mrs Bickford's determination to reach an impartial decision about the rose. It also complicates the story formally, because it points to the impossibility of justice in the storyteller's art; for every story that does get told, there is another that stays hidden.

Close attention has been given to 'The Only Rose' as a fine instance of a story which immobilizes its characters in a simple setting. Location is firmly established at the outset, and then referred to only allusively when dialogue is insufficient to express what is going on between the characters. Another reason for studying this type of story very carefully is that Jewett's techniques and preoccupations reappear, often more boldly and disturbingly, in many of Kipling's Sussex stories. There are obvious similarities between the way Kipling personifies the brook in 'Friendly Brook' (1917), making it a crucial character in the story, and Jewett's use of the stream's sounds in 'Miss Tempy's Watchers' to punctuate the rhythm of confidences and silences that carries the two women through to morning, when 'the brook's voice was not nearly so loud as it had been in the midnight darkness'.[94] At the end of Kipling's story, where the brook plays a more central part narratively and thematically, the same image of nature's benign volubility occurs: 'The Brook had changed her note again. It sounded as though she were mumbling something soft.'[95] Perhaps the resemblance is unsurprising, given the rural settings of both stories, and the ancient lineage of ideas about river gods, but it is worth noting that while he was living in Vermont, Kipling read Jewett's *The Life of Nancy* – the volume of stories which included 'The Only Rose' – and described her work as, 'immense – it is the very life.'[96]

It is in Kipling's stories which aim to capture 'the very life' of rural communities that a case for Jewett's direct influence here seems more than tenuous. When 'The Wish House' (1926), for example, is read alongside 'The Only Rose', striking similarities emerge, though these are masked by the later writer's greater expertise in handling structure and avoiding sentimentality. Interpretations of 'The Wish House' usually concentrate on its supernatural aspects, and understandably so; the validity of Grace Ashcroft's belief that she has been given the suprahuman power to take all her lover's suffering upon herself is the crux of the story. Less attention is given to the introductory frame which Kipling supplies for Mrs Ashcroft's frank but essentially mysterious account, perhaps because here he seems to be merely adopting a conventional method of establishing a background of normality against which the supernatural will seem all the more startling. The frame, however, is more important than this: it enriches the overall complexity of the story by binding theme and setting so closely that intimacy becomes both topic and manner, involving the reader and yet simultaneously offering distancing ironies like those found in 'The Only Rose'.

For 'The Wish House' Kipling chooses the simple plot device so favoured by Sarah Orne Jewett: he brings two rural characters together as hostess and guest and restricts narrative time to the duration of a visit: time is then extended backwards by the retrospective cast of the women's conversation. The visit is not casual; Mrs Fettley has travelled thirty miles to see Mrs Ashcroft, her friend since childhood, and by the end of the story it is evident that the two women do not expect to meet again. As in the Jewett story, the character of the hostess, who is to dominate the action, is established first, though Kipling does this much more rapidly, foregoing description and compressing information about Grace Ashcroft into a single sentence. The facts given emphasis are that Mrs Ashcroft is 'an elderly, experienced, and pensioned cook', able to use standard English for formal callers like the Church Visitor who has just left as the story opens. In contrast, 'ancient Sussex' dialect is the speech appropriate for friends on first-name terms, as Liz Fettley and Grace Ashcroft are, a privilege which is not shared by the omniscient author, who consistently refers to the women by their married titles.

As in 'The Only Rose', conversation begins without a specific aim: 'Much was to be said, and many ends, loose since last time, to be ravelled up on both sides, before Mrs Fettley, with her bag of quilt-patches, took the couch beneath the window commanding the garden, and the football ground in the valley below.' With splendid economy, Kipling has set the quiet room apart from everything that lies outside; inside the room all is peaceful, the characters immobile except for the handwork which, as in so many Jewett stories, provides a gentle accompaniment to talk. It is in fact from the outer world that the conversation begins its gradual movement inwards to deeply personal concerns, touching first on easy topics – Mrs Fettley's discomfort on the bus after it emptied for the football match, leaving her no one 'to cushion agin'; the respective merits of the women's Church Visitors (one not gossipy enough, the other 'full o' words an' pity' but a poor listener, and herself food for scandal), and the ingratitude of the young who neglect work for leisure. An atmosphere of likemindedness is established, particularly by the shared disapproval of idleness, which is reminiscent of the unity with which Miss Pendexter and Mrs Bickford, in 'The Only Rose', scorned lazy women who spring-clean one room at the beginning of March, brag of it to everyone else's shame, and then never let on when (if ever) they finish the job.

Kipling enhances the calm atmosphere inside the cottage by counterpointing dialogue with the confused sounds of a modern Saturday afternoon going on outside: two heavy buses taking people to the football match make the cottage 'tremble'; another, bound for the county's capital, 'fumes' behind them, and from the crowded pubs yet another vehicle backs out, adding to the congested 'stream of through pleasure-traffic'. Sealed off from this bustling activity, the two women, whose lives have included little enough leisure-time, can disclose secrets to one another, speaking with an openness denied them in their outer spheres: when Mrs Ashcroft observes that her friend is 'as free-tongued as ever', Mrs Fettley replies, 'Only when I'm with you. Otherwhiles, I'm Granny – three times over.' And an exploited granny at that, constantly badgered for money, and in this respect like Miss Binson in Jewett's 'Miss Tempy's Watchers'.

Kipling uses the women's desultory chatter about their grandchildren to edge them towards the real topic of his story, remembered pleasures beside which organized delights like football matches or village whist drives look tame and contemptibly public. Youthful modernity interrupts briefly when Mrs Ashcroft's grandson dashes in and snatches the picnic-basket she has been lining, and from this moment on, questions, hints and evasions push the talk into deeper and deeper intimacy. Mrs Fettley spots the grandson's resemblance to Jim Batten, whose wife once went for Mrs Ashcroft with a hay-fork, and she promptly begins to investigate:

'Now 'oo the dooce do he remind me of, all of a sudden?'
'They must look arter theirselves – 'same as we did.' Mrs Ashcroft began to set out the tea.

181

'No denyin' *you* could, Gracie', said Mrs Fettley.

'What's in your head now?'

'Dunno . . . But it come over me sudden-like – about dat woman from Rye – I've slipped the name – Barnsley, wadn't it?'

'Batten – Polly Batten, you're thinking of.'

The moves are calculated according to the conventions of gossip, but these are no conventionally sweet grannies but women of passion whose pleasures have been seized illicitly with masterful men expected to 'take all and give naught'. Mrs Ashcroft, like Jewett's Mrs Bickford, carries flowers to her husband's grave, but purely 'for the look o' the thing'.

Each woman has her memories to recount, but Kipling astutely postpones the central story of Grace's extraordinary sacrifice until all of the social rituals have been completed: a meal of stewed tea, bitter as leather, and a cold boiled pig's tail elicits 'all the proper compliments' from the guest. Out of the ordinariness of this scene (where discussing indigestion is as proper as paying compliments) emerges the information that Mrs Ashcroft is dying. But as soon as Kipling delivers this shock, he diverts attention to Mrs Fettley: 'you've *your* back-lookin's too', her friend reminds her, offering a cue which Kipling emphasizes by halting his characters and positioning them against the contrasting scene outside: 'Mrs Fettley stared, with jaw half-dropped, at the grocer's bright calendar on the wall. The cottage shook again to the roar of the motor-traffic, and the football-ground below the garden roared almost as loudly; for the village was well set to its Saturday leisure.' The moment recalls pauses in 'The Only Rose' where talk must either cease or go boldly into private territory, but Kipling makes the crisis more portentous still by breaking the eavesdropping process at this point, something never attempted by Sarah Orne Jewett. The effect is similar to an unexpected cut in a film: the image of Mrs Fettley 'with jaw half-dropped' is held, and then, instead of leading to speech, it is instantly replaced by a picture of her wiping her eyes and concluding a story which, like Miss Pendexter's in 'The Only Rose', we will never hear and can only infer. For Kipling's purposes, it is enough to know that, again like Abby Pendexter, Mrs Fettley has endured an ordeal of love concealed. Admittedly, Mrs Fettley's passion has been requited in the past, but the pain of not being able to display it publicly now by visiting the dead lover's grave is identical to Abby's hidden suffering. Furthermore, in both stories the sole witness to these confidences makes a brisk response; Mrs Ashcroft resembles Jewett's widow in the facility with which she offers consolation: 'But you've 'ad your satisfactions? . . . Then you've naught to cast-up about. 'Nother cup o' tea?'

Once again Kipling cuts then resumes, using objective description to register changes of light and air as the sun, previously filtering through the geraniums on the window-sill, descends, creating a chill against which the two elderly women close the kitchen door; it is a reminder that, however fiery their remembered love affairs, they are now old and frail. As a prelude to confessions, this time Mrs Ashcroft's, this return to setting parallels the earlier one, but with the important difference that now it is nature, not men and machines, which produces noise, discordant but curiously appropriate to tales of sexual possessiveness and rivalry: 'A couple of jays squealed and skirmished through the undraped apple-tree in the garden.' Located anew in the scene, the reader is given a thread of conversation which teasingly conveys the fictional listener's excitement: '"Well I never! But what did your 'usband say to that?" Mrs Fettley asked.' Through Mrs Fettley the reader is to benefit from the candour she showed in telling her friend whatever it was Kipling omitted: the age-old logic of gossip, according to which one good confidence deserves another, turns Grace Ashcroft's confession of her bargain with a supernatural Token into the fulfilment of another kind of bargain: 'I'm payin' ye for what you told me just now', she says, unconsciously indicating the theme of her narrative – 'payment' or recompense for suffering.

More than two-thirds of 'The Wish House' is devoted to conveying this theme through Mrs Ashcroft's weird account of how she gained and controlled the power to suffer all of her lover's pains and illnesses for him. Kipling's proportioning of the story as a whole is reflected by the subsidiary role now taken by Mrs Fettley, whose interjections resemble Abby Pendexter's as tactics for keeping the confidences flowing. There is the same concern for circumstantial thoroughness as in the Jewett story: when, for example, Mrs Ashcroft dates her return to London as 'the year you shifted to Portsmouth', she must be put right ('"Cosham"', Mrs Fettley corrected'); and irrelevant to us or not, it matters to the teller that it was on 'The fourth – no, the fifth day, Wednesday that she saw 'Arry again.

Like Mrs Bickford's reminiscences in 'The Only Rose', Mrs Ashcroft's narrative is virtually a monologue, though her listener's social equality and sexual knowingness make her quicker than Abby Pendexter to anticipate and direct the drift of memories. Astutely, she deflates Mrs Ashcroft's musing – 'We've only a backwent view of our proceedin's' – with a sharp question, 'Oo was it?' She knows there must be a man somewhere in the story, and having waited until now to learn secrets unguessed at all these years, she has little patience with philosophizing. Mrs Fettley's probing questions (described at one point as merciless) are alternated with various indications of how she reacts to Grace's disclosures: atmosphere is intensified or relaxed simply by varying the words 'asked' and 'said' to 'demanded', 'insisted', 'gasped', 'clucked sympathetically', and many others, the most eloquent being reserved for the crucial question about Grace's decision to suffer for 'Arry: ' "But what did *you* get out of it, Gra'?" Mrs Fettley almost wailed.' The cadencing could almost be Henry James's.

Largely because Kipling has given 'The Wish House' such a definite setting in the early part of the story, he can at this stage dispense entirely with allusions to the cottage kitchen, concentrating instead on dialogue. Action becomes almost completely verbal, the only noticeable physical movement being the listener's compassionate stretching of one arm across the table to finger the speaker's sleeve, a gesture that is not 'permitted' by Grace until her passion reaches an unbearable peak. So totally is everything outside forgotten, that the Nurse's arrival at the end of the story has the force of a violent intrusion. One of the young generation to whom picnics and Institute dances represent pleasure enough, the Nurse is perfectly unaware of the irony in her glib remark, 'When old ladies get together they talk a deal too much, I've noticed'. Her patronizing attitude displays a stereotyped outlook of precisely the sort Kipling has been undermining throughout 'The Wish House'. But that is not to say that he upholds the old women's superstitious interpretation of events either; Grace's illness, after all, could be explained, though not exalted, in strictly pathological terms. While Mrs Fettley's quick sympathies allow the word 'cancer' to remain unspoken amidst such a profusion of words, her literal-mindedness deters easy acceptance of Grace's certainty that she has kept 'Arry alive by regulating her wound exactly as she would her kitchen range. At times, Mrs Fettley's obtuseness is comic, cutting across her friend's dramatic flights:

> '. . . Then I fussed apiece with the child, to force him past me, like.
> So 'e 'ad to come past. 'E just says "Good evenin'"', and goes on.
> tryin' to pull 'isself together.'
> 'Drunk, was he?' Mrs Fettley asked.
> 'Never! S'runk and wizen; 'is clothes 'angin on 'im like bags . . .'

Elsewhere Mrs Fettley is more cautious, especially when she challenges Grace's convictions: 'But – just for de sake o' sayin' somethin' – 'spose 'Arry *did* get married?' The question is a pertinent one which calls attention to the precariousness of Mrs Ashcroft's theory that 'Arry will belong to no one sexually while he is hers spiritually. The old woman's faith in the efficacy of her self-inflicted agonies is certainly not vindicated by Kipling in any simple way; he does not offer a choice between naturalistic or supernatural interpretations, preferring ambiguities which recall James in 'The Turn of the Screw'. Positive value is clearly meant to be seen in Grace Ashcroft's creation of a personal religion to assuage the emotional pain caused by 'Arry's rejection of her (an outcome she foresees as soon as he repays the money she has spent on him); her ability to make a virtue out of the fated intermingling of love and suffering does give her a kind of secular 'grace'. But Kipling also indicates, as Jewett had done, that ambiguities complicate such lonely determinations; the need to be justified in lonely absolutism can turn intimate confidences into desperate bids for reassurance, unmindful of the confidante's own needs. Without diminishing sympathy for his major character, Kipling uses his minor figure Mrs Fettley in the same way as Jewett used Abby Pendexter to suggest that insensitivity is the counterpart of openness in Mrs Bickford's self-justifications. Mrs Fettley asks her friend how long she expects to live, and when told, 'if I don't set eyes on ye 'fore next hoppin' this'll be good-bye Liz', she reveals fears that by then she will need a dog to lead her, 'For de chillern, dey won't trouble, an' – O' Gra'! – I'm blindin' up – I'm blindin' up!' Mrs Ashcroft's response is chillingly matter-of-fact, veering away from the emotion in Mrs Fettley's outburst and back to her own obsession: 'Oh, *dat* was why you didn't more'n finger with your quilt-patches all this while! I was wonderin' . . . But the pain *do* count, don't ye think, Liz? The pain *do* count to keep 'Arry – where I want 'im. Say it can't be wasted, like.' It is hard to decide which of the two women deserves the most compassion at this moment, but there is at least the ironic possibility that Mrs Fettley's reply, 'I'm sure of it – sure of it, dearie. You'll 'ave your reward', is in its way as selfless as Grace's sacrifice for 'Arry, who is to stay unconsciously 'where she wants 'im'.

Like 'The Only Rose', Kipling's 'The Wish House' conveys a sense that the intimacy assumed and reinforced by the setting is finally limited by the human egotism which makes confessional conversations interesting in the first place. The paradox touches the reader who is invited into congenial surroundings, permitted to share fictional characters' secrets, but simultaneously reminded that the human beings so candidly displayed are also performers to one another, their words and actions concealing motives, perhaps even from themselves. Kipling takes ironies and ambivalences much farther than Sarah Orne Jewett, and this is in keeping with his greater structural audacity and his avoidance of sentimentality. Where Jewett goes on to supply a resolution to Mrs Bickford's dilemma, ending the story with the old woman's words about her first husband ('the flower he first give me was a rose') Kipling finishes a story which has been full of direct speech by substituting gesture for words. Having met Grace's insistence that she look at the cancerous wound while it is being dressed, Mrs Fettley answers the urgently reiterated question, 'It *do* count, don't it – de pain?' by kissing 'the lips that still kept trace of their original moulding', avoiding the explicit, and as it were blessing with *caritas* a mouth shaped for passion as well as for truth-telling.[97] Mrs Fettley's own story remains untold: the cocky formula Kipling scattered throughout *Plain Tales* – 'That's another story' – has been transformed into a mature acknowledgement of every short story's incompleteness.

Throughout his mature fiction, Kipling employs similar methods of indirection, but although his use of setting in his later stories is far more allusive than anything to be found among the garish, densely-peopled landscapes of his Indian tales, the principle of showing characters in transit remains constant. In 'The Wish House', the journey is backwards in memory for the two old women, and as we follow them, an extra dimension is added – profundity of compassion and understanding. The journey that encompasses the entire narrative has for its destination the approaching death of Mrs Ashcroft, a meaning which Kipling reinforces by emphasizing the stillness of his characters as they talk. To make his readers stay equally still and listen to a story which scarcely has a plot at all, Kipling must create a special ambience of intimacy. And for this, his deft way of making the setting of the story produce its own atmosphere cannot be bettered. Here, atmosphere is not an element added to the story, it is a necessary condition without which the story simply could not be told. In this respect, Kipling unifies aspects of narrative art that other writers treat separately. Stevenson, for example, saw a number of choices facing the storyteller, or so Graham Balfour records his saying:

> 'There are, so far as I know, three ways, and three ways only, of writing a story. You may take a plot and fit characters to it, or you may take a character and choose incidents and situations to develop it, or lastly – you must bear with me while I try to make this clear' – (here he made a gesture with his hand as if he were trying to shape something and give it outline and form) – 'you may take a certain atmosphere and get action and persons to express and realize it.'[98]

The word 'realize' is well-chosen here, though it is not in Stevenson's own work but in that of his successors that we find the perfect integration of atmosphere, action, and characters he indicates. 'Shaping' something, so as to 'give it outline and form', as in the gesture Stevenson makes to express his meaning, becomes the conscious aim of the modern short-storywriter, who is likely to disdain the travelogue-like colourism of the genre's founding fathers (Irving, Mitford and Jewett, for example), but who loses power if he fails to recognize the wisdom of Elizabeth Bowen's remark, 'Nothing happens nowhere.' The constancy of short-story writers' attention to the places, fictional or real, in which stories are set, is exemplified by James Joyce, in many people's minds the paradigm of the modern artist. Joyce's brother Stanislaus talked about the epiphanies written early in Joyce's career as 'brief sketches', where depth and accuracy of observation were paramount, 'the matter being so slight': collected, the epiphanies 'served him as a sketch-book serves an artist or as Stevenson's note-book served him in the formation of his style'.[99] Not only should this remind us that 'sketch' is not a word to be despised when talking about short fiction, but it offers another instance of the barrier between pre-modern and modernist writing proving flimsy, at least in the case of the short story.

NOTES AND REFERENCES.

1. See *London Magazine* (Mar. 1970), p. 16.
2. *Afterthought*, p. 78 and p. 79.
3. 'Notes on Writing a Novel', *Pictures and Conversations* (1975), p. 177.
4. *Ibid.*, p. 178.
5. *Ibid.*
6. *Ibid.*, p. 179.
7. *Letters on the Short Story*, p. 74 (4 Feb. 1895).
8. Bowen, *Pictures and Conversations*, p. 175 and p. 179.
9. *Letters on the Short Story*, p. 86 (3 Jan. 1899).
10. *Ibid.*, p. 70 (10 May 1886).
11. *Lawrence in Love*, p. 49 (23 Jan.).
12. *Pictures and Conversations*, p. 179.
13. Ibid., p. 178.
14. See *Points of View*, p. 185.
15. *Pictures and Conversations*, pp. 41–2.
16. Ibid., p. 44.
17. *Ibid.*
18. *Sherwood Anderson's Notebook* (New York, 1926; repr. 1970), p. 76.
19. *Ibid.*
20. *Many Inventions*, p. 261.
21. *Life's Handicap*, p. 183.
22. Introduction to *A Choice of Kipling's Prose*, p.v.
23. *Wee Willie Winkie and other stories*, p. 202. 'The Man Who Would be King' was first collected in *The Phantom Rickshaw*.
24. 'The Rise of the "Short Story"', *The Cornhill Magazine*, New Series, VII, 3.
25. 'The Outcasts of Poker Flat', *Complete Works*, II, 107–20 *passim*.
26. *Letters to Eminent Hands*, p. 13.
27. 'The Death of Simon Fuge', *The Grim Smile of the Five Towns*, Penguin pbk edn (Harmondsworth, Middx, 1946; repr. 1975), pp. 133–87 *passim*.
28. *William Dean Howells as Critic*, p. 117.
29. *Ibid.*

30. *Ibid.*, p. 117 and p. 118.
31. 'L'Envoy', *The Sketch Book of Geoffrey Crayon, Gent.*, ed. Haskell Springer (Boston, 1978), p. 299. All subsequent page references to *The Sketch Book* are to this edition, which is Vol. VIII of *The Complete Works of Washington Irving*.
32. *The Life and Letters of Washington Irving*, ed. Pierre Irving (4 vols, 1862–64), II, 182 and 183.
33. *The Spectator*, I, No. 1, (1 Mar. 1711), 4. See also Irving's epigraph for *The Sketch Book*; taken from Robert Burton's *The Anatomy of Melancholy*, this introduces the author as 'a mere spectator of other men's fortunes and adventures'.
34. 'The Author's Account of Himself', *The Sketch Book*, p. 8.
35. *Ibid.*, p. 9.
36. *Ibid.*
37. *Ibid.*, p. 10.
38. 'The Christmas Dinner', *ibid.*, p. 181.
39. *Ibid.*
40. See Afterword to *The Sketch Book*, Signet Classic pbk edn (New York, 1961), p. 376.
41. *The Sketch Book*, p. 196.
42. See 'Explanatory Notes', *ibid.*, p. 319.
43. *Ibid.*, p. 120.
44. *Wessex Tales*, p. 33.
45. *Ibid.*
46. Introduction to Washington Irving, *Tales of a Traveller* (Philadelphia, 1824; Longman edn, 1896), p. viii.
47. *The Sketch Book*, p. 263.
48. *Tales of Horsemen*, ed. Alexander Maitland (Edinburgh, 1981), p. 92. The volume of Cunninghame Graham's fiction in which 'El Lazo' first appeared was *The Ipané*.
49. Preface (1884) to *Tales of a Traveller*, p. 6.
50. *Life and Letters*, II, 182; 183.
51. 'Stratford-on-Avon', *The Sketch Book*, pp. 210–11.
52. 'The Christmas Dinner', *ibid.*, p. 191.
53. 'Elia-Geoffrey Crayon', *The Spirit of the Age, or Contemporary Portraits*, ed. E. D. Mackerness (1969), p. 292.
54. *Ibid.*, p. 293.
55. See *The Short Story in English*, Ch. 11, esp. pp. 230–1.
56. P. J. Keating, Introduction to *Working-class Stories of the 1890s* (1971), p. xiii.
57. *W. D. Howells as Critic*, p. 116.
58. 'Our Village', *Our Village* (1947; White Lion edn, 1976), p. 21. All subsequent page references to *Our Village* are to this edition, which is based on the 3 vol. edn of 1836 and, unlike many selections published under the same title, includes all (and only) the sketches relating to the Berkshire village of Three Mile Cross.
59. *The Spectator*, I, No. 10 (12 Mar. 1711), 45.
60. 'Our Village', *Our Village*, pp. 21–2.
61. 'The Dell', *ibid.*, p. 94.
62. 'The Cowslip-Ball', *ibid.*, p. 46.

63. Mitford, 'Violeting', *ibid.*, p. 43; Gaskell, *Cranford and Cousin Phillis*, ed. Peter Keating, Penguin pbk edn (Harmondsworth, Middx, 1976), p. 316.
64. 'Our Village', *ibid.*, p. 29.
65. For a detailed study of 'the localised story' in post-Civil-War American fiction, see Robert D. Rhode, *Setting in the American Short Story of Local Color 1865–1900* (The Hague, 1975).
66. *Sarah Orne Jewett Letters*, ed. Richard Cary (Waterville, Maine, 1967), p. 84 (22 May 1893).
67. Preface to *Stories of American Life; by American Writers*, ed. Mary Russell Mitford (3 vols, 1830), I, vi and iv.
68. *The Works of Samuel Johnson*, IV, *The Rambler*, eds. W. J. Bates and Albrecht B. Strauss (New Haven, Conn., 1969), p. 365.
69. *Ibid.*
70. 'Dialect in Literature', *W. D. Howells as Critic*, p. 241.
71. *Letters*, p. 84.
72. See Barbara H. Solomon, Introduction to *Short Fiction of Sarah Orne Jewett and Mary Wilkins Freeman*, Signet Classic edn (New York, 1979), p. 3.
73. 'The Return', *The Country of the Pointed Firs*, in *The Best Stories of Sarah Orne Jewett*, selected by Willa Cather (2 vols bound in one, Gloucester, Mass, 1965), p. 2. Unless otherwise indicated, all subsequent page references to Jewett's fiction are to the Mayflower Edition.
74. See F. O. Matthiessen, *Sarah Orne Jewett* (Boston, 1929), p. 67.
75. IRVING HOWE, *Celebrations and Attacks: Thirty Years of Literary and Cultural Commentary* (1979), p. 132.
76. 'The Queen's Twin', *The Country of the Pointed Firs*, p. 257.
77. 'The Bowden Reunion', *ibid.*, p. 156.
78. *Ibid.*, pp. 173–4.
79. *Ibid.*, p. 174.
80. *Not Under Forty* (1936), p. 101. Cather's essay partly duplicates her 1925 Preface to *The Best Stories of Sarah Orne Jewett*.
81. 'Along Shore', *The Country of the Pointed Firs*, p. 194.
82. 'Martha's Lady', *ibid.*, p. 161.
83. 'Where Pennyroyal Grew', *ibid.*, p. 78.
84. 'The Backward View', *ibid.*, p. 304.
85. *Letters*, p. 120 (11 June 1899).
86. See Matthiessen, *Sarah Orne Jewett*, p. 67.
87. 'Mr and Mrs Fields', *The Cornhill Magazine*, New Series, XXXIX (July 1915), 42.
88. *Ibid.*
89. 'Sarah Orne Jewett's Tales' (1903) in *Friday Nights: Literary Criticisms and Appreciations*, First Series (1922), p. 194.
90. 'A White Heron', *The Best Stories of Sarah Orne Jewett*, II, 1–21 *passim*.
91. 'The Only Rose', *ibid.*, pp. 109–36 *passim*.
92. *The Only Rose and other tales*, Travellers' Library edn (1937), p. 103.
93. 'The Only Rose', *The Best Stories of Sarah Orne Jewett*, II, 109–36 *passim*.

94. *Ibid.*, p. 137.
95. *A Diversity of Creatures*, p. 62.
96. Quoted Matthiessen, *Sarah Orne Jewett*, P. 108.
97. 'The Wish House', *Debits and Credits*, pp. 113–38 *passim*.
98. *The Life of Robert Louis Stevenson* (2 vols, 1901), II, 141–2.
99. *My Brother's Keeper*, ed. Richard Ellmann (New York, 1958), pp. 124–5.

Chapter 7

SUBJECT-MATTER

The meaning of a story has to be embodied in it, has to be made concrete in it. A story is a way to say something that can't be said any other way, and it takes every word in the story to say what the meaning is. You tell a story because a statement would be inadequate. When anybody asks what a story is about, the only proper thing is to tell him to read the story. The meaning of fiction is not abstract meaning but experienced meaning, and the purpose of making statements about the meaning of a story is only to help you to experience that meaning more fully.

(Flannery O'Connor)

V. S. Pritchett concluded his first volume of autobiography, *A Cab at the Door*, with a picture of himself as a young man in Paris, traipsing from one job to another, yet at the same time poised to begin his true career: 'I became a foreigner. For myself that is what a writer is – a man living on the other side of a frontier.'[1] The image of the exiled artist is especially compelling when related specifically to the short-storywriter, since there is a view that the experience of 'living on the other side of a frontier' is often carried over whole into his choice of subject-matter. Arguing that the short story is partly defined by the material it treats, Frank O'Connor has pointed out how appropriate the form is to subjects like the intransigent romantic self, fugitive from society or belonging to a 'submerged population group'.[2] The stories discussed in O'Connor's study *The Lonely Voice* are principally modern treatments of 'frontier experiences' in a metaphoric sense, conveying an uneasy feeling of alienation as a widespread human phenomenon which transcends geographical boundaries. But early on in the evolution of short fiction, 'frontiers' in the literal meaning of the word provided staple material.

Bret Harte's tales about the opening up of the American West are clear instances of what could be done fictionally with the unknown: having found a ready audience for his Californian stories, Harte could write them virtually to order, even while living in London. So keen was the demand for Harte's evocations of the Wild West that he was given a free hand to write a story of any sort for *Graphic* magazine, as long as it included 'a real live bear'; even a 'half-grown' grizzly, in the editor's opinion, was 'better than no bear at all'.[3] Later in the nineteenth century, Kipling's Anglo-Indian stories established a British prototype for numerous colonial pieces, notably Somerset Maugham's Malayan stories which depicted people living in 'an alien land, a temporary rather than a permanent habitation' and (especially before aviation changed everything) finding their ties with the homeland 'insensibly loosened and sometimes broken asunder'.[4] Similarly, though more romantically, when Katherine Mansfield felt an impulse to write about her homeland New Zealand she recorded that in order to 'make our undiscovered country leap into the eyes of the Old World' she wanted to evoke a breathtaking island, 'mysterious, as though floating'.[5] This subject has actually been seen by Elizabeth Bowen as bringing Mansfield's descriptive powers to a peak; in her New Zealand stories, so Bowen argues, Mansfield became truly an Impressionist painter in words: 'we see her moving into the story, from its visual periphery to its heart, recognizing the "why" as she penetrates'.[6]

In diverse ways, all of these writers are concerned with experiences of foreignness, depicting life in its unfamiliar aspects and so leading their readers beyond familiar territory. The principle involved is typified by H. E. Bates's story entitled 'The Frontier' (1951): the reader is taken on a journey through misty Eastern distances where mountains mark frontiers with closed states. The story traces the central character's movement towards the human frontier, death, but Bates also uses his narrative to explore the topic of India's independence, foreseen in the story as 'the creation of yet another frontier' about to be created by the birth of a new nationalism.[7] Political and personal vistas are constantly changing, sometimes appearing to enlarge, like the hero's distant view of Kangchenjunge, at other times to become blurred and hazy.

A frontier is most simply defined as the part of one country that borders on another. It is a notion which we understand by seeing the relationship between two areas, though the frontier itself is a borderland, a third entity. Applying this to the aesthetic of the short story, it can be proposed that the combination of chiselled definiteness and tantalizing suggestiveness inherent in the form, makes it ideally suited to exploring that third entity, which is itself both a distinct line and a borderland whose features are shadowy and indistinct. Politically crucial, frontiers may be unmarked by any discernible changes in the natural landscape. If it were not for the human institutions which make the concept 'national frontier' physically real, the traveller would constantly be crossing invisible lines, finding himself without warning in unfamiliar circumstances; it is the position in which many short-storywriters want to put their readers, imaginatively at least. The types of experiences treated in short fiction are so many and various that it would be misguided to suggest that 'frontier subjects' are definitive of the genre, or even of a distinctive sub-genre. What can be claimed, however, is that these subjects have a special appeal for storytellers because they are often inherently dramatic, yielding conflicts which can be encompassed in a brief narrative. Furthermore, form and content do collaborate particularly closely in stories evoking a sense of barriers and boundaries; watching a character cross a frontier, literal or metaphorical, the reader can be made to feel that he too is discovering something new, experiencing in a short time-span the dislocating sensation of entering a foreign state, unlike the one he normally inhabits.

It has already been noted that short stories often work towards a single moment of revelation, frequently described in Joycean terms as an epiphany, or instant of radiant insight; suddenly the fundamental secret of things is made accessible and ordinary circumstances are tranfused with significance. The moment exists on a boundary between the ordinary and the mysterious, though what makes it miraculous, or even mystical, is that it fleetingly dissolves that boundary. Described as the lifting of a veil or as a moment which lays bare 'the burthen of the mystery', the epiphany obviously has spiritual affinities, but secret intimations can induce wonder without being at all otherworldly.[8] Whether it is a shameful secret confessed, a clue brilliantly interpreted by Sherlock Holmes while Dr Watson and the reader pant to keep up with his deductions, or a moral insight freshly grasped by the central character (sometimes, but not always, seized by the reader at the same instant), many stories disclose a definite meaning, often referred to as 'the point of the story'.

Despite the annoyance it causes a writer like Frank O'Connor, 'What is the point?' is actually a fair question.[9] It is as natural and proper for the reader of a polished short story to ask it, as for a listener to wonder where a friend's informal anecdote or humorous story is leading. In all cases, no one wants to be left waiting for an answer after the storyteller, literary or oral, has finished; success for the teller and satisfaction for the receiver depend on the answer – however complicated – being delivered in the story itself. Every story should provide the key to its own elucidation, solving its own puzzles, even if the solution consists of an aura of suggestiveness which actually expresses the elusiveness of certainties, or the instability of human perceptions. Indeed, the 'point' may be all the more powerful for its capacity to reverberate in the mind, outlasting the story's ending and multiplying significances, so that 'point' will seem a paltry term for what has been realized. But it is essential not to mistake the vague for the mysterious, and most worthwhile short stories do contain a definite moment at which understanding is attained, sometimes involving a response no deeper than, 'So it *was* the butler who killed Lord Mountjoy', but often turning the reader inward to reassess his own moral or ethical standpoint.

To emphasize such moments of newly perceived significance, many twentieth-century writers use symbolic methods, crystallizing meaning on a level other than plot, and making a symbol take over the part hitherto played by action and analysis. John Updike does this at the end of 'Pigeon Feathers' (1962); the beautifully patterned feathers of the birds David has shot, produce in the boy feelings which are reminiscent of the wonder expressed in a Hopkins poem. David recognizes the 'controlled rapture' with which the 'idle designs of color, no two alike' and the 'infinitely adjusted yet somehow effortless mechanics of the feathers' must have been created, and this perception leads naturally to wonderment at his own existence.[10] The story brings the hero to an epiphanic moment, and there is a corresponding change in the reader's activity: interest in narrative action falls away to be replaced by thoughtfulness about what the entire story signifies. A boundary is crossed, but not felt as a barrier, because the ending is stylistically and tonally in harmony with the rest of the piece. This harmony is essential, and it cannot be faked, despite the attempts noted by H. S. Canby, who in 1915 referred to the vogue for 'last suspirations' among magazine story-writers who hoped that 'a beautiful descriptive sentence charged with sentiment' would pass for a satisfactory conclusion.[11]

For the novel's more diffused and cumulative methods of conveying meaning, a story like 'Pigeon Feathers' substitutes an episode which culminates in a single moment of perception. It is inappropriate to look for the kinds of narrative and thematic development found in longer works, since where the story's meaning resides is in the one momentous event depicted. Naturally, this affects the way human experience and individual progress are treated in short fiction: people's lives do not unfold gradually, they either change, often abruptly and violently, or they pass through a crisis, leaving the story's main character to readjust to altered circumstances, though outwardly everything may go on as before. Because one phase, or even a single decisive moment, is isolated by the writer, fictional time tends to be conceived in terms of discrete stages or periods rather than as a process or flow. These segments of time can be likened to the countries which are separated by a definite yet only faintly perceptible frontier, the writer's task being to convince us that the phase he selects from his character's complete life-span is a crucial one, genuinely a period of rapid transitions, foreshortenings, or expansions.

This seems to put the short-storywriter at a disadvantage when compared with the novelist: choice of subject is inevitably restricted by the impossibility of patterning a short story according to a slow progress from youth to maturity as in the *Bildungsroman*; nor can the complex processes which lead, say, a Jane Austen heroine to eventual self-knowledge be compacted easily into the story's abbreviated form. For these reasons, it is natural that short-storywriters should focus on periods of life which can be held in a steady light, or be shown to have definite horizons. Beyond, lies either the future or the past, inaccessible, though perhaps not remote in time. A limited viewpoint is required, and to the extent that childhood and old age can be seen as threshold periods which are nevertheless entire unto themselves, they are 'frontier subjects' ideally suited to treatment in short stories. The writer can extract these periods from a network of variables and complicated issues of moral responsibility: between childhood and old age occur those maturing changes depicted by many novelists, the complicated changes which short-storywriters circumvent. Instead of investigating responsible action, the storyteller can emphasize stages in which physical circumstances largely determine what can be expected of a character in the way of action and individual choice. There are benefits for the writer in the child's reliance on adults and the increasing likelihood of an old person's immobility, always a godsend when unity of place is made a priority.

Active or not, elderly characters in short fiction can be portrayed through habitual actions which give a credible impression of life's permanent aspects and at the same time compress narrative by summarizing a life-time in the rituals and routines of its closing phase. The influence of the past can be conveyed by collecting up memories and scrutinizing them through the mind's eye of an old character who looks back on key episodes in his life, perhaps explaining in the process the quirk which makes him notable in the present. The Scottish writer Fred Urquart, for example, uses retrospection in his story 'Cuckoo' (1967) to account for the more than curmudgeonly bitterness displayed by an old man towards his neighbour's child.[12] Urquart's story also demonstrates that if separately children and old people provide ready-made short-story material, together they offer countless narrative possibilities. An early H. E. Bates story, 'Fear' (1928) is another case in point: it brings together a small boy and his grandfather for a single stormy night; when dawn breaks the child feels exhilarated and adventurous, while for the old man the sight of a falling star is a certain portent of death. The melancholy effect produced by juxtaposing these characters and their divergent emotions was one which Bates was to repeat later in 'Old' (1940), where we are left with the final image of a little girl brushing her grandfather's thin white hair in silent restitution for the callous way her parents are treating him.

A wide range of effects can be derived (or in some cases milked) from combining youth and age, and showing how they influence one another: at one end of the spectrum there is Katherine Mansfield's realistic depiction of a little girl's closeness to her grandmother in 'The Voyage' (1922), and at the other the eerie supernaturalism of Mrs Gaskell's 'The Old Nurse's Story' (1855), where a child is the catalyst for revelations about an old woman's past cruelty, and hence becomes an agent of moral retribution. In 'The Old Nurse's Story' the little girl's unclouded sensitivity to supernatural forces achieves a result which she is too young to understand or judge, and the effect is to challenge the way adults deal with emotions, a theme dealt with in another powerful Gaskell tale, 'The Half-Brothers' (1859). Parallels and piquant contrasts between children and old people, sometimes uniting them through mutual simplicity (or, according to the author's outlook, guile), and at other times suggesting an antithesis between innocence and experience, occur frequently in short stories of all nations. The American writer Willa Cather's 'Old Mrs Harris' (1932), and Walter de la Mare's uncanny story 'Seaton's Aunt'(1923), along with his gentler 'Miss Miller' (1936) and 'Miss Duveen' (1923), are notable instances of what virtually constitutes a sub-genre of short fiction. In stories of this kind the extremes of innocence and experience are brought together, perhaps in a single encounter, but often over a period long enough for the child's reliance on instinct to be tempered, and for him to learn something important about the terrain that he must cross before entering his 'second childhood'.

Having chosen a particular phase of life to depict, a writer can of course give his material still further concentration by selecting a crisis point within that phase, or, as frequently happens, at its outer edge, the line that marks both its fruition and its fading. Like Browning when he shows a character emerging as it were from a fissure between two distinct stages of experience, the short-story-writer often selects for attention an episode which pushes his major character on towards a boundary between the known and the unknown. Stories dealing with childhood frequently end with their principal character teetering on the brink of adulthood, and certainly in the case of writers who would be classified as realists it is usually more accurate to say that the concern is with adolescence, rather than childhood.

Superficially, Katherine Mansfield's story 'Prelude' appears to be predominantly concerned with childhood, but although much of the narrative is taken up with a child's view of the unsettling experience of moving house, the story ends with a gesture that seems to mark the end of a guileless era for the child-heroine. Kezia's vain Aunt Beryl has just been chastising herself for the constant play-acting which has obliterated 'the real Beryl' – if in fact such a being ever existed. Kezia comes in, clutching a grubby calico cat, and tells

Beryl that the grown-ups are waiting for her downstairs. When her aunt has left the room, Kezia is left alone at the dressing-table, which is as much of an altar for Beryl as it was for Pope's Belinda in 'The Rape of the Lock'. The way Mansfield describes what happens conveys precisely Kezia's desultory curiosity – unscrewing a little pot of cold cream and sniffing it – while her aunt is in the room, and later her spontaneous playfulness when she is alone. Sticking the top of the cosmetic jar over the calico cat's ear and then commanding it sternly to look at itself in the mirror is an accurately observed piece of childhood behaviour, all the more convincing for its element of adult mimicry. So too is Kezia's panic when the top falls and rolls 'like a penny in a round on the linoleum'. The top does not break, 'But for Kezia it had broken the moment it flew through the air, and she picked it up, hot all over, and put it back on the dressing table. Then she tiptoed away, far too quickly and airily . . .' Taken together with the story's recurrent images of violence, broken dreams and emotional guilt, these final sentences of 'Prelude' express far more than a child's momentary fear of being found out. It is left to the reader to make the connection between the little girl's apprehensiveness and the deficiencies of the adult world as it is presented throughout the story. The suggestion is that Kezia is tiptoeing into a straitened sphere where cold cream is the appropriate anointment: it certainly seems probable that the acute sensitivity she has inherited from her sexually withdrawn mother will have similarly negative results. The buoyant delight with which earlier in the story Kezia found 'a pill box black and shiny outside and red in, holding a blob of cotton wool' has faded; in the old abandoned house, the box was something to treasure ('"I could keep a bird's egg in that", she decided'), but the impression left by the story is that a change of home also means a new stage in growing up.[13]

Of course this theme was not new in literature, and other short-story writers had already written about girls reaching a boundary between innocence and self-consciousness. Sarah Orne Jewett made this theme central to 'A White Heron', although her treatment of it is rather coy; the story's insight into what it feels like for the young heroine to find a man she disapproves of attractive, is not its strongest feature. Jewett seemed to be more comfortable with the adult point of view, and in 'The Hiltons' Holiday' (1895) she evokes the mixture of pride and regret with which devoted parents acknowledge that their two daughters are at an age to 'see somethin' more o' the world'.[14] The story leaves no doubt that the little Hilton girls will be eased into adulthood by loving parents, a benign view of family life which is not shared by the later writer Elizabeth Bowen, whose female characters tend to resist leaving childhood. Bowen's stories frequently depict characters who are reluctant to grow up, and who carry a kind of defiant innocence into their adult lives, sometimes with disastrous consequences. In diverse ways, women are shown clinging to pre-adolescent simplicities in 'Mysterious Kôr' (1945), and in several of the stories collected in *The Cat Jumps* (1934): the female types depicted in stories like 'The Apple Tree' and 'The Disinherited' are epitomized by Valeria Cuffe in 'Her Table Spread', one of the best stories in the same volume. Valeria is said to be 'still detained in childhood', a phrase which applies equally well to other Bowen women who are totally out of place in the present.[15]

Unsurprisingly, however, female adolescents in short fiction are far outnumbered by their male counterparts. The theme of initiation is more prominent in stories dealing with boys, one reason being that their transitions into adulthood can be readily matched by events and settings which recall the conventions of narrative 'adventures'. Ernest Hemingway's Nick Adams stories offer perhaps the most clear-cut examples of stories which dramatize the experience of growing up from one moment to the next, using the framework of a male world of action to enhance the inward shock felt by the adolescent hero. In 'Indian Camp' (1925) Nick literally 'discovers' death when an Indian, unable to stand his wife's suffering in childbirth, kills himself. Birth and death coexist, and Nick has to adjust to the new knowledge into which he is admitted, traumatically and irrevocably. Though totally dissimilar in style and outlook, this story and Updike's 'Pigeon Feathers' resemble one another in their use of violence as the means by which the young heroes learn about mortality, a lesson which for Updike's hero is bound up with thoughts about an immortal creator.

Adolescent 'boy heroes' also occur frequently in Kipling's stories, which are insistently concerned with thresholds of every kind – between life and death; sanity and madness; farce and tragedy. In 'Thrown Away' Kipling emphasizes the central character's inexperience, and his inability to cope with the strains of Indian life, by calling him 'The Boy'; and the very title of 'The Brushwood Boy' (1898), which deals with the relationship between dreams and reality, draws attention to the hero's youthfulness, an important aspect of this romantic piece. More worldly are the discoveries made by the heroes of a less fanciful writer like Sherwood Anderson, who, in single stories as well as in the *Winesburg, Ohio* sequence, focuses on adolescent awakenings, often sexual, and usually disillusioning. In 'I'm a Fool' (1923) and 'I Want to Know Why' (1921), Anderson uses monologue form to express the bafflement felt by his teenage protagonists as they describe what seems to them wayward adult behaviour. These stories depend on a rather disingenuous irony produced by the deliberate misalignment of the character's realization and the reader's; the monologist fails to see the implications of what he is recounting, but while he puzzles away it becomes obvious that he is already part of the community he is so reluctant to join. It gives the narrator of 'I Want to Know Why' the 'fantods' to think about his idol, the trainer Jerry Tillford, watching a marvellous horse run and then the same day kissing a 'lean and hard-mouthed' woman: 'What did he do it for? I want to know why.'[16] The price of an answer is, of course, the loss of the already waning sexual innocence which has shaped the angry question in the first place, and this irony, though rather heavily handled by Anderson, is in key with his naturalistic view of life.

In these single stories, Anderson was returning to the theme which had dominated *Winesburg, Ohio*, where the progressive movement of young George Willard towards maturity is traced, and made to coincide with his increasingly jaundiced view of small-town life. In that particular work, a pervasive condition of unhappiness is reflected in the way characters see one another through closed windows in airless rooms; and it is the closed window of a train that eventually 'frames' Winesburg for George Willard when he leaves. Oppressive silences between people are accentuated by the sounds of feet tramping on board sidewalks or evening trains pulling out of the stationyard; streets are dimly lit so that characters find their way 'half lighted, half darkened, by the lamps and by the deepening shadows cast by the low-branched trees'.[17] In this suffocating atmosphere, a yearning for 'adventure' (a word which recurs throughout the book) is expressed by sudden decisions to walk, often in the rain or while a storm is brewing: repeatedly, Anderson uses banal details to evoke scenes in which characters experience unexpected moments of radiance akin to Joycean epiphanies. Typical is a story pointedly called 'An Awakening' in which, aroused by a visit to a pool room full of Winesburg boys who 'talked of women', George walks in 'dimly lighted streets', not knowing 'where he was going or what he wanted to do'. A dark and narrow alleyway in a sordid area of town produces a melée of sounds – pigs grunting, women clattering dishes, dogs barking and children crying – unfamiliar enough to Willard, and with a sufficiently dangerous ambience, to make him seem, 'as he lurked in the darkness, oddly detached and apart from all life'. As George stands alone looking up at the sky he feels 'unutterably big and remade by the simple experience through which he had been passing. The desire to say words overcame him and he said words without meaning, rolling them over on his tongue and saying them because they were brave words, full of meaning. "Death", he muttered, "night, the sea, fear, loveliness".' But the elevated sensation 'that all of the people in the little street must be brothers and sisters to him', is, like all such moments in these stories, short-lived, and George soon finds the day-labourers' neighbourhood dwindling back to something 'utterly squalid and commonplace'.[18]

Anderson's intention is of course to show that the cycle of epiphany followed by a collapse into drabness is endlessly repeated, and his realism obliges him always to acknowledge the disappointing sequel as well as the revelation. But reading the Winesburg stories as a sequence does highlight a problem common to all *collections* of epiphanic narratives, as opposed to single, unified stories. How many epiphanies can a reader take in succession without feeling that they are merely literary tricks with little bearing on actual experience?

It is difficult to renew involvement each time another obsessed character is introduced and shown to be undergoing an essentially similar crisis, when at the same time we are being asked to follow George Willard through successive phases of his development. At one and the same time Anderson wants to show Willard growing up and Winesburg standing still, so he tries to interweave signs of change and patterns made up of repetitions. The impression left is that he is torn between two literary forms, the novel and the short story.

What the unsatisfactoriness of *Winesburg, Ohio* considered as a totality suggests, is that it is difficult to sustain interest in an adolescent hero through a series of linked narratives when the setting is static. A comparison with Joyce's *Dubliners*, where thematic echoes, and increasing formal complexity, perform impersonally the function ascribed to Anderson's single hero, is instructive in this regard. Joyce's principal concern is also the 'awakening' of consciousness, but he does not tie the process down to only one period of life; young, middle-aged, or elderly – the characters are all trapped in Dublin's narrow parochialism, and there is no observing figure to provide a critical point of view as Anderson's Willard is made to do. Conversely, the way Anderson's Winesburg stories work better singly than as a group, indicates how appropriate short-story form is when a writer does want to concentrate on a discrete epoch of personal history, eliminating a 'before' and an 'after'.

Whatever the narrative techniques employed, stories dealing with stages of individual lives depict episodes which are seen as significant in themselves, but which are also important because of their relationship with areas of experience lying outside the confines of the actual story. When the subject is childhood, there is very often a quasi-Wordsworthian element of judgement on what lies ahead – the adulthood which is the supposed reader's own condition. That judgement is given satiric force in stories where the child character is denied his step into maturity: Lawrence, for example, indicts a money-crazed environment in 'The Rocking-horse Winner' (probably written early in 1926), by showing the little boy's premature death; and in his powerful story 'The Pupil' (1892), Henry James offers a moving deathbed scene which can be read as a critique of all sentimental child-deaths in Victorian fiction, and which augments his censure of what he saw as a barbarous society, intent on virtually murdering the fine spirits born into it.

Death is the epitome of 'frontier subjects', and it is not surprising that many short-storywriters' fascination with moments of change emerges in a preoccupation with this, the most unequivocal transition from the known to the unknown. Death is a subject which is amenable to the short story's aesthetic interest in those perceptual split-seconds that intrigued Walter Pater, moments like the exact instant at which light changes to darkness, or conversely, the precise moment when a reader's puzzlement clears and understanding dawns. No matter how the writer tries to present it, death remains the unknown, the unexperienced, and it is therefore especially affronting to any artist who believes that nothing is beyond his imagination. Attempts to capture the very sensations of death usually have an obsessive quality, prime examples of this being Poe's stories about the shadowy boundaries between life and death. 'The Premature Burial', first published in 1844, is one example; it plays on the morbid terrors arising from the possibility that the frontier can be misidentified. Less sensationally and with greater thematic depth, William Faulkner too exploits the gothic potential of death as a subject for fiction. This interest is evident in the first of Faulkner's stories to be published in a national magazine: 'A Rose for Emily' (1931) reveals that, in order to keep her Yankee lover, Miss Emily has killed him and slept with his corpse beside her until her own death. What saves Faulkner's piece from being merely a Poe-like horror story is the symbolic level on which his narrative also works, conveying that the only way Miss Emily can preserve the traditional Southern values she cherished is by denying the reality of death and decay.

There are, however, plenty of stories which explore attitudes to death more realistically than either Poe's or Faulkner's. This is something which by and large the novel has not attempted until very recently. And even in contemporary novels the emphasis tends to be an almost sociological one, often concentrated on so-called 'taboo subjects' like terminal illness or bereavement. The metaphysical reach of Beckett's *Malone Dies* (1959) is a rarity in longer fiction, but a fairly common feature of the short story. Walter de la Mare's fiction yields some very fine instances: 'The House' (1936) shows a dying man accepting with dignity the irony that the most important experience in the life he has consciously shaped is its unavoidable ending; and in the earlier piece 'Out of the Deep' (1923) a supernatural element is blended with an acute psychological investigation of a dying man's mind as he relives his unhappy childhood. Both stories promote the comforting fiction that death can be met in anticipation, each character exerting some control over the uncontrollable, a theme which is reflected in de la Mare's techniques of indirection; his compressed, oblique expressing of inner states and moments of retrospection imply a metaphysical perspective which illumines the metaphoric structure of each story. There are affinities with James here, partly of style, but also of theme: in a sense, 'The House' is a rewriting of 'The Beast in the Jungle' (1903) from an optimistic viewpoint. And it should be remembered that James's *The Wings of the Dove* (1902) is one of the only novels in English to place all of its narrative events in relation to death as an absolute, making Milly Theale's death far more than an incident within a fictive plot.

The short story's pressure to move resolutely towards a climax makes it an ideal form in which to juxtapose life and death in striking ways. But as always with short-storywriting, striking effects can easily turn into gimmickry. The reader's common-sense assumption that a character who is conscious is also alive, exposes him to all sorts of authorial tricks, in which the American writer Ambrose Bierce became an adroit specialist. Among the pieces collected in Bierce's *Tales of Soldiers and Civilians* (1891), the famous story 'An Occurrence at Owl Creek Bridge' presents much of its action through the consciousness of a man hovering between life and death; and the ending of 'One of the Missing', which consists mainly of the minute-by-minute thoughts of a soldier trapped in the debris of a fallen building, is designed to surprise and shock: 'Dead a week', says the officer who discovers the soldier.[19] The intricacy of Bierce's time scheme in 'One of the Missing' allows him to move across normal boundaries between consciousness and its extinction, but although the story is cleverly articulated, the reader feels swindled. He has been persuaded to admire the lucidity with which the central character's every movement is recorded, but then any basis for caring about all this is whipped away from him. The reaction is likely to be similar to the resentment felt at an O. Henry 'trick ending', where applause for the author's ingenuity is demanded, killing the story once and for all.

Estimates of Bierce's achievement vary, but whether or not H. E. Bates's opinion that he just misses being an American Maupassant is accepted, it remains true that for all their faults, Bierce's stories do exemplify the short story's inherent capacity to stretch narrative conventions and range widely in its search for fresh subject-matter.[20] Crossing boundaries that normally categorize historical and experiential time, Bierce showed an interest in technique which was advanced for his time. The trouble is that, especially to modern eyes, his technical experiments seem out-moded and incapable of contributing anything of lasting value to the growth of fiction. Indeed, along with O. Henry, Bierce was a harmful influence, providing an honoured example for magazine writers with nothing of their own to say.

The cheated, emotionally empty-handed feeling a Bierce story leaves behind is partly due to the theoretical nature of his interests, and it would be wrong to suppose that a surprise death occurs only in stories contrived to catch the reader out. Less experimentally bold, but just as concerned with shifting categories of experience, is Chekhov's early story 'Grief', first published in 1885. This traces the thoughts of a peasant who is taking his wife to hospital through a snowstorm so bad that it is 'impossible to say whether the snow came from the sky or from the ground'. As he drives along, Grigory admits to himself the dreadful cruelties he has inflicted on the ailing woman during the past forty years of living in a drunken fog. But any inclination towards self-reform is suddenly deflated when Grigory discovers that his wife has already died; denied the luxury of penitence, he reacts with totally credible irritation: 'She would have lived another ten years, the silly woman, and now, I shouldn't wonder, she thinks I'm really like that.' Chekhov mingles comedy and tragedy, creating ironies which do not depend on authorial slickness. Grigory falls asleep in the bitter cold, and the story ends with the information that he will not recover: 'You've had your life, haven't you?' says the doctor curtly, underlining the theme of missed chances, a recurrent topic in short fiction – notably in James's 'The Beast in the Jungle', which gives tragic force to the irony of neglected opportunities.[21] This theme reappears closer to our own time in Elizabeth Bowen's work, where the risks carried by too much detached observation of life are embodied in Jamesian figures like Humphrey Carr in 'The Secession' (1926), and Alban in the later story 'Her Table Spread'.

On the other hand, the short story's power to sustain an unbroken mood makes it equally hospitable to a more serene attitude to death, recommending stoic acceptance rather than fierce resistance. In 'Living Relic' (1852), for example. Turgenev manages to make believable the courage, almost the gaiety, with which a withered peasant beauty faces an appalling death. The success of the story lies in the sheer compassion of its style, and this perhaps influenced one of Turgenev's admirers, Sarah Orne Jewett, when she wrote 'Miss Tempy's Watchers', which expresses a similarly calm view of death. The dialogue between the two women who watch over their friend's body evokes Miss Tempy's presence vividly, creating a bond of sympathy and restful security so firm that the watchers sleep and – or so Jewett hints – become the watched; perhaps Tempy is standing nearby, seeing her former existence in a new light. In keeping with the homely realism of the setting and characterization, the brief touch of supernaturalism introduced by Jewett towards the end of the story is tentative and whimsical, but it underlines discreetly her theme of the mysterious links between the living and the dead.

The short story in general lends itself to supernatural effects because these readily produce the desired 'unity of impression'. That is why ghost stories were amongst the first types of distinctive short fiction to emerge, making up the dominant strain in Victorian storywriting. In the specific instances of stories dealing with childhood or old age (or both, as in de la Mare's 'Miss Miller' and 'Miss Duveen') otherworldly elements often occur, the most interesting being mystical experiences which fulfil very much the same unifying purpose as the appearance of a ghost in overtly supernatural stories. The boundaries between youth and adulthood, old age and death, are frequently explored within a fictional framework which evokes yet another borderland, the hazy area between fantasy and reality, dreaming and waking.

H. G. Wells makes the problem of telling the real and the fantastic apart central to his story 'The Door in the Wall' (1911). The principal character, Lionel Wallace, tells a sceptical listener about the green door, set in a white wall, through which he walked into an enchanted garden when he was five years old. Now entering middle age, his entire life has been haunted by the image of this paradisal garden, with its purring panthers and kindly people; but each time the door has reappeared invitingly, he has chosen to pass it and go on with his successful public career in 'the grey world'. The more eminent he becomes (and he has recently been appointed to the Cabinet) the deeper grows the sorrow with which he grieves for what he has lost – or rather, rejected. Wells's device of the dream-like garden creates a compound image of regret and longing, directly challenging 'our daylight standard' by which 'we see our world fair and common'. By this standard, Wallace's death, which the outer narrator discloses in the last section of the story, is an accident: a workman has simply left a doorway in a hoarding unfastened, and Wallace has fallen into a railway excavation; he has 'walked out of security into darkness, danger, and death'. But it is equally possible that Wallace, possessing an 'abnormal gift', saw 'an outlet, a secret and peculiar passage of escape into another and altogether more beautiful world.' The outer narrator's mind is left 'darkened with questions and riddles' to which there can be no certain answers; the story is not offering fantasy and reality as alternatives, but showing how they intertwine within the 'mystery of these dreamers, these men of vision and the imagination'. Wallace, it is inferred, has a great contribution to make to English politics, and Wells is very careful not to present him as a pushy careerist: the pity of the situation touches the whole of society, for it lies in the realization that one man's vision, a basis for Utopianism, is at odds with reality.

Wells succeeds in giving this story an allegorical flavour without simplifying his material to the extent required by true allegory. The story's power to disturb depends on convincing the reader, through the initially disbelieving outer narrator, that to Wallace 'The Door in the Wall was a real door, leading through a real wall to immortal realities.' A fabular quality comes from Wells's skilful construction and potent imagery: there are echoes of magic and fairy-story in Wallace's declaration that he has passed the green door 'three times in the last years'; the velvety panthers in the garden suggest mythic beasts tamed as if by Orphic harmonies, and of course the colour of the door alone recalls traditional associations of green with the land of faery.[22] But through the outer narrator's personal testimony and, more persuasively still, the authoritative precision of Wells's style, fantasy and reality are so inextricably combined that it is impossible to dismiss Wallace's experiences as illusory. The unembellished quality of Wells's language places him in the tradition of Swift, as was noted by the Argentinian writer Borges, who in his own stories 'tried to be faithful to the example of H. G. Wells in combining a plain and at times colloquial style with a fantastic plot'.[23]

A similar strategy seems to be at work in Kipling's '"They"' (1904), where an adult narrator enters an enchanted landscape which again is linked with ideas of childhood innocence. Like Wells, Kipling keeps the 'daylight standard' of normality in play throughout the story, even giving it prominence by assigning a central role to the narrator's motorcar, indisputably an emblem of modernity. The narrator's vision, again like Wallace's (and indeed all such glimpses into eternity) is temporary: he knows that he must wrench himself away from the blind woman and the child-presences that surround her, back to ordinary life and its responsibilities.[24] The story brings the narrator through strange experiences to the point where he is on the verge of leaving them behind, as though he were standing on another threshold, but enabled by the healing insights he has gained to make a fresh and hopeful departure.

The success of '"They"' depends largely on Kipling's presentation of an episode which is complete in itself, yet at the same time implies a future for its protagonist. Many short stories aim for a similar effect, and the aura of mystery conveyed by Kipling's finely graded transitions from the normal into the strange, and then beyond that into the marvellous, are found in totally realistic stories. too. Both Wells and Kipling are employing heightened versions of a constant principle in storytelling, according to which nothing is stranger than the ordinary: 'Its unexpectedness, its singularity, its infinite variety', wrote Somerset Maugham of the ordinary, afford 'unending material'.[25] Wallace and the narrator of '"They"' both wander by chance into the landscapes which move them so deeply and surprise them into emotion. Walking along a West Kensington road full of 'mean dirty shops', Wells's hero comes upon the green door; driving across the Sussex downs, Kipling's narrator shuts off his car engine and 'slides' through tangled woods into the sunshine and immaculate lawns of an enclosed magical garden.[26] The sense of wonder aroused by these stories is due to the way rich meaning is conferred on an apparently random event which is not consciously willed by the character. But even in realistic stories without any reminiscences of Alice falling down the rabbit-hole, wonder is often the response aimed for; many realistic writers will try to justify what seems an arbitrary choice of subject by presenting it in such a way as to bring out its latent significance, or, to use V. S. Pritchett's term, its 'indwelling value'.[27] To transform the normal into the wonderful (not to be confused with the beautiful) is what every storyteller wants to do. Differences lie in the intrinsic unusualness of the material, but even when the writer keeps within what Wells called 'our daylight standard', he is hoping that, by virtue of his attention to it, his subject will be endowed with specialness. If this hope could not be realized, then Gogol's realistic portrayals of 'little men' would be social documents, not stories: the very act of telling the story of one government clerk, to a reader presupposed to be able to see his human importance, makes him already exceptional, though still representative. Furthermore, as Maugham noted, great men may be too consistent, too lacking in conflict for short-storywriters' purposes: 'it is the little man that is a bundle of contradictory elements'.[28]

The piquancy of revealing interest where, according to appearances or prejudices, it is least to be expected, is of course not the short story's monopoly, but it is a province where it does function especially well. Effects range from the hair-raising to the poignant, though basically the assumption is that the reader can only be made to look beneath surfaces for short intense periods. The reward may be thrilled nerves, as in Algernon Blackwood's tale of atavistic vengeance, 'The Doll' (1946), which concludes:

> Thus in the suburbs, where great spaces between the lamps go dead at night, where the moist wind comes whispering through the mournful branches of the silver-pines, where nothing happens and people cry 'Let's go to town!' there are occasional stirrings among the dead dry bones that hide behind respectable villa walls. . . .[29]

Blackwood simultaneously returns his audience to its familiar safe surroundings and enhances the weirdness of the occurrences he has just depicted. The unusual flows back into the normal, leaving a residue of strangeness behind, and producing the 'delicious shudder' in which Blackwood specialized.[30] Blackwood actually described his interest in psychic matters as a concern with 'questions of extended or expanded consciousness', and he suggested that what made his type of fiction more than the 'homespun "ghost-story"' was the way he presented 'an average man who, either through a flash of terror or beauty, becomes stimulated into extra-sensory perception'.[31]

But however strange the escape from 'average' existence, the short story's characteristic final movement is a return to normality.

This is perhaps as close as the form can come to the Aristotelian catharsis in tragedy or the joyful atmosphere which seals comedy. And for some people, that is not nearly close enough. The tendency of many stories to end with an adjustment rather than a purgation or celebration of emotion is often seen as a serious limitation. Herbert Ellsworth Cory in 1917 put the case against the short story in the strongest possible terms, accusing it of being pathological in technique; overconcerned with unity of abnormally artificial and intense kinds; lacking in any healing catharsis, and too dependent on a feverish excitement which made it 'blood kinsman of the quick-lunch'.[32] No wonder Cory was nostalgic for the three-decker as well as for the essay, which he saw foundering because 'teachers and quacks' found in the short story a ready supply of 'facile material'.[33] Cory's attack was launched specifically at what he saw as 'an artificially stimulated demand' for short stories in America in the early twentieth century, and so it should not be given too wide an application; he was, after all, writing before the heyday of Fitzgerald and Hemingway, and at a time when there was genuine worry that the short story reflected a deplorable speed mania which writers ought to discourage.[34] But the objection that the short story is a trivializing genre which cultivates the extremes of the sensational and the mundane in its subject-matter, and encourages negative moods by its method, deserves to be taken seriously.

The problem seems to be most acute when assessing realistic stories about humble people, often in a rural setting; the brand of fiction which is typified by the mid-nineteenth-century *Dorfgeschicht*. A significant figure here is the Swiss writer Jeremias Goffhelf, whose vast output included 'The Black Spider', which appeared in 1842 and was later greatly admired by Thomas Mann. Drawing on Bernese legends as well as the work of Walter Scott, Gotthelf attempted to give a kind of mythic grandeur to the everyday, and the tendency apparent in his writing was continued by other practitioners of the *novelle*, most notably Gottfried Keller. In his many stories about the people of Seldwyla, Keller (also a Swiss) mythicized communities, basing his fiction on closely observed 'fringe elements of society', and providing a model for the twentieth-century German writer, Hermann Hesse, particularly during the pre-1912 period referred to as Hesse's Swabian period.[35] Like Keller – and before him, Gotthelf – Hesse was interested in creating imaginatively an 'everyday world of ordinary human beings', so as to convey an impression of 'life's little comedies and paradoxes'.[36]

But this kind of storytelling is by no means confined to German literature, and although it was not until Keller was entering his last phase in the second half of the 1870s that any equivalent to his method became evident outside Germany, various countries did produce writers with similar aims. Among these are some of the writers already considered in Chapter 6 (Sarah Orne Jewett, for instance, and in some moods, Kipling) and to theirs could be added the names of other 'regional' writers like Faulkner in America, or Eden Phillpotts in England. By the time Faulkner began publishing his work, however, a writer like Hesse had abandoned traditional storytelling, and it must be asked whether the regional short story is not essentially narrow in its possibilities. What is wrong with stories in the *Dorfgeschicht* tradition, according to its critics, might be summarized by recalling the premise which William Empson identified as basic to pastoral literature, namely that everything about 'complex feelings, involving all kind of distant matters' can be said by depicting humble life.[37] The pastoral process, according to Empson, consists of 'putting the complex into the simple' an activity which is 'in itself a great help to the concentration needed for poetry'.[38] Such help is equally welcome to the writer of short stories, and in view of the form's restraints on fullness, in the sense of exhaustiveness, it is obvious why 'simple' people should hold particular attraction for him. But it is exactly this effort to make the simple represent the complex (what Empson calls 'the essential trick of the old pastoral'), which is often felt to falsify human potential and betray the idealism literature should serve.[39]

It is unarguable that the tendency of the short story's tightly controlled quality is to reduce the possibility of showing characters making free, let alone complicated, choices. Willpower often seems to have become the privilege of the author alone: paradoxically, his desire to give a story inevitability may have the effect of depriving his characters of any self-determining power, making them appear to be locked in a structure which has been specially designed to fate them to passivity and sameness. In view of this, it is understandable that the realist writer should favour subjects and situations which plausibly restrict his characters' opportunities for bold action, and which require a minimum of overt authorial manipulation. Naturally, the compactness of the short story attracts writers to material that reduces the Many to the One, relying on the 'idea of everything being included in the humble thing'.[40] Associated with this is a tendency, already discerned in writers considered earlier in this study, to select topics which can be presented credibly through the description of recurrent actions: 'So it went on every day', writes Chekhov of 'The Butterfly's' selfish quotidien round of visits; and in 'Ward Number Six' (1893) he begins a résumé of Dr Ragin's actions with a summarizing statement: 'His routine was as follows'.[41] The impression left is of existence following unvarying patterns, irrespective of the individual character's motives and intentions, and it is to this, and to the jaded view of life epitomized by the ending of another Chekhov story, 'The Duel' (1892) that detractors of short-story form object. 'It began to drizzle' are the last words of the story, and as so often in Chekhov's fiction, insight seems to have been gained momentarily only to be lost.[42]

For admirers of Chekhov, the natural answer to all this is to say that his fidelity to his characters' waverings and unfulfilled yearnings are marks on his humane artistry, and it is a point that can be taken further and applied to the short story in general. The short story's wisdom, when it claims to have any at all, consists largely of accepting monotony, limitations, and compromises. And there are in fact advantages of many kinds in this situation, particularly if the writer can make acceptance seem a defining aspect of individual will, rather than a bowed submission. Here the portrayal of people whose characters are expressed through their attitude to work becomes as asset to the writer. Short stories frequently depict manual labour, perhaps gaining over other genres in this respect. And while by no means always joyless, work and manual tasks of the sort described by, among others, Sherwood Anderson, Coppard, and Chekhov, do tend to conform to believably repetitive patterns which reflect a melancholy outlook.

H. E. Bates offers some fine examples of this type of fiction, which is often rural in its setting, though not always concerned with the peasant life so memorably captured by the Russian writers he most admired – Turgenev and Chekhov. In 'The Ox' (1939), for example, the central character has no direct contact with the land, but her stoic endurance and resolute obedience to habit are given the force of a law of nature. The woman maintains her determination throughout, and in spite of, the melodramatic sequence of events that makes up Bates's narrative. Cumulatively, stature is attributed to the recurrent image of Mrs Thurlow pushing her bicycle, never riding it, because it is burdened with objects which identify her as a working woman. It is with this image, clearly intended to awe the reader, that the story ends: 'She struggled up the hill. The mud of the track seemed to suck at her great boots and hold her down. The wheels of the bicycle seemed as if they would not turn, and she could hear the noise of the air dying once again in the tyre.'[43] Out of context, this seems to bear out the criticisms made by opponents of the short story, but related to the story's subject and the objective point of view sustained by Bates, it is eloquent. In 'The Ox' Bates achieves exactly what he sets out to do, meeting high standards of organization and pacing, and fitting his language deftly to his subject. There is no pretence that Mrs Thurlow (who is perhaps a literary descendant of Flaubert's Félicité) is a complex person in disguise, or that her 'simplicity' is representative of civilized mankind. Instead of divided feelings and intricate motives, Bates presents the dignity of the woman's extremism. The events which occur in the story are sensational, but Bates declines to make them the pretext for releasing his main character from mechanical time, which is her habitat. There is no stunning moment or epiphany for Mrs Thurlow, no flash of recognition which raises her to tragic greatness, yet her willed anti-sensationalism has the force of an absolute within the story.

Ultimately, there are no literary rules by which to settle whether the muted emotions aroused by short stories of this kind make them negligible. The genre does not display any single characteristic shape or philosophy which makes it possible to outline its properties and conventions, or to rank it definitively in a hierarchy of genres. The absence of any fixed disposition towards comedy or tragedy has undoubtedly helped to lower the short story's prestige, but here too there may be hidden benefits. The genre's unattached quality can be seen as a valuable facet of its freedom, as Arnold Bennett indicated at the end of the 1920s, a decade in which he found plenty to admire about the British short story. Disagreeing with 'the lettered élite' who felt that editors were hampering artistic progress by an undue insistence on 'the convention of the happy ending', Bennett proclaimed that such opinions were not only inaccurate (editors, he said, were not so biased), they were narrowing: 'A genuine creative artist can and does fit his work to any convention. And a story with a happy ending can be just as true, or even just as sad, as a story with an unhappy ending. Also the unhappy ending can be just as sentimental and conventional as the happy.'[44] Preoccupation with the happiness or unhappiness of story-endings is probably carried over from discussions of the novel, and Bennett is right to set it aside in his commonsensical way. If there is any single mode corresponding to short-story form, then it is neither the comic nor the tragic, but the ironic. Once more, the metaphor of a frontier is a useful one. Untheoretically defined, irony can be described as the effect produced by bringing two entities together with the aim of drawing attention to the line of demarcation between them, and showing that proximity involves disparities, not sameness. All types of irony require a division; thesis is opposed to antithesis, and apprehending ironies is a matter of seeing the relationship between two ideas, statements or events. To grasp ironies it is necessary to be aware of contrasts and substitutions; there would, for example, be no point in the unmasking of a Somerset Maugham hypocrite unless the reader were thinking in paired terms – mask and face. The basic simplicity underlying ironic patterns makes them particularly conducive to the compression desired by the storywriter: an initial situation, potentially complex enough to be the beginning of a lengthy novel, can be cut back by a single ironic reversal which abruptly but convincingly curtails development.

In his aptly titled collection *Life's Little Ironies* (1894), Hardy repeatedly uses a decisive irony to reduce all sense of life opening out. Phyllis's misinterpretation of Gould's overheard words just as she is about to elope with 'The Melancholy Hussar' locks her from that moment on in a desolate situation; the single ironic occurrence is crucial and irrevocable. And in 'The Son's Veto' Sophy's marriage of convenience is a denial of nature that recoils on her, closing forever her prospects of happiness with the true man of nature, Sam Hobson. Misery taking the place of wished-for happiness provides an economical plot which can be unfolded rapidly, using the central ironic reversal as a pivot, the frontier within the story between comedy and tragedy.

In these stories the loss of hope as loneliness replaces anticipated joy has a melancholy effect in keeping with Hardy's belief that human beings are essentially powerless. But the short story is equally receptive to more robust moods, particularly when 'justice' is not dispensed by fate but by the characters themselves. There is a large class of story in which an ironic structure is used to deal with the intrinsically lawless subject of revenge. Vengeance thrives as a short-story subject because it carries with it elements of clearly delineated conflict, vivid emotion and urgency. Revenge is a notion that collapses if its outlines are blurred, and for the storyteller the positive side of this is that a vendetta successfully accomplished can be described in a taut story which ends with a satisfying turnabout of the characters' positions. In Maupassant's bloodthirsty tale 'Vendetta' (1885), a frail old widow triumphs over the ostensibly stronger man who murdered her son; the story merely records the strategy by which the widow gains her revenge, strength and weakness changing places. Fascination with crafty stratagem is also apparent in a much later story, Borges's Kiplingesque 'The Bribe' (1975), though here the revenge theme is given an extra twist, since it is 'the vanity of not seeking revenge' which makes one scholar play into the hands of his cunning academic rival.[45]

There is a lighter side to the revenge pattern, as numerous stories about practical jokes testify. The reader is often flatteringly made privy to the trick while the target of the joke is made to seem ridiculous by being kept unaware of what is going on. Here, the narrative conforms to the type of irony which conveys inner meaning to a small group of *cognoscenti*, and only outer meaning to the rest. Kipling is the modern writer most closely associated with practical joking as a topic for humorous fiction, but the literary hoax can be traced back through centuries and is not confined to any single period or country. Its roots probably lie in the classical taste for witty sayings, puns, understatements and double meanings, a favourite target being literal-minded individuals, like the pedant who wanted to see what he looked like when asleep, and so stood in front of the mirror with his eyes closed. Jests also had a place in epic, some having to do with witty 'things said', and others with 'things done' a distinction which Quintilian formalized in his instructions on rhetoric.[46] In later periods, however, the tendency was away from 'literariness'; jestbooks of the fifteenth and sixteenth centuries cultivated instead links with the vernacular and went out of their way to seem artless. P. M. Zall points out that *A Hundred Merry Tales* (1526), which was full of jests aimed against logic-chopping and scholastic dogmatizing, appears to have been 'compiled from jests circulating by word-of-mouth'.[47] These jests, in which common sense invariably won the day, can be seen as anarchic substitutes for the amusing exempla used by medieval preachers to keep their audiences awake. As Zall shows, tales which had in the twelfth century been used for sacred purposes passed gradually into secular use, until in the fifteenth century moral tags either disappeared completely or remained only to be parodied. An important aspect of these changes was an increasing concern with realism, and eventually a rudimentary interest in artistic form. It was the impulse to shape stories that finally displaced the jest, admitting a greater fictional element, and taking a longer view of narrative development. Thomas Deloney's translation of Des Périers' *Mirrour of Mirth* (1583) is seen as a landmark by Zall: 'Plot, setting, characters, are focused on achieving the humorous effect, where in the "pure" jest little is important other than the incident or the punch line, and there is no time for development.'[48] Four centuries later, these remain alternative possibilities for the writer of humorous short stories: the 'jest' writer will emphasize the 'snapper', making the whole story depend on its final line, while a writer like Kipling will make everything in the story contribute to the total impression; for him, every stage of the writing matters just as every step in their plans matters to his practical jokers.

It must be admitted that the satisfactions of watching a hoax being carried out are limited, and many readers find that the more gleefully successful the tricksters are, the less rewarding the story. Kipling's *Stalky and Co.* (1899), for example, can arouse distaste virtually unparalleled in literature. Many people share Somerset Maugham's view that, 'A more odious picture of school life can seldom have been drawn.'[49] What this suggests is that in humorous stories as well as in serious ones, too much overt authorial control is unwelcome; readers prefer stories to keep something back, to have an undisclosed reserve. The most memorable hoax stories are consequently those which deviate from the norm, perhaps by withholding information from the reader until late on in the story, or, more subtly, by exploiting his trustfulness. Leonard Merrick's 'The Judgment of Paris' (1920) is one remarkable instance of a story that does both: it tricks the reader along with the characters, and all without any unfair play whatsoever. The way the story works is to trip the reader up on his trusting belief that he is being kept one step ahead of the characters, and that if a character assumes a disguise, there will be some way of knowing who is behind the disguise. Merrick's characters are all professional comic actors, and this enables him to divert attention to the idea of stage performances, encouraging the reader to forget that masquerade can also go on offstage. Another clever strategy is to make the reader concentrate on the more forceful of the two rival tricksters without realizing that in doing so he is underestimating the power of quiet guile.[50]

Merrick's story is a comic *tour de force* that remains fresh after many readings, but it has no pretensions other than to amuse and intrigue. The hoax, however, can be put to more serious uses. Mark Twain's story 'The Man Who Corrupted Hadleyburg' (1900) is at one and the same time a dexterously perpetrated trick and an exposé of fundamental human dishonesty: the title itself is a rueful conundrum, since the outwardly virtuous citizens of Hadleyburg need no external agency to corrupt them. They are human – that alone is sufficient. Kipling too was capable of elevating the hoax-story above the level of the Stalky pranks, as his mature story 'Dayspring Mishandled' (1932) shows. Here Kipling transforms the revenge-pattern into a complex investigation of moral corruption and the tragic ways in which, despite itself, artistic conscience becomes implicated with sexual irrationalities. The story has an intricacy and profundity worthy of late James, and indeed the economy with which it conveys several layers of meaning in less than ten thousand words surpasses anything James attempted in short fiction.

Ostensibly, the subject of 'Dayspring Mishandled' is the revenge which Manallace makes it his life-work to gain when a fellow man-of-letters Castorley insults the memory of a woman once loved by both men. Castorley's offensive remark is not actually recorded, which increases the reader's belief that Manallace's vengeful mission transcends personal motives. The biblical pronouncement, 'Vengeance is mine, saith the Lord', is swept aside as Manallace takes upon himself the task of defending honour and dispensing justice. And it is very much an Old Testament 'eye for an eye, tooth for a tooth' type of justice he adopts, mercilessly constructing a trap for Castorley, whose scholarly and social vanity provide additional reasons for wanting to see him destroyed. These unpleasant attributes also lead Castorley to collaborate in the downfall Manallace plans for him. For about two-thirds of the story the reader is kept busy spotting clues, and by the time Castorley has published his expert opinion on 'a fragment of a hitherto unknown Canterbury Tale', and received his coveted knighthood, the reader is likely to be congratulating himself on knowing who actually did write the Chaucer manuscript. In line with the hoax-pattern, a reversal is expected: Manallace will reveal the truth about his forgery at the height of Castorley's triumph, and the story can end with the mixture of laughter and moral righteousness which properly accompanies a deserved come-uppance successfully completed. What Kipling in fact does is to make the point at which the reader and Manallace are both anticipating this reversal the occasion for a totally unexpected twist. The reader is congratulating himself on being so much quicker on the uptake than the first-person narrator who has watched Manallace assemble the materials for the forgery; meanwhile, Manallace is enjoying an understandable thrill at having produced a manuscript which will lure Castorley to his doom only because it really is a superbly convincing imitation of Chaucer. Suddenly these pleasures turn sour when, daringly late in the story, Kipling introduces two new characters, Lady Castorley and her lover, Gleeag; it is a tactical step which in itself mocks the reader for expecting a storyteller to limit his important characters to those in the spotlight at the beginning.

Instead of a tipping of the scales which will resolve the conflict between Manallace and Castorley, conflict is renewed and transferred. Lady Castorley is now the enemy, and a truly vicious one. She wants Castorley dead as much as Manallace does, but for baser reasons. Manallace has not reckoned on forces external to his own scheme, and what he confronts now is the independent existence of evil far deeper than anything represented by Castorley's lack of gallantry. '*She's* the devil', Manallace remarks, partly exonerating her adulterous conspirator Gleeag from blame, and testifying to the dire power of female sexuality.[51] From the moment he realizes that he is not alone in deceiving Castorley, Manallace's task becomes to save rather than destroy. By altering the direction of his narrative and adjusting sympathies in the closing phase of the story, Kipling chastens the reader's potentially smug pleasure in the hoax; eager complicity in Manallace's vindictive action against a man who is shown increasingly as a pathetic victim now seems shabby. Castorley is already dying, and all human ploys to punish him look niggardly when seen alongside what disease is accomplishing in its own course. Perhaps vengeance is to be the Lord's after all.

At the end of the story, as Castorley's coffin slides out of sight, Lady Castorley exchanges a silent look with Gleeag, knowing that Manallace sees them both in their true light. Only from this vantage point is it possible to begin a full interpretation of all that has gone before. Reconsidered in this perspective, 'Dayspring Mishandled' becomes far more than the account of a practical joke gone dreadfully wrong. It *is* that, but at a deeper level it is a fable about a man who profanes his creative gifts by using them to exact a brutal kind of justice. On the surface, Kipling tells how a trickster is outfoxed by deviousness beyond his imagining, and by death itself, but the story's real twists are not to do with plot; they concern complex themes of mercy, betrayal, and – in the fullest Chaucerian sense – '*gentilesse*'.

That Manallace should use Chaucer's Christian epic *The Canterbury Tales* as the material for his pitiless hoax is just one of many oblique hints used to warn the reader that piecing the plot together is only the first stage of understanding this story's implications. Manallace disregards, even abuses, the spirit of Chaucer's writing while imitating its letter wonderfully well, and it is significant that the spoof 'Canterbury Tale' he invents is a secular one about a knight who does *not* want to go to the crusades. There is a further irony in the fact that several of Chaucer's tales (the Miller's and the Reeve's, for instance) deal specifically with the anarchic sexual passions which Manallace forgets about until he finds them working against him, embodied in Lady Castorley. It is also relevant that Manallace's Chaucerian fragment concerns a girl with two suitors, a predicament which belongs as much to the Gilbert and Sullivan operas alluded to early in 'Dayspring Mishandled' as it does to the medieval fabliau tradition he is imitating. Triangular situations, so the story indicates, are truly eternal, but Manallace's obsession with Castorley's wrongdoing (his failure to be a 'parfit gentil knight in the past) blinds him to anything and anybody except his enemy.

The network of allusions and ironies in 'Dayspring Mishandled' is so intricate as to be inexhaustible, and the recurrence of triangular relationships is only one of a number of motifs that echo throughout the story, giving it a richly dense texture. Extended outwards to the story as a whole, the fake Chaucerian triangle embedded deep in the narrative can be seen as the pattern which unifies constantly shifting perspectives. The initial triangle consists of Castorley, Manallace and 'Vidal's mother', a deliberately shadowy figure whose main role is to inspire Manallace's chivalric idealism and its counterpart – his savage hatred of Castorley. With Vidal's mother a mere memory, attention can be concentrated on the two men as rivals, though here perhaps the most intriguing triangular relationship of the story comes in – the trio of Castorley, Manallace and Chaucer. Three entirely different literary men, they constitute the triangle which Kipling perhaps saw as the one that ought to be the finest, binding two scholars through their shared work on a third, and vastly greater, figure. This triangle is warped by Castorley's self-seeking and Manallace's hidden motive, and so it is fitting that in the later stages of the story yet another three-cornered relationship should supervene – the triangle created by an adulterous love affair. Interestingly, Kipling minimizes attention to the relationship between Castorley, his wife, and Gleeag (who is his doctor as well as his cuckolder) and focuses instead on the bizarre and totally unconventional triangle made up by Castorley, Lady Castorley, and Manallace. Tensions put strains on all three lines of force, and the only thing that keeps the triangle stable is the paradox that Lady Castorley is at one and the same time united with Manallace against her husband, and opposed to him in enmity. With Castorley dead, yet another triangle shapes itself, comprising Manallace, Lady Castorley and Gleeag. The final implication seems to be that, as he pulls on his black mourning gloves, Manallace is meditating how he will keep the outward forms of these relationships intact and punish the she-devil. None of the triangular groupings in the story, except, ironically, for the unfulfilled ideal relationship between the two scholars and their subject, can be publicly avowed; all of them involve secrecy, treachery, and, above all, strain. The effort required to keep unbroken the outward forms of marriage, friendship, and even a doctor/patient relationship like Gleeag's to Castorley is enormous, depending on carefully suppressed information, such as Lady Castorley's knowledge that Manallace's discovery is a fake, or conversely Manallace's insight, sharpened by vengefulness, into her true character. This aspect of 'Dayspring Mishandled', its dramatization of the sheer concentration required to keep surfaces smooth, while all the time lawless passions are threatening to surge through, tearing all 'forms' apart, is reminiscent of the task given to Maggie Verver in James's novel *The Golden Bowl*. In Kipling's story, the seeming harmony of the Castorleys' marriage is kept undisturbed since both Manallace's subterfuge and Lady Castorley's adultery remain secrets; and indeed it is by restraining her in the publicly decorous category of 'widow' that Manallace will delay her remarriage – or so it is implied at the end of the story. The characters, like James's, gain power by knowing, but not admitting *what* they know, about one another; they work for their own moral and emotional ends behind calm social façades, never breaking the taut skin which conceals subversive irrationalities, keeping passions hidden, though only just.

There is of course the vital difference that James seems to justify Maggie Verver's deviousness while Kipling's characters are shown to be degraded by theirs; the prospect of Manallace's future cat-and-mouse game with Lady Castorley is especially depressing; he cannot be said to be 'saving' cherished values as James's heroine is attempting to do. The only deviousness which is justified in 'Dayspring Mishandled' is Kipling's own artistry: the hoax element of his story is itself a façade behind which he conducts a disturbing exploration of highly complicated questions. The story asks, among other things, what exactly is the relationship between the social institutions which 'pair' people into couples (man and wife; knight and lady) and the individual will, which is forever pushing tidy lines into triangular shapes that threaten social norms?

Kipling's fascination with unorthodox threesomes has been emphasized here because it illustrates forcefully a preoccupation which is widespread among short-storywriters. Form as well as content is involved in this; it is possible to see 'Dayspring Mishandled' as following a three-phase movement consisting of thesis (Manallace will gain revenge), antithesis (Lady Castorley will thwart his purpose) and an implied synthesis (neither Lady Castorley nor Manallace will achieve the full satisfaction of their wishes). On the level of plot, synthesis is represented by Manallace's adjustment to a new set of circumstances at the end of the story, but a measure of the story's greatness is that a true synthesis is only possible within the reader's imagination as he tries to see the precise relationship between the various strands of the completed narrative. It is at this stage that 'Dayspring Mishandled' fully reveals its ambiguities as well as the artistry of its structure.

Some theorists have argued that a story cannot come into being until three events or phases of development have been combined, an additional requirement being that linkage is not simply a matter of sequence, 'Once upon a time . . . and then . . . and then.' Building on the work of the Russian formalist Vladimir Propp, who demonstrated in the 1920s that folktales are constructed according to regular patterns and sequences, Gerald Prince has proposed that 'no more than three conjoined events are required to constitute a story', but that a 'causal relationship between certain events' and a chronological order of events are essential before a story can come into being.[52] The exact nature of the links between one event and another in the short story is probably impossible to establish once for all, and, as 'Dayspring Mishandled' shows, the logic of any story worth reading is likely to be far from obvious. Nevertheless, it is worth noting that patterns of three are constantly evinced in short stories of various degrees of sophistication from fairy-tales (where wishes, bears, and almost everything else come in threes) upwards. Ian Reid has suggested that the 'deep-rooted aesthetic preference' for a 'tripartite sequence' in simple stories is related to Aristotle's ruling that a plot must have a beginning, middle and end; but it may be possible to extend this comment beyond 'simple' stories.[53]

In complicated stories too, patterns of threes are present, though rarely obtrusive. It may be that they are concealed by subtle manipulation of chronology, for as Flannery O'Connor has observed, 'there has to be a beginning, a middle and an end, though not necessarily in that order'.[54] 'A good short story', O'Connor insists, 'should not have less meaning than a novel, nor should its action be less complete', a comment that suggests a particular use to which the three-phase action of short fiction can be put: it could be that in the short story's ability to handle triangular human situations lies one of the principal ways in which it can rival the traditional novel.[55]

Early on in short-story criticism, Brander Matthews pointed out that the short-storywriter was gloriously free in comparison with the novelist, who apparently had little choice, either of subject-matter or about how to conclude his narrative. Hero and heroine there must be, and, according to Matthews, they were fated to meet one or other of four ends: either they married; she married someone else, or else *he* did; or, as a last sad alternative, she died. Matthews undoubtedly takes his scorn too far, and anyway what he really fears is the plotless novel he sees on the horizon, and in which there will be no formulaic marriages or broken hearts to complain about. But he does have sound reasons for observing with satisfaction that, although 'a short-story in which nothing happens at all is an absolute impossibility', a good story 'need not be a love-story', and so 'it is of no consequence at all whether they marry or die'.[56] The words 'need not' are well chosen; although it is sometimes supposed that the short story cannot handle the themes of love and marriage, there is plenty of evidence to the contrary. Many excellent stories treat the subjects of courtship and marriage with a degree of social consciousness sometimes thought to be inimical to the genre as a whole. As the juxtaposition of a compact story like 'Dayspring Mishandled' and a lengthy novel like *The Golden Bowl* suggests, the short story is actually free to enter the domain of the novel at any point, the most important differences lying in patterning, pacing, and the terms in which endings are conceived, rather than in the nature of the material treated. All of the endings listed by Matthews carry a sense of finality and closure, and although the modern novel has superannuated his examples, making open-endedness a far more regular feature of long fiction, it is probably true to say that the short story was quicker to break with the practice of supplying a definite ending. The extended narrative span of the traditional novel made desirable the kind of conclusion Elizabeth Bowen had in mind when she wrote: 'Completed action is marked by the exhaustion (from one point of view) of the character. Throughout the novel, each character is expending potentiality. This expense of potentiality must be felt.'[57] In comparison, the short story is freer because it is not obliged to show 'the effects both of action and of the passage of time' or to trace the gradual 'diminution of the character's alternatives', effects without which, Bowen found, plot could not advance evenly.[58] Perhaps too because of its origins in the supernatural tale, where an aura of mystery was essential, the short story cultivated, early on in its history, endings which were convincingly inevitable and yet capable of prolonging an atmosphere of strangeness. In this respect, the short story's emancipation from novelistic interest in 'couples' and their ultimate destinies was an especially important factor, allowing treatment of less conventional relationships, and in some cases providing a vehicle for controversial views about sexual morality. Hardy's short stories, usually disqualified from inclusion in the genre because of their lack of form, are somewhat neglected instances of short fiction's power to examine social conventions and to provide endings which express a sense of wasted, rather than exhausted potentiality. And for this purpose it was appropriate to choose as subject-matter unorthodox 'triangular' situations which could be resolved by reducing the number three to one, proposing solitariness as the inevitable outcome of rivalries and three-cornered relationships within a society where marriage was deemed the only acceptable context for sexuality.

Many of Hardy's shorter pieces take the basic ingredients of a romantic love plot and then dispose them in such a way as to undermine conventional views about 'right choices' and the equation of 'moral' behaviour with happiness. In 'The Melancholy Hussar', for instance, Phyllis is the familiar figure of a girl with two suitors, Tina and Gould, but by the end of the story fine-spirited Tina is dead and Gould has married for shallow prudential reasons, leaving Phyllis facing lifelong loneliness. The triangular plot-situation favours rapidly established contrasts between the two men, and introduces conflict into the story by placing the heroine in a dilemma. But where a conventional, romantic approach would insist that the moral soundness of the heroine's choice be rewarded by happiness, here she loses both the man she chooses for emotional reasons, and the man to whom she feels morally bound. Three-cornered relationships are particularly conducive to Hardy's brand of irony: in 'The Son's Veto', for example, the inflexible hostility of Sophy's son perpetuates the consequences of her first choice of husband, reflecting at plot level a larger irony which fates Sophy and Sam, the story's 'couple' by nature and disposition, to remain permanently apart.[59] 'To please his Wife', another story collected in *Life's Little Ironies*, varies the pattern by attributing rivalry to two women, gentle Emily Hanning and envious Joanna Phippard, the third corner of the triangle being Captain Joliffe. Here the unhappy love-story is amalgamated with a retribution theme: Joanna, who marries Joliffe out of spite, is left desolate while the woman she deprived of happiness prospers financially, though not emotionally.[60]

In the twentieth century A. E. Coppard took the two-men-and-a-girl situation as the starting point for 'Tribute' (1923) a tale about the divergent fortunes of rivals in love. Like Hardy, Coppard uses fiction to document social attitudes and the power of convention; 'Tribute' is a bitter attack on class divisions and bogus patriotism, and it attains impressive brevity and concision. The story recalls Hardy too in the folktale quality it derives from a plain 'once upon a time' manner. The opening sentence of 'Tribute' simultaneously evokes a modern industrial setting and captures the timelessness of a fairy-tale: 'Two honest young men lived in Braddle, worked together at the spinning mills of Braddle, and courted the same girl in the town of Braddle, a girl named Patience who was poor and pretty.'[61]

Marriage in the short story is seldom the token of hope and

renewed social harmony it is in the line of romantic comedy which descends from Shakespeare through centuries of drama and fiction. When courtship does have a happy outcome in short fiction, it tends to have something offbeat about it, like the shy romance between two elderly people in Sarah Orne Jewett's comic tale 'Miss Esther's Guest' (1893); or, perhaps the *reductio ad absurdum* of courtship stories involving three characters, Eden Phillpotts's 'The Twins' (1927). Here 'Nature', said to be 'famous for her jokes', contrives to make identical twins the genial competitors for a man who cannot for the life of him choose between them.[62] Only by squaring the triangle and introducing a cousin who sweeps the man off his feet is the stalemate broken, with no hard feelings anywhere.

More frequently, courtship make melancholy reading, as in Coppard's powerful story 'The Higgler' (1925), where the central character's suspicions about the amazing proposal he receives on behalf of a quiet girl who would have brought him those fairly-tale rewards, love and a fortune, lead him to marry unadventurously – and unhappily. Once again the dominant influence on Coppard is Hardy, who treats an unconventional courtship tragically in 'For Conscience' Sake'. The main character is Mr Millborne, a contented bachelor who feels compelled to propose to Leonora, the woman he wronged and deserted twenty years previously. In a curious scene which inverts all of the associations usually carried by marriage proposals in literature, a confirmed bachelor woos a woman who is equally reluctant to sacrifice her well-organized independence. Millborne's motive is the direct opposite of the revenge motive discussed earlier; he wishes to make reparation, and it is doubly ironic that the only argument to sway Leonora is his assurance that their marriage will help their illegitimate daughter's match with a somewhat reluctant curate. The actual consequence of marrying purely 'for conscience' sake' is to threaten, not promote, the daughter's engagement. Nobody profits, least of all Millborne who, after years of comfortable shuttling back and forth between his lodgings and his Bond Street club, now finds that to be married is truly to be homeless. When the recriminations of his wife and daughter become unbearable, he escapes to his club, but finds that he cannot, 'as formerly, settle down into his favourite chair with the evening paper, reposeful in the celibate's sense that where he was his world's centre had its fixture. His world was now an ellipse, with a dual centrality, of which his own was not the major.' Hardy's choice of a geometrical image to convey Millborne's feeling of displacement is perfectly in accord with the story's central irony: by creating a domestic circle in the accepted sense, Millborne has uprooted Leonora and his daughter from the rural social circle where they were 'known and respected', and has brought them to London, where they feel lonely and anonymous watchers of glamorous society 'flashing past'.

It is a striking case of the wrong thing done for the 'right' reason, and finally Millborne can remedy the situation only by going into self-imposed exile abroad and fading into 'dishonourable laxity'. Instead of following a straight and comfortingly unvarying route between lodgings and club, Millborne is last seen lurching back to his Brussels rooms from the *Cercle* he frequents, 'having imbibed a little too much liquor to be able to take care of himself'. Far from being the dawn of a joyful era, marriage in 'For Conscience' Sake' marks a dire step which reduces an independent but sociable being to a pathetically 'harmless' and secretive recluse who needs his servant's help to get home.[63] If Frank O'Connor is correct to say that loneliness is the experience best-suited to short fiction, then it remains to distinguish between types of loneliness, differentiating as, for instance, Hardy does here, benign from desolate solitariness.

'For Conscience' Sake' is only one example of short fiction which takes up where the traditional romantic novel leaves off, and which uses a neatly structured plot to challenge contemporary social and moral assumptions. Many short stories ask questions put aside by novels with 'happy endings': How does married life differ from 'marriage' as a personal and social ideal? What is the sequel to the novelistic ending which radiates social hope through the symbolism of weddings? Failed marriages abound in the short story. Nor are they confined to nineteenth-century fiction as might be supposed from H. S. Canby's observation that 'slowly developing incongruity in married life' was beyond the scope of the modern story because 'like a film in the moving pictures' the emphasis was on speed.[64] Illustrations might be drawn readily from the work of writers as diverse as Hemingway, Maugham, Elizabeth Bowen and Katherine Mansfield. H. E. Bates too portrays numerous disillusioned couples and strained marriages: in 'The Evolution of Saxby' (1955) he evokes the agonized bondage of a home-loving man whose febrile wife has a passion for buying one house after another, perfecting the interior décor and then selling out to ghastly people. Another distinguished Bates story, 'The Good Corn' (also collected in *The Daffodil Sky*, 1955), deals with a childless marriage, transforming a triangular situation which is actually a stereotype of music-hall comedy – the husband who has an affair with the over-prolific servant girl – into a moving story which combines psychological acuteness and powerful nature-description. A. E. Coppard is yet another twentieth-century writer to offer fictional portraits of marriage, using the way characters behave in their marriages to exemplify individual traits. In 'The Wife of Ted Wickham' (1923), it is again a stereotype that is given realistic force: Molly is a grimly believable version of the nagging wife, an 'unresting woman', 'for ever on at' her husband, even when he is dying.[65]

But although there is plenty of evidence to suggest that marriage did not cease to preoccupy short-storywriters of generations later than Edith Wharton's or Henry James's, as Austin McGiffert Wright has argued it did, it is true that possibly the most striking contribution to the genre of marriage-stories was made by a Victorian writer better known for his novels – Anthony Trollope.[66] Seldom if ever thought of as a short-storywriter, and cited by Brander Matthews to prove his rule that novelists are no good at writing short pieces, Trollope's name has become virtually synonymous with mid-Victorian fiction at its most leisurely and reactionary.[67] More recent critics have been more discerning. V. S. Pritchett has acknowledged that Trollope is an exception among nineteenth-century writers; a 'compulsively novelizing' artist, Trollope did manage to 'discover the short story when he became a traveller', and so he avoided the pitfall of writing stories which 'read like crowded episodes of a continuing novel, or like novels that have been started and then given up'.[68] But although Pritchett takes an important step towards correcting the view that Trollope was only at home with novelistic conventions, he does not mention what is perhaps Trollope's best short story, 'Mrs General Talboys' (1861).[69] Here, the titular heroine exploits her status as a married woman (whose husband is conveniently absent in another country) to combine enjoyable flirtations and bold ideological pronouncements about freedom, both political and personal. It is evident from the skilful pacing of this story that Trollope's social comedy does not always require the broad canvas of a three-decker novel to make its comments tell; indeed the social observation in 'Mrs General Talboys' has an especially sharp edge to it precisely because it contains none of the padding and sentimental compromises which sometimes weaken Trollope's novels. It is very much as though Trollope felt freer in the shorter form to indulge his interest in unorthodox female behaviour, a topic he treats more sporadically and tentatively in his novels: feminists in his novels are not treated as a complete joke, but they are usually given minor comic roles and subjected to authorial teasing.

Before very long, the topic which Trollope had handled with such a light touch in 'Mrs General Talboys' was to be given far more serious treatment, and short stories became vehicles for the expression of the advanced views which actually made Trollope's heroine morally disreputable. During the 1890s there was discernible what H. G. Wells later described as 'a rebel undertow of earnest and aggressive writing and reading, supported chiefly by women and supplied very largely by women, which gave the lie to the prevailing trivial estimate of fiction'.[70] Though not confined to the short story, this new militancy had a ready outlet in a form which, as Derek Stanford has indicated, provided a suitable medium for depicting clashes between the old morality and the 'egalitarianism of the erotic senses' which characterized the thinking of the period.[71] The short story 'could offer the reader the bare essentials of the encounter, the dilemma, the choice: a victory for love or a victory for class. In the same way the short story could highlight, with no inartistic argumentation, the debate on the claims of erotic attraction and the demands of a sexual morality geared to marriage and solely marital intercourse.'[72] Using the short story to urge social change, or as the feminist writer of the 1890s, George Egerton, does, to encapsulate visions of the 'new woman's' hoped-for future, affords one more instance of the genre's adaptability and its disposition towards 'frontier subjects'. When women as a class saw themselves reaching a threshold, so it might be argued, they turned to a form which allowed them to combine 'greater artistic stringency, and a broader moral permissiveness'.[73] Seen in this light, the late nineteenth-century feminist short story is part of the wide interest in bohemian and déclassé existence which was evident in the work of writers like George Gissing, whose story about a despairing spinster, 'The Foolish Virgin', appeared in *The Yellow Book*, January 1896. This concern has its twentieth-century counterpart in Jean Rhys's collection *The Left Bank* (1927), provocatively sub-titled 'sketches and studies of present-day Bohemian Paris'.[74]

In narrower terms of its specific goals, however, the feminist short story of the kind referred to by Stanford takes the genre perilously close to a frontier beyond which lies oversimplified propaganda, raising the question of whether the 'story with a purpose' is always bound to fail in an artistic sense. Ironically, many of the most compelling depictions of women's experiences have come from male writers who have no overt feminist aim: female eroticism is perhaps nowhere more powerfully evinced than in Coppard's story 'The Field of Mustard' (1926), which reveals astutely the limitations of heterosexual love conventionally viewed. And in 'Breeze Anstey' (1937) H. E. Bates used the situation of a triangular relationship between two girls and a man to trace his heroine's movement towards a fresh start. The story's closing sentence puts her on a threshold to independence: 'And she knew that the rest, whatever it was, lay with herself.'[75]

Irrespective of the author's personal ideology, the short story is inherently suited to dealing with the unconventional, in relationships, in attitudes, in behaviour. A large part of the genre's appeal, to readers as well as writers, lies in its detachment, and the freedom it gives by encouraging improvisation and experimentation. For although certain subjects are more conducive than others to the intensity aimed for in short fiction, there is really no limit to the topics a short-storywriter can select for treatment. Fashions and preoccupations alter, but this ought not to be turned into a basis for legislative pronouncements like the one made by Cyril Connolly, who outlawed romantic fiction from *Horizon*, because 'the love story

. . . is not a story, but a confession'.[76] At the other extreme is the reader described by Flannery O'Connor in her essay 'Writing Short Stories': 'I have an aunt who thinks nothing happens in a story unless somebody gets married or shot at the end of it.'[77] Neither of these ideas about what a story should, or should not do, can be totally supported – or finally discountenanced. Connolly the editor, in touch with artistic and intellectual developments, and the aunt whose tastes are completely unsophisticated, both have the right to what they think is a good story, so long as their preferences are not exalted into presciptions. It is one particular strength of the short story to be capable of ranging so widely among subjects and methods that both these types of reader, and everybody in between, can be satisfied. 'We all write', says Flannery O'Connor, 'at our own level of understanding, but it is the peculiar characteristic of fiction that its literal surface can be made to yield entertainment on an obvious physical plane to one sort of reader while the selfsame surface can be made to yield meaning to the person equipped to experience it there.'[78] The short story shows a marked disposition towards the kinds of subjects discussed in this chapter, but what we have seen are tendencies, strengthened by technical considerations, rather than laws. In the broader sense intended by O'Connor, the subject-matter of a short story is, like that of all art with any representational purpose at all, whatever makes the writer's meaning concrete, allowing us to experience it for ourselves, at *our* own level of understanding.

NOTES AND REFERENCES

1. *A Cab at the Door* (1968), Penguin pbk edn (Harmondsworth, Middx, 1970), p. 207.
2. Introduction to *The Lonely Voice*, p. 18 and *passim*.
3. Quoted Stanley Weintraub, *The London Yankees: Portraits of American Writers and Artists in England 1894–1914* (1979), p. 50.
4. Preface to *Complete Stories*, III, iv.
5. *Letters and Journals*, p. 65 (22 Jan. 1916).
6. *Afterthought*, p. 58.
7. *Colonel Julian and Other Stories* (1951), p. 251. The placing of 'The Frontier' last in the collection emphasizes indirectly the story's concern with endings and new beginnings.
8. Harry Levin, *James Joyce: a Critical Introduction* (1960), p. 37.
9. See above, p. 56.
10. *Pigeon Feathers and Other Stories* (1962), p. 149.
11. 'Free Fiction', *Atlantic Monthly*, CXVI (July 1919), 61.
12. Written in March 1961, Urquhart's story is included in *The Dying Stallion* (1967), which is Vol. I of his *Collected Stories*.

13. 'Prelude', *Collected Stories*, pp. 11–60 *passim*.
14. *The Best Stories of Sarah Orne Jewett*, II, 278.
15. *The Collected Stories of Elizabeth Bowen* (1980), p. 418. All subsequent page references to Bowen's short stories are to this edition.
16. *The Triumph of the Egg: A Book of Impressions from American Life in Tales and Poems* (New York, 1921), pp. 5–20 *passim*.
17. 'The Thinker', *Winesburg, Ohio*, Viking Press pbk edn (New York, 1960; repr. 1964), p. 138.
18. 'An Awakening', *ibid.*, pp. 179–89 *passim*.
19. *In the Midst of Life: Tales of Soldiers and Civilians*, 1st English edn (1892), p. 81. The amplified title did not appear in the first, San Francisco, edition of Bierce's collection, and was chosen by the publisher.
20. See *The Modern Short Story*, p. 56.
21. 'Grief', *Lady with Lapdog*, pp. 15–20 *passim*.
22. 'The Door in the Wall', *Complete Short Stories*, pp. 144–61 *passim*.
23. Author's Note, *The Book of Sand*, p. 2.
24. For discussion of poetic analogues to the mystical experience in '"They"', see Julia Briggs, *Night Visitors: The Rise and Fall of the English Ghost Story* (1977), pp. 206–7.
25. *The Summing Up*, p. 4.
26. Wells, 'The Door in the Wall', *Complete Short Stories*, p. 147; Kipling, '"They"', *Traffics and Discoveries*, p. 304.
27. 'The Short Story', *London Magazine* (Sept. 1966), p. 6.
28. *The Summing Up*, p. 4.
29. 'The Doll', *The Doll and One Other* (Sauk City, Wisconsin, 1946), p. 71.
30. Author's Preface, *Selected Tales of Algernon Blackwood* (1964; repr. 1970), p. 12.
31. *Ibid.*, p. 8 and p. 9.
32. 'The Senility of the Short-Story', *Dial* LXII (3 May 1917), 380.
33. *Ibid.*
34. *Ibid.*
35. Joseph Mileck, *Hermann Hesse: Life and Art* (Berkeley, Calif., 1978), p. 48.
36. *Ibid.*
37. *Some Versions of Pastoral* (1935; 1950 edn), p. 11.
38. *Ibid.*, p. 23.
39. *Ibid.*, p. 11.
40. *Ibid.*, p. 21.
41. *The Oxford Chekhov*, VI, 64 and 132.
42. *Ibid.*, V, 224.
43. *The Flying Goat* (1939), p. 315. This story was also included by Bates in his collections *Thirty-One Selected Tales* (1947) and *Seven by Five* (*1963*). All the Bates stories referred to can be found in *Seven by Five*, which has been frequently reprinted in paperback form.
44. *The Evening Standard Years*, pp. 312–13 (10 Oct. 1929).
45. *The Book of Sand*, p. 77.
46. See Introduction to *A Hundred Merry Tales and Other English Jestbooks of the Fifteenth and Sixteenth Centuries*, (Lincoln, Nebraska, 1963), p. 3.
47. *Ibid.*, p. 2.

48. *Ibid.*, p. 9.
49. *A Choice of Kipling's Prose*, p. vi.
50. 'The Judgment of Paris' is included in *A Chair on the Boulevard* (1920), a collection of Merrick stories about bohemian life in Paris.
51. 'Dayspring Mishandled', *Limits and Renewals*, pp. 3–32 *passim*.
52. *A Grammar of Stories: An Introduction* (The Hague, 1973), p. 21 and p. 24. Propp's study was made in 1928 and later translated into English; see *Morphology of the Folktale*, 2nd rev. edn (Bloomington, 1968).
53. *The Short Story* (1977), p. 6.
54. *Mystery and Manners: Occassional Prose*, eds Sally and Robert Fitzgerald (1972), p. 93.
55. *Ibid.*
56. *The Philosophy of the Short-story*, p. 35. Matthews makes a similar point earlier, pp. 18–19.
57. *Pictures and Conversations*, p. 188.
58. *Ibid.*
59. 'The Son's Veto' was first published in December 1891; in 1896 Hardy said that it was his best short story (see *Life's Little Ironies* and *A Changed Man*, ed. F. B. Pinion (1977), p. 489).
60. For another version of the ending, see Hardy's poem 'The Sailor's Mother'.
61. *The Black Dog and Other Stories* (1923), p. 133.
62. *It happened Like That* (1927), p. 13.
63. 'For Conscience' Sake', *Life's Little Ironies*, pp. 47–61 *passim*.
64. 'Free Fiction', p. 62.
65. *The Black Dog*, p. 201.
66. Wright, *The American Short Story in the Twenties* (Chicago, 1961) *passim*.
67. For Matthews's comments on Trollope as a writer who offers only 'excellent specimens of the story which is short', see *The Philosophy of the Short-story*, pp. 24–5.
68. Introduction to *The Oxford Book of Short Stories* (Oxford, 1981), p, xii.
69. 'Mrs General Talboys' was first published in *The London Review*, Feb. 1861, and then collected later the same year in *Tales of All Countries*. It is included in *Nineteenth Century Short Stories*.
70. *Henry James and H. G. Wells*, p. 134.
71. *Short Stories of the 'Nineties: A Biographical Anthology* (1968), p. 29.
72. *Ibid.*
73. *Ibid.*, p. 13.
74. *The Left Bank* was Rhys's first book, and she later considered many of the sketches unworthy of republication. A selection, approved by the author was, however, made and published in 1968; it was included in *Tigers are Better-Looking*, Penguin pbk edn (Harmondsworth, Middx, 1972; repr. 1981).
75. *Something Short and Sweet,* p. 266.
76. Introduction to *Horizon Stories* (1943), p. 5.
77. *Mystery and Manners*, p. 94.
78. *Ibid.*, p. 95.

Chapter 8

'THE SPLINTERING FRAME'

> The Novel in English was produced in an atmosphere of security for
> the entertainment of secure people who liked to feel established and
> safe for good. Its standards were established within that apparently
> permanent frame and the criticism of it began to be irritated and
> perplexed when, through a new instability, the splintering frame began
> to get into the picture.
>
> (H. G. Wells)

When Virginia Woolf described the power of great essays to 'haunt
the mind and remain entire in the memory', she was using terms
which apply equally well to the short story.[1] Yet although the short
story was prospering at the time Woolf made this comment, the conversational essay apparently enjoyed no comparable vogue; if anything, it had declined, eclipsed rather than assisted by the fresh
interest in short fiction which led Elizabeth Bowen to say that in the
1920s the short story gained new acceptance as a 'free form'.[2] Even
before the start of the decade, interest in the essay seemed to be
waning: in 1919 Woolf lamented that the art of essay-writing was
already lost, Max Beerbohm, 'our solitary essayist', providing an
exception that made it all the more perplexing that such a rewarding
form should be neglected.[3] One reason for this situation is offered
by Woolf herself when she conjectures that 'it is in the nature of
these short pieces that they need unity and a mind at harmony with
itself', commodities which were in short measure for the contemporary writer: 'The essays of Montaigne, Lamb, even Addison',
writes Woolf, 'have the reticence which springs from composure, for
with all their familiarity they never tell us what they wish to keep
hidden.'[4]

The blend of detachment and individuality which Virginia Woolf
identified as the mark of good essay-writing seemed with hindsight
to have depended on serenity and confidence, although the complaint that these had vanished from modern life was not new with
the twentieth century. W. E. Henley had made a very similar point

in the late nineteenth century when he recorded the demise of 'your true essayist', a candid and independent-minded creature who is, 'in a literary sense the friend of everybody'.[5] Henley too blamed the pace of modern life: 'In these hysterical times life is so full, so much is asked and so much has to be given, that tranquil writing and careful workmanship are impossible'.[6] What resulted, according to Henley, was precisely that excess and self-display which in an earlier chapter we saw Chekhov condemning in the short-storywriter; authors began to compete for attention by writing in an eye-catching way, working, so Henley says, 'as men paint for exhibitions: with the consciousness that we must pass notice if we do not exceed in colour and subject and tone'.[7]

Yet the forces which lowered regard for the essay or, as Henley and Virginia Woolf believed, made it virtually impossible to write good essays from the late nineteenth century onwards, are actually those which are cited as giving the modern short story its prime impetus. In 1938, H. E. Bates, for example, could proclaim that the short story's 'flexibility, almost unlimited range of subject and sympathy, and its very brevity, make it as perfectly suitable to the expression and mood of this age as the heroic couplet was to the age of Pope'.[8] It was the very fragmentariness of the genre which gave it a unique and distinguished role, upsetting previous notions about the relative greatness of different literary kinds and, to Bates's mind at least, offering 'in every way a finer means of expression of our age of unrest, disbelief and distrust, than either the novel or poetry'.[9] Others agreed that the traditional novel was incapable of registering the 'new instability' referred to by H. G. Wells in the passage which provides the epigraph for this chapter: 'the splintering frame' was pushing further and further into the picture, and one obvious answer was to dispense with the weakened frame and let the splinters *be* the picture, each short story presenting a different shard, with no pretence of wholeness beyond itself.[10] This is surely what lies behind Nadine Gordimer's statement that, 'The short story is a fragmented and restless form, a matter of hit or miss, and it is perhaps for this reason that it suits modern consciousness – which seems best expressed as flashes of insight alternating with near-hypnotic states of indifference.'[11] This view of the short story as 'the art of the only thing one can be sure of – the present moment' has produced a dominant strand in twentieth-century short fiction: many writers have chosen to imitate the restlessness they see around them by fragmenting the very forms in which they work.[12]

But this type of realism is not the only possibility to emerge from the new sense of the inadequacy of the novel, as is indicated by Mary McCarthy's observation that the novel, rooted in common sense and rationality, is 'of all forms the least adapted to encompass the modern world, whose leading characteristic is irreality'.[13] Here we take a step beyond the 'unrest' noted by Bates and Gordimer, and the short story as an alternative form is implicitly given an even fuller task to perform: it will not only reflect the disturbed, fragmentary quality of modern life, it will deal with 'irreality', a project which clearly includes the possibility of replenishing the elements of fantasy and the supernatural that have been associated with short fiction since its inception.

Individual responses to the dislocations which characterize the modern writer's situation vary widely, but two main tendencies are discernible, corresponding to alternative strategies and different notions of the artist's possibilities. On the one hand, the short-storywriter may conceive his task to be the charting of a reality which is essentially alien and baffling, while on the other, he may believe that it is the artist's job to confront and challenge the 'irreality' of modern existence by positing alternative worlds – realms of order which perhaps exist only in fantasy but which nonetheless express defiance of the way actual life squanders ideals. In this chapter a number of twentieth-century writers will be considered within the broad categories, 'realist' and 'romantic', which are suggested by these divergent, but not irreconcilable, tendencies. Central to the question of what kind of story a modern writer feels he can (and should) be writing is the issue of 'personality' raised by Virginia Woolf in her discussion of the essay as a dying form: for both realist and romantic, the matter of the writer's relation to his material is crucial and problematic; after all, the decade in which Virginia Woolf watched the personal yet reticent essay disappear was also the period which saw the publication of major modernist texts like Eliot's *Waste Land* and Joyce's *Ulysses* (both published in 1922), and during which the doctrine of artistic impersonality gained enormous power. To a large extent the stories of writers like Virginia Woolf and Katherine Mansfield can be seen as attempts to participate in, while at the same time withstand, developments which moved the artist further and further towards the stance famously described by Joyce as that of an aloof god who pares his fingernails, remote from the contingencies of created life.

In part, both Virginia Woolf and Katherine Mansfield were motivated by a well-founded feeling that in discussions of literature, poetry was capturing the most attention. Their defensiveness on behalf of prose recalls Brander Matthews's objection that late nineteenth-century aesthetic debates were too narrowly concentrated on the novel, and their comments display similar determination to correct an imbalance. Reviewing Logan Pearsall Smith's anthology *A Treasury of English Prose* in 1920 Virginia Woolf struck a side-blow against the supremacy of poetry, claiming that writers who keep 'beautiful English prose alive' deserve the highest honour, and adopting a mock-respectful attitude towards poetry:

> For though English poetry was a fine old potentate – but no, I dare
> not breathe a word against English poetry. All I will venture is a sigh
> of wonder that when there is prose before us with its capacities and
> possibilities, its power to say new things, make new shapes, express
> new passions, young people should still be dancing to a barrel organ
> and choosing words because they rhyme.[14]

For Katherine Mansfield; modern poetry was less a cumbrous dance
to the sound of a barrel-organ than a 'Masked Ball' where identities
were never revealed: she complained that the poetry of her contemporaries was unsatisfying because its impersonality never allowed us
to see behind the mask, and she too marvelled at the neglect of
prose.[15] Reading Jules Laforgue, so she noted in her Journal in July
1919, 'only makes one feel how one adores English prose, how to
be a writer – is *everything*. . . . People have never explored the
lovely medium of prose. It is a hidden country still – I feel that so
profoundly.'[16]

   Yet the novel no longer seemed the genre in which best to
explore 'the lovely medium of prose'. Almost despairingly, and temporarily forgetting that Henry James ever existed, Virginia Woolf
wrote in a 1925 letter: 'What is form? What is character? What is
a novel? . . . The truth is of course that no one for 100 years has
given a thought to novels, as they have done to poetry; and now we
wake up, suffocated, to find ourselves completely in the dark.'[17] For
the sake of future generations, Woolf's generation must, as she had
earlier put it, 'break its neck', accepting that 'the beauty which
comes from completeness' – the beauty of *War and Peace*, or Sten-
dhal, or Jane Austen – must be renounced.[18] All that the present
generation could hope to achieve would be 'fragments – paragraphs –
a page perhaps: but no more'.[19] But if these 'fragments' were to
attain their own kind of beauty, then it would be by indirection, and
not by producing 'little daisies and forget-me-nots – simpering sweet-
nesses – true love-knots'.[20]

   For Virginia Woolf, models of the kind of storytelling she felt
modern literature needed came not from France or England, where
even the best stories struck her as dull because 'events seem
threaded like beads on a string', but from Russia.[21] Reviewing
Constance Garnett's translation of *The Bishop and other Stories* by
Chekhov in 1919, Virginia Woolf pointed out that expectations and
assumptions about what constitutes a story had changed: no one, she
comments, is likely to complain that Chekhov's 'The Bishop' (which
first appeared in 1902) is not a story at all but a 'vague and inconclusive account of a bishop who was distressed because his mother
treated him with respect, and soon after died of typhoid'.[22] What
Chekhov offered was perfectly in tune with the new mood of instability, and yet his stories could provide a measure of solace too:

We are by this time alive to the fact that inconclusive stories are legitimate; that is to say, though they leave us feeling melancholy and perhaps uncertain, yet somehow they provide a resting-point for the mind – a solid object casting its shade of reflection and speculation. The fragments of which it is composed may have the air of having come together by chance.[23]

In her own short fiction Virginia Woolf aimed at the same effects of inconsequentiality and inconclusiveness that she admired in Chekhov, composing stories out of fragments which 'have the air of having come together by chance' and which provide a narrative of sensation and sense-impressions instead of a narrative of events. In a story like 'Kew Gardens' the random qualities of life, and the unsatisfactory nature of human attempts to communicate inner experience, are conveyed by focusing now on one, now on another human relationship; people wander in a desultory way past the flowerbed, which is evoked, (almost literally embodying a Chekhovian 'solid object casting its shade of reflection and speculation'), in the densely textured opening paragraph. In this connection, it is important to note that as first published by the Hogarth Press, 'Kew Gardens' was itself a discrete aesthetic object, appearing within its own covers, illustrated with Vanessa Bell's woodcuts and providing the Woolfs with a runaway success.[24]

'Kew Gardens' satisfied Virginia Woolf's demand for indirection in art by depending for its unity on the consciously wrought quality of its prose-style rather than on the stated presence of a narrating consciousness. The writer's thought is expressed obliquely through impassively recorded visual and aural perceptions and through the interweaving of images, notably images of movement, which are contrasted to the static rigidity of objects within the story – the brass candlestick, for example, or the walking-stick and parasol used by different characters at moments when the unspoken threatens to overwhelm outwardly calm appearances. The style of this piece clearly owes a good deal to Virginia Woolf's belief that the distinction between prose and poetry was being made too strenuously, and that what modern prose required was to have rhapsody restored to it. Part of the blame, she maintained, lay with critics who exaggerated the differences between poetry and prose, but another factor was the rise of realism in fiction which disdained lyricism in favour of facts, seeming to work on the assumption that 'if only the egg is real and the kettle boils, stars and nightingales will somehow be thrown in by the imagination of the reader'.[25] What she predicted was that the fact-recording power of fiction would decline, and fiction would more and more resemble poetry; it would recapture the power exemplified by Sterne in *Tristram Shandy*, giving once more 'the relation of the mind to general ideas and its soliloquy in soli-

tude' and involving the writer and reader together in close intimacy.[26] Sterne's fascination with 'fancies and sensibilities' of his own
mind was the source of a brand of intimacy which Virginia Woolf
also associated with the essay form, where hard fact could be dis-
solved into distant prospects, 'cloudlike and supple', and where reason and rhapsody were assimilated rather than set at variance.[27]

Interestingly, one of the essayists Virginia Woolf admired most,
De Quincey, could be described with equal accuracy as a writer of
prose poems: his *Autobiographic Sketches* (1834–53), which Woolf
praised for the way they use prose to shift 'the values of familiar
things', belong very properly in an anthology of *English Prose Lyrics*
like the one edited by Wilhelm Füger in 1976.[28] De Quincey, as
Füger reminds us; 'not only developed an influential theory that
strongly defended prose as a legitimate and by no means inferior
medium of poetic expression, but also successfully practised this
mode of writing in many of his works'.[29] 'Kew Gardens', along with
the four plotless prose-sketches ('Monday or Tuesday'; 'The String
Quartet', 'A Haunted House', and 'Blue and Green') written by
Woolf around 1920 and collected in *Monday or Tuesday* (1921),
clearly owe a good deal to the tradition of the prose poem as it
descended to her through De Quincey and, closer to her own
period, Oscar Wilde and Ernest Dowson, whose 'studies in sentiment' treated subjects usually associated with poetry. In fact, she
makes De Quincey sound very much like a prototype for herself
when she says, in her essay on 'Impassioned Prose' that in his writing
'it is not the actual sight or sound itself that matters, but the rever-
berations it makes as it travels through our minds'.[30]

Seen in this context, Virginia Woolf represents one side of the
prose/poetry controversy which engrossed numerous writers on both
sides of the Atlantic in the first two decades of the twentieth century,
and in which the influence of European writers like Baudelaire and
Rimbaud played a significant part. New possibilities were opened
to all imaginative writers, irrespective of the medium they were
working in, by French symbolism, which drew its images from
ordinary life and then treated them with such intensity that they
became suggestive of an entire world behind surface appearances.
Even T. S. Eliot, who resolutely opposed the idea of 'poetry in
prose', wrote a prose poem 'Hysteria' (1917) early in his career.
Here the preoccupation with random fragments of experience which
characterizes both the modern short story and Eliot's major poetry is
evident. As the last bizarre sentence of 'Hysteria' alone demonstrates,
there is the same obsession with linking disparate perceptions: 'I decided that if the shaking of her breasts could be stopped; some of the
fragments of the afternoon might be collected, and I concentrated my
attention with careful subtlety to this end.'[31]

Within the same genre belong the 'epiphanies' which James Joyce wrote between 1901 and 1905, where sharply registered sense-impressions create an atmosphere of unease, as in the dream-like encounter with 'an arctic beast with a rough yellow coat'; the first-person narrator thrusts at the creature with a stick: 'He moves his paws heavily and mutters words of some language which I do not understand.'[32] But of course for Joyce, as for Woolf and Eliot, the prose lyric was merely apprentice work, their greatest endeavours appearing in major forms which reveal affinities with, but do not depend on, the material explored in early short pieces. In the case of Woolf, what matters most in our consideration of the short story as a genre is that a piece like 'Kew Gardens', a work which E. M. Forster described as 'vision unalloyed' (without a moral, with no philosophy and no form in the usual sense) exemplifies a type of neo-romantic writing which aims to poeticize prose, and to disengage it from everyday language.[33] Forster related the deliberate aimlessness and long loose sentences of 'Kew Gardens' to innovatory developments in English prose when he reviewed the piece in 1919, and twenty-five years later, lecturing on 'The Development of English Prose between 1918 and 1939', he cited Virginia Woolf, along with Lytton Strachey, as an example of a writer who led prose in esoteric directions.[34]

The other trend identified by Forster, the popular tendency to replenish prose with contemporary speech and colloquial idiom, deserves equal attention, and is probably of more lasting significance to the history of the short story. In this instance, Forster's chosen example was Ernest Hemingway, whose style, though no less deliberately contrived than Virginia Woolf's, offered far more reminders that prose, unlike poetry, serves practically useful purposes in daily life as well as creating art. Partly as a result of his experience as a journalist, Hemingway's style keeps the reader constantly in touch with the diction and rhythms of ordinary speech; his stories are structured on repetitions artfully interwoven and given an intensity which combats limitations of length by exploiting language's other dimension, its depth. What is produced is an arrangement of words which in themselves are unremarkable but which, through Hemingway's patternings, yield images as vibrant as those captured in an imagist poem.

Hemingway's technique is especially suitable for recounting what has been described as 'the inevitable doom that overtakes nearly anonymous people in nearly anonymous settings'.[35] The way in which his unemotional presentation of isolated people, often trapped in a personal neurosis, can become timeless and universal in its impact is illustrated by the stories in the volume significantly entitled *Men Without Women* (1927). Among these, 'Now I Lay Me', displays markedly the features which give Hemingway's prose a mythic quality reminiscent of ancient fable. The title itself is allusive, although the omission of the final words in the quotation 'Now I lay me down to sleep' provides a hint that the reassuring associations of the original expression have been lost and that the story is to provide an ironic context for a familiar ritual of prayer and sleep. The four simple lines of the anonymous verse, which was first printed in a late edition of the *New England Primer* (1781), afford a striking contrast to the story's dominant mood:

> Now I lay me down to sleep;
> I pray the Lord my soul to keep.
> If I should die before I wake,
> I pray the Lord my soul to take.

In Hemingway's story, there is none of this calm spiritual readiness, nor any of the self-acceptance which marks King Lear's moving words; 'I'll pray, and then I'll sleep' in Act III, scene iv of Shakespeare's play. The mood of 'Now I Lay Me' is one of restlessness, and if there is any calm, then it is the calmness of despair. This impression is borne out by the first sentence, which combines a colloquial tone with a strange effect of abnormally heightened sense-perception: 'That night we lay on the floor and I listened to the silk-worms eating.' Initially, interest seems to be concentrated on what is heard rather than on the listener, and the second sentence conveys an effort to capture precisely the qualities of the sound: 'The silk-worms fed in racks of mulberry leaves and all night you could hear them eating and a dropping sound in the leaves.' Attention is diverted from the 'I' of the story, postponing any explanation of his wakefulness until the third, and far longer, sentence which informs us that, 'I myself did not want to sleep because I had been living for a long time with the knowledge that if I ever shut my eyes in the dark and let myself go, my soul would go out of my body.' The understated language, with its repetition of the colourless mono-syllable 'go', adds indirectly to the feeling that the narrator's experience is truly horrifying, and that he is trying to articulate an almost metaphysical fear in ordinary terms. The verb 'go', or one of its variants, occurs no less than five more times in the next three sentences which complete the opening paragraph, by the end of which the reader is not only acquainted with the narrator's predicament but also attuned to Hemingway's rhythm of repetitions.

The entire story progresses by means of these repetitions and the echoes they create. Various words and phrases denoting time in the first paragraph ('That night'; 'all night'; 'a long time'; 'ever since'; 'ever'; 'never'; 'since'; 'now'; and 'then') establish an atmosphere of disquiet and on this Hemingway builds an extended account of the narrator's private rituals, all of them reversing the traditional purpose of prayer since they are tactics for staying awake, not preludes to healing rest. Mentally reconstructing fishing trips made in boyhood, the narrator simultaneously compresses his experiences for the reader while prolonging them for himself, lingering on details which will quell his fear of oblivion. This double effect arises from Hemingway's patterning of frequently repeated words like 'sometimes', 'always', 'often', 'once', words which are banal in themselves yet, in the way they are deployed to punctuate the narrator's thoughts, are essential parts of a complex psychological excursion into the past. Significantly, as the narrator recalls the traumatic moment when he once used a lovely salamander for bait, the words denoting time press against one another, producing a dense texture which still manages to be authentic as recorded speech: 'He had tiny feet that tried to hold on to the hook, and *after* that *one time* I *never* used a salamander, although I found them very *often*' (my italics).

The reader is closely involved in sharing the narrator's memories, yet it is not until the next phase of the story that the word 'remember' is mentioned, and when it does come it seems entirely prepared for by what has already been dramatized through the narrator's consciousness. Once it has been uttered, 'remember' becomes a key word in the story, occurring eighteen times in the course of seven paragraphs (one short paragraph of less than sixty words has 'remember' four times, a frequency which would be startling in a stanza of poetry), and reaching a hectic pitch at the point where memory actually fails and we are brought back to the opening situation. It is also at this point that the word 'sleep' takes over the role of carrying meaning forward through repetitions. To demonstrate Hemingway's technique here, the passage needs to be quoted in full:

> Some nights, though, I could not remember my prayers even. I could only get as far as 'On earth as it is in heaven' and then have to start all over and be absolutely unable to get past that. Then I would have to recognize that I could not remember and give up saying my prayers that night and try something else. So on some nights I would try to remember all the animals in the world by name and then fishes and then countries and cities and then kinds of food and the names of all the streets I could remember in Chicago, and when I could not remember anything at all any more I would just listen. And I do not remember a night on which you could not hear things. If I could have a light I was not afraid to sleep, because I knew my soul would only go out of me if it were dark. So, of course, many nights I was where I could have a light and then I slept because I was nearly always tired and often very sleepy. And I am sure many times too that I slept without knowing it – but I never slept knowing it, and on this night I listened to the silk-worms. You can hear silk-worms eating very clearly in the night and I lay with my eyes open and listened to them.

Here, there are not only echoes of earlier patterns ('Some nights'; 'go out of me'; 'silk-worms') but the transition from memory as the dominant concept, to the story's central preoccupation – sleep. It is as much a recoil as a transition; at this moment of apparent impasse it is as though the narrator has no inner resources left for fighting sleep, and relief is felt when he mentions (for the first time since the unexplained 'we' of the opening sentence) the other occupant of the room. Now the repeated word is 'awake', easing the story into a passage of dialogue between the narrator and his orderly, during which bland words like 'good' and 'nice' recur, with 'sleep' returning to prominence, and then, in the story's last phase, 'married' (first used early in the dialogue and providing the only social reference so far) becoming dominant. And it is the idea of marriage which brings the story to a natural close. The orderly has insisted:

> 'A man ought to be married. You'll never regret it. Every man ought to be married.'
> 'All right', I said. 'Let's try and sleep a while.'
> 'All right Signor Tenente. I'll try it again. But you remember what I said.'
> 'I'll remember it', I said. 'Now let's sleep a while; John.'
> 'All right', he said. 'I hope you sleep, Signor Tenente.'

The themes of memory and sleep, never far apart at any point in the story, are brought together again, and with this the story's opening situation recurs. John falls rapidly to sleep: 'Then he started to snore. I listened to him snore for a long time and then I stopped listening to him snore and listened to the silk-worms eating. They ate steadily, making a dropping in the leaves'. All that has changed is that the narrator has 'a new thing to think about', although he soon finds that in comparison with dearly loved trout-streams 'all the girls I had ever known and what kinds of wives they would make' lack sufficient clarity as images to stave off sleep. But the human contact with the orderly endures, and it is with an almost envious, though ironic, comment on John's simple convictions that the story ends: 'He was going back to America and he was very certain about marriage and knew it would fix up everything'. The story demonstrates that there is no procedure sure to 'fix up everything', not social relationships like marriage, and not, either, the supposed balm, sleep, the image which, carrying with it a host of figurative associations within literary tradition, provides the story's encompassing ironic allusion.[36] Hemingway has drawn obliquely on a reservoir of echoes, using the historical dimension of language to give his story depth and complexity.

The impression left by 'Now I Lay Me' is a mixture of intimacy and detachment: we are close to the narrator, and yet he remains distant, locked in his own anxieties. We do not see anything of his war experiences, the events which remain unspoken, precisely because they block the flow of memory the narrator is so desperate to preserve. The story's effect is largely due to its cool prose style, flat tone, and dispassionate manner. Structure is not a matter of linear development, but of building up sequences consisting of repetitions; each stage introduces, often unobtrusively, words and phrases which are to play a central part in the next, acquiring cumulative significance while always referring back to the initial situation. Similar devices are evident throughout Hemingway's work; in another story from *Men Without Women*, 'Hills Like White Elephants', the innocuous colloquialism 'fine' is used repeatedly to create a rhythm which expresses ironically the stasis of the relationship between man and girl. Hemingway's style works superbly well for the presentation of detached, emotionally atrophied characters, or, with more approval, stoics like the soldiers in 'In Another Country' (1927), where grim chance is shown to be stronger than bonds of fellowship: 'We were all a little detached, and there was nothing that held us together except that we met every afternoon at the hospital'.[37]

Although based on contemporary situations and mediated by recognisably twentieth-century voices, Hemingway's stories still recall imaginative forms which pre-date the existence of a highly literate reading public. Their objectivity of approach conforms very closely to Virginia Woolf's account of artistic anonymity in an uncompleted essay which was to be the opening chapter of a book about 'the universality of the creative instinct'.[38] In this piece she explores ways in which 'Anon', the outsider whose social isolation gives him the freedom to articulate emotions embedded in the human psyche, charts 'the world beneath our consciousness, the anonymous world to which we can still return', and so speaks for the community as a whole.[39] Strangely enough, Woolf could be describing Hemingway, not Malory, when she says that *Morte D'Arthur* is 'told with a child's implicit belief. It has a child's love of particularity. Everything is stated. The beauty is in the statement, not in the suggestion. . . . The world is seen without comment.'[40] People often talk of the tough masculinity of Hemingway's style, and yet it is often marked by a naive acceptance of things as they are, a child-like quality which is reflected by the simplicity of style and the absence of authorial comment. Equally applicable to Hemingway is Woolf's statement that once Caxton had taken the irrevocable step and printed 'the old dream', bringing to the surface 'the old hidden world' and killing 'Anon' with the very invention designed to preserve him, writers risked being seen as standing behind rather than in their work: 'Of the writer', Woolf writes, still talking about Malory, 'the scholar can find something. But Malory is not distinct from his book. The voice is still the voice of Anon.'[41] Similarly, Hemingway is not distinct from his stories, overcoming what Woolf saw as the silencing of a 'nameless wandering voice' throughout the centuries after Spenser, when 'the thing the writer has to say' became 'increasingly cumbered', and 'to disengage the song from the effect of the audience' became a task for the critic, 'that specially equipped taster'.[42] Hemingway's melancholy 'songs' are attached to no single audience, in fact they seem totally unaware of any audience at all, and they pare away all encumbrances from 'the thing the writer has to say'. In almost every respect Virginia Woolf's itemization of the freedoms enjoyed by 'Anon' corresponds to features of Hemingway's art:

> Anonymity was a great possession. It gave the early writing an impersonality, a generality. It gave us the ballads; it gave us the songs. It allowed us to know nothing of the writer: and so to concentrate on the song. Anon had great privileges. He was not responsible. He was not self conscious. He can borrow. He can repeat. He can say what everyone feels. No one tries to stamp his own name, to discover his own experience in his work. He keeps at a distance from the present moment. Anon the lyric poet repeats over and over again that flowers fade; that death is the end.[43]

Hemingway's style is aloof in the same way as a ballad-maker's language is, and yet at the same time it is in harmony with the most advanced developments in literary prose during the early part of the twentieth century. A view of Hemingway as a latter-day 'Anon' is perfectly compatible with a depiction of him as an American James Joyce. Certainly, Frank O'Connor's analysis of Joyce's style highlights qualities to be found in many of Hemingway's stories too. With both writers, 'style ceases to be a relationship between author and reader and becomes a relationship of a magical kind between author and object. . . . It is not an attempt at communicating the experience to the reader, who is supposed to be present only by courtesy, but at equating the prose with the experience'.[44] By basing his prose style on what Forrest Read has called 'the form of an emotion rather than the form of a short story', Joyce had invented a kind of prose imagism which was, Read claims, 'perfectly adapted to register modern life both objectively and as it struck the sensitive individual'; again, the description fits Hemingway's technique well.[45] Alternatively, Hemingway's prose can be seen as exemplifying the compressed juxtapositioning of ideas which Ezra Pound discerned in Japanese seventeen-syllable poems, *hokku*. Through affinities like these the short story manifests its ability to transcend both national and generic boundaries; it was Pound's conviction that good modern poetry would be an evolution of the prose written by nineteenth-century realists like Flaubert and Maupassant, and so it is possible to trace for Hemingway a literary lineage in which poetry and prose exert a combined influence. There are undoubtedly many reminiscences of Flaubert, as well as of Pound, in Hemingway – the visual method; the way transitions are achieved by means of a phrase, and above all the objective technique which presents but does not analyse. For the 'generality' aimed at in his stories, Hemingway's method was perfectly adapted, but the movement away from plot exemplified by his work and that of other writers in the 1920s should not be seen as a permanently fruitful tendency in short-storywriting. Elizabeth Bowen was right to feel, in the 1960s, that the 'free form' story had run its course; and she was honest in her admission that for many writers, herself included, the fashion for plotlessness was a convenience rather than an opportunity to make genuine innovations: 'Impressionism lightly laced with psychology bought one out of needing to have a plot. At that time that suited me, as it did others.'[46] Perhaps Bowen's mature preference for 'narrative short stories, with a beginning, a crisis, and an end' seems a disappointingly conservative return to the old ways sanctioned by Poe, but this would be a shallow response.[47] No matter how experimental the short story becomes in different periods and in different hands, the narrative impulse is never totally displaced or superannuated, and in fact the most exciting experiments in twentieth-century fiction have come from writers who have attempted to give their stories the fabular, sometimes mythic, impersonality evident in Hemingway, while adhering to the venerable narrative pattern of 'beginning, crisis, and end'. Impersonality, as Bowen recognized, can be an excuse for lack of inventiveness, and there is the further danger that it can be used, not to express a view of life, but to disguise the fact that the author does not actually have a view of life to express. There is a world of difference between choosing to convey personal beliefs by artistically impersonal methods and using objectivity as a mask which covers a blank face; the difference is between gaps and elisions which actually mean something, and mere empty spaces, voids which constitute evasions instead of essential, though silent, statements by the author.

The issue here is that of individual voice, what Eudora Welty calls 'the writer behind the writing', or the 'individual and personal factor' which is ultimately what determines 'the way emphasis falls, the value of a story'.[48] Similarly, the Irish writer Sean O'Faolain calls the short story a 'personal exposition', arguing that, 'What one searches for and what one enjoys in a short story is a special distillation of personality, a unique sensibility which has recognized and selected at once a subject that, above all other subjects, is of value to the writer's temperament and to him alone.'[49] There is no yearning for anonymity here; on the contrary, these writers, to whose names many others could be added, see the short story as valuable in so far as it conveys a view of life inalienably linked with the writer's individual make-up. And this is a purpose which no amount of technical expertise can adequately fulfil; technique can be acquired, learned from other writers, but it is not what finally gives value and lasting importance to a short story.

The feeling that the high degree of technical proficiency displayed by a writer like Hemingway actually militates against the expression of a personal vision is perhaps what accounts for the waning of his influence, which was dominant between the wars and by the late forties had diminished considerably. By 1949, as the American short-storywriter Caroline Gordon noted, the position occupied by Hemingway in the twenties now belonged to a writer who had died in 1924 but whose work was little known until after the second world war – Franz Kafka. Here was a writer who, like Hemingway, gave stories a naturalistic surface, but whose grasp was wider, showing up Hemingway's symbolism as narrow, his characters as childish in their reflective moments. In Hemingway's stories, Caroline Gordon argued, a 'symbolic plane of action' is only glimpsed intermittently and fitfully, neither underlying the 'Naturalistic plane of action solidly', nor managing to 'over-arch it grandly, as Kafka's symbolism does'.[50] As a result, Hemingway is to the writer of 1949 what Maupassant was to James's generation, a 'lion in the path', but a lion perhaps not fearsome enough; the 'best contemporary writers', according to Caroline Gordon, were taking an altogether different path, following Kafka into 'a deeper jungle' than Hemingway had explored.[51]

The extent to which Kafka's fiction was rooted in his own experiences is well-established, but what concerns us here are not autobiographical traces but the artist's capacity to communicate a vision which is at once personal and universal. A letter to his publisher about the story 'In the Penal Colony' (completed in 1914), is characteristic of the way Kafka saw in his own experience a heightened image of the age in which he was living; from reference to the particular story in question he expands outward until he has conceived himself as a kind of symbol:

> Your criticism of the painful element accords completely with my opinion, but then I feel the same way about almost everything I have written so far. Have you noticed how few things are free of this painful element in one form or another? By way of clarifying this last story, I need only add that the painfulness is not peculiar to it alone but that our times in general and my own time as well have also been painful and continue to be, and my own even more consistently than the times.[52]

It is, therefore, not as an idiosyncratic sensibility that Kafka offers his personality in his stories, but as an almost prophetic voice which discloses man's own reality to him, an activity which involves fantasy rather than documentation, since 'the dream reveals the reality, which conception lags behind'.[53] One photographs things, Kafka says, 'in order to get them out of one's mind'; in contrast, his stories 'are a kind of closing one's eyes'.[54] This keen internal vision involves a distancing effect which in Kafka is the equivalent of the objectivity sought by writers following the Flaubertian tradition: distancing in this case is not to be confused with detachment. When Kafka pronounces that 'one speaks best about what is strange to one', he is not renouncing the right to express his own individuality through the strange situations he depicts; rather, he finds in the realms of fantasy, where the rationally impossible becomes commonplace, ways of confronting truths which are hidden when anyone stands too close to what is there, waiting to be perceived.[55] His story 'The Stoker' (1913), which he insisted should be subtitled 'A Fragment', may have been 'the remembrance of a dream, of something that perhaps never really existed', but the crucial thing is that it is a dream seen all the more clearly because of its remoteness.[56] It was for this reason, no doubt, that Kafka had misgivings about the use of an illustrated frontispiece depicting the Ferry at Brooklyn: his objection was not that the picture would harden the images of his story into too clear-cut lines, but that it 'had the advantage over my story since it produced its effect before my story did, and a picture is naturally more concentrated than prose'.[57] On reflection, however, Kafka came to feel that his prose was enriched by the illustration, and 'that already an exchange of strengths and weaknesses has taken place between picture and book'; opinions like these ones accentuate Kafka's desire to give his style the vivid immediacy of pictorial art, even when treating situations the essence of which is isolation from ordinary human society.[58] In 'Metamorphosis' (1915) dislocation is figured by the initial situation – the boundaries between human and insect life are transgressed – but although the basic premise of the story is fantastic, Kafka's method is rigorously attentive to realistic detail. It is the seer, man transformed into beetle, and not the seen which is extraordinary in this story; that is why Kafka anxiously insisted that the illustrator must on no account draw the insect itself: 'Not that, please not that! I do not want to restrict [the illustrator], but only to make this plea out of my deeper knowledge of the story. The insect itself cannot be depicted. It cannot even be shown from a distance.'[59] Kafka's own suggestions for the illustration emphasize his concern to keep in focus the pathetic inadequacies of the well-meaning human beings who have to cope with the bizarre presence in their house: the parents and the head clerk in front of the locked door, he suggests, would make a good title-page drawing, or, with more sinister effect, the parents and Gregor's beloved sister 'in the lighted room, with the door open upon the adjoining room that lies in darkness'.[60]

The pictorial style to which Kafka's prose displays affinities is graphic and bold, the antithesis of the subjective manner he disliked in the Kokoschka drawings he was shown on one occasion recorded in *Conversations with Kafka*: 'I do not understand them', Kafka remarked, 'Drawing derives from to draw, to describe, to show. All they show me is the painter's internal confusion and disorder.'[61] Kafka 'draws' people, things, buildings in exactly the sense he means here, and for him 'to show' is also to relinquish the clutter which egoism carries around with it. In his advice to the young writer Gustav Janouch we can discern the combination of firmness and scepticism with which Kafka expressed these beliefs: 'You say far more about the impressions which things inspire in you than about the things and objects themselves. That is lyrical poetry. You caress the world, instead of grasping it.'[62] And then, having reassured his young friend that stories are not worthless just because they are so personal, Kafka goes on to tell him that his writing is 'not yet art':

> 'This description of feelings and impressions is most of all a hesitant groping for the world. The eyes are still heavy with dreams. But in time that will cease and then perhaps the outstretched groping hand will withdraw as if caught by fire. Perhaps you will cry out, stammer incoherently, or grind your teeth together and open your eyes wide, very wide. But – these are only words. Art is always a matter of the entire personality. For that reason it is fundamentally tragic.'[63]

The notion here of the short story delivering its meaning in little shocks like burns inflicted on a 'groping hand' has already been encountered in earlier chapters of this study, but where Kafka differs from other writers who share his sense that 'the ordinary is itself a miracle!' is in his radical doubts about the power of language to 'record' the miracle.[64]

'But – these are only words', Kafka tells Janouch, and in 1923 he explains to his closer friend Max Brod that his failure as a correspondent is due to 'strategic' reasons connected with his distrust of 'words and letters, my words and letters'.[65] Characteristically, the personal explanation leads to a general reflection: 'It sometimes seems to me that art in general, the existence of art, is explicable solely in terms of such "strategic considerations", of making possible the exchange of truthful words from person to person.'[66] All of Kafka's stories can be seen as strategies for transmitting a view of life as problematic, an undertaking that is concerned with truth in very much the same way as the ancient biblical parables were. But as Roy Pascal has pointed out, where religious parables use the simple story-line of an illustrative anecdote to promote an unambiguous meaning, in Kafka's work the expectation of significance aroused by straightforward narrative unfolding and 'type' characters is frustrated: instead of a didactic message, we find a 'baleful riddle', and no abstract formulation of the story's 'meaning' is possible.[67]

Kafka's characters inhabit a secular world, and although his talking animals derive from the world of fable, they do not jauntily convey exemplary moral lessons; instead, they share Kafka's predicament, wondering how to 'solder fragments together into a sweeping story'.[68] For Kafka, the answer often lay in choosing a central metaphor or a single unalterable set of circumstances from which the entire structure of the story would naturally follow, the situation itself frequently taking the form of an apparently endless quest, like that of the dog in 'Investigations of a Dog' (written in 1922) who poses an unanswerable question; or the scholarly narrator of the unfinished story 'The Great Wall of China' (probably dating from the winter of 1916–17) whose findings lead him to abandon his enquiry. There are no answers that can be expressed, but in the short stories at least this is not the tragic circumstance it is in Kafka's novels; Roy Pascal's comment that the stories and fables cast a more tender, humorous light on the dilemmas which destroy the heroes of the novels is well-judged. What is more, the shorter form is highly amenable to Kafka's awareness that human learning is something which occurs piecemeal, not progressively, and by quite other means than rational investigation.

In the face of mysteries which even the most tenacious investigator cannot penetrate satisfactorily, the artist becomes very properly a craftsman, acknowledging that 'the struggle against chance is always a struggle against ourselves, which we can never entirely win', yet calmly getting on with the task in hand.[69] It is significant that several of Kafka's metaphors for his own activity should have come from the manual crafts which he admired so much and which seem often to be associated in his mind with a particular kind of quietness and self-effacement. Seeing Gustav Janouch with a book of Johannes Becher's poems, for example, he remarked: 'They are so filled with noise and verbal uproar, that one cannot get away from oneself. Instead of bridges, the words form high unscalable walls. . . . The words never condense into language. They are a shriek and nothing more.'[70] To build bridges instead of walls meant for Kafka being like a carpenter who wants 'to hammer a table together in a painstaking and craftsmanlike way yet at the same time do nothing: but not so that people might say, "Hammering is nothing to him", but "Hammering is real hammering to him and at the same time it is nothing."'[71] This is Kafka's analogy for his artistic desire 'to achieve a view of life (and necessarily connected with this, of course, to make other people believe in it by writing) in which life would both retain its natural, heavy rise and fall and at the same time and with equal clarity be recognized as a nothing, a dream, a hovering'.[72] Such duality, offering simultaneously the familiar rhythms of life, like the regular rise and fall of the hammer, and the incalculable fluctuations of dream, can only be achieved by retaining calmness and quietness, the qualities which Kafka said 'make one free – even on the scaffold'.[73]

Within the stories, characters contemplate with wonder the prospect of such delicious freedom. Typical is the narrator of 'The Burrow' (written in 1923), who describes 'the loveliest imaginable haunt' he would acquire if only he could 'isolate his Castle Keep from its surroundings', leaving 'a free space' all around. He envisages the delights that would come to him: 'to avoid the Castle Keep, to rest one's eyes from it whenever one wanted, to postpone the joy of seeing it until later and yet not have to do without it, but literally hold it safe between one's claws, a thing that is impossible if you only have an ordinary open entrance to it'. There are no 'open entrances' in Kafka's fictional constructions, and in 'The Burrow' secrecy becomes an aspect of confident possession, one of the necessary strategies for defying society's restlessness:

> Then there would be no noises in the walls, no insolent burrowing up to the very keep itself; then peace would be assured there and I would be its guardian; then I would not have to listen with loathing to the burrowing of the small fry, but with delight to something that I cannot hear now at all: the murmurous silence of the Castle Keep.

Yet this project can never be fully realized, and having savoured in imagination the pleasures of standing guard over his own creation, the narrator tells himself that his 'beautiful dream is past and I must set to work . . .'[74]

It is in this sense, of perfection glimpsed then acknowledged as unattainable, that we should understand Kafka's statement that art expresses the *entire* personality. By being able 'to make friends with [his] own ignorance', the writer can manifest himself and so reach out beyond himself; 'how can one find another, by losing oneself?' Kafka asks.[75] What is more, 'the other – that is, the world in all its magnificent depths – only reveals itself in quietness'.[76] So although 'there is passion behind every art' it is expressed with reticence, that quality so frequently honoured by short-storywriters.[77]

To argue, as Kafka did, that all art is the expression of the *entire* personality does not entail acceptance of self-display. Quite the reverse; it involves a type of self-transcendence which is achieved by rejecting idiosyncrasies and ostentatious cleverness in favour of the austere task indicated by Kafka's admirer, Borges, when he wrote, 'now, having past seventy, I believe I have found my own voice'.[78] For an artist like Borges, this voice is not stridently personal or individualistic, but an expression, with its own cadences and tones, of a cultural inheritance shared by everyone: 'Each language is a tradition, each word a shared symbol, and what an innovator can change amounts to a trifle; we need only remember the splendid but often unreadable work of a Mallarmé or a Joyce.'[79] Where the individual voice is evident, then, is not in narrative 'surprises' or stylistic 'variations and novelties', but in the writer's selection and disposition of elements which he makes peculiarly his own by tapping what belongs to all of history and all of mankind.[80]

Borges is an especially important figure in the history of the short story because his eminence as a writer is based entirely on short pieces, and also because, in the course of a long literary career, he has moved from one genre to another. Until about 1930 his principal writing medium was poetry, although he also wrote many essays which recalled the work of G. K. Chesterton in their compactness and their startling use of paradox. In the thirties, Borges turned to short fictional narratives, bringing together the analytical quality of his essay-writing and the imaginative freedom of his poetry within a single form, and achieving a compression which was to be increased still further when his near-blindness led him to concentrate on even shorter forms (parable, for example) which could be dictated. The stories collected in 1970 under the title *Dr Brodie's Report* are therefore in the nature of a return to the genre Borges had abandoned for almost twenty years, and it is a return which is characterized by a determination not to show off or tease the reader: 'I have given up the surprises inherent in a baroque style as well as the surprises that lead to an unforeseen ending. I have, in short, preferred to satisfy an expectation rather than to provide a startling shock.'[81] There is a concern here for intimacy between writer and reader, calling to mind the sense of an audience or a group of listeners which preoccupied the 'artless' storytellers discussed in Chapter 4. The links between Borges' fiction and the oral tradition are very strong, providing him in fact with grounds for explaining without bashfulness why a long prose work is beyond him: why spend five hundred pages, he asks, 'developing an idea whose perfect oral exposition is possible in a few minutes?'[82] And in 'The Duel' he wittily reduces what might have been a Henry James novel to seven tightly-written pages which create an atmosphere of colloquial ease and implicitly overcome the breach between lofty writer and lonely reader so often associated with modernism.

Borges's emphasis on human solidarity, rather than on the isolation often associated with modern short fiction, reflects his vehement rejection of insular nationalism in literature. Both his European education and his conviction that twentieth-century European history was profoundly resonant for South Americans made him increasingly critical of Argentinian writers who maintained that, 'we are essentially alone and cannot play at being Europeans'.[83] In his essay 'The Argentine Writer and Tradition', Borges scorns the idea that 'we Argentines find ourselves in a situation like that of the first days of Creation', an opinion he finds to be 'unfounded', although

'I find it understandable that many people should accept it, because this declaration of our solitude, of our loss, of our primeval character, has, like existentialism, the charm of the pathetic. Many people can accept this opinion because, once they have done so, they feel alone, disconsolate, and in some way or another, interesting.'[84] Against such weary soulfulness, Borges proposes that Argentina, precisely because it is 'a new country', should assert its claim to a tradition that cannot be narrowed into provinciality: 'I believe', he affirms, 'our tradition is all of Western culture, and I also believe we have a right to this tradition, greater than that which the inhabitants of one or another Western nation might have.'[85] Recalling Thorstein Veblen's argument that Jews are pre-eminent in Western culture because they act within that culture without feeling devoted to it, Borges finds a comparable case in the part played by the Irish in English culture:

> We have no reason to suppose that the profusion of Irish names in British literature and philosophy is due to any racial pre-eminence, for many of these illustrious Irishmen (Shaw, Berkeley, Swift) were the descendents of Englishmen, were people who had no Celtic blood; however, it was sufficient for them to feel Irish, to feel different, in order to be innovators in English culture. I believe that we Argentinians, we South Americans in general, are in an analogous situation; we can handle all European themes, handle them without superstition, with an irreverence which can have, and already does have, fortunate consequences.[86]

The argument is reminiscent of William Dean Howells's observation that it was Mark Twain's ability to treat inherited solemnities irreverently that made him so important an innovator in American literature; and in wider terms, it recalls Frank O'Connor's appreciation of the short story's 'romantic, individualistic and intransigent'qualities.[87] But O'Connor's description of the advantages of cultural remoteness contains an irony which diminishes the appeal of his theory: not only should the ideal short-storywriter be born at an outpost of civilization, he should stay there. If O'Connor's argument is valid, then it is incumbent on the short-storywriter to remain obscure and unrecognized, the alternative being the kind of recurrent obsolescence he discerns in the genre's history, regionally speaking: 'I have seen the Irish crowded out by Indian storytellers, and there are plenty of indications that they, in their turn, having become respectable, are being outwritten by West Indians.'[88] In comparison, Borges's belief in the outsider's 'greater right' to 'all European themes', serves a confidence that transcends national boundaries: 'our patrimony', he declares with greater flamboyance still, 'is the universe; we should essay all themes, and we cannot limit ourselves to purely Argentine subjects in order to be Argentine

. . . I believe that if we surrender ourselves to that voluntary dream which is artistic creation, we shall be Argentine and we shall also be good or tolerable writers.'[89]

Borges's position is like that of the character Fischbein in his story 'The Unworthy Friend': Fischbein opposes Zionism, 'which he held would turn the Jew into a man like anyone else – tied down to a single tradition and a single homeland, and no longer enriched by strife and complexities'.[90] And what Borges recommended to his fellow Argentine writers in the 1950s he has practised in his own writing, where he compensates himself for lacking a spiritual homeland by creating imaginary and symbolic worlds, realms of order which are fantastic and yet rooted in his own experience, notably his experience of literature and legend. From his literary 'patrimony' he draws a personal legacy comprising the sympathies and affinities he feels with various European writers, including, among others, Kafka, H. G. Wells, Stevenson, Kipling, and G. K. Chesterton. In Chesterton, Borges finds a capacity to combine fantastic horror and the detective story, elements invented but kept separate by Poe. Borges is perhaps most deeply impressed by the way Chesterton can use detective mysteries as vehicles for metaphysical ideas, but in fact all of the writers he reveres display in their writing a fascination with the boundaries between the real and the imaginary, varying from the nightmarish uncertainties of Kafka's stories to the deep sense of man's ambiguous moral nature in Stevenson's.

Given the nature of his literary allegiances, it is not surprising to find that even when he offers stories as being realistic, Borges is concerned to keep alive the notion of 'romance' in the sense of an invented story meant to create wonder. His aim seems constantly to be that of startling his reader into amazement at the nature of existence, an activity which for Chesterton was ultimately religious, but which for Borges involves the discovery of order amidst confusion in a secular universe. And with Borges this is an activity which requires insight on the part of readers who, despite the author's disclaimer, 'I do not aspire to be Aesop', are assumed to be looking for profundity as well as entertainment.[91] Borges's morality undoubtedly does not fulfil itself in Aesopian moral tags or conclusions which can be learned and retained; it is, as might be expected in a modern writer, oblique and concealed, mediated through fictions which suggest that there is significance in the artistic discovery of order. The writer is no less at the mercy of life's complexities than is the reader, and so writer and reader collaborate in the process of discovering order: this is why Borges finds special delight in following Cervantes and 'confusing the objective and the subjective, the world of the reader and the world of the book' in order to produce a 'play of strange ambiguities'.[92] Borges carries the principle of allusiveness far beyond local effects or momentary echoes, and even when he sets out to write 'straightforward stories' he 'dare' not call them 'simple', since the nature of all existence is 'complexity'.[93] In view of all this, Borges's comparison of the stories in *Dr Brodie's Report* to 'those of the Thousand and One Nights', which 'try to be entertaining or moving but not persuasive' has a twist to it.[94] His narratives resemble Scheherazade's stories in being strongly plotted, but they proclaim their own artifice far more deliberately; in a way, they fulfil the unrealized potential of their ancient model, which Borges described in his short piece 'Partial Magic in the *Quixote*' as having accidentally created a counterpoint between a real prosaic world and an imaginary poetic world:

> This collection of fantastic tales duplicates and reduplicates to the point of vertigo the ramifications of a central story in later and subordinate stories, but does not attempt to gradate its realities, and the effect (which should have been profound) is superficial, like a Persian carpet. The opening of the story is well known: the terrible pledge of the king who every night marries a virgin who is then decapitated at dawn, and the resolution of Scheherazade, who distracts the king with her fables until a thousand and one nights have gone by and she shows him their son. The necessity of copying a thousand and one sections obliged the copyists of the work to make all manner of interpolations. None is more perturbing than that of the six hundred and second night, magical among all the nights. On that night, the king hears from the queen his own story. He hears the beginning of the story, which comprises all the others and also – monstrously – itself. Does the reader clearly grasp the vast possibility of this interpolation, the curious danger? That the queen may persist and the motionless king hear forever the truncated story of the *Thousand and One Nights*, now infinite and circular.[95]

The story-within-the-story, the play-within-the-play, the map-within-a-map: these 'inversions' hold special fascination for Borges because of their power to disturb us by suggesting that, 'if the characters of a fictional work can be readers or spectators, we, its readers or spectators, can be fictitious'.[96] So as to disturb as well as entertain us, Borges writes stories which are not flat in design like a Persian carpet but which 'gradate realities' in such a way as to give an effect at once 'infinite and circular'. It is a method which depends on calculated indirection, although in Borges's case this often involves candour and gravity of manner, simplicity of style, and sometimes the presence of a seemingly guileless first-person narrator, who bears resemblance to Kafka's scholarly investigators – themselves relations to Cervantes's tenacious seeker Don Quixote.

The oblique, 'masked' qualities of Borges' writing are the result of humility in the face of previous artistic achievements, presenting us with the paradox of a writer who is totally distinctive and yet elusively absorbed into the fabric of literature of all ages, genres, and countries. Borges declares his affiliations with other writers in a variety of ways, most noticeably by an allusive method of bringing identifiable artistic voices into the texture of his own writing. Sometimes this is done by direct quotation, or by referring to other writers as representatives of alternative possibilities in the art of storytelling. It is early Kipling who is proposed in the preface to *Dr Brodie's Report* as the book's prime originator, and on several occasions Borges imitates Kipling's way of beginning a story with a marvellously atmospheric description of the setting, out of which a 'choric' narrator's voice emerges. Yet in the same collection a highly sophisticated predecessor, Henry James, is also invoked, and we are told at the beginning of 'The Duel' that James's complex fictional world was first disclosed to Borges by one of the story's two characters. The teasing suggestion is that Borges's own storytelling activity has given him insights into works which pre-date that activity. At the same time as alerting us to the timelessness and universality of the story he is now about to tell (it could, he says, be set in London or Boston equally probably as in Buenos Aires) Borges brings into play our awareness of the entirely different treatment James would have given this story of two women rivals. The situation and characters as James would have developed them hover over the story as Borges chooses to tell it, providing a mysterious sense of the unuttered and unenacted, as though James's unwritten version were haunting and commenting on Borges's straightforward language and his chic ruthless characters. We are also compelled to remember that James himself was constitutionally incapable of commenting on a contemporary work without in a sense 'rewriting' it according to his own interest; and brought to mind too are James's marvellous Prefaces, where he offers his own account of the choices, eliminations and selections made by him among multiple possibilities of artistic method. In the Prefaces, where James relives the experience of composing various works, we find 'the story of the story', a layering that is constantly present in Borges's work too.

'The Duel', and each moment within it, constitute a kind of hieroglyph which enigmatically expresses a totality, conforming on a reduced scale to Borges's description of every novel as 'an ideal plane inserted into the realm of reality'.[97] At the same time as offering his own brand of mystery story, Borges here manages to challenge the orthodoxy of historical time: not only does he set this and other stories 'some distance off in time and space' so that 'the imagination can operate with greater freedom', but he invites us to rearrange the normal sequence in which Henry James is his predecessor, already entering his final phase when Borges was born in 1899.[98] Just as Browning's 'Fears and Scruples' can be seen as foretelling Kafka's work but also, according to Borges, is perceptibly sharpened and deflected for us by our reading of the later writer, so James's treatments of covert 'duels' and veiled hostilities are illuminated by 'The Duel'.[99] Similarly, in 'The Gospel According to St Mark' a new perspective is offered on the biblical text by means of Borges's chilling and deeply ironic dramatization of sacred history becoming actual truth on a South American ranch in the spring of 1928; at the end of the story we know that the Crucifixion is to be re-enacted, and we are reminded that Christ's passion is continuously happening, an idea also explored by Kafka in 'The Hunter Gracchus' (written in 1917).

For Borges, to the extent that every writer's work 'modifies our conception of the past as it will modify the future', every literary artist actually '*creates* his own precursors'.[100] Seen in this way, language is really a network of quotations and 'what we now call tradition is made up of centuries-old web of adventures'.[101] What is thrilling about these 'adventures' is that they can take place in the study or the library, requiring no involvement in the world of action: they are imaginative flights which implicitly defeat contingency in a way exemplified for Borges by the French writer Paul Valéry, 'a man who, in an age that worships the chaotic idols of blood, earth, and passion, preferred always the lucid pleasures of thought and the secret adventures of order'.[102]

Described rather than experienced first-hand, Borges's fiction can sound like esoteric and formalist game-playing, and the mention of Valéry here might seem to associate Borges with the doctrine of impersonality propounded by Eliot, another admirer of the French poet, and another writer who enriched the texture of his language with allusion and quotation.[103] But this would be to miss the point that for Borges personality is not something to be extinguished in a work of art; rather, it is something 'behind the work', a fact that is not diminished by 'the circumstance that personality is, in some way a projection of the work'.[104] Valéry's fictional character Edmond Teste is not, Borges insists, a 'mere Doppelgänger' of the poet; and although surpassed in technical achievement by writers like Yeats, Rilke and Eliot, Valéry is to be valued above his followers for his incomparable personality, the force that made his 'mission' of proposing lucidity in an era of cultural and political chaos a 'noble' one.[105] Again we encounter a paradox: Valéry's texts are admirable because they 'do not exhaust, do not even define, their all-embracing possibilities', and it is because he 'transcends the differential traits of the self' that he is uniquely himself.[106]

Rather similarly, Borges's 'personality' is evident in his 'mission' to defy the confusion and disorder of perceived reality, a purpose which is discernible in single pieces and also in correspondences, echoes and variations between one work and another. Never is this intention palpable; on the contrary, it depends for its fulfilment on the pretence that the author is not aware of the significance of the story he is telling. The effect is reminiscent of the workings of parable, where, according to Frank Kermode, sacred mysteries are protected by the incorporation of 'very dubious interpretations, which help to make the point that the would-be interpreter cannot get inside, cannot even properly dispose of authoritative interpretations that are more or less obviously wrong': in the Parable of the Sower, Mark, like one of Borges' narrators, protects a mystery without understanding it; he mediates but he does not, cannot, explain.[107] For Borges the mystery is not religious, though his pursuit of it has the seriousness of a religious quest, and to this purpose the plenitude of the created world provides copious material. Borges's description of Valéry taking every phenomenon as 'a stimulus capable of provoking an infinite series of thoughts' applies to himself too, and it is through this sense of intellectual and imaginative excitement that much of the pleasure of reading Borges comes.[108] The reader partakes of some of the quester's dignified animation: V. S. Pritchett catches the effect precisely when he says that 'Borges has the power to burst the anecdote open. He seems to say that the story must be open, because I, too, am like my characters, part of an endless series or repetitions of the same happenings.'[109] Because the emphasis is on the delights of the chase, Borges does not feel any need to strain for new ideas: his comparatively small repertoire of plots, situations, and 'type' characters (many of them used to explore themes of revenge and compensation) actually seems to allow him exceptional freedom to investigate the possibilities of short fiction and to improvise a huge range of tones and techniques. The same ideas occur again and again – the notion of recurrence and repetition; the eerie indeterminacy of time, as in 'Guayaquil' where the identities of the two dead generals and their historians seem to merge; the impossibility of telling dream from reality, or, as in 'Juan Muraña', distinguishing a talismanic object from its owner and user. Similarly, certain age-old devices reappear in several of the stories: the anecdotal framework of 'Rosendo's Tale'; the story recounted to the narrator while on a journey, as in 'Juan Muraña', where we are warned that 'certain devices of a literary nature and one or two longish sentences' make the tale recorded seem suspiciously well-rehearsed; the fortuitous discovery of a manuscript like the Swiftian 'Doctor Brodie's Report', which is, appropriately enough, tucked in to the heavily annotated copy of *Arabian Nights' Entertainments* belonging to the prosaic Scottish missionary Dr Brodie.[110] There are Kiplingesque elisions, and a playful preoccupation with the lineage and accuracy of stories, as in the lengthy introductory paragraph of 'The Intruder', a story which began long ago when 'someone got it from someone else' and is now, after passing through various versions, to be told by a narrator who foresees that he is bound to 'give in to the writer's temptation of emphasizing or adding certain details'.[111] The storyteller in 'The End of the Duel' is equally scrupulous yet tentative, promising to 'transcribe' details collected by someone else from oral accounts, and admitting to his own misgivings, 'since both forgetfulness and memory are apt to be inventive'.[112]

Chastening inventiveness in the usually accepted sense of the word, Borges dissolves the boundaries by which experience is habitually categorized. 'I no longer know whether the events I am about to relate are effects or causes', he declares in 'The End of the Duel': this story about two rival gauchos, as the title suggests, echoes and brings to a conclusion the themes of the preceding story, 'The Duel' – though in such a different setting and with such totally opposite character-types that the very idea of 'concluding' is made to seem untenable.[113] And in 'The Meeting' (a story resembling so many others by Borges and centuries of storytellers before him in the way it discloses a long-held secret) the narrator admits, 'I do not know whether there were two or three emptied bottles on the floor or whether an excess of movies suggest this false memory to me.'[114] There is often uncertainty too about how much finality a story can attain: 'who knows whether the story ends here', are the last words of 'The Meeting', suggesting, of course, that the events described are capable of endless repetition and re-enactment.[115]

But the relatively small number of situations, and the venerability of Borges's narrative techniques, like Kipling's, in no way limit the stories' scope or the width of their purpose. Just as he believes that 'common metaphors are the best because they are the only true ones', and that the small number of inventions of which man is capable can mean everything to everyone, so a single story can be read differently according to the reader's disposition.[116] 'Guayaquil', for example, offers two alternative experiences: it can be treated rationally, 'as a symbol of the meeting of the famous generals', or, 'if the reader is in a magical mood, as the transformation of the two historians into the two dead generals'.[117] The reader is free to make his own choice, to define the limits of his own faith in the irrational and magical.

The short story for Borges is not simply a product, an ingeniously crafted artistic object as it was in Poe's account of it, but an imaginative adventure in which enjoyment always precedes, and endures beyond, interpretation and explication. These excursions can, like 'The Duel', make their way 'in darkness and end in darkness'; or exorcize a painful memory, like 'The Unworthy Friend', which Borges calls 'really a confession' of his own boyhood treachery, and in which he uses the device of dramatic monologue.[118] The principle of confession pervades the stories, and is enunciated in 'Guayaquil': 'to confess to a thing is to leave off being an actor in it and to become an onlooker – to become somebody who has seen it and tells it and is no longer the doer'; the blend of personal involvement and aesthetic detachment could be taken as a description of the aim and effect of all Borges's stories, and not only the overtly 'confessional' ones.[119] Here again there are reminiscences of Kafka who, when asked what he meant by describing 'The Judgment' as 'the spectre of a night', explained that the writing of the story was 'merely the verification, and so the complete exorcism of the spectre'.[120] Complete detachment is constantly prevented by Borges's emphasis on the processes of telling and understanding a story, a concern which often takes the form of false starts and self-corrections like those in 'Guayaquil' where a flowing opening paragraph is instantly deflated and our expectations unsettled: 'Rereading the above paragraph preparatory to writing the next, its at once melancholy and perhaps pompous tone troubles me. . . . My opening paragraph, I suspect, was prompted by the unconscious need to infuse a note of pathos into a slightly painful and trivial incident.'[121]

On such displays of honesty and humility cordial relations between storyteller and listener have always depended. Borges complies with time-honoured custom in the way he makes his stories reveal the Many in the One; we accept, trustfully, illusion as reality, and are restored to a condition of wholeness that is comforting, though inevitably fleeting. Whether it is by retrieving for us, through allusion, the work and values of past authors, or by showing us that no incident, if thought about and explored for its possibilities, can be accurately written off as trivial, Borges attempts to break down the modern reader's isolation. 'A book', he asserts, 'is more than a verbal structure or series of verbal structures; it is the dialogue it establishes with its reader, and the intonation it imposes upon his voice and the changing and durable images it leaves in his memory. This dialogue is infinite.'[122] The reader in fact may be able to complete what the author is forced to abandon, rather like the imagined 'you' in the parable embedded in Kafka's thought-provoking story 'The Great Wall of China': the messenger sent by the Emperor from his deathbed 'to you alone' has no hope of fighting his way out of the palace, but yet in solitariness 'you' complete the journey.[123] The parable ends with a call to the reader's willing collaboration: 'Nobody could fight his way through here even with a message from a dead man. – But you sit at your window when evening falls and dream it to yourself.'[124]

It is as a verbal magician who can give to the real the suggestiveness of romance, and make the outrageously romantic seem real, that Borges takes the short story out of the trap created for it by those modernist writers who assume that fragmentation of reality compels them to fragment the forms in which they record that reality. Borges does not accept, as Virginia Woolf has been seen to do, that the most a story can do is to take a fragment of experience and hold it up to the light: he takes fragments by the handful, arranges, then rearranges them, until they begin to reveal their hidden coherence and unity.

Borges's stories are 'done' artistically in precisely the sense intended by Henry James when he proclaimed in his Preface to *The Awkward Age* that in a 'really wrought work of art' the 'grave distinction between substance and form' breaks down and gives way to a unity which defies fragmentation of any kind.[125] The passage is worth quoting in full, since it voices so energetically a determination to resist atomism, and to exalt the literary artist's role as deft illusionist, in ways that do seem to make James and Borges contemporaries, in spirit at least:

> The thing 'done', artistically, is a fusion, or it has not *been* done – in which case of course the artist may be, and all deservedly, pelted with any fragments of his botch the critic shall choose to pick up. But his ground once conquered, in this particular field, he knows nothing of fragments and may say in all security: 'Detach one if you can. You can analyse in *your* way, oh yes – to relate, to report, to explain; but you can't disintegrate my synthesis; you can't resolve the elements of my whole into different responsible agents or find your way at all (for your own fell purpose). My mixture has only to be perfect literally to bewilder you – you are lost in the tangle of the forest. Prove this value, this effect, in the air of the whole result, to be of my subject, and that other value, other effect, to be of my treatment, prove that I haven't so shaken them together as the conjurer I profess to be *must* consummately shake, and I consent but to parade as before a booth at the fair.'[126]

The 'synthesis' of a Borges story is 'perfect' in just these respects, and although the critic will be able to point out that there is just as much Kipling and H. G. Wells in his 'mixture' as there is Henry James, he will find it impossible to detach fragments or 'disintegrate' the whole. In fact he will find that the perfection of Borges's mixture consists in the way writers as diverse as James and Kipling have been 'consummately shaken' together. Within the 'straightforward' method of *Dr Brodie's Report*, Borges dissolves all rivalry between the Jamesian artist, priest-like in his 'haunted study', and the convivial Kiplingesque storyteller who addresses a group rather than the solitary reader.

Because, if order is to be found anywhere, it will not for Borges emanate from the sensibility or single ego of the observer, his narratives often have a quality of dream-like reminiscence, conveying a feeling of involuntariness yet inevitability. Like his own fictional narrators, he worries about spoiling his ideas for stories with 'changes that my fancy or my reason judged fitting', but he reassures himself with the comment that 'after all, writing is nothing more than a guided dream'.[127] Behind this is the conviction that 'the art of writing is mysterious', not an 'act of the intelligence', but something much closer to Kipling's obedient reliance on his personal daemon.[128] In fact Borges praises Kipling in the preface to *The Unending Rose* (1975) for acknowledging that no artist 'knows entirely what he is doing' and that prime obligation is owed to 'the imagination, and not to the mere ephemeral circumstances of a supposed "reality"'.[129] Reliance on instinctive promptings must not, however, be exaggerated to the neglect of careful deliberation on Borges's part: this has particular importance in view of the fact that both as scholar and writer he moves outside the confines of his native language, Spanish. Translation, a highly conscious activity, is an essential aspect of his work, and his comments on the aims and methods involved in preparing the English texts to his stories afford interesting insights into his art, and perhaps into short-storywriting in general. The principle followed in translating *The Aleph and Other Stories 1933–1969*, Borges tells us, was to try 'to make the text read as though it had been written in English', an attempt which quickly showed him and his collaborator that 'the English and Spanish languages are not, as is often taken for granted, a set of interchangeable synonyms but are two possible ways of viewing and ordering reality'.[130] There is, then, a kind of multiple potentiality about any story written in a particular language, and a translation constitutes the realization of one set of possibilities inherent in the material. In the case of the stories collected in *Dr Brodie's Report*, the processes of composition and of translation were 'more or less simultaneous', easing the translator's task, according to Borges, because 'we were always under the spell of the originals' and so 'stood in no need of trying to recapture past moods'.[131] What this suggests is not only the obvious point that a good translation retains the mood and atmosphere of the original, but that an awareness of more than one set of linguistic possibilities for a story may become closely involved in the preparation of the 'original' – and not in any mechanical sense either.

There are numerous instances of writers eminent in the field of short-storywriting whose fiction demonstrates that the capacity to work in more than one language can be a definite advantage, often giving the writer a keen sense of the different 'possible ways of viewing and ordering reality' described by Borges. Here the business of writing in a 'second', acquired language (as Conrad did, or Isak Dinesen, or Nabokov in his English stories), and the practice of writing in a native language with the prospect of translation in mind, lie very close together. Kafka's situation is relevant here: a Jewish writer living in Czechoslovakia and using Prague German, the language of the influential, largely upper-class minority into which his father wanted to be assimilated, he stood at double remove from the mass of his compatriots. Add to this Kafka's fascination with the grotesque and fantastic, his use of animal fable and dream, and it is possible to see how various factors combiined to give him the distanced feeling which is perhaps essential to all good storywriting. Furthermore, Kafka felt that his Jewishness endowed him with a natural sense of narrative movement: 'we Jews', he said, 'cannot depict things statically. We see them always in transition, in movement, as change. We are story-tellers.'[132] And the kind of story told was in his view also determined by Jewry, which was not just a matter of faith but 'a question of the practice of a way of life in a community conditioned by faith', making storytelling more a matter of ritual founded in historical lore than of ideology, and so giving the folktale particular durability and appeal.[133]

Writers like Kafka who are linguistically and spiritually exiled in their native country occupy a comparable position to those who actually leave the environment in which they grew up, departing physically yet taking elements of their cultural inheritance with them. Much of the finest short fiction has come from emigré writers who adopt, but do not renounce themselves entirely to, a foreign language; a notable example is Isaac Bashevis Singer, whose stories are often about immigrants in the United States, the country he himself went to when he left Poland in 1935. In Singer we have the intriguing case of a writer who writes stories in Yiddish, translates them into English, and then sees the same stories go into foreign-language editions prepared from the English versions. For Singer as for Borges, writing and translation are closely connected: his translators, he says in his note to *A Friend of Kafka and Other Stories* (1972), are his 'first readers'.[134] Believing as he does that translation is 'the greatest problem and challenge of literature', Singer associates translation with criticism, presenting it as a beneficial way of achieving the directness and concision which we have seen as essential to good storytelling:

> The 'other' language in which the author's work must be rendered does not tolerate obscurity, puns, and linguistic tinsel. It teaches the author to deal with events rather than with their interpretation and to let the events speak for themselves. The 'other' language is often the mirror in which we have a chance to see ourselves with all our imperfections and, if possible, to correct some of our mistakes.[135]

A writer with such a durable mirror is perhaps at a decided advantage when it comes to resisting the gimmickry which mars so much storywriting, and Singer's achievement stands as testimony to the proposition that allowing events to speak for themselves is the best way of stimulating a reader to supply his own interpretation, and also the most eloquent way of conveying a belief like that expressed at the end of one Singer story: 'if there is such a thing as truth it is as intricate and hidden as a crown of feathers'.[136]

So although Singer's stories bristle with people and things, seeming to be packed to bursting point with noises, smells, colours, and often involving violent events or clashes between the natural and the supernatural, there is also something austere about them: words spill out in profusion, but nothing is totally explained; characters wear a mantle of unknowability over the sometimes gaudy, sometimes shabby, but almost always eccentric appearances they offer to the world around them. It is an effect of mystery which many short-storywriters aim to achieve, and it might be argued that Singer's consciousness of his 'second' language represents a disciplining sense of 'foreignness' which helps all writers to control their writing of short fiction. What may be attained in the way of unelaborated tautness for the writer working with a second language has its equivalent in the bracing restrictions felt by a writer who uses his native language, but chooses subjects which are in some way alien or mysterious. This may be the reason for the popularity of super-natural themes, and latterly of neo-gothic situations, among twentieth-century writers who want to go beyond the impressionism of the 1920s but find documentary realism an unpromising alternative.

Despite the scientific and intellectual advances which have narrowed the province of the unknowable and inexplicable, the super-natural has continued to have a place in short fiction. It could even be said that because of these very advances many imaginative writers have felt the need to assert the value of intuition, registering their belief that reason and logic yield only partial or abstract truths about human experience. Perhaps the more people find themselves being 'explained' to themselves, physiologically, psychoanalytically, sociologically, the more it is incumbent on artists to cherish a sense of mystery, not propitiating ancient superhuman gods, necessarily, but still warning us against making new secular gods out of machines, intellectual systems or conceptual schemes. Seen in this way, the modern supernatural story has an honourable role to fulfil; not attempting to displace rationality, it can nevertheless put in a counterclaim for the irrational and the subliminal, forces which have their glories as well as their horrors. This tendency seems to be particularly marked in English writing. Introducing stories of his, written between 1906 and 1912, Algernon Blackwood asserted what to him was a first principle of imaginative creation: 'The true "other-worldly" story should issue from that core of superstition which lies in every mother's son of us, and we are still close enough to primitive days with their terror of the dark for Reason for abdicate without too violent resistance.'[137]

Thirty years later, Blackwood observed, the findings of modern physicists like Eddington and Whitehead were actually making the 'abdication' of reason less necessary, bringing about a 'rapprochement' between modern science and 'so-called psychical and mystical phenomena'.[138] In the 1930s and 1940s, however, supernaturalism continued to have a special function in short fiction, and its power is by no means extinguished today. Among writers of the first half of the century, Elizabeth Bowen offers an illustrative case of an artist who wrote novels as well as short stories, but who deliberately restricted the use of the supernatural to the shorter form. Although she asserted that the supernatural was 'inseparable (whether or not it comes to the surface) from my sense of life', Bowen was clear in her mind about the novel not being the form in which to let her belief in otherworldly forces 'come to the surface'.[139] The novel's demands, she felt, were 'calmer, stricter' than those of the short story, requiring the writer to depict human behaviour in its rational aspects.[140] In comparison, the short story was freer, able to deal with extremes, and admitting into fiction 'what is crazy about humanity: obstinacies, inordinate heroisms, "immortal longings"'.[141] To introduce supernatural elements which made 'some of the happenings' in her stories 'unable to be rationally explained' was not, therefore, a lazy 'get-out', but a means of expanding her scope beyond the social portraiture to which she felt tied when writing a novel.[142] It is a view which seems to have been shared by E. M. Forster, in whose short stories freer rein is given to the supernatural than was permissible in the novels, where mysticism had to be assimilated into a framework of social realism.

For these writers the supernatural story does not involve conjuring ghosts out of thin air in order to chill the reader; their purpose is rather to indicate human impulses, often associated with places rich in atmosphere or history, which a rationally ordered society neglects at its peril. Instead of sensationalism, the aim is, as Bowen puts it, to 'raise some issue' and to convey 'the valid central emotion and inner spontaneity of the lyric', requirements which she makes of all worthwhile short stories: 'However plain or lively or unpretentious be the manner of the story, the central emotion – emotion however remotely involved or hinted at – should be austere, major. The subject must have implicit dignity.'[143] These standards, and Elizabeth Bowen's concern for 'tautness and clearness', are apparent even when her use of the supernatural seems on the surface to be playful.[144] In an early story like 'The Cat Jumps' (1934) we can see her superimposing an awareness of atavistic forces on the briskly 'normal' attitudes cultivated by her main characters, the Harold Wrights. This inordinately sensible and fashionably intellectual couple is made to contend with powers which they have deliberately suppressed when they buy a house where a lavishly gruesome murder has been committed. Other buyers have been deterred by the place's 'dreadful associations', a squeamishness ridiculed by the Harold Wrights as they set about redecorating the house, congratulating themselves on their strong nerves: looking into 'the unfortunate bath

– *the* bath, so square and opulent, with its surround of nacreous tiles', Jocelyn Wright laughs lightly and supposes, 'anyone *else* would have had that bath changed. "Not that that would be possible", she added; "the bath's built in . . . I've always wanted a built-in bath."' A weekend-party is arranged to 'warm the house', but rationality and smart conversation are brittle defences against the fears which begin to invade the guests, whose personalities appear to be progressively 'attacked by some kind of decomposition'. At the climax of the story all the characters find themselves behind locked doors, but although a rational explanation for this is offered, the story leaves the lingering impression that the passion and sheer joy with which the murderer (also named Harold) disposed of his wife are as built-in as the bath. The tensions evaded by the passionless intellectuality of the Harold Wrights' marriage are briefly revealed as husband approaches wife: 'Forces he did not know of assembling darkly, he had faced for untold ages the imperturbable door to his wife's room. She would always be there, densely, smotheringly there, like a great cat, always, over the mouth of his life.'[145]

In a later story like 'The Demon Lover' (1941), Bowen is more daring in her use of the supernatural, dispensing with the mood of social satire and the rational clarification which lighten 'The Cat Jumps' into comedy. Here the supernatural power attained by inextinguishable passion is more fully explored and the situation is more deftly fitted to the theme, extraneous characters being dispensed with so as to create a sustained mood of uncertainty mingled with inevitability. The woman who returns to her shut-up house in blitzed London, to collect several things for her family in the country, finds waiting for her a letter which recalls her to the past she betrayed by marrying sensibly some years after her fiancé was reported missing in the First World War. Setting plays a major part in creating the macabre atmosphere of the story and also in providing oblique comment on the failure of passion for which the central figure Mrs Drover is now called to account. Her home, but not the place where she is living, the London house with its cracks in the structure is a metaphor for her desertion; she felt no real grief when her soldier lover vanished from her life 'presumed killed', and now that his stern letter reminding her of their pledge has mysteriously arrived, the house resembles in her mind 'a cracked cup from which memory, with its reassuring power, had either evaporated or leaked away'. Detail is skilfully used to capture the anguish of a woman who cannot even remember the face of the man who now reclaims her – the draught from the basement which tells her that someone has chosen this moment to leave the house; the intense silence and the 'damaged stare' of the unoccupied houses opposite: these images of emptiness convey powerfully the dreadful blankness of her mind and emotions. As in 'The Cat Jumps', it is a case of common sense showing its insufficiencies when faced with the merciless absolutism of passion, and appropriately it is from 'the ordinary flow of life' into which Mrs Drover hopes to escape, that the real terror strikes; the taxi which represents safety turns out to be a kind of chariot of vengeance speeding off with her into 'the hinterland of deserted streets'.[146] This story is a splendid instance of what Elizabeth Bowen meant when she defended stories which leave the reader to conjecture 'exactly what happened next (or in some cases, exactly what *had* happened)', her explanation being that she expects the reader to be 'as (reasonably) imaginative' as herself.[147] It is an expectation which touches on the very theme of 'The Demon Lover', since it is a deficiency of imagination in Mrs Drover which is felt to be the ghostly lover's reason for exacting retributive justice twenty-five years after he first disclosed his rough extremism to her. She has compromised, despite the memory of the way he pressed her hand, 'without very much kindness, and painfully, on to one of the breast buttons of his uniform', while he was telling her, 'I shall be with you sooner or later. You won't forget that. You need do nothing but wait.'[148] It is almost as though the comfortable evenness of her present life in a period of conflict and suffering has unleashed the supernatural against her – as though her betrayal touches all of the soldiers fighting in this Second World War and not just a single individual lost in the first one.

The strength of 'The Demon Lover' arises in large part from the way it fuses supernatural elements with the theme of war, producing a heightened feeling of irreality which is evident in the work of many other writers who treat similar topics. Kipling's stories 'A Madonna of the Trenches', 'The Gardener' (both included in *Debits and Credits*, 1926) and to some extent 'Mary Postgate' (1917), all have an almost hallucinatory effect somewhere within them, the assumption seeming to be that the disorientating and violent experience of war puts people in touch with non-human forces, sometimes benignantly, as in 'A Madonna of the Trenches', where the battlefield becomes the place in which illicit lovers can be reunited, and perhaps even sanctified. The separation between the men who fight and the women who stay at home is treated in a variety of ways by Kipling in these stories, but what they share is a suggestion that there is a non-human (or in Mary Postgate's case an inhuman) level on which communion with the dead is possible.

For many twentieth-century writers the dislocations epitomized by two world wars were historical analogues to the modern artist's predicament. Finding it difficult to write, yet believing it somehow crucial to go on trying in the unsettled war years, Elizabeth Bowen remarked in 1942 that 'these years rebuff the imagination as much by being fragmentary as by being violent'.[149] One way of countering the rebuff was to document imaginatively the events and experiences which so palpably demonstrated that violence and fragmentariness were aspects of the same widely diffused situation, and many writers did exactly that. But despite the continuance of the realist tradition in storytelling during the decades following the end of the Second World War, it is from writers who draw on ancient romance patterns that the most vivid insights into turbulence have come in recent years. Kafka once pronounced that, 'There are no bloodless fairy stories. Every fairy story comes from the depths of blood and fear.'[150] It is by plunging into those depths while still retaining a modern consciousness that a recent writer like Angela Carter has transformed old fairy-tales, familiarized and softened by pantomime and nursery cosiness, into shapes that are recognizable and yet entirely new. A kind of translation is involved, but instead of the result being archaism or nostalgia, the fusion of Angela Carter's own modern idiom with figures drawn from fantasy literature, unobtrusive Shakespearean allusions and faintly heard echoes of songs and nursery rhyme, produces a delicately woven literary texture which makes it impossible to separate present-day reality from time immemorial, when storytelling first began. The stories in *The Bloody Chamber and Other Stories* (1979) are not 'new versions' of old tales; they are completely new stories which retain the magical qualities of the originals, but are free to highlight qualities submerged by rationalism – and in particular by nineteenth-century morality. So the Beast in 'The Courtship of Mr Lyon' inhabits a world which includes motor cars, telephones, photographs and dinner-parties, but is still Beast, a lion whose muzzle grazes the heroine's skin and who needs Beauty's love to transform him and thus to reveal his true identity. Compassionate grief is a powerful agent in the working of Angela Carter's magic, but so too is that post-Freudian obsession – sexuality. The 'blood and fear' captured in her stories accommodate twentieth-century acknowledgements of erotic fantasy as gracefully as they assimilate diverse figures from popular culture, merging Rossini's Figaro with Puss-in-Boots to create a mixture of self-interest and rascality; making the Erl-King both sensuously irresistible and terrifying; and creating a snow maiden whose loveliness is violently ravished even after sexual jealousy has killed her.

This is not to say that Carter is offering psycho-analytic versions of old folktales: on the contrary, she is restoring the kind of atmosphere that surrounded, for example, the seventeenth-century Neapolitan story which became Charles Perrault's 'La Belle au Bois dormant', the first tale in his *Histoires ou Contes du Temps Passé* (1697). In Basile's *Pentamerone* (1636), the sleeping beauty was raped, left, and forgotten.[151] Many of the features of the classic fairy-tale are evident in *The Bloody Chamber* collection, which fully bears out Angela Carter's comment that each century 'tends to create or re-create fairy tales after its own taste'.[152] The stories here display in an entirely individual way the 'consummate craftsmanship' and 'good-natured cynicism' noted by Carter as characteristic of Perrault, whose seventeenth-century versions of ancient tales became 'standard ones and entered back into the oral tradition of most European countries, especially that of England'.[153] Admiration for Perrault's elegance and wit is clearly evident in Carter's style, which is equally 'marked by concision of narrative . . . precision of language; irony; and realism', qualities which she sees as having prefigured the eighteenth-century enlightenment.[154] But although there are affinities between Carter's stories and Perrault's, the later writer displays far less confidence in the powers of rationality than her predecessor: consolation is not offered by 'worldly security', and indeed an ironic footnote is being added to Perrault's original note telling us that no modern husband could behave like Bluebeard.[155] There are no comforting moral tags to suggest that 'the succinct brutality of the traditional tale is modified by the application of rationality': and of course these are not stories for children ('apprentice adults' as Perrault sees them) but for grown-ups who are also attuned to the 'savagery and wonder and dark poetry' which entered the fairy-tale tradition in the romantic age with Grimms' *Kinder- und Hausmärchen* (*Household Tales*, 1812–14).[156] Carter's fiction exemplifies the tendency which she discerns when she says that after Perrault 'fairy tales and tales of wonder became increasingly adult and literary forms'.[157] It is the word 'literary' that needs emphasis here: there is no question of a Carter story like 'The Tiger's Bride' entering back into the oral tradition from which it derives some of its strength. There is a well-educated literary awareness and a rich imagination stocked with images drawn from Western culture behind Angela Carter's work, and although, like Perrault's, her tales are told with the kind of art 'that conceals art', retaining 'the simplicity of form and the narrative directness of a country story-tale', they depend for full appreciation on responsiveness to a range of allusions far wider than any 'country story-tale' could contain.[158]

The eclecticism of Angela Carter's allusions lends her work a complex texture which is given the appearance of utter simplicity by the combination of sumptuousness and sparsity in her style: events and characters are both animated and stilled by the precision and astonishing beauty of her language. Understatement, along with resolute attention to banal detail and the immediacy of sensory experience, play an important part in her stories, creating a mood of calm, often irradiated with humour. It is in this mood that many of the tales close, leaving the reader contemplating an image towards which the entire narrative has been moving. At the end of 'The Tiger's Bride' a wonderful transformation occurs, but the girl who undergoes, and describes, the magical process, retains an unexpected sprightliness of language: 'He dragged himself closer and closer to me, until I felt the harsh velvet of his head against my hand, then a tongue, abrasive as sandpaper. "He will lick the skin off me!"'[159] Because the girl's alarm is so robustly expressed, there is all the more glamour about the image with which the story ends: 'And each stroke of his tongue ripped off skin after successive skin, all the skins of a life of the world, and left behind a nascent patina of shining hairs. My earrings turned back to water and trickled down my shoulders; I shrugged the drops off my beautiful fur.'[160] There is a similar modulation from almost jaunty realism to subdued lyricism at the end of 'The Courtship of Mr Lyon', where Beauty's tears effect a 'soft transformation' of the dying Beast:

> And then it was no longer a lion in her arms but a man, a man with an unkempt mane of hair and, how strange, a broken nose, such as the noses of retired boxers, that gave him a distant, heroic resemblance to the handsomest of all beasts.
> 'Do you know', said Mr Lyon, 'I think I might be able to manage a little breakfast today, Beauty, if you would eat something with me.'

> Mr and Mrs Lyon walk in the garden; the old spaniel drowses on the grass, in a drift of fallen petals.[161]

For all their sensuousness, Carter's stories display something of the reticence which Virginia Woolf thought had vanished along with the essay. The stories in *The Bloody Chamber* exemplify the enlivening role short narrative still has to play in 'the long evolution of fiction' described by another writer whose work reflects the appeal of ancient romance, and who has made his own adaptation of Perrault's 'Cendrillon' – John Fowles. In his 'Personal Note' to 'Eliduc' (1974), the amplified retelling of a very old Celtic tale, Fowles comments that the development of fiction 'has been very much bound up with finding means to express the writer's "voice" – his humours, his private opinions, his nature – by means of word manipulation and print alone'.[162] So adroit is the concentrated 'word manipulation' in stories like Angela Carter's, or indeed Fowles's own, that the private voice is entirely absorbed into the fabric of the prose, remaining 'private' in the best sense of that word.

It is the degree and nature of the reticence conveyed by the short story at its best that gives the genre its own decorum, a tactfulness consisting of respect for silences or unstated feelings, and displaying itself formally in the 'artful compromise' by which, as Henry James proposed, the 'space-hunger and space-cunning' of a writer's material can be 'kept down'.[163] The surface of a story, James explained, was made 'irridescent, even in the short piece, by what is beneath it and what throbs and gleams through', and it is this that produces 'the only compactness that has a charm, . . . the only spareness that has a force, . . . the only simplicity that has a grace – those, in each order, that produce the *rich* effect'.[164] In many of the stories presented in this study as attaining a 'rich effect', silence is of paramount significance: sometimes it is silence between characters, as in Sarah Orne Jewett's stories, or the wordless understanding that passes between characters in Kipling's mature fiction. Examples could be drawn too from Turgenev, or from Herman Melville, whose story 'Bartleby the Scrivener' (1856) is almost a requiem for silence. Bartleby's extreme reticence, his withdrawal from the noisy world of commerce and chatter, represent an heroic determination to preserve that core of mystery which is destroyed by modern society's emphasis on communication; unable to force Bartleby into self-explanation, society must retaliate by deeming him insane. His predicament recurs, though less tragically, in Heinrich Böll's story 'Murke's Collected Silences' (1958) where a young man who works in Broadcasting House retrieves left-over scraps of tapes: '"When I have to cut tapes", he explains to a colleague, "in the places where the speakers sometimes pause for a moment – or sigh, or take a breath, or there is absolute silence – I don't throw that away, I collect it."'[165] Here what is being cherished is the scepticism about language which characterized Kafka's narrator in 'Investigations of a Dog'; the dog wants only 'to be stimulated by the silence which rises up around me as the ultimate answer'.[166]

Sometimes it is not the characters, but the author who is silent, leaving things unsaid and unexplained, partly because of the demands of the form he has chosen to work in, but also – and more importantly – because he wants to convey a view of life in which things felt but left unstated have value. The perception that we are all, as Kafka's dog puts it, 'bulwarks of silence', informs much of the finest storytelling in all languages.[167] It is what lies behind Sarah Orne Jewett's remark in a letter to a friend: 'You bring something to the reading of a story that the story would go lame without; but it is these unwritable [sic] things that the story holds in its heart, if it has any, that make the true soul of it, and these must be understood.'[168] The short story's success often lies in conveying a sense of unwritten, or even unwriteable things: the storyteller accepts the limitations of his art, and makes his freedom an aspect of those same restrictions. And if his story succeeds, that freedom is passed on to us through the fiction – though it is human, not artistic, limitation from which as readers we are temporarily set free. Henry James believed that so long as people continued to gather impressions of life, the novel would remain the best way of communicating those impressions. His comments might be modified and applied to the short story: as long as a sense of limitation is prominent among people's impressions of life, the short story will be the best way of expressing this sense and, for a brief spell at least, allaying the worries that it brings with it. The sometimes confidential, sometimes hoarse, piping of Kafka's 'Josephine the Singer' is perhaps the most fitting analogue we have for the storyteller's power. The narrator of the story observes that, 'here piping is set free from the fetters of daily life and it sets us free too for a little while. We certainly should not want to do without these performances.'[169] No more would we want to do without the performances given by the diverse short-storywriters whose many and various works form an essential part of our culture.

NOTES AND REFERENCES

1. *Collected Essays* I, 158.
2. Preface to *A Day in the Dark*, p. 8.
3. *Collected Essays*, I, 94.
4. *Ibid.*, p. 158.
5. *Views and Reviews: Essays in Appreciation; Literature* (1890), p. 189.
6. *Ibid.*, p. 192.
7. *Ibid.*
8. Introduction to *Country Tales* (1938); p. 10.
9. *Ibid.*
10. *An Experiment in Autobiography* (2 vols, 1934), II, 494.
11. 'The International Symposium on the Short Story', *Kenyon Review*, (1968), 460.
12. *Ibid.*, p. 459.
13. *On the Contrary*, p. 267.
14. *Books and Portraits*, p. 17.
15. *Letters and Journals*, p. 136 (28 June 1919).
16. *Ibid.*
17. *Letters*, III, 211 (18 Sept.).
18. *Letters*, II, 598 and 599 (25 Dec. 1922).
19. *Ibid.*, p. 598.
20. *Ibid.*, p. 599.
21. *Ibid.*, III, 66–7 (10 Aug. 1923).
22. *Books and Portraits*, p. 123.
23. *Ibid.*
24. See *The Diary of Virginia Woolf*, ed. Anne Olivier Bell, I (1977), 280.
25. *Collected Essays*, I, 166.
26. *Ibid.*, II, 225.
27. *Ibid.*; II, 92 and I, 169.
28. *Ibid.*, I, 172.
29. *English Prose Lyrics: An Anthology*, ed. Wilhelm Füger (Heidelberg, 1976), p. 39.
30. *Collected Essays*, I, 172.
31. *The Complete Poems and Plays* (1969), p. 32. 'Hysteria' was included in *Prufrock and Other Observations* (1917), but had already appeared in *Catholic Anthology 1914–1915*, ed. Ezra Pound (1915).
32. 'Epiphany 16' (probably written in 1901) in *The Workshop of Daedelus: James Joyce and the Raw Materials for a Portrait of the Artist*

as a Young Man, eds Robert Scholes and Richard M. Kain (Evanston, Illinois, 1965), p. 26.

33. *Daily News*, 31 July 1919, p. 2; repr. in *Virginia Woolf: The Critical Heritage*, eds Robin Majumdar and Allen McLaurin (1975), p. 69.

34. The W. P. Ker Memorial Lecture, 1944; repr. in *Two Cheers for Democracy*, Penguin pbk edn (Harmondsworth, Middx, 1965), pp. 277–88.

35. Jackson J. Benson, 'Ernest Hemingway as a Short Story Writer', *The Short Stories of Ernest Hemingway*, ed. Jackson J. Benson (Durham, North Carolina, 1975), p. 287.

36. 'Now I Lay Me', *Men Without Women*, Penguin pbk edn (Harmondsworth, Middx, 1955, repr. 1969), 151–60 *passim*.

37. *Ibid.*, p. 46.

38. '"Anon" and "The Reader": Virginia Woolf's Last Essays', ed. Brenda R. Silver, *Twentieth Century Literature*, XXV (1979), 370.

39. *Ibid.*, p. 385.

40. *Ibid.*, p. 384.

41. *Ibid.*, p. 385.

42. *Ibid.*, p. 390.

43. *Ibid.*, p. 398.

44. *The Mirror in the Roadway: A Study of the Modern Novel* (1957), p. 304. See also *The Lonely Voice*, p. 115.

45. 'Pound, Joyce and Flaubert: the Odysseans', *New Approaches to Ezra Pound*, ed. Eva Hesse (1969). p. 131.

46. Preface to *A Day in the Dark*, p. 8.

47 *Ibid*.

48. 'The Reading and Writing of Short Stories', *Atlantic Monthly* (Mar. 1949) p. 49.

49. *The Short Story* (1948), pp. 37–8.

50. 'Notes on Hemingway and Kafka', *Sewanee Review*, LVII (1949), 226.

51. *Ibid*.

52. *Letters to Friends, Family, and Editors*, trans. Richard and Clara Winston (1978), p. 127 (11 Oct. 1916).

53. Gustav Janouch, *Conversations with Kafka: Notes and Reminiscences*, trans. Goronwy Rees (1953), p. 35.

54. *Ibid.*; p. 34.

55. *Ibid.*; p. 33.

56. *Ibid*.

57. *Letters to Friends*, p. 98 (25 May 1913). The illustration was taken from a book published in 1838, and Kafka's initial objection was that, 'it refuted me, since I had after all presented the most up-to-date New York'.

58. *Ibid*.

59. *Ibid.*, pp. 114–15 (25 Oct. 1915).

60. *Ibid.*, p. 115.

61. *Conversations*, p. 51.

62. *Ibid.*, p. 38.

63. *Ibid*.

64. *Ibid.*, p. 44.

65. *Ibid.*, p. 38 and *Letters to Friends*, p. 387 (postmarked on arrival, 25 Oct. 1923).

66. *Letters to Friends*, p. 387.
67. 'Kafka's Parables: Ways Out of a Dead End', *The World of Franz Kafka*, ed. J. P. Stern (1980), p. 113.
68. Quoted Joachim Beug, 'The Cunning of the Writer', *The World of Franz Kafka*, p. 130.
69. *Conversations*, p. 55.
70. *Ibid.*, pp. 56–7.
71. *Beschreibung eines Kampfes: Novellen, Skizzen, Aphorismen aus den Nachlass*, 2nd edn, ed. Max Brod (New York, 1954), p. 294. My translation.
72. *Ibid.*, pp. 293–4.
73. *Conversations*, p. 106.
74. *Metamorphosis and Other Stories*, trans. Willa and Edwin Muir, Penguin pbk edn (Harmondsworth, Middx, 1961; repr. 1964), p. 152.
75. *Conversations*, p. 93; p. 91.
76. *Ibid.*, p. 91.
77. *Ibid.*, p. 107.
78. Preface to *Dr Brodie's Report*, p. 13.
79. *Ibid.*
80. *Ibid.*
81. *Ibid.*
82. Prologue to *The Garden of Forking Paths* (1941); in *Ficciones*, ed. Anthony Kerrigan (1962), p. 15.
83. *Labyrinths*, p. 183. Originally a lecture, 'The Argentine Writer and Tradition' is also contained in the revised edition of the collection *Discusión* (1957).
84. *Ibid.*
85. *Ibid.*, p. 183 and p. 184.
86. *Ibid.*, p. 184.
87. Introduction to *The Lonely Voice*, p. 21.
88. *Ibid.*, p. 20.
89. *Labyrinths*, p. 185.
90. *Dr Brodie's Report*, p. 23. All the Borges stories discussed in this chapter are from the *Dr Brodie's Report* collection.
91. *Ibid.*, p. 11.
92. 'Partial Magic in the *Quixote*', *Labyrinths*, p. 194.
93. Preface to *Dr Brodie's Report*, p. 11.
94. *Ibid.*
95. *Labyrinths*, p. 195.
96. *Ibid.*, p. 196.
97. *Ibid.*, p. 194.
98. Preface to *Dr Brodie's Report*, p. 14.
99. 'Kafka and his Precursors', *Labyrinths*, p. 201.
100. Ibid.
101. 'The Duel', *Dr Brodie's Report*, p. 35.
102. 'Valéry as Symbol', *Labyrinths*, p. 198.
103. For a warning against the risk that 'criticism of Borges will become an accretion that will force us to see his stories as conceits alone', see V. S. Pritchett, *The Myth Makers* (1979), p. 184.
104. *Labyrinths*, p. 198.
105. *Ibid.*

106. *Ibid.*
107. *The Genesis of Secrecy* (Cambridge, Mass, 1979), p. 28.
108. *Labyrinths*, p. 198.
109. *The Myth Makers*, p. 184.
110. 'Juan Muraña', *Dr Brodie's Report*, p. 67.
111. *Ibid.*, p. 52.
112. *Ibid.*, p. 38.
113. *Ibid.*, p. 39.
114. *Ibid.*, p. 69.
115. *Ibid.*; p. 65.
116. 'The Elder Lady', *ibid.*, p. 75.
117. Afterword, *ibid.*, p. 102.
118. *Ibid.*, p. 37 and p. 102.
119. *Ibid.*, p. 81.
120. *Conversations*, p. 34.
121. *Dr Brodie's Report*, p. 81.
122. 'A Note on (toward) Bernard Shaw', *Labyrinths*, p. 213.
123. *Metamorphosis*, p. 77.
124. *Ibid.* The parable appears separately as 'A Message from the Emperor' in *A Country Doctor* (1919) and is included in *Wedding Preparations in the Country and Other Stories*, Penguin pbk edn (Harmondsworth, Middx, 1978; repr. 1982).
125. *The Art of the Novel*, p. 115.
126. *Ibid.*, p. 116.
127. Preface to *Dr Brodie's Report*, p. 12 and p. 13.
128. *Ibid.*, p. 12.
129. *The Book of Sand*, p. 99. The preface is translated by Alastair Reid.
130. Foreword to *Dr Brodie's Report*, p. 9.
131. *Ibid.*
132. *Conversations*, pp. 86–7.
133. *Ibid.*, p. 66.
134. Author's Note, *A Friend of Kafka* (1972) Penguin pbk edn (Harmondsworth, Middx, 1975).
135. *Ibid.*
136. 'A Crown of Feathers', *A Crown of Feathers and Other Stories* (1974), Penguin pbk edn (Harmondsworth, Middx, 1977), p. 32.
137. Author's Preface to *Selected Tales*, p. 12.
138. *Ibid.*
139. Preface to *A Day in the Dark*, p. 9.
140. *Afterthought*, p. 80.
141. *Ibid.*
142. Preface to *A Day in the Dark*, p. 9.
143. Preface to *The Faber Book of Modern Stories*, p. 15 and p. 14.
144. *Ibid.*, p. 14.
145. 'The Cat Jumps', *Collected Stories*, pp. 362–70 *passim*.
146. 'The Demon Lover', *ibid.*, pp. 661–6 *passim*.
147. Preface to *A Day in the Dark*, p. 8 and p. 9.
148. *Collected Stories*, p. 663.
149. 'Contemporary', *New Statesman* XXIII (23 May 1942), 340. See also *Collected Impressions*, where Bowen recalls the 'state of lucid abnor-

mality' (p. 48) in which she and her contemporaries lived during the war.

150. *Conversations*, p. 58.
151. See Iona and Peter Opie, *The Classic Fairy Tales*, (1974) Granada pbk edn (1980), pp. 102–4.
152. *The Fairy Tales of Charles Perrault*, p. 17.
153. *Ibid.*, p. 18 and p. 13.
154. *Ibid.*, p. 17.
155. *Ibid.*, p. 18.
156. *Ibid.*; p. .17.
157. *Ibid.*, p. 14.
158. *Ibid.*, p. 15.
159. *The Bloody Chamber*, Penguin pbk edn (Harmondsworth, Middx, 1981), p. 67.
160. *Ibid.*
161. *Ibid.*, p. 51.
162. *The Ebony Tower* (1974), p. 121.
163. *The Art of the Novel*, p. 278.
164. *Ibid.*
165. *Absent without Leave and Other Stories*, trans. Leila Vennewitz, p. 294.
166. *Metamorphosis*, p. 99.
167. *Ibid.*, p. 100.
168. Quoted Matthiessen, *Sarah Orne Jewett*, p. 148.
169. *Wedding Preparations*, p. 184.

BIBLIOGRAPHY

This bibliography does not aim to encompass the available critical material relating to individual writers. Rather, it is intended to provide information about the texts used and to offer a select bibliography for the use of students of the short story.

1. BIBLIOGRAPHICAL RESOURCES

BOYLE, ANDREW. *An Index to the Annuals, 1820–1850.* Worcester, 1967.

COOK, DOROTHY E., and ESTELLE A. FIDELL. *Short Story Index, Supplement 1950–54.* New York, 1956. (Further supplements, 1960, 1971).

FIRKINS, INA TEN EYCK. *Index to Short Stories.* New York, 1923. (Supplements 1929 and 1936).

HANNIGAN, FRANCIS J. *The Standard Index of Short Stories.* Boston, 1918.

THURSTON, JARVIS, and others. *Short Fiction Criticism: A Checklist of Interpretation since 1925 of Stories and Novelettes (American, British, Continental) 1800–1958.* Denver, 1960. Since the establishment of the periodical *Studies in Short Fiction* (published by Newberry College, South Carolina) in 1964, Thurston's bibliography has been continued annually, beginning with a *Bibliography of Short Fiction Criticism since 1960*, in *Studies in Short Fiction* I and II (Summer 1964 and Summer 1965).

WALKER, WARREN S. *Twentieth-Century Short Story Explication: Interpretations 1900–1960 inclusive of Short Fiction since 1800.* Hamden, Conn., 1961.

——. *Twentieth-century Short Story Explication: Interpretations 1900–1975, of Short Fiction since 1800.* 3rd edn 1977.

2. AUTHOR COLLECTIONS

The following titles are limited to volumes from which examples of short stories were selected for discussion, and to volumes containing prefaces or introductions referred to in the text.

ANDERSON, SHERWOOD. *The Triumph of the Egg: A Book of Impressions of American Life in Tales and Poems*. New York, 1921.
——. *Winesburg, Ohio: A Group of Tales of Ohio Small Town Life* (1919). Viking Press edn, New York, 1960; repr. 1964.
BATES, H. E. *The Beauty of the Dead and Other Stories*. 1940.
——. *Colonel Julian and other stories*. 1951.
——. *Country Tales: Collected Short Stories*. 1938.
——. *The Daffodil Sky*. 1955.
——. *The Flying Goat*. 1939.
——. *Seven by Five: A Collection of Stories 1926–61* (1963). Penguin pbk edn, Harmondsworth, Middx, 1972.
——. *Something Short and Sweet*. 1937.
——. *Thirty-One Selected Tales*. 1947.
BENNETT, ARNOLD. *The Grim Smile of the Five Towns* (1907). Penguin pbk edn. Harmondsworth, Middx, 1946; repr. 1975.
BIERCE, AMBROSE. *Can Such Things Be?* (1893). 1926.
——. *In the Midst of Life: Tales of Soldiers and Civilians*. 1st Eng. edn 1892.
BLACKWOOD, ALGERNON. *The Doll and One Other*. Sauk City, Wisconsin, 1946.
——. *Selected Tales*. 1964; repr. 1970.
BÖLL, HEINRICH. *Absent Without Leave and other stories*, trans. Leila Venewitz. 1967.
BORGES, JORGES LUIS. *The Book of Sand* (1975), trans. Norman Thomas di Giovanni. Penguin pbk edn. Harmondsworth, Middx, 1979.
——. *Dr Brodie's Report* (1970), trans. Norman Thomas di Giovanni in collaboration with the author. Penguin pbk edn, Harmondsworth, Middx, 1976.
——. *Ficciones* (1956), ed. Anthony Kerrigan. 1962.
——. *Labyrinths: Selected Stories and Other Writings*, ed. Donald A. Yates and James E. Irby. New Directions pbk edn, New York, 1964.
——. *A Universal History of Infamy* (1954), trans. Norman Thomas di Giovanni. Penguin pbk edn, Harmondsworth, Middx, 1975.
BOWEN, ELIZABETH. *Collected Stories*, introd. Angus Wilson. 1980.
——. *A Day in the Dark and Other Stories*. 1965.
——. *Early Stories*. New York, 1951.
CAPOTE, TRUMAN. *A Tree of Night and Other Stories*. 1950.
CARTER, ANGELA. *The Bloody Chamber and Other Stories* (1979). Penguin pbk edn, Harmondsworth, Middx, 1981.
CATHER, WILLA. *Obscure Destinies* (1932). 1st British edn, 1956.
CHEKHOV, ANTON. *Lady with Lapdog and Other Stories*, trans. David Magarshack. Penguin pbk edn, Harmondsworth, Middx, 1964; repr. 1970.
——. *The Oxford Chekhov*, trans. and ed. Ronald Hingley. 9 vols, 1964–80.
——. *The Schoolmistress and other Stories*, trans. Constance Garnett. 1920.

COPPARD, A. E. *The Black Dog and Other Stories*. 1923.

——. *The Field of Mustard: Tales*. 1926.

——. *Fishmonger's Fiddle: Tales*. 1925.

DE LA MARE, WALTER. *The Connoisseur and other stories*. 1926.

——. *On the Edge*. 1930.

——. *The Riddle and Other Stories*. 1923.

FLAUBERT, GUSTAVE. *Three Tales*, trans. Robert Baldick. Penguin pbk edn, Harmondsworth, Middx, 1979.

GASKELL, ELIZABETH. *Tales of Mystery and Horror*, ed. Michael Ashley. 1978.

GOGOL, NIKOLAI. *Diary of a Madman and Other Stories*, trans. Ronald Wilks. Penguin pbk edn, Harmondsworth, Middx, 1972.

——. *The Mantle and other stories*, trans. Claud Field and introd. Prosper Mérimée. No date.

GRAHAM, R. B. CUNNINGHAME. *Tales of Horsemen*, ed. Alexander Maitland. Edinburgh, 1981.

HARDY, THOMAS. *Life's Little Ironies and A Changed Man*, ed. F. B. Pinion. 1977 (Vol. II of New Wessex Edition of the *Stories of Thomas Hardy*).

——. *Wessex Tales and A Group of Noble Dames*, ed. F. B. Pinion. 1977 (Vol. I of New Wessex Edition of the *Stories of Thomas Hardy*).

HARRIS, JOEL CHANDLER. *Uncle Remus and His Friends: Old Plantation Stories, Songs, and Ballads, with Sketches of Negro Character*. 1893.

HARTE, FRANCIS BRET. *Complete Works*, collected and rev. by the author. 10 vols, 1880.

——. *The Luck of Roaring Camp and other sketches*, introd. Tom Hood. 1887.

HEMINGWAY, ERNEST. *Men Without Women* (1927), Penguin pbk edn, Harmondsworth, Middx, 1955; repr. 1969.

HENRY, O. *Complete Works*. 2 vols, New York, 1953.

IRVING, WASHINGTON. *The Sketch Book of Geoffrey Crayon, Gent.* ed. Haskell Springer. Boston, 1978.

——. *The Sketch Book of Geoffrey Crayon, Gent.*, with Afterword by Perry Miller. Signet Classic pbk edn, New York, 1961.

——. *Tales of a Traveller* (1824), introd. Brander Matthews. Longman edn 1896.

JAMES, HENRY. *Novels and Tales*. 'New York edition', 24 vols, New York, 1907–9.

JEWETT, SARAH ORNE. *The Best Stories of Sarah Orne Jewett*, selected and arranged with a preface by Willa Cather. 2 vols bound in one. Gloucester, Mass., 1965.

——. *The Only Rose and Other Tales*, introd. Rebecca West. Traveller's Library edn 1937.

——. *Short Fiction of Sarah Orne Jewett and Mary Wilkins Freeman*, ed. Barbara H. Solomon. Signet Classic pbk edn New York, 1969.

JOYCE, JAMES. *Dubliners*. 1914.

KAFKA, FRANZ. *Beschreibung eines Kampfes: Novellen, Skizzen, Aphorismen aus den Nachlass*, ed. Max Brod. New York, 1954.

——. *Metamorphosis and Other Stories*, trans. Willa and Edwin Muir. Penguin pbk edn Harmondsworth, Middx, 1961; repr. 1964.

——. *Wedding Preparations in the Country and Other Stories*. Penguin pbk edn Harmondsworth, Middx, 1978; repr. 1982.

KIPLING, RUDYARD. *Debits and Credits*. 1926.

——. *A Diversity of Creatures*. 1917.

——. *Life's Handicap: Being Stories of Mine Own People*. 1891.

——. *Limits and Renewals*. 1932.

——. *Many Inventions*. 1893.

——. *Plain Tales From the Hills*. Calcutta, 1888; London, 1890.

——. *Soldiers Three*. Allahabad, 1888; London, 1890.

——. *Traffics and Discoveries*. 1904.

——. *Wee Willie Winkie and Other Child Stories*. Allahabad 1888; London, 1890.

LARDNER, RING. *The Best Stories of Ring Lardner*. 1959.

——. *How to Write Short Stories (with samples)*. 1926.

LAVIN, MARY, *The Stories of Mary Lavin*. 2 vols, 1964–74.

LAWRENCE, D. H. *The Collected Short Stories*. Phoenix edn, 1974

LESKOV, NIKOLAI. *The Enchanted Wanderer and other Stories*, trans. George H. Hanna and ed. Julius Katzer. Moscow 1958; repr. 1974.

MACLAVERTY, BERNARD. *A Time to Dance and Other Stories*. 1982.

MANSFIELD, KATHERINE. *Collected Stories*. 1945.

——. *34 Short Stories*, introd. Elizabeth Bowen. 1957.

MAUGHAM, WILLIAM SOMERSET. *The Complete Short Stories*. 3 vols, 1951.

——. *The Mixture as Before*. 1940.

MAUPASSANT, GUY DE *The Complete Short Stories*. Cassell edn, 3 vols, 1970.

——. *Tales from Maupassant*, introd. R. B. Cunninghame Graham. 1926.

MELVILLE, HERMAN. *The Piazza Tales*. New York, 1856.

MERRICK, LEONARD. *A Chair on the Boulevard*, introd. A. Neil Lyons. No date.

MITFORD, MARY RUSSELL. *Our Village*. White Lion edn, 1976.

MOORE, GEORGE. *The Untilled Field*. 1903.

PHILLPOTTS, EDEN. *It Happened Like That: A New Volume of Short Stories*. 1927.

POE, EDGAR ALLAN. *Collected Works*. ed. Thomas Ollive Mabbot. Cambridge, Mass 1969–(Vols II and III include Poe's *Tales and Sketches*).

——. *Complete Works*, ed. James A. Harrison. 17 vols, New York, 1902; repr. 1965.

——. *The Works of the Late Edgar Allan Poe*, with a memoir by R. W. Griswold. 4 vols, New York, 1859.

PORTER, KATHERINE ANNE, *Collected Stories*. New York, 1965.

RHYS, JEAN. *Tigers are Better-Looking*. Penguin pbk edn Harmondsworth, Middx, 1972; repr. 1981.

SINGER, ISAAC BASHEVIS. *A Crown of Feathers and Other Stories* (1974). Penguin pbk edn Harmondsworth, Middx, 1977.

——. *A Friend of Kafka and Other Stories* (1972). Penguin pbk edn Harmondsworth, Middx, 1975.

STEVENSON, ROBERT LOUIS. *Works*. Tusitala edition. 35 vols. 1924.

STRONG, L. A. G *Travellers: Thirty-One Selected Short Stories*, introd. Frank Swinnerton. 1945.

TURGENEV, IVAN. *Sketches from A Hunter's Album*, trans. Richard Free-born. Penguin pbk edn Harmondsworth, Middx, 1979.

TWAIN, MARK. *The Celebrated Jumping Frog of Calaveras County and other Sketches*, ed. John Paul. 1867.

——. *Complete Works*. 'Definitive edition'. 37 vols, New York, 1923–5.

UPDIKE, JOHN *Pigeon Feathers and Other Stories*, Eng. edn, 1962.

URQUART, FRED. *The Collected Stories*. 2 vols, 1967–8.

WELLS, H. G. *The Complete Short Stories*. 1927; repr. 1970.

——. *The Country of the Blind*. 1911.

WELTY, EUDORA. *A Curtain of Green*. New York, 1941; London, 1943.

WOOLF, VIRGINIA. *Monday or Tuesday*. 1921 (includes 'Kew Gardens' and rev. version of *The Mark on the Wall*).

3. ANTHOLOGIES

In addition to anthologies referred to in the text, this section includes a selection of anthologies which offer useful introductory material or in some other way highlight particular aspects of short-storywriting. Titles are arranged alphabetically by name of editor or of the person responsible for the selection of stories.

BOWEN, ELIZABETH, ed. *The Faber Book of Modern Stories*. 1937.

BREWSTER, DOROTHY, ed. *A Book of Modern Short Stories*. New York, 1928.

BURNETT, WHIT and HALLIE, eds. *Great Short Stories of the World*. 1965. First published in USA under the title *Story Jubilee* to celebrate the twenty-third anniversary (in 1964) of the Burnetts' editorship of the magazine *Story*, which was originally started in Vienna in 1931.

——. *The Modern Short Story in the Making*. New York, 1964.

CANBY, HENRY SEIDEL, and ROBESON BAILEY, eds. *The Book of the Short Story* (1903). New and enlarged edn, ca. 1970.

CONNOLLY, CYRIL. *Horizon Stories*. 1943.

CROSS, ETHAN ALLEN. *A Book of the Short Story: Selected and Edited, With the History and Technique of the Short Story, Notes and Bibliographies*. New York, 1934.

CURRENT-GARCIA, EUGENE, and WALTON R. PATRICK, eds. *Short Stories of the Western World*, Glenview, Illinois, 1969.

——. *What is the Short Story? Case Studies in the Development of a Literary Form*. Glenview, Illinois, 1961.

DOLMETSCH, CARL R. *'The Smart Set': A History and Anthology*. New York, 1966.

FAGIN, N. BRYLLION. *America Through the Short Story*. Boston, 1938.

FÜGER, WILHELM, ed. *English Prose Lyrics: An Anthology*. Heidelberg, 1976.

GARDNER, JOHN, and Lennis Dunlap, eds. *The Forms of Fiction*. New York, 1962.

GORDON, GILES, ed. *Beyond the Words: Eleven Writers in Search of a New Fiction*. 1975.

GORDON, ROBERT. *The Expanded Moment: A Short Story Anthology*. Boston, 1963.

HAMMERTON, J. A. ed. *The Masterpiece Library of Short Stories: The Thousand Best Complete Tales of all Times and all Countries*. 10 double-volumes. No date.

HEILMAN, ROBERT B., ed. *Modern Short Stories*. New York, 1950.

KEATING, PETER, ed. *Nineteenth Century Short Stories*. Longman English Series, 1981.

——. *Working-Class Stories of the 1890s*. 1971.

MATTHEWS, BRANDER. *The Short Story: Specimens Illustrating its Development*. New York, 1907.

MAUGHAM, W. SOMERSET. *A Choice of Kipling's Prose*. 1952.

——. *Introduction to Modern English and American Literature*. Philadelphia, 1943.

——. *Tellers of Tales: 100 Short Stories from the United States, England, France, Russia and Germany*. New York, 1939.

MERCIER, VIVIAN. *Great Irish Short Stories*. New York, 1964.

MITFORD, MARY RUSSELL, ed. *Stories of American Life by American Writers*. 3 vols, 1830.

MOFFETT, JAMES, and KENNETH R. McELHENY, eds. *Points of View: An Anthology of Short Stories*. Signet Classic pbk edn, New York, 1966.

O'BRIEN, EDWARD J. *Best British Short Stories*. Annually 1922–40. These volumes also offered a yearly index of stories by British and Irish authors in American as well as English periodicals, and listed articles on the short story along with volumes of short stories published in Britain and Ireland.

——. *The Best Short Stories of 1915 and the Yearbook of the American Short Story*. Boston, 1916. This annual anthology continued under different editorship after O'Brien's death in 1940.

PRITCHETT, V. S. *The Oxford Book of Short Stories*. Oxford, 1981.

PUDNEY, JOHN. *Pick of Today's Short Stories*. Annually 1949–62.

ROSS, ALAN. *London Magazine Stories*. Annually 1966–.

ROWLAND, JOHN. *Path and Pavement: Twenty New Tales of Britain*. 1937.

SCHORER, MARK, ed. *The Story: A Critical Anthology*. New York, 1950.

STANFORD, DEREK. *Short Stories of the 'Nineties: A Biographical Anthology*. 1968.

TRASK, GEORGIANNE, and CHARLES BURKHART, eds. *Story-tellers and Their Art*. Garden City, New York, 1963.

Various eds. *O. Henry Memorial Award Stories*. Garden City, New York, annually 1920–.

——. *Scottish Short Stories*, ed. Scottish Arts Council. Annually 1973–.

——. *Winter's Tales*. Annually 1955–. Originally established to offer an additional vehicle for the 'long short story', a form which writers find difficult to place in periodicals.

WYATT, WOODROW, ed. *English Story*. Annually 1941–50.

ZALL, P. M. ed. *A Hundred Merry Tales and Other English Jestbooks of the Fifteenth and Sixteenth Centuries*. Lincoln, Nebraska, 1963.

4. STUDIES OF THE SHORT STORY

Also included in this section are related studies of other short fictional forms.

ALBRIGHT, EVELYN MAY *The Short Story: Its Principles and Structure*. New York, 1931.

ALLEN, WALTER. *The Short Story in English*. Oxford, 1981.

ANONYMOUS, 'The art of story-telling', *Fraser's Magazine*, LIII (June 1856), 722–32.

BAKER, FALCON O. 'Short stories for the millions', *Saturday Review of Literature*, XXXVI (19 Dec. 1953) 7–9 and 48–9.

BAKER, HOWARD. 'The contemporary short story', *Southern Review*, III (1938), 576–96.

BALDESHWILER, EILEEN. 'The lyric short story: The sketch of a history', *Studies in Short Fiction*, VI (Summer 1969), 443–53.

BATES, H. E. *The Modern Short Story: A Critical Survey*. 1941.

——. 'A note on the English short story', *Lovat Dickson's Magazine*, II (1934), 145–8.

BEACHCROFT, T. O. *The English Short Story*. Writers and their Work series. 1964.

——. *The Modest Art: A Survey of the Short Story in English*. 1968. Includes a guide to collections of stories and sources before the Eighteenth Century.

BECK, WARREN. 'Art and formula in the short story', *College English*, V (1943), 55–62.

BENNETT, E. K. and H. M WAIDSON. *A History of the German 'Novelle'*, Cambridge, 1961.

BOLAND, JOHN. *Short story technique*. Enlarged rev. edn, Crowborough, Sussex, 1973. Previously published as *Short Story Writing*, 1960.

BOWEN, ELIZABETH. 'The search for a story to tell', *Harper's Bazaar*, XLIX (June 1953), 102–3.

BOYCE, BENJAMIN. 'English short fiction in the eighteenth century: a preliminary view', *Studies in Short Fiction*, V (Winter 1968), 95–112.

BREWSTER, DOROTHY, and ANGUS BURRELL. *Dead Reckonings in Fiction*. New York, 1924 (Chs 3 and 4).

BRICKELL, HERSHEL. 'What happened to the short story', *Atlantic Monthly*, CLXXX VII (Sept. 1951), 74–6. At this juncture, Brickell was in charge of selecting the O. Henry Memorial Award Prize Stories.

BUNGERT, HANS, ed. *Die Amerikanische Short Story: Theorie und Entwicklung*. Darmstadt, 1972. Includes many items in English.

CABLE, GEORGE WASHINGTON. 'Speculations of a story-teller', *Atlantic Monthly* LXXVII (July 1896), 88–96.

CANBY, HENRY SEIDEL. 'Free fiction', *Atlantic Monthly*, CXVI (July 1915), 60–8.

——. 'On the short story', *Dial*, XXXI (16 Oct. 1901), 271–3.

——. *The Short Story in English*. New York, 1909.

CLEMENTS, ROBERT J. and JOSEPH GIBALDI. *Anatomy of the Novella: The European Tale Collection from Boccaccio and Chaucer to Cervantes*. New York, 1977.

CODY, A. SHERWIN. *How to Write Fiction, Especially the Art of Short Story Writing: A Practical Course of Instruction after the French Method of Maupassant*. New York, 1894.

CONANT, MARTHA PIKE. *The Oriental Tale in England in the Eighteenth Century*. New York, 1907; repr. 1966.

CORY, HERBERT ELLSWORTH. 'The senility of the short-story', *Dial*, LXII (3 May 1917). 379–81.

CROSS, ETHAN ALLEN. *The Short Story: A Technical and Literary Study*. Chicago, 1914.

ESENWEIN, J. BERG. *Writing the Short-Story: A Practical Handbook on the Rise, Structure, Writing, Sale of the Modern Short-Story*. New York, 1909.

EVANS, WALTER. 'Nineteenth century American theory of the short story: the dual tradition', *Orbis Literarum*, XXXIV (1976), 314–30.

FAGIN, N. BRYLLION. *Short Story-Writing: An Art or a Trade?*. New York, 1923.

FRIEDMAN, NORMAN. 'What makes a short story short?', *Modern Fiction Studies*, IV (Summer 1958), 103–17.

FULLER, HENRY B. 'New forms of short fiction', *Dial*, LXII (8 Mar. 1917), 167–9.

GEORGE, A. J. *Short Fiction in France 1800–1850*. Syracuse, 1964.

GERALD, GREGORY FITZ. 'The satiric short story: a definition', *Studies in Short Fiction*, V (Summer 1968), 349–54.

GILLESPIE, GERALD. 'Novella, nouvelle, novelle, short novel?: a review of terms', *Neophilologus*, LI (July 1967), 225–30.

GORDIMER, NADINE. 'The international symposium on the short story', *Kenyon Review*, XXX (1968), 457–63. Part II of this Symposium can be found in Kenyon Review, XXXI. See also below, Lanning, *The Short Story Today*.

GORDON, CAROLINE. 'Notes on Chekov and Maugham', *Sewanee Review*, LVII (1949), 401–19.

——. 'Notes on Hemingway and Kafka', *Sewanee Review* LVII (1949), 215–26.

GRABO, CARL. *The Art of the Short Story*. New York, 1913.

GULLASON, THOMAS H. 'The short story: an underrated art', *Studies in Short Fiction*, II (Fall, 1964), 13–31.

HARLAND, HENRY. 'Concerning the short story', *The Academy and Literature*, LI (5 June 1895), 6.

HARRIS, WENDELL V. 'English short fiction in the nineteenth century', *Studies in Short Fiction*, IV (1968–69),1–93.

HARTE, FRANCIS BRET. 'The rise of the "short story" ', *The Cornhill Magazine*, New Series, VII (July 1899), 1–8.

HOWELLS, WILLIAM DEAN. 'Some anomalies of the short story', *North American Review*, CLXXIII (Sept. 1901), 422–32.

JAMES, HENRY. 'The story-teller at large: Mr Henry Harland', *The Fortnightly Review*, New Series, LXIII (Apr. 1898), 650–4.

JONES, WILLIAM M. 'The plot as search', *Studies in Short Fiction*, V (Fall 1967).

LANNING, GEORGE, and ELLINGTON WHITE, eds. *The Short Story Today: A Kenyon Review Symposium*. Kent, Ohio, 1970.

LEIBOWITZ, JUDITH. *Narrative Purpose in the Novella*. The Hague, 1974.

LEVIN, GERALD. *The Short Story: An Inductive Approach*. New York, 1967.

MATTHEWS, BRANDER. *The Philosophy of the Short-story*. New York, 1901.

MAUGHAM, W. SOMERSET. 'How I write short stories', *Saturday Review of Literature*, 28 July 1934: repr. in *How Writers Write: Essays by Contemporary Authors*, ed. N. S. Tillett (Oxford, 1937), pp. 69–82.

——. 'The short story', *Nash's Magazine*, Oct. 1934; repr. as Introduction to *East and West* (1934).

——. 'The short story'. In *Points of View*, 1958.

MORRISON, ARTHUR. 'How to write a short story', *Bookman* (New York), V (Mar. 1897), 45–6.

NEAL, R. W. *Short Stories in the Making: a Writer's and Student's Introduction to the Technique and Practical Composition of Short Stories*. New York, 1914.

——. *To-day's Short Stories Analyzed: an Informal Encyclopaedia of Short Story Art*. New York, 1918. (A companion volume to *Short Stories in the Making*).

O'BRIEN, EDWARD J. *The Advance of the American Short Story*. New York, 1923.

O'CONNOR, FRANK. *The Lonely Voice: A Study of the Short Story*. 1963.

O'FAOLAIN, SEAN. 'Are you writing a short story?', *The Listener*, LIX (13 Feb. 1958), 282–3.

——. *The Short Story*. 1948.

OVERSTREET, BONARO. 'Little story, what now?', *Saturday Review of Literature*, XXIV (22 Nov. 1941), 3–5 and 25–6.

PAIN, BARRY. *The Short Story*. 1914.

PATTEE, F. W. *The Development of the American Short Story: An Historical Survey*. New York, 1923; repr. 1966.

PEDEN, WILLIAM. *The American Short Story: Front Line in the National Defense of Literature*. Cambridge, Mass, 1964. Includes a checklist of 100 notable American short-storywriters, 1940–63.

PERRY, BLISS. 'The short-story', *Atlantic Monthly*, XC (Aug. 1902), 246.

PHILLIPS, H. A. *Art in Short Story Narration*. New York, 1913.

PITKIN, WALTER B. *The Art and Business of Story Writing*. New York, 1912.

PORTER, KATHERINE ANNE. 'An interview', *The Paris Review*, XXIX (1963), 87–114.

——. 'No plot, my dear, no story' (1942). In *The Days Before*, 1st Eng. edn (1953), pp. 133–6.

PRITCHETT, V. S. 'Books in general', *New Statesman and Nation*, New Series, XXIII (10 Jan. 1942), 28. (Review of Bates's *The Modern Short Story*).

——. 'Books in general', *New Statesman and Nation*, New Series, XXIII (17 Jan. 1942), 43.

——. 'Books in general', *New Statesman and Nation*, New Series, XXXI (2 Feb. 1946), 87. (Review of Katherine Mansfield's *Collected Stories*.)

——. 'A sense of strangeness', *Book Choice*, IX (Sept. 1981), 20–1.

——. 'Short stories', *Harper's Bazaar* (New York), LXXXVII (July 1953), 31 and 113.

——. William Sansom, and Francis King. 'The short-story', *London Magazine*, New Series, VI (Sept. 1966), 6–12.

REID, IAN. *The Short Story*. Methuen Critical Idiom Series. 1977.

SAROYAN, WILLIAM. 'What is a story?', *Saturday Review of Literature*, XI (5 Jan. 1935), 409.

STERN, JAMES, and others. 'Some notes on writing stories', *London Magazine* (Special Short Story Issue), IX (Mar. 1970), 6–16.

STRONG, L. A. G. 'Concerning short stories', *Bookman* (New York LXXV (Nov. 1932), 709–12.

——. *Instructions to Young Writers*. 1958.

——. 'The short story: notes at random', *Lovat Dickson's Magazine*, II (Mar. 1934), 281–91.

——. *The Writer's Trade*. 1953.

SWALES, MARTIN. *The German 'Novelle'*. Princeton, New Jersey, 1977.

VOSS, ARTHUR. *The American Short Story: A Critical Survey*. Norman, Oklahoma, 1973.

WAIDSON, H. M. 'The German short story as a literary form', *Modern Languages*, XL (1959), 121–7.

WARD, A. C. *Aspects of the Modern Short Story*. 1924.

WEDMORE, FREDERIC. 'The short story', *The Nineteenth Century*, XLIII (Mar. 1898), 406–16.

WELTY, EUDORA. 'The reading and writing of short stories', *Atlantic Monthly*, CLXXXIII (Feb. 1949), 54–8 and CLXXXIII (Mar. 1949), 46–9.

WEST, JR., RAY B. *The Short Story in America: 1900–1950*. Chicago, 1952.

WHARTON, EDITH. 'Telling a short story'. In *The Writing of Fiction* (New York, 1925: repr. 1966), pp. 31–58.

WILLIAMS, BLANCHE COLTON. *A Handbook on Story Writing*. 1921.

——. *Our Short Story Writers*. New York, 1920.

WRIGHT, AUSTIN McGIFFERT. *The American Short Story in the Twenties*. Chicago, 1961.

ZOLA, EMILE. 'Alexis et Maupassant', *Oeuvres Complètes*, (Vol. XIV), édn établie sous la direction de Henri Mitterand. Paris, 1966–.

5. OTHER LITERARY WORKS

AITKEN, GEORGE A. ed. *The Tatler*. 4 vols, 1899.

ALLEN, MICHAEL. *Poe and the British Magazine Tradition*. 1969.

ALPERS, ANTONY. *Katherine Mansfield*. 1954.

——. *The Life of Katherine Mansfield*. 1980.

ANDERSON, SHERWOOD. 'Man and his imagination'. In *The Intent of the Artist*, ed. Augusto Centano (1941).

——. *Notebook, Containing Articles Written During the Author's Life as a Story Teller, and Notes of his Impressions from Life Scattered through the Book*. New York, 1926; repr. 1970.

——. *A Story Teller's Story*. New York, 1924.

AUBRY, GÉRARD JEAN, Joseph Conrad, *Life and Letters*. 2 vols, 1927.

BALDICK, ROBERT, ed. and trans. *Pages from the Goncourt Journal*. 1962.

BALFOUR, GRAHAM. *The Life of Robert Louis Stevenson*. 2 vols, 1901.

BARNES, HOMER F. *Charles Fenno Hoffman*. New York, 1930.

BENNETT, ARNOLD. *The Author's Craft*. 1914.

——. *Books and Persons*. New York, 1917.

——. *The Evening Standard Years: 'Books and Persons' 1926–31* ed. Andrew Mylett. 1974.

BENSON, JACKSON J., ed. *The Short Stories of Ernest Hemingway*. Durham, North Carolina, 1975.

BOND, DONALD. *The Spectator*. 5 vols, Oxford, 1965.

BOND, RICHMOND P. *The Tatler: The Making of a Literary Journal*. Cambridge, Mass, 1971.

BOWEN, ELIZABETH, *Afterthought: Pieces about Writing*. 1962.

——. *Collected Impressions*. 1950.

——. 'Contemporary', *New Statesman and Nation*, XXIII (23 May 1942), 340.

——. *Pictures and Conversations*. 1974.

——. GRAHAM GREENE, and V. S. PRITCHETT *Why Do I Write?: An Exchange of Views*. 1948.

BRIGGS, JULIA. *Night Visitors: The Rise and Fall of the English Ghost Story*. 1977.

BROWNING, ROBERT. *Poetical Works 1833–1864*, ed. Ian Jack. 1970.

——. *The Ring and the Book*, ed. Richard D. Altick. Penguin pbk edn, Harmondsworth, Middx, 1971.

CADY, EDWIN H. *W. D. Howells as Critic*. 1973.

CATHER, WILLA. *Not Under Forty*. 1936.

CHEKHOV, ANTON. *Letters on the Short Story, the Drama and other Literary Topics*, ed. Louis S. Friedland. 1965.

CHESTERTON, G. K. *Charles Dickens*. 1906.

CONRAD, JOSEPH. *Notes on Life and Letters*. 1921.

COPPARD, A. E. *It's Me, O Lord!: An Abstract and Brief Chronicle of Some of the Life with Some of the Opinions of A. E. Coppard, Written by Himself*. 1957.

CUSHMAN, KEITH. *D. H. Lawrence at work: the Emergence of the Prussian Officer Stories*. Hassocks, 1978.

DE LA MARE, WALTER, ed. *The Eighteen Eighties*. 1930.

EDEL, LEON, and GORDON RAY, eds. *Henry James and H. G. Wells: A Record of their Friendship, their Debate on the Art of Fiction, and their Quarrel*. 1958.

ELIOT, T. S. 'The borderline of prose', *New Statesman*, V (19 May 1971), 157–9.

——. *The Complete Poems and Plays*. 1969.

——. Frederic Manning, and Richard Aldington. 'Poetry in prose: three essays', *The Chapbook: A Monthly Miscellany*, XXII (Apr. 1921), 1–24.

EMPSON, WILLIAM. *Some Versions of Pastoral* (1935). 1950.

FORSTER, E. M. *Two Cheers for Democracy*. Penguin pbk edn Harmondsworth, Middx, 1965.

FOWLES, JOHN. *Cinderella: Adapted from Perrault's Cendrillon of 1697*. 1974.

——. *The Ebony Tower*. 1974.

FRIERSON, WILLIAM C. *The English Novel in Transition 1885–1940*. 1942.

GARD, ROGER, ed. *Henry James: The Critical Heritage*. 1968.

GARNETT, EDWARD. *Friday Nights: Literary Criticisms and Appreciations*. 1st Series. 1922.

GASKELL, ELIZABETH. *Cranford and Cousin Phillis*, ed. Peter Keating. Penguin pbk edn Harmondsworth, Middx, 1976.

GEISMAR, MAXWELL. *The Last of the Provincials: the American Novel 1915–1925*. New York, 1959.

GERHARDIE, WILLIAM. *Anton Chehov: A Critical Study* (1923). Definitive edn with a preface by Michael Holroyd. 1974.

GILBERT, ELLIOT L. *The Good Kipling: Studies in the Short Story*. Manchester, 1972.

GLENDINNING, VICTORIA. *Elizabeth Bowen: Portrait of a Writer*. 1977.

GREEN, ROGER LANCELYN, ed. *Kipling: The Critical Heritage*. 1971.

GUIGET, JEAN. *Virginia Woolf and her Works* (1962), trans. Jean Stewart. 1965.

HAMILTON, IAN. *The Little Magazines: a Study of Six Editors*. 1976.

HARDEN, O. ELIZABETH McWHORTER. *Maria Edgeworth's Art of Prose Fiction*. The Hague, 1971.

HARDY, FLORENCE EMILY. *The Life of Thomas Hardy 1840–1924*. Macmillan pbk edn, 1965.

HARRIS, WENDELL V. 'An approach to Gissing's short stories', *Studies in Short Fiction*, I (Winter 1965),137–44.

——. 'Identifying the decadent fiction of the 1890s', *English Fiction in Transition*, V (1962), 1–13.

HAZLITT, WILLIAM. *The Spirit of the Age, or Contemporary Portraits*, ed. E. D. Mackerness. Collins Annotated Student Texts. 1969.

HENLEY, W. E. *Views and Reviews: Essays in Appreciation; Literature*, 1890.

HESSE, EVA, ed. *New Approaches to Ezra Pound: A Co-ordinated Investigation of Pound's Poetry and Ideas*. 1969.

HINGLEY, RONALD. *A New Life of Anton Chekhov*. 1976.

HOFFMAN, FREDERICK J., CHARLES ALLEN, and CAROLINE F. ULRICH. *The Little Magazine: A History and a Bibliography*. Princeton, 1947.

HOWE, IRVING. *Celebrations and Attacks: Thirty Years of Literary and Cultural Commentary*. 1979.

IRVING, PIERRE, ed. *The Life and Letters of Washington Irving*. 4 vols, 1862–64.

JAMES, HENRY. *The Art of the Novel: Critical Prefaces*. New York, 1962.

——. *Letters*, ed. Leon Edel. 1974–.

——. *The Letters of Henry James*, ed. Percy Lubbock. 1920.

——. *Literary Reviews and Essays on American, English, and French Literature*, ed. Albert Mordell. New York, 1957.

——. 'Mr and Mrs Fields', *The Cornhill Magazine*, New Series, xxxix (July 1915) 29–43.

——. *The Notebooks of Henry James*, ed. F. O. Matthiessen and Kenneth B. Murdock. New York 1947.

——. *Partial Portraits*. 1888.

JANOUCH, GUSTAV. *Conversations with Kafka: Notes and Reminiscences*, trans. Goronwy Rees. 1953.

JEWETT, SARAH ORNE. *Letters*. Enlarged and rev. edn, with introd. and notes by Richard Cary. Waterville, Maine, 1967.

JOHNSON, SAMUEL. *The Rambler*, ed. W. J. Bate and Albrecht B. Strauss. Yale Edition. 3 vols, New Haven, 1969. (Vols III–V of Yale edn).

JOYCE, JAMES. *The Workshop of Daedelus: James Joyce and the Raw Materials for A Portrait of the Artist as a Young Man*, collected and ed. Robert Scholes and Richard M. Kain. Evanston, Illinois, 1965.

JOYCE, STANISLAUS. *My Brother's Keeper*, ed. Richard Ellmann. New York, 1958.

KAFKA, FRANZ. *Letters to Friends, Family and Editors*, trans. Richard and Clara Winston. 1978.

KEATING, P. J. *The Working Classes in Victorian Fiction*. 1971.

KERMODE, FRANK *The Genesis of Secrecy: On the Interpretation of Narrative*. Cambridge, Mass, 1979.

KIPLING, RUDYARD. *From Sea to Sea and other Sketches: Letters of Travel*. 2 vols, 1900.

——. *Something of Myself: For My Friends Known and Unknown*. 1937.

LAW, MARIE HAMILTON *The English Familiar Essay in the Early 19th century: The Elements Old and New Which Went into its Making as Exemplified in the Writings of Hunt, Hazlitt, and Lamb*. Philadelphia, 1934.

LAWRENCE, D. H. *Lawrence in Love: Letters to Louie Burrows*, ed. James T. Boulton. Nottingham, 1968.

——. *The Letters of D. H. Lawrence*, ed. James T. Boulton. Cambridge, 1979–.

——. *Selected Literary Criticism*, ed. Anthony Beal. Heinemann pbk edn 1967.

——. *Studies in Classic American Literature* (1924). Phoenix edn 1964.

LEVERTOV, DENISE. 'What is a prose poem?', *The Nation*, CXCIII (Dec. 1961), 518–9.

LEAVIS, Q. D. *Fiction and the Reading Public*. 1932.

LEVIN, HARRY. *James Joyce: a Critical Introduction*. 1960.

MACAULAY, THOMAS BABINGTON *Critical and Historical Essays Contributed to the Edinburgh Review*, ed. F. C. Montague. 3 vols, 1903.

McCARTHY, MARY. *On the Contrary*. 1962.

McCULLERS, CARSON. *The Mortgaged Heart*, ed. Margarita G. Smith. 1972.

MAJUMDAR, ROBIN, and ALLEN McLAURIN, eds. *Virginia Woolf: The Critical Heritage*. 1975.

MANSFIELD, KATHERINE. *Letters and Journals: A Selection*, ed. C. K. Stead. 1977.

——. *Novels and Novelists*, ed. J. Middleton Murry. 1930.

——. *The Scrapbook of Katherine Mansfield*, ed. J. Middleton Murry. 1939.

MASON, PHILIP. *Kipling: The Glass, the Shadow and the Fire*. 1975.

MATTHIESSEN, F. O. *The James Family*. New York, 1947.

——. *Sarah Orne Jewett*. Boston. 1929.

MAUGHAM, W. SOMERSET. *Selected Prefaces and Introductions*. 1963.

——. *The Summing Up* (1938). 1944.

——. *A Writer's Notebook*. 1949.

MAUPASSANT, GUY DE. *Pierre and Jean*, trans. Leonard Tancock. Penguin pbk edn, Harmondsworth, Middx, 1979.

MAYO, ROBERT D. *The English Novel in the Magazines 1740–1815*. Evanston, Illinois, 1962.

MILECK, JOSEPH. *Hermann Hesse: Life and Art*. Berkeley, Calif., 1978.

MONEGAL, EMIR RODRIGUEZ. *Jorge Luis Borges: A Literary Biography*. New York, 1978.

MORRISON, ARTHUR. 'What is a realist?', *New Review*, XVI (1897), 326–36.

MOTT, FRANK LUTHER. *A History of American Magazines, 1741–1850*. New York, 1930.

O'CONNOR, FLANNERY. *The Habit of Being: Letters*. 1979.

——. *Mystery and Manners: Occasional Prose*, selected and ed. Sally and Robert Fitzgerald. 1972.

O'CONNOR, FRANK. *The Mirror in the Roadway: A Study of the Modern Novel*. 1957.

O'CONNOR, RICHARD. *Ambrose Bierce: A Biography*. 1968.

'OLGIVANNA'. 'The last days of Katherine Mansfield', *Bookman* (New York), LXXIV (Mar. 1931), 6–13.

OPIE, IONA and PETER. *The Classic Fairy Tales* (1974). Granada pbk edn, 1980.

OWENS, GRAHAM, ed. *George Moore's Mind and Art: Essays*. Edinburgh, 1968.

PATER, WALTER. *Letters*, ed. Lawrence Evans. Oxford, 1970.

PAULSON, RONALD, ed. *The Novelette before 1900*. Englewood Cliffs, 1965.

PERRAULT, CHARLES. *The Fairy Tales*, trans. Angela Carter. 1977.

PERRY, BLISS. *A Study of Prose Fiction*. Rev. edn, New York, 1920.

POE, EDGAR ALLAN. *Poems and Essays*. Everyman pbk edn, 1927; repr. 1969.

PORTER, KATHERINE ANNE. *The Days Before*. 1st English edn, 1953.

PRAWER, S. S. *Caligari's Children: The Film as Tale of Terror*. 1980.

PRAZ, MARIO. *The Hero in Eclipse in Victorian Fiction*, trans. Angus Davidson. Oxford pbk edn 1969.

PRINCE, GERALD. *A Grammar of Stories: An Introduction*. The Hague, 1973.

PRITCHETT, V. S. *Books in General*. 1953.

——. *A Cab at the Door* (1968). Penguin pbk edn, Harmondsworth, Middx, 1970; *Midnight Oil* (1971). Penguin pbk edn Harmondsworth, Middx, 1974. (Autobiography).

——. *The Myth Makers: Essays on European, Russian and South American Novelists*. 1979.

——. *The Tale Bearers: Essays on English, American and Other Writers*. 1980.

PROPP, VLADIMIR. *Morphology of the Folktale*. 2nd rev. edn, Bloomington, 1968.

RAITT, A. W. *Prosper Mérimée*. 1970.

RAKNEM, INGVALD. *H. G. Wells and His Critics*. Oslo, 1962.

RHODE, ROBERT D. *Setting in the American Short Story of Local Color 1865–1900*. The Hague, 1975.

ROSENFELD, PAUL. 'What has happened to the prose-poem?', *The Satur-*

day *Review of Literature*, XXVI (24 July 1943), 9–11.

ROURKE, CONSTANCE. *American Humor: A Study of National Character*. New York, 1931.

SALE, ROGER. *Fairy Tales and After: from Snow White to E. B. White*. Cambridge, Mass, 1978.

SCARBOROUGH, DOROTHY. *The Supernatural in Modern Fiction*. New York, 1917.

SCHOLES, ROBERT. 'Towards a poetics of fiction (4): an approach through genre', *Novel*, II (Winter 1969), 101–11.

STERN, J. P., ed. *The World of Franz Kafka*. 1980.

STEVENSON, ROBERT LOUIS. *Letters*, ed. Sidney Colvin. 5 vols, 1924.

STURROCK, JOHN. *Paper Tigers: The Ideal Fictions of Jorge Luis Borges*. Oxford, 1977.

SULLIVAN, EDWARD D. *Maupassant: The Short Stories*. 1962.

SWEARINGEN, ROGER G. *The Prose Writings of Robert Louis Stevenson: A Guide*. 1980.

TREVELYAN, JANET PENROSE. *The Life of Mrs Humphry Ward*. 1923.

TROYAT, HENRI. *Gogol: The Biography of a Divided Soul*, trans. Nancy Amphoux. 1974.

TWAIN, MARK. *The Complete Essays*, ed. Charles Neider. New York, 1963.

WEINTRAUB, STANLEY. *The London Yankees: Portraits of American Writers and Artists in England 1894–1914*. 1979.

WELLS, H. G. *An Experiment in Autobiography: Discoveries and Conclusions of a very ordinary brain (since 1866)*. 2 vols, 1934.

WEYGANDT, ANN M. *Kipling's Reading*. 1939.

WHITE, GLEESON. *Letters to Eminent Hands*. 1892.

WOOLF, VIRGINIA. ' "Anon" and "The Reader": Virginia Woolf's last essays', ed. Brenda R. Silver, *Twentieth Century Literature*, XXV (1979), 356–441.

——. *Books and Portraits*, ed. Mary Lyon. 1977.

——. *Collected Essays*. 4 vols, 1966–67.

——. *The Diary of Virginia Woolf*, ed. Anne Olivier Bell. 1977–.

——. *Letters*, ed. Nigel Nicolson. 6 vols, 1975–80.

——. *Walter Sickert: a Conversation*. 1934. (Published by Leonard and Virginia Woolf at the Hogarth Press).

YATES, NORRIS. *The American Humorist: Conscience of the Twentieth Century*. Ames, Iowa, 1964.

ZABEL, MORTON DAUWEN. *Craft and Character: Texts, Method, and Vocation in Modern Fiction*. 1957.

ZIPES, JACK. *Breaking the Magic Spell: Radical Theories of Folk and Fairy Tales*. 1979.

INDEX

THE SHORT STORY
A CRITICAL INTRODUCTION

After years of critical neglect the short story is at last coming into its own as an important and distinctive literary form. For too long it has been dismissed as a relatively inconsiderable genre which rates little more than a passing glance on the critic's way to the serious business of the novel. Serious study of the short story has, moreover, been bedevilled by the difficulty of finding and using appropriate critical tools: are the criteria we use in assessing the effects of a novel automatically relevant to a genre quite different in scale and character?

In this stimulating introduction, Valerie Shaw asserts the claims of the short story as an art form in its own right – international, timelessly appealing, supremely flexible, and with a unique capacity to create its own brand of intimacy between the reader and the fictional world it depicts.

She addresses herself throughout to two key questions: 'What are the special satisfactions afforded by reading short stories?' and 'How are these satisfactions derived from each story's literary techniques and narrative strategies?'. To answer them she draws on stories from different periods and countries – by authors who were also great novelists, like Henry James, Flaubert, Kafka and D. H. Lawrence; by authors who specifically dedicated themselves to the art of the short story, like Kipling, Chekhov and Katherine Mansfield; by contemporary practitioners like Angela Carter and Jorge Luis Borges; and by unfairly neglected writers like Sarah Orne Jewett and Joel Chandler Harris.

Although this book offers a critical rather than historical approach to the subject, the emergence of the modern form of the short story is fully discussed. Dr Shaw also investigates the short story's nature and elements, its basic types of narrative effect, presentation of character, evocation of place, its appropriate subject-matter, and the short story's preference for the instinctual over the intellectual, for the reticent over the explicit.

Valerie Shaw is a lecturer in the Department of English Literature at the University of Edinburgh.

Cover illustration by Liz Pyle.

ISBN 0 582 48687 4

LONGMAN